ZAGAT SURVEY

Back in 1979, we never imagined that an idea born during a wine-fueled dinner with friends would take us on an adventure that's lasted three decades – and counting.

The idea – that the collective opinions of avid consumers can be more accurate than the judgments of an individual critic – led to a hobby involving friends rating NYC restaurants. And that hobby grew into Zagat Survey, which today has over 350,000 participants worldwide weighing in on everything from airlines, bars, dining and golf to hotels, movies, shopping, tourist attractions and more.

By giving consumers a voice, we – and our surveyors – had unwittingly joined a revolution whose concepts (user-generated content, social networking) were largely unknown 30 years ago. However, those concepts caught fire with the rise of the Internet and have since transformed not only restaurant criticism but also virtually every aspect of the media, and we feel lucky to have been at the start of it all.

And that wasn't the only revolution we happily stumbled into. Our first survey was published as a revolution began to reshape the culinary landscape. Thanks to a host of converging trends – the declining supremacy of old-school formal restaurants; the growing sophistication of diners; the availability of ever-more diverse cuisines and techniques; the improved range and quality of ingredients; the rise of chefs as rock stars – dining out has never been better or more exciting, and we've been privileged to witness its progress through the eyes of our surveyors. And it's still going strong.

As we celebrate Zagat's 30th year, we'd like to thank everyone who has participated in our surveys. We've enjoyed hearing and sharing your frank opinions and look forward to doing so for many years to come. As we always say, our guides and online content are really "yours."

We'd also like to express our gratitude by supporting **Action Against Hunger,** an organization that works to meet the needs of the hungry in over 40 countries. To find out more, visit www.zagat.com/action.

Nina and Tim Zagat

ZAGAT®
CELEBRATING 30 YEARS

New Jersey
Restaurants
2009/10

LOCAL EDITORS
Mary Ann Castronovo Fusco and Pat Tanner

LOCAL COORDINATOR
Brooke Tarabour

STAFF EDITOR
Sharon Gintzler

Published and distributed by
Zagat Survey, LLC
4 Columbus Circle
New York, NY 10019
T: 212.977.6000
E: newjersey@zagat.com
www.zagat.com

ACKNOWLEDGMENTS

We thank Heather Harr, Cody Kendall, Rosie Saferstein and Steven Shukow, as well as the following members of our staff: Caitlin Eichelberger (assistant editor), Brian Albert, Sean Beachell, Maryanne Bertollo, Jane Chang, Sandy Cheng, Reni Chin, Larry Cohn, Bill Corsello, Carol Diuguid, Alison Flick, Jeff Freier, Andrew Gelardi, Justin Hartung, Roy Jacob, Garth Johnston, Ashunta Joseph, Cynthia Kilian, Natalie Lebert, Mike Liao, Dave Makulec, Andre Pilette, Kimberly Rosado, Becky Ruthenburg, Jacqueline Wasilczyk, Yoji Yamaguchi, Sharon Yates, Anna Zappia and Kyle Zolner.

The reviews in this guide are based on public opinion surveys. The ratings reflect the average scores given by the survey participants who voted on each establishment. The text is based on quotes from, or paraphrasings of, the surveyors' comments. Phone numbers, addresses and other factual data were correct to the best of our knowledge when published in this guide.

Contents

Ratings & Symbols

Zagat Top Spot	Name	Symbols	Cuisine	Zagat Ratings			
				FOOD	DECOR	SERVICE	COST

Area, Address & Contact

Z Tim & Nina's ◗ *Portuguese*   ▽ 23 | 9 | 13 | $15

Atlantic City | 5678 Pacific Ave. (Atlantic Ave.) | 609-555-1212 | www.zagat.com

Review, surveyor comments in quotes

"Miles from the boardwalk but still not far enough away", this "never-closing" AC "eyesore" "single-handedly" started the "saltwater-taffy pizza craze" that's "sweeping the casino capital" like "a run of bad luck"; don't forget to "visit the all-you-can-stomach buffet" – "it's to die for" (or from) – but don't look for ambiance because "T & N don't know from design", or service, for that matter.

Ratings   **Food, Decor** and **Service** are rated on the Zagat 0 to 30 scale.

0 – 9	poor to fair
10 – 15	fair to good
16 – 19	good to very good
20 – 25	very good to excellent
26 – 30	extraordinary to perfection
▽	low response	less reliable

Cost   Our surveyors' estimated price of a dinner with one drink and tip. Lunch is usually 25 to 30% less. At prix fixe–only places we show the charge for the lowest-priced menu plus 30%. For unrated **newcomers** or **write-ins,** the price range is shown as follows:

I	$25 and below	E	$41 to $65
M	$26 to $40	VE	$66 or more

Symbols

Z	highest ratings, popularity and importance
◗	serves after 11 PM
☒	closed on Sunday
M	closed on Monday
⊄	no credit cards accepted

About This Survey

Here are the results of our **2009/10 New Jersey Restaurants Survey,** covering 1,003 eateries. Like all our guides, this one is based on the collective opinions of avid consumers – 6,377 all told. As a companion to this guide, we also publish *New Jersey Shore Restaurants.*

WHO PARTICIPATED: Input from these enthusiasts forms the basis for the ratings and reviews in this guide (their comments are shown in quotation marks within the reviews). These surveyors are a diverse group: 49% are women, 51% men; 5% are in their 20s; 19%, 30s; 23%, 40s; 28%, 50s; and 25%, 60s or above. Collectively they bring roughly 946,000 annual meals' worth of experience to this Survey. We sincerely thank these participants – this book is really "theirs."

HELPFUL LISTS: Our top lists and indexes can help you find exactly the right place for any occasion. See Key Newcomers (page 7), Most Popular (page 9), Top Ratings (pages 10–15), Best Buys (pages 16–17) and the 44 handy indexes starting on page 171.

OUR EDITORS: Special thanks go to our local editors, Mary Ann Castronovo Fusco, a freelance food editor and writer published in *The New York Times, The New York Daily News* and *The Star-Ledger*; Pat Tanner, a restaurant critic for *New Jersey Life magazine*; and to our local coordinator Brooke Tarabour, a food columnist at *The Star-Ledger.*

ABOUT ZAGAT: This marks our 30th year reporting on the shared experiences of consumers like you. Today we have over 350,000 surveyors and now cover airlines, bars, dining, entertaining, fast food, golf, hotels, movies, music, resorts, shopping, spas, theater and tourist attractions in over 100 countries.

INTERACTIVE: Up-to-the-minute news about restaurant openings plus menus, photos and more are free on **ZAGAT.com** and the award-winning **ZAGAT.mobi** (for web-enabled mobile devices). They also enable reserving at thousands of places with just one click.

VOTE AND COMMENT: We invite you to join any of our surveys at **ZAGAT.com.** There you can rate and review establishments year-round. In exchange for doing so, you'll receive a free copy of the resulting guide when published.

AVAILABILITY: Zagat guides are available in all major bookstores as well as on **ZAGAT.com.** You can also access our content when on the go via **ZAGAT.mobi** and **ZAGAT TO GO** (for smartphones).

FEEDBACK: To improve this guide, we invite your comments about any aspect of our performance. Tell us if we missed one of your favorite restaurants. Just contact us at **newjersey@zagat.com.**

New York, NY
May 6, 2009

Nina and Tim

Nina and Tim Zagat

What's New

While eating out remains a way of life for New Jersey residents, the shaky economy has clearly had an impact. Nearly three-quarters of survey respondents say they've made cost-saving adjustments such as dining out less frequently, choosing less-expensive places and forgoing extras like alcohol or dessert. The new focus on value makes sense given that the average cost of a meal in NJ is now $39.24, a 3.1% annualized increase since our last Survey and well above the national average of $34.49. But while the downturn has no doubt contributed to some restaurant closings, newcomers continue to appear, many geared to today's financial realities.

TOP TOQUES TRIM DOWN: Celeb chef Bobby Flay turns his attention from grilling steaks at Atlantic City's ritzy **Bobby Flay Steak** to cooking burgers at his new **Bobby's Burger Palace** in Eatontown, the second location of a planned national chain. Impresario Stephen Starr, whose dramatic signature restaurants include AC's **Buddakan** and **Continental,** does an about-face at **Teplitzky's** – a tuna melt and tomato soup diner at the Chelsea Hotel in AC. And Michael Cetrulo has opened Asbury Park's **Stella Marina,** a stylish Italian serving pizza and more at prices that are well below his prix fixe dinner tab at **Scalini Fedeli** in Chatham.

MORE CULINARY COMFORT: Newcomers **Avenue Bistro Pub** in Verona, **9 North** in Wayne, **Backyards Bistro** in Hoboken and **The Orange Squirrel** in Bloomfield are banking on attracting business with homey, affordable fare like mac 'n' cheese and frittatas. Meanwhile, value-priced grilled-chicken chains with a Latin accent are spreading their wings, among them **Pollo Campero** in West New York and **Pollo Tropical** in several North Jersey locations.

GOINGS AND COMINGS: The abrupt shuttering earlier this year of Arthur's Landing, a Weehawken waterfront fixture for almost two decades, took many by surprise, as did the closing of Amazing Hot Dog in Bound Brook. Likewise, the historic Ho-Ho-Kus Inn closed its doors, though is reportedly planning to reopen in summer 2009 with a dual concept combining upscale and casual dining.

SURVEY STATS: Service remains the biggest irritant associated with NJ dining, cited by 72% of respondents. Yet some places clearly get it right: Middletown's **Nicholas** is celebrating its seventh consecutive year as No. 1 for Service (and its fifth year as No. 1 for Food and third as Most Popular). **Rat's,** located on the Grounds for Sculpture in Hamilton, is in its ninth year as No. 1 for Decor . . . Despite complaints about service, NJ diners are among the nation's highest tippers, leaving an average of 19.4%, on the heels of the nation's top tippers, Philadelphians, at 19.6% . . . On the green front, 49% say that they will fork out more green for food that has been sustainably produced, while 46% will pay more for organic.

New Jersey
May 6, 2009

Mary Ann Castronovo Fusco
Pat Tanner
Brooke Tarabour

Key Newcomers

Our editors' take on the year's top arrivals. See page 220 for a full list.

Avenue Bistro Pub | *American*

Boulevard Five 72 | *American*

Char Steak | *Steak*

Chelsea Prime | *Steak*

Cubanu | *Cuban*

Delicious Heights | *American*

Due Mari | *Italian*

elements | *American*

Eno Terra | *Italian*

Farm 2 Bistro | *American*

Il Fiore | *Italian*

Il Mulino NY | *Italian*

JL Ivy | *French/Japanese*

LaPrete's | *Italian*

Limani | *Greek*

9 North | *American*

Nisi Estiatorio | *Greek*

Orange Squirrel | *American*

Prairie | *American*

Resto | *French*

Stamna | *Greek*

Steakhouse 85 | *Steak*

The coming year promises a spate of new eateries. Princeton will soon welcome **BT Bistro**, from one of the city's beloved chefs, Bobby Trigg (of **The Ferry House**). It will feature classic bistro dishes plus American comfort food, a raw bar and lounge. Trigg is also preparing for a late-2009 unveiling of his top-to-bottom renovation of Princeton's historic Peacock Inn, including an upscale new restaurant, **BT 20 @ The Peacock Inn.** (The 20 reflects Trigg's 20th anniversary in the food business.) Meanwhile, chef-owner Chris Roman will move his seasonal Avalon restaurant Blackfish Avalon – sister of the highly regarded Conshohocken, PA, spot, **Blackfish** – to Stone Harbor this spring, where he'll dish up his acclaimed contemporary American cuisine with an emphasis on seafood. Unlike the previous location, the newly named **Blackfish Stone Harbor** will be open year-round. And the Harvest Restaurant Group (**Ciao, Huntley Tavern, 3 West**) expects to debut the Italian **Grato** this spring in Morris Plains, across the parking lot from its **Tabor Road Tavern.** The executive chef will be John Schaefer, formerly of Irving Mill and Gramercy Tavern, and a Tom Colicchio acolyte.

Greek restaurants are becoming ever more popular on the NJ dining scene. The two **Greek Taverna** restaurants (in Edgewater and Montclair) will welcome a third sibling in Glen Rock in late spring 2009. At press-time, **Santorini Taverna,** specializing in seafood, debuted in Fort Lee.

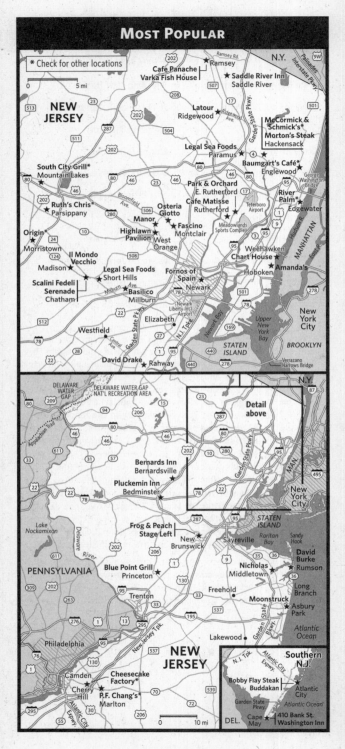

MOST POPULAR

* Check for other locations

0   5 mi

NEW JERSEY

Ramsey Rd
Ramsey
Cafe Panache
Varka Fish House
★ Saddle River Inn
Saddle River

N.Y.
Palisades Interstate Pkwy.

Latour
Ridgewood

McCormick & Schmick's*
Morton's Steak
Hackensack

Legal Sea Foods
Paramus

Baumgart's Café*
Englewood

George Washington Bridge

South City Grill*
Mountain Lakes

Park & Orchard
E. Rutherford
Cafe Matisse
Rutherford

River Palm*
Edgewater

Ruth's Chris*
Parsippany

Osteria Giotto
Manor
Fascino
Montclair
Highlawn Pavilion
West Orange

Teterboro Airport

Meadowlands Sports Complex

Weehawken
Chart House
Hoboken

Amanda's

MANHATTAN

Origin*
Morristown

Il Mondo Vecchio
Madison

Legal Sea Foods
Short Hills
Scalini Fedeli
Serenade
Chatham
Basilico
Millburn

Fornos of Spain
Newark

Newark Liberty Int'l Airport

Upper New York Bay

New York City

BROOKLYN

Westfield

Elizabeth

STATEN ISLAND

David Drake
Rahway

Verrazano Narrows Bridge

DELAWARE WATER GAP
DELAWARE WATER GAP NAT'L RECREATION AREA

Appalachian Trail

N.Y.

Detail above

New York City

MAN.

Bernards Inn
Bernardsville
Pluckemin Inn
Bedminster

STATEN ISLAND

Sandy Hook

Lake Nockamixon

Frog & Peach
Stage Left
New Brunswick

Sayreville

Raritan Bay

David Burke
Rumson

PENNSYLVANIA

Delaware River

Blue Point Grill
Princeton

Nicholas
Middletown

Long Branch

Trenton

Freehold

Moonstruck

Asbury Park

Atlantic Ocean

Lakewood

NEW JERSEY

Philadelphia

Camden

Cheesecake Factory*

Cherry Hill

P.F. Chang's*
Marlton

New Jersey Tpk.

Southern N.J.

Bobby Flay Steak
Buddakan
Atlantic City

Atlantic Ocean

DEL.

Cape May

410 Bank St.
Washington Inn

0   10 mi

Menus, photos, voting and more – free at ZAGAT.com

Most Popular

1. Nicholas | *American*
2. River Palm | *Steak*
3. Cafe Panache | *Eclectic*
4. Ruth's Chris | *Steak*
5. Cheesecake Factory | *American*
6. Scalini Fedeli | *Italian*
7. Highlawn Pavilion | *American*
8. P.F. Chang's | *Chinese*
9. Saddle River Inn | *Amer./French*
10. Legal Sea Foods | *Seafood*
11. Amanda's | *American*
12. Frog and the Peach | *American*
13. Serenade* | *French*
14. Cafe Matisse | *Eclectic*
15. Bernards Inn | *American*
16. Pluckemin Inn | *American*
17. Baumgart's | *Amer./Pan-Asian*
18. Bobby Flay Steak | *Steak*
19. Latour | *French*
20. Buddakan | *Pan-Asian*
21. Fascino* | *Italian*
22. Manor | *American*
23. Morton's Steak* | *Steak*
24. Blue Point | *Seafood*
25. David Drake | *American*
26. McCormick/Schmick's* | *Sea.*
27. Park & Orchard | *Eclectic*
28. Il Mondo | *Italian*
29. Moonstruck* | *American/Med.*
30. Origin | *French/Thai*
31. Osteria Giotto | *Italian*
32. 410 Bank St. | *Creole*
33. Washington Inn | *American*
34. South City Grill | *American*
35. Fornos of Spain | *Spanish*
36. Varka | *Greek/Seafood*
37. David Burke | *American*
38. Stage Left | *American*
39. Basilico | *Italian*
40. Chart House | *American*

It's obvious that many of the above restaurants are among New Jersey's most expensive, but if popularity were calibrated to price, we suspect that a number of other restaurants would join their ranks. Thus, we have added two pages of Best Buys starting on page 16.

---

* Indicates a tie with restaurant above

Top Food Ratings

Excludes places with low votes.

28
Nicholas | *American*
Lorena's | *French*
David Drake | *American*
Ajihei | *Japanese*
Cafe Panache | *Eclectic*
Saddle River Inn | *Amer./French*
Serenade | *French*

27
Scalini Fedeli | *Italian*
Washington Inn | *American*
SeaBlue | *Seafood*
Whispers | *American*
Bay Ave. Tratt. | *Amer./Italian*
Sagami | *Japanese*
CulinAriane | *American*
André's | *American*
Ebbitt Room | *American*
DeLorenzo's Pies | *Pizza*
Tre Figlio | *Italian*
Cafe Matisse | *Eclectic*
Chef Vola's | *Italian*

Blue Bottle Cafe | *American*
Piccola Italia | *Italian*

26
Pluckemin Inn | *American*
Bernards Inn | *American*
Chef's Table | *French*
Augustino's | *Italian*
Latour | *French*
Tisha's | *American*
Il Mulino NY | *Italian*
Drew's Bayshore | *American*
Karen & Rei's | *American*
Fascino | *Italian*
White House | *Sandwiches*
Vivas | *Nuevo Latino*
Peter Shields | *American*
La Isla | *Cuban*
Chez Catherine] *French*
Yellow Fin | *American*
Rosemary & Sage | *American*
410 Bank St. | *Creole*

BY CUISINE

AMERICAN (NEW)
28
Nicholas
David Drake
Saddle River Inn
27
Whispers
CulinAriane

AMERICAN (TRAD.)
27
Washington Inn
25
Ram's Head Inn
A Toute Heure
24
Bistro 44
Manor

CHINESE
24
Hunan Taste
Chengdu 46
Lotus Cafe
23
Wonder Seafood
Chez Elena Wu

COFFEE SHOP/DINER
20
Skylark
Mastoris
18
Nifty Fifty's
Ponzio's
Tick Tock

CONTINENTAL
23
Farnsworth House
Stony Hill Inn
Café Gallery
22
Black Forest Inn
Court Street

CUBAN
26
La Isla
25
Rebecca's
23
Mi Bandera
22
Cuba Libre
Martino's

ECLECTIC
28
Cafe Panache
27
Cafe Matisse
25
Gables
Little Café
Frenchtown Inn

FRENCH
28
Lorena's
Saddle River Inn
Serenade
26
Latour
Chez Catherine

FRENCH (BISTRO)

26 Chef's Table
   Le Rendez-Vous
25 Le Fandy
   Verjus
24 Bistro 44

GREEK

26 Varka
23 Stamna
   Pithari Taverna
   Axia Taverna
22 Limani

INDIAN

25 Moghul
24 Mehndi
   Karma Kafe
   Mantra
23 Chand Palace

ITALIAN

27 Bay Ave. Trattoria
   Tre Figlio
   Chef Vola's
   Piccola Italia
26 Il Mulino NY
   Fascino
   Girasole
   Laceno
   Ombra
   Il Capriccio

JAPANESE

28 Ajihei
27 Sagami
26 Yumi
25 Aozora
   Shumi

MEDITERRANEAN

25 Moonstruck
   Hamilton's
   Vine
24 Sage
   Frescos

MEXICAN

24 El Meson
22 Charrito's
   Los Amigos
   Tortilla Press
   Taqueria

MIDDLE EASTERN

23 Lodos
   Beyti Kebab
   Samdan
22 Seven Hills
21 Pamir

PAN-ASIAN

26 Yumi
25 Buddakan
24 Ritz Seafood
   Nouveau
23 Elements Asia

PIZZA

27 DeLorenzo's Pies
24 Conte's
   Grimaldi's
23 Brooklyn's Pizza
   Kinchley's Tavern

SEAFOOD

27 SeaBlue
26 Laceno
   Varka
   Dock's
25 Atlantic B&G

S. AMERICAN/
PAN-LATIN

25 Cucharamama
   Casa Solar
24 Zafra
22 Lua
21 Brasilia

SPANISH/
PORTUGUESE

24 Bistro Olé
23 Casa Vasca
   Fornos of Spain
   Tony Da Caneca
   Fernandes Steak

STEAKHOUSES

26 Old Homestead
25 Bobby Flay Steak
   Morton's Steak
   Palm
   Roots

THAI

26 Origin
24 Siri's
   Thai Kitchen
   Chao Phaya
   Mie Thai

BY SPECIAL FEATURE

BREAKFAST
24 Zafra
23 Hobby's
Mad Batter
22 Nana's Deli
Meil's

BRUNCH
26 Anthony David's
25 Amanda's
Moghul
Verjus
Rat's

CHILD-FRIENDLY
27 Sagami
André's
Tre Figlio
26 White House
Rosemary & Sage

HOTEL DINING
27 SeaBlue (Borgata)
Ebbitt Room (Virginia Hotel)
26 Il Mulino NY (Trump Taj Mahal)
Old Homestead (Borgata)
Ombra (Borgata)

NEWCOMERS (RATED)
26 Il Mulino NY
23 Stamna
22 Limani
21 Delicious Heights
19 JL Ivy

OFFBEAT
27 Chef Vola's
26 La Isla
25 Cucharamama
Makeda
20 Ali Baba

PEOPLE-WATCHING
28 David Drake
26 Pluckemin Inn
Bernards Inn
25 Bobby Flay
Cucharamama

POWER SCENES
28 Cafe Panache
27 SeaBlue
25 David Burke
24 Daryl
23 Catherine Lombardi

QUICK BITES
24 Bobby Chez
Nha Trang Place
23 Hobby's Deli
22 Kibitz Room
Nana's Deli

SINGLES SCENES
25 Atlantic B&G
Cucharamama
Buddakan
Shipwreck Grill
Mia

TRENDY
28 Lorena's
27 SeaBlue
DeLorenzo's Pies
Cafe Matisse
22 Lua

WINNING WINE LISTS
28 Nicholas
David Drake
Serenade
27 Scalini Fedeli
Washington Inn

WORTH A TRIP
28 Cafe Panache
Ramsey
Saddle River Inn
Saddle River
Serenade
Chatham
27 Scalini Fedeli
Chatham
SeaBlue
Atlantic City

BY LOCATION

ATLANTIC CITY

27 SeaBlue
   Chef Vola's
26 Il Mulino NY
   White House
   Old Homestead

CAPE MAY AREA

27 Washington Inn
   Ebbitt Room
26 Tisha's
   Peter Shields
   410 Bank St.

CHERRY HILL

25 Mélange
24 La Campagne
   Siri's
   Bobby Chez
   Caffe Aldo

COLLINGSWOOD

27 Sagami
26 Blackbird
25 Word of Mouth
24 Nunzio
   Bobby Chez

HOBOKEN

26 Augustino's
   La Isla
   Anthony David's
25 Amanda's
   Cucharamama

LAMBERTVILLE

26 No. 9
25 Manon
   Hamilton's
22 DeAnna's
   Ota-Ya

MIDDLETOWN

28 Nicholas
25 Anna's Kitchen
   Sono Sushi
20 Crown Palace
   Neelam

MONTCLAIR

27 CulinAriane
26 Fascino
25 Aozora
   Osteria Giotto
24 Nouveau

MORRISTOWN

26 Grand Cafe
   Origin
25 Copeland
   Tim Schafer's
24 Mehndi

NEWARK

23 Casa Vasca
   Hobby's Deli
   Fornos of Spain
   Tony Da Caneca
   Fernandes Steak

NEW BRUNSWICK

26 Frog and the Peach
   Stage Left
25 Makeda
24 Daryl
23 Delta's

PRINCETON

28 Ajihei
25 Blue Point
   Ferry House
   Ruth's Chris
24 Conte's

RED BANK

24 Dish
   Siam Garden
23 Molly Pitcher
   Bienvenue
22 Sogno

RIDGEWOOD

26 Latour
25 Sakura-Bana
24 Gazelle Café
23 Village Green
   Brooklyn's Pizza

SOMERVILLE

26 Origin
25 Shumi
   Wasabi
24 Chao Phaya
23 da Filippo

VOORHEES

26 Laceno
25 Little Café
   Catelli
24 Ritz Seafood
23 Chez Elena Wu

Top Decor Ratings

28 Rat's	Gables
Highlawn Pavilion	Chakra
	Ombra
27 Pluckemin Inn	**25** Serenade
Buddakan	Equus
Nicholas	Chart House
Hotoke	Molly Pitcher
	Mehndi
26 Catherine Lombardi	Sirena
Peter Shields	Manor
Bernards Inn	Scalini Fedeli
Avenue	Inn at Millrace
Grand Cafe	Bobby Flay Steak
Daryl Wine Bar	Il Capriccio
Ebbitt Room	Chophouse
SeaBlue	Raven & Peach*
Stonehouse	Tabor Rd. Tavern
Red Square	Cuba Libre
Stony Hill Inn	Cafe Matisse
Saddle River Inn	Union Park
Washington Inn	
Ram's Head Inn	

OUTDOORS

Cafe Matisse	Matisse
Inlet	Rat's
La Campagne	Rebecca's
Liberty House	Stella Marina
Lilly's on the Canal	Windansea

ROMANCE

Atlantic B&G	Harvest Moon
Avenue	Raven & Peach
Black Trumpet	Scarborough Fair
David Drake	Sergeantsville Inn
Ebbitt Room	Sirena

ROOMS

Bernards Inn	Madeleine's
Chakra	Manor
Gables	Nicholas
Hamilton's	Serenade
Highlawn Pavilion	Stonehouse

VIEWS

Atlantic B&G	McLoone's
Avenue	Mr. C's
Chart House	Rat's
Liberty House	Sirena
Matisse	Stella Marina

Menus, photos, voting and more – free at ZAGAT.com

Top Service Ratings

29 Nicholas	Casa Giuseppe
27 Lorena's	Highlawn Pavilion
26 Bernards Inn	Tre Figlio
David Drake	Le Petit Chateau
Grand Cafe	Tisha's
Saddle River Inn	Capriccio
Ebbitt Room	Catherine Lombardi
Serenade	Rat's
Scalini Fedeli	Merion Inn
SeaBlue	**24** Stage Left
Washington Inn	Frog and the Peach
Cafe Matisse	Piccola Italia
Pluckemin Inn	Ombra
25 Ram's Head Inn	Girasole
Il Capriccio	Chez Catherine
Cafe Panache	Chef's Table
Whispers	Fascino
Karen & Rei's	CulinAriane
Latour	Gables
Peter Shields	Union Park

Best Buys

Everyone loves a bargain, and New Jersey offers plenty of them. All-you-can-eat options are mostly for lunch and/or brunch. For prix fixe menus, call ahead for availability.

ALL YOU CAN EAT

- 25 | Moghul
- 24 | Mehndi
- Karma Kafe
- 23 | Bistro di Marino
- Chand Palace
- Cinnamon
- Fernandes Steak
- 22 | Black Forest Inn
- Saffron
- Raagini
- Aangan
- Rod's Steak
- 21 | Brasilia Grill
- Hunt Club
- 19 | Minado

BYO

- 28 | Lorena's
- Ajihei
- Cafe Panache
- Saddle River Inn
- 27 | Whispers
- Bay Ave. Trattoria
- Sagami
- CulinAriane
- DeLorenzo's Pies
- Cafe Matisse
- Chef Vola's
- Blue Bottle Cafe
- 26 | Chef's Table
- Latour
- Tisha's

FAMILY-STYLE

- 23 | Wonder Seafood
- Jimmy's
- Mi Bandera
- Risotto House
- 22 | Spanish Tavern
- Dinallo's
- 21 | Pad Thai
- Carmine's
- 20 | Swanky Bubbles
- 19 | Michael's
- 18 | Meson Madrid
- Cuban Pete's

PRIX FIXE LUNCH

- 28 | Saddle River Inn ($25)
- 26 | Frog and the Peach ($25)
- 25 | Le Fandy ($21)
- Wasabi ($9)
- Madeleine's ($20)
- David Burke ($25)
- Copeland ($23)
- Vine ($21)
- 24 | Chengdu 46 ($15)
- Mie Thai ($8)
- 23 | Mikado ($9)
- RoCCA ($10)
- Perryville Inn ($23)
- Village Green ($19)
- Eccola ($15)

PRIX FIXE DINNER

- 27 | André's ($43)
- 26 | Drew's Bayshore ($25)
- Peter Shields ($38)
- Frog and the Peach ($30)
- 25 | Manon ($30)
- Catelli ($30)
- Madeleine's ($29)
- 24 | Ritz Seafood ($35)
- 23 | Farnsworth House ($19)
- Labrador ($35)
- Bank 34 ($34)
- Bienvenue ($35)
- 21 | La Cipollina ($39)
- 20 | Cafe at Rosemont ($24)
- Avenue ($29)

PUB GRUB

- 23 | Light Horse
- 21 | Barnacle Bill's
- 20 | Quiet Man
- 19 | Black Horse
- 18 | Irish Pub
- Inn of the Hawke
- Brickwall Tavern
- 17 | Allendale B&G
- Ugly Mug
- 16 | Alchemist & Barrister
- P.J. Whelihan's
- Chickie's & Pete's

BEST BUYS: BANG FOR THE BUCK

In order of Bang for the Buck rating.

1. Five Guys
2. White House
3. Benny Tudino's
4. Hiram's Roadstand
5. WindMill
6. Hale & Hearty
7. Rutt's Hut
8. Pop Shop
9. Nifty Fifty's
10. Baja Fresh Mex. Grill
11. Surf Taco
12. DeLorenzo's Pies
13. Taqueria
14. Holsten's
15. Johnny Rockets
16. Nana's Deli
17. Tony Luke's
18. Hobby's Deli
19. Country Pancake
20. Tacconelli's
21. Richard's
22. Tom Sawyer
23. Irish Pub
24. Grimaldi's
25. Conte's
26. Gotham City
27. Norma's
28. Brooklyn's Pizza
29. Nha Trang Place
30. Thai Kitchen
31. Sri Thai
32. Eurasian Eatery
33. Tick Tock
34. El Azteca
35. Kibitz Room
36. El Meson
37. Ali Baba
38. Hunan Chinese
39. A Mano
40. Kinchley's Tavern

BEST BUYS: OTHER GOOD VALUES

Aby's
Allen's Clam Bar
Avenue Bistro Pub
Backyards Bistro
Bell's
Bistro 44
Crab House
Delicious Heights
DiPalma
E & V
Far East Taste
Farm 2 Bistro
Federici's
Fedora Cafe
Fishery
Forno
Frankie Fed's
Freshwater's
Hard Grove
Il Fiore

It's Greek To Me
Je's
La Isla
La Sorrentina
Little Food Café
Lotus Cafe
Marmara
Martino's
Mastoris
Mexico Lindo
Moksha
Ponzio's
Pop's Garage
Raymond's
Royal Warsaw
Sister Sue's
Skylark
Somsak
Teresa Caffe
Tortuga's

RESTAURANT DIRECTORY

| | | FOOD | DECOR | SERVICE | COST |

Aamantran Ⓜ *Indian* ▽ 21 | 16 | 21 | $26

Toms River Township | Victoria Plaza | 1594 Rte. 9 S. (Church Rd.) |
732-341-5424 | www.aamantrancuisine.com
Set in a Toms River strip mall, this Indian BYO offers an "extensive
variety" of "well-made" fare (including an "excellent lunch buffet")
in a pleasant setting complete with tandoor ovens and a "gracious"
staff; if a few find it "light on spices", it still stands out "in a veritable
no man's land" of culinary options.

Aangan *Indian* 22 | 17 | 18 | $27

Freehold Township | A&M Plaza | 3475 Rte. 9 N. (Three Brooks Rd.) |
732-761-2900
This Freehold strip-mall Indian BYO purveying "well-prepared"
dishes (both "standard" and "inventive") "never disappointments" –
especially the "bargain" lunch buffet; it's "not much on frills" and
"service can be slow", but it's a "solid performer" nonetheless;
N.B. it shares a kitchen with Ginger Thai, and guests can order
from either menu.

Aby's Mexican Restaurant *Mexican* 20 | 12 | 18 | $23

Matawan | 141 Main St. (Ravine Dr.) | 732-583-9119 |
www.abysrestaurant.com
"Friendly" and "family-run", this BYO storefront in Downtown
Matawan serves "good Mexican for the money" (including "interesting specials") and features a guitarist on Saturdays, which allows
many to overlook "modest portions" and "kitschy" environs; parents
consider the children's menu a "bonus."

Acacia Ⓜ *American* 23 | 21 | 22 | $48

Lawrenceville | 2637 Main St. (bet. Craven Ln. & Phillips Ave.) |
609-895-9885 | www.acaciacuisine.com
Advocates affirm this "upscale" American BYO "mainstay" in
Lawrenceville has experienced "no change in quality or reliability"
since coming under new ownership in late 2007; the food is "well
prepared" and "adventurous", the service "superior" and the decor
"imaginative"; still, dissenters find the vibe "a bit stuffy."

Acquaviva delle fonti *Italian* 22 | 20 | 20 | $45

Westfield | 115 Elm St. (Broad St.) | 908-301-0700 |
www.acquaviva-dellefonti.com
Well-heeled Westfielders head to this "upscale" "staple" in a former
bank for "artfully presented" Northern Italian cuisine that "always
hits the mark", complemented by "hospitable" service; though "the
din" can be daunting at times and prices aren't cheap, most find it
"worth the occasional splurge"; N.B. you can BYO if you dine alfresco in the summertime.

Adega Grill *Portuguese/Spanish* 21 | 21 | 21 | $39

Newark | 130-132 Ferry St. (bet. Madison & Monroe Sts.) | 973-589-8830 |
www.adegagrill.com
A "good-looking crowd" bellies up to "enormous portions" of
"amazing fish dishes" and the "best sangria ever" at this "lively"

Ironbound Iberian that's "one of the fancier offerings in Newark"; a "friendly staff" works the "very romantic", faux grapevine–swathed dining rooms (*adega* means 'wine cellar' in Portuguese), as well as the bar and "hip" adjacent lounge.

ⓩ Ajihei Ⓜ *Japanese* 28 | 12 | 17 | $34

Princeton | 11 Chambers St. (Nassau St.) | 609-252-1158
For "fish so fresh it swims to your table" step into this Japanese BYO in Princeton and let Koji Kitamura, "a real sushi master from Japan", make the selection for you; the "no-gimmicks" fare trumps the lack of ambiance and "spotty service" at this "tiny" spot that "won't let in groups larger than four."

Akai Lounge *Japanese* 25 | 20 | 21 | $39

Englewood | 11 N. Dean St. (bet. Bergen St. & Palisades Ave.) | 201-541-0086 | www.akailounge.com
"Finally, a sushi restaurant that gets it" praise fans of this "lively" Englewood lounge, a "red den of hipster chic" offering "beautifully presented", "extremely creative" food (e.g. tuna guacamole); the staff is "courteous and knowledgeable", and if it's "a little pricey", there's always the "great lunch deal."

Akbar *Indian* 19 | 17 | 18 | $32

Edison | 21 Cortland St. (Patrick Ave.) | 732-632-8822 | www.theakbarrestaurant.com
This venerable Edison Indian, which seats up to 500 and "doubles as a wedding hall", may be "a little down at the heels" but it's "trying hard" with "a good selection of well-prepared fare" including a "wonderful lunch buffet"; P.S. "service is attentive", and "children are welcome."

Alan@594 ⓏⓂ *Italian* 21 | 18 | 19 | $37

Upper Montclair | 594 Valley Rd. (Bellevue Ave.) | 973-744-4120
Portions are "large" but the seating is "tight" at this "friendly" Upper Montclair Italian BYO where the "good" eats include what fans call "the best eggplant in North Jersey"; some find the menu "limited" and there's debate over the cost ("fair" vs. "a bit pricey"), but the overall consensus is "solid"; P.S. warm-weather dining is best "in the front room with the French doors open" or in the backyard garden.

Alchemist & Barrister *American* 16 | 17 | 17 | $37

Princeton | 28 Witherspoon St. (Nassau St.) | 609-924-5555 | www.theaandb.com
"Have a burger", "your favorite ale" and some "random conversation about quantum physics" at this "old mainstay" Princeton American where most regulars opt for pub grub at the "fun bar" or in the enclosed patio, rather than "mediocre dinner entrees" in the formal dining room; either way, it's "a comfortable neighborhood place."

Al Dente Ristorante *Italian* 23 | 20 | 23 | $47

Piscataway | 1665 Stelton Rd. (Ethel Rd.) | 732-985-8220 | www.aldenteristorante.com
"Impeccably prepared and seasoned food" in an "overdone but lovely setting" (think "kitschy charm") is the hallmark of this

Piscataway strip-mall Italian staffed by an "entertaining" and "attentive" crew; "expensive but worth it" is the majority view; N.B. there's a newly enhanced patio for alfresco dining.

Aldo & Gianni *Italian* | 21 | 15 | 20 | $40 |

Montvale | A&P Shopping Ctr. | 108 Chestnut Ridge Rd. (Grand Ave.) | 201-391-6866 | www.aldoandgianni.com ✉
South Hackensack | 268 Huyler St. (bet. Dinallo & Hoffman Sts.) | 201-487-4220

These "old-world" Italian "standbys" no longer share a proprietor but loyalists still endorse their "consistently good", "traditional" fare and "warm service"; while tabs can be "on the pricey side" and aesthetes feel that both the South Hackensack BYO (which changed owners in 2007) and strip-mall Montvale location could use a decor boost, regulars appreciate their pleasant "family feel."

Alessio 426 Ⓜ *Italian* | 19 | 19 | 21 | $39 |

Metuchen | 426 Main St. (New St.) | 732-549-6464 | www.alessio426.com

"Good value", a "friendly atmosphere" and "warm" service keep fans coming back to this "simple but nice" Northern Italian–influenced Continental BYO in "bustling Downtown" Metuchen that does "a good job with pastas, fish" and "creative specials"; P.S. "the excellent weekday buffet lunch is very reasonably priced."

Alexander's Ⓜ *French* | ▽ 26 | 26 | 26 | $45 |

Cape May | Alexander's Inn | 653 Washington St. (bet. Franklin & Ocean Sts.) | 609-884-2555 | www.alexandersinn.com

"*Très bien*" is the consensus on both the "excellent" French fare and "white-glove service" provided by tuxedo-clad waiters at this "charming" and "romantic" Cape May B&B restaurant set in a restored 1883 Victorian mansion just blocks from the beach; N.B. closed from January 1 to February 13.

Ali Baba *Mideastern* | 20 | 11 | 16 | $21 |

Hoboken | 912 Washington St. (bet. 9th & 10th Sts.) | 201-653-5319

"Solid" Middle Eastern fare with an "authentic taste" "never disappoints" at this family-run BYO, a "neighborhood standby" (since 1983) on Hoboken's main drag; you may want to "avert your eyes from the Arabian nights kitsch that covers the walls."

Aligado *Japanese/Thai* | ▽ 24 | 15 | 24 | $29 |

Hazlet | 2780 Rte. 35 (Miller Ave.) | 732-888-7568

The "most inventive" sushi and "consistently delicious" Thai fare are purveyed at this "odd and easily overlooked" building on Route 35 in Hazlet, where "hands-on" owner-chef George Zhenz keeps prices "affordable" and "makes time to welcome all patrons"; it works for anything from "family night" to "a date or a ladies' night out."

Allendale Bar & Grill ◗ *Pub Food* | 17 | 13 | 17 | $24 |

Allendale | 67 W. Allendale Ave. (bet. Demercurlo Dr. & Maple St.) | 201-327-3197 | www.mahwahbarandgrill.com

"Pub grub done right" in an "energetic atmosphere" makes this "unpretentious" circa-1935 Allendale "institution" a "local tradition", whether for "family dining" or "casual dates"; the food is "reliable and reasonable" ("best burgers in Bergen"), service is "friendly" and there's "fresh popcorn while you're waiting"; N.B. the menu includes heart-healthy 'Lite Choice' entrees.

Allen's Clam Bar Ⓜ⇗ *Seafood* ▽ 19 | 11 | 18 | $24

New Gretna | 5650 Rte. 9 (Garden State Pkwy.) | 609-296-4106
Experience an "old-time", "no-frills" Jersey clam house at this New Gretna BYO serving "pretty good" seafood (e.g. "the best fried whole-belly clams"); the "rustic" setting features a "comfortable dining room", seasonal "outdoor picnic tables" – and a shark's head at the entrance.

Alstarz Sports Pub *Eclectic* ▽ 16 | 22 | 16 | $31

Bordentown | 140 Rte. 130 S. (Hwy. 206) | 609-291-0200 | www.alstarzsportspub.com
Fans cheer the "fun vibe" at this "upscale" Bordentown sports bar, an offshoot of the landmark Mastoris Diner just across the parking lot; with a vast Eclectic menu and 24 TVs, it's a "place to go to watch a game", but those who maintain "the room outshines the food" recommend that you "stick to the basics" for best results.

⒵ Amanda's *American* 25 | 24 | 24 | $49

Hoboken | 908 Washington St. (bet. 9th & 10th Sts.) | 201-798-0101 | www.amandasrestaurant.com
"Attention to detail is everywhere" at this "classy and elegant" New American in a "charming" 1895 Hoboken brownstone, where a "well-heeled clientele" enjoys "outstanding food that matches the wonderful ambiance" and "always A+ service"; it's "pricey but worth it", particularly for the "best-value early-bird in NJ" ($28 for two) and the "excellent Sunday brunch"; P.S. "a local garage comps patrons for up to three hours."

A Mano *Italian* 21 | 17 | 18 | $24

Ridgewood | 24 Franklin Ave. (Chestnut St.) | 201-493-2000 | www.amanopizza.com
"The crust is genuine Italian but the price is genuine Ridgewood" at this "great-looking" (for the genre) pizzeria with 30-ft.-high ceilings and handcrafted, twin-domed wood-fired ovens from which the "painstakingly authentic" pies emerge; you'll also find salads, appetizers and gelato at this "very easygoing place", though service is too easygoing for some ("could use a boost").

Amarone *Italian* 21 | 15 | 22 | $41

Teaneck | 63 Cedar Ln. (bet. Broad St. & Teaneck Rd.) | 201-833-1897 | www.amaroneristorante.net
"Locals revel in the warmth of the welcome" from "friendly" staffers who provide "old-fashioned white-glove service" at this "cozy" Teaneck Italian serving "consistently delicious" food in "good-size portions" at "fair prices"; contrarians contend it "needs a spark" and even some fans wish for "more stylish" decor, but it's nonetheless a firm "neighborhood favorite."

	FOOD	DECOR	SERVICE	COST

Amelia's Bistro *American*
20 | 20 | 19 | $30

Jersey City | 187 Warren St. (bet. Essex & Morris Sts.) | 201-332-2200 | www.ameliasbistro.com

This "comfortable" New American with a "lively bar scene" in Jersey City's Paulus Hook section earns praise for its "reliable comfort food" and "great brunch"; if a few quibblers note room for improvement and feel "the kitchen tries too hard to be trendy sometimes", its "cool decor", "do-it-yourself hummus" and "outdoor seating in summer" help win over most.

Amici Milano *Italian*
22 | 18 | 21 | $38

Trenton | 600 Chestnut Ave. (Roebling Ave.) | 609-396-6300 | www.amicimilano.com

"Each meal is a memorable experience" at this "old-school" Italian, a "staple" of Trenton's Chambersburg section, with "a tight but cozy setting", live piano some evenings and "convenient parking"; the "staff knows the menu inside and out" and "treats you like family", so most customers leave feeling "happy."

Amiya *Indian*
19 | 17 | 18 | $27

Jersey City | Harborside Financial Ctr. | 160 Greene St. (Christopher Columbus Dr.) | 201-433-8000 | www.amiyarestaurant.com

A "great assortment of Indian cuisine" in a "nice-looking" setting distinguishes this casual, contemporary Jersey City eatery in the Harborside Financial Center; while some find it "a bit pricey", the "lunch buffet is excellent and very reasonable" (as is the validated parking); N.B. there's outdoor seating in warm weather.

Andaman Ⓜ *French/Thai*
∇ 23 | 15 | 19 | $26

Morristown | 147 Morris St. (bet. Elm & King Sts.) | 973-538-5624

"You'll get over the lack of decor with your first bite" of the "reasonably priced, consistently delicious dishes" at this Thai-French BYO "across the street from the Morristown train station"; whether you find the service "indifferent" or "courteous", it's a "reliable alternative to the more expensive spots in the area."

🅉 André's Ⓜ *American*
27 | 21 | 24 | $53

Newton | 188 Spring St. (bet. Adams & Jefferson Sts.) | 973-300-4192 | www.andresrestaurant.com

It's "worth the trip" to this "romantic" storefront in Newton for "super-talented" chef-owner Andre de Waal's "inventive" American cuisine, enhanced by a "wonderful" wine selection (there's also an on-site wine boutique open Wednesdays–Sundays) and "pleasant if not always polished" service; a less-pricey bistro menu is also available; N.B. a sidewalk cafe was added in 2008.

Angelo's Fairmount Tavern *Italian*
21 | 15 | 20 | $33

Atlantic City | 2300 Fairmount Ave. (Mississippi Ave.) | 609-344-2439 | www.angelosfairmounttavern.com

"You can't go to Atlantic City without stopping in" at this "informal", "old-world" Italian "institution" that's been feeding aficionados

| | FOOD | DECOR | SERVICE | COST |

"real red sauce" "just like mama's" and homemade red wine ("a must") for over 70 years; for most it's "a reprieve from the casinos", though not always an escape from the "noise"; P.S. reservations accepted for large parties only, so "expect long waits at the crowded bar."

Anjelica's Ⓜ *Italian*   24 | 17 | 19 | $46

Sea Bright | 1070 Ocean Ave. (bet. Peninsula Ave. & River St.) | 732-842-2800 | www.anjelicas.com

"Consistent", "high-quality" Italian fare – the "delightful" specials in particular – more than compensates for the "cramped quarters", "crowds" and "way loud" decibels at this "upscale" brick-walled Sea Bright BYO that's a "favorite" of many; P.S. in season, "get there early or plan to wait", even with reservations.

Anna's Italian Kitchen Ⓜ *Italian*   25 | 15 | 20 | $48

Middletown | Fountain Ridge Shopping Ctr. | 1686 Rte. 35 S. (Old Country Rd.) | 732-275-9142 | www.annasitaliankitchen.com

As the ratings attest, "the main attraction" at this Middletown BYO "is definitely the food" of chef-owner Anna Perri – "authentic", "homestyle" Italian that's "cooked to perfection", from "Dover sole to dessert crêpes"; if the "price is high" for a strip-mall location, "attentive" service helps compensate.

Anthony David's *Italian*   26 | 19 | 22 | $43

Hoboken | 953 Bloomfield St. (10th St.) | 201-222-8399 | www.anthonydavids.com

The "inventive" Northern Italian food is "spot on" at this "revamped", "intimate" (some say "cramped") Hoboken BYO with "efficient, smiley service", where seating options include the more "formal" dining room, a "casual bistro setting" (in the storefront gourmet market) or sidewalk tables; it's "always a hit" for brunch (served daily), and you're advised to "save room" for its "heavenly" dessert doughnuts.

Anthony's Ⓜ *Italian*   23 | 18 | 21 | $34

Haddon Heights | 512 Station Ave. (White Horse Pike) | 856-310-7766 | www.anthonyscuisine.com

"South Jersey has many good Italian restaurants – and this is one of them" declare devotees of owner Anthony Iannone's "neighborhood" BYO, a "staple" of the Downtown Haddon Heights dining scene; chef John Pilarz's "innovative" cooking is "always fresh", "never boring" and served in a "pretty" storefront setting – in all, it's likely to delight even the most difficult to please family members.

Antonia's by the Park *Italian*   ▽ 20 | 18 | 20 | $40

North Bergen | 9011 Palisade Ave. (Woodcliff Ave.) | 201-868-0750 | www.antoniasbythepark.com

Steps from Hudson County Park in North Bergen, this "reliable neighborhood Italian" in a "lovely setting" has "something for everyone" according to fans – "huge portions" of "solid, good food", a "kind, attentive" staff, full bar service, weekend entertainment and "plenty of parking", all of which explains why the few who find the fare "ordinary" are easily outvoted.

Anton's at the Swan Ⓜ *American*   22 | 23 | 21 | $48

Lambertville | Swan Hotel | 43 S. Main St. (Swan St.) | 609-397-1960 | www.antons-at-the-swan.com

"Atmosphere" abounds at this "charming and romantic" Lambertville New American "tucked away" in the "beautiful, old" Swan Hotel; while some extol the dining room's "delightful" but "expensive" menu, others prefer the "casual" pub fare and a brew in the "cozy" bar with a fireplace that looks out onto an "enchanting" patio.

Aozora ⊘ *French/Japanese*   25 | 20 | 21 | $43

Montclair | 407 Bloomfield Ave. (Seymour St.) | 973-233-9400 | www.aozorafusion.com

Offering "a brilliant mix of Asian and French cuisines", the "broad", "innovative" menu at this "contemporary" Montclair BYO boasts Nelson Yip's "exotic sushi" and the "best-cooked meats and seafood" served by an "earnest" staff; just note that the "Zen-like atmosphere" can morph into "very noisy" and "crammed", so "go midweek to avoid the crowds" – or opt for delivery in the Montclair area (cash only).

Aquila Cucina *Italian*   22 | 19 | 23 | $41

New Providence | 30 South St. (Springfield Ave.) | 908-464-8383 | www.aquilarestaurant.com

"Still delightful after all these years" say admirers of this New Providence BYO and its "traditional Italian with a twist" fare, "prepared with a very deft imagination" and served by a "polite, efficient" staff in a "comfortable", "never rushed" atmosphere; if a few label it "average", more consider it "reliable for a nice quiet meal."

Armando's *Italian*   18 | 16 | 18 | $41

Fort Lee | 144 Main St. (Parker Ave.) | 201-461-4220

It's "been around forever" but "this "friendly" Fort Lee Italian is "still going strong", with "reliable" "old-world cooking" ("full meals" or "good pizza") and a "warm, friendly" environment; some argue that it's "nothing exceptional", but at least "the kitchen is cooperative", portions "ample" and the staff "makes you feel very welcome."

Aroma Royal Thai *Thai*   ▽ 21 | 19 | 20 | $29

Franklin Park | 3175 Rte. 27 (Delar Pkwy.) | 732-422-9300

A "very varied and interesting menu" awaits diners at this "accommodating" BYO Thai tucked in a Franklin Park strip mall; dishes are "well prepared and artfully presented" in a setting that reminds some of a "boardroom" ("heavy wood tables and chairs") – and any board would be pleased with the "reasonable prices" and amiable service.

	FOOD	DECOR	SERVICE	COST

Arthur's Steakhouse & Pub *Steak* | 19 | 13 | 17 | $34 |

North Brunswick | 644 Georges Rd. (Ashland Pl.) | 732-828-1117 |
www.arthurssteakhouse.org

"Value" abounds at this "very noisy but enjoyable" North Brunswick
steakhouse where carnivorous cravings are assuaged by "huge portions" of "very good steaks and burgers" complemented by an "endless" supply of pickles and coleslaw; the "no-frills" atmosphere
("plenty of paper plates") is "all part of the charm"; N.B. it's now
serving a selection of sandwiches and desserts from Harold's NY
Deli of Lyndhurst.

Arthur's Tavern *Steak* | 18 | 13 | 16 | $31 |

Hoboken | 237 Washington St. (3rd St.) | 201-656-5009
Morris Plains | 700 Speedwell Ave. (Littleton Rd.) |
973-455-9705
www.arthurstavern.com

"Go early or be prepared to wait" at these "loud", "bare-bones"
"throwbacks" in Hoboken and Morris Plains serving "giant" beers
and steaks that are "sized to challenge competitive eaters" and
"priced to sell"; if some sniff "a little updating" is in order, partisans
proclaim "you go for the food not the atmosphere"; N.B. an Emerson
location has closed.

Arturo's Ⓜ *Italian* | 23 | 20 | 21 | $47 |

Midland Park | 41 Central Ave. (bet. Greenwood & Madison Aves.) |
201-444-2466 | www.arturos-restaurant.com

"A hometown classic", this Midland Park Southern Italian "won't
disappoint" with its "extensive" menu of "dishes like mama used
to make", even if they are "on the expensive side"; "elegant
tuxedoed service" adds to the "classy atmosphere", making it
perfect "for a special occasion"; P.S. some contend "it helps to
be a regular."

Assembly Steak House *Steak* | 17 | 17 | 17 | $53 |

Englewood Cliffs | 495 Sylvan Ave. (Palisade Ave.) | 201-568-2616 |
www.assemblysteakhouse.com

This Englewood Cliffs steakhouse divides the assembly: while
advocates say aye to its "good" cuts, "smart-casual" atmosphere
and "fair-value" prices, opponents veto "mediocre" fare that's
"too pricey for what you get"; but both sides high-five "the hectic
bar scene that keeps this place going", complete with free
happy-hour hors d'oeuvres.

A Tavola Ⓜ *Italian* | 19 | 14 | 18 | $33 |

Old Bridge | Deep Run Shopping Ctr. | 3314 Rte. 9 S. (Ferry Rd.) |
732-607-1120 | www.atavola1.com

Fans say this Italian BYO in an Old Bridge strip mall remains a "local
gem" for "homestyle food" prepared in an "action-filled open
kitchen" and delivered by a "helpful" staff in "tight" quarters; but
dissenters feel it lost some luster with staff changes, citing "inconsistent" cooking and service – "it could be a keeper if they get
their act together."

	FOOD	DECOR	SERVICE	COST

Athenian Garden ⓜ *Greek* ▽ 24 | 13 | 19 | $33

Galloway Township | 619 S. New York Rd. (bet. Brook Ln. & Holly Brook Dr.) | 609-748-1818 | www.athenian-garden.com
"Shout *opa!*" – "when you're in the mood for good ethnic food", aficionados say this "excellent" Galloway Greek has "the real stuff", right down to the rustic taverna setting; it's especially "fun with a group" – and "BYO adds to the value."

Atlantic Bar & Grill *American/Seafood* 25 | 22 | 22 | $49

South Seaside Park | Central & 24th Aves. (J St.) | 732-854-1588 | www.atlanticbarandgrillnj.com
Thanks to its "floor-to-ceiling windows", you "can't beat the ocean view" at this "beach-chic" Shore American seafooder where the fare is "always on the money" (if "a bit pricey") and purveyed by "educated servers"; N.B. closed January–February, with live music Thursdays and Fridays in season.

A Toute Heure ⓈⓂ *American* 25 | 19 | 22 | $45

Cranford | 232 Centennial Ave. (Elm St.) | 908-276-6600 | www.atouteheure.com
"Fresh on every level" is how advocates describe this "charming" Cranford American BYO with French and Spanish accents that makes "terrific use" of "market-driven" ingredients in "creative yet comforting dishes" (which some find "a little pricey for the portions"); it's run by "friendly, attentive" owners, and though no reserving means waits are "often long", it's "worth it" – "so bring a bottle of wine and relax."

🅩 Augustino's Ⓢ🍴 *Italian* 26 | 16 | 21 | $46

Hoboken | 1104 Washington St. (bet. 11th & 12th Sts.) | 201-420-0104 | www.augustinosrestaurant.com
"Reservations are a must" ("months in advance for weekends") at this "cramped", "cash-only", 10-table Hoboken Southern Italian, aka "the Rao's of NJ", serving "incredible homemade specialties" at "realistic prices" – and there's no charge for the "side of swearing" from "the spirited staff"; N.B. walk-ins can try for a seat at the small bar.

🅩 Avenue *French* 20 | 26 | 18 | $57

Long Branch | 23 Ocean Ave. (Cooper Ave.) | 732-759-2900 | www.leclubavenue.com
"Step into St. Tropez" and "mingle with the beautiful people" at this "gorgeous" French brasserie in Long Branch with "breathtaking" ocean views and a "trendy" upstairs lounge – just "bring plenty of money or Daddy's AmEx"; some say service "could be better" but the food draws mostly good reviews, with special kudos for the "not-to-be-missed" raw bar and "superb" cocktails; N.B. the presence of a new chef may outdate the above scores.

🆕 Avenue Bistro Pub *American* - | - | - | I

Verona | 558 Bloomfield Ave. (bet. Gould St. & Park Pl.) | 973-239-7444
Everybody knows your name at this friendly, upscale tavern on Bloomfield Avenue in Verona serving New American comfort food

and an affordable wine list; the work of local artists is on display and the bar's bustling with regulars – Norm and the gang would feel right at home.

Avon Pavilion *American*   19 | 16 | 17 | $31

Avon-by-the-Sea | 600 Ocean Ave. (bet. Norwood & Woodland Aves.) | 732-775-1043 | www.avonpavilion.com

The "ocean view is priceless" at this seasonal American BYO on the boardwalk in Avon, where fans line up for "surprisingly good" breakfasts, lunches and dinners served by a "spunky" staff; regulars recommend that you "sit outside" for "perfect people-watching."

Axelsson's Blue Claw *Seafood*   23 | 20 | 21 | $49

Cape May | 991 Ocean Dr. (Rte. 109) | 609-884-5878 | www.blueclawrestaurant.com

"The seafood is out of this world" at this "pricey", "off-the-beaten-path" "classic" in a "quaint" Cape May boatyard sporting a "yachting theme" and an "attractive" bar; those with an ax to grind say the food's "unimaginative", but the majority maintains it's "always a great experience"; N.B. there's piano music on weekends.

Axia Taverna *Greek*   23 | 24 | 21 | $49

Tenafly | 18 Piermont Rd. (bet. Central Ave. & Jay St.) | 201-569-5999 | www.axiataverna.com

Surveyors are smitten by the "extraordinary interpretations of Greek classics" and the "gorgeous interior design" at this "upscale" bi-level Greek in Tenafly also boasting "gracious service"; though the din can be "deafening" and the tab "very pricey", for most it's a "lovely experience"; P.S. "live music on Tuesdays is always fun."

Azúcar Ⓜ *Cuban*   21 | 20 | 19 | $40

Jersey City | 495 Washington Blvd. (Thomas Gangemi Dr.) | 201-222-0090 | www.azucarcubancuisine.com

"Informal and fun" – "especially on an expense account"– this "upscale" "slice of Havana in Jersey City" serves "generous portions" of "real-deal Cuban cooking" "in a kitschy atmosphere" that includes an "upstairs cigar room" and "dancing in a kicky little bar"; "service with a smile" is also *"muy bueno."*

NEW Backyards Bistro *American*   - | - | - | I

Hoboken | 732 Jefferson St. (8th St.) | 201-222-2660 | www.backyardsbistro.com

Far off the beaten track, this quirky BYO newcomer in Hoboken attracts a laid-back crowd in the mood for creative Americana from a reasonably priced menu filled with playful possibilities like pretzel-bread sandwiches, Bada Bing burgers, salads and more; there's weekend brunch and takeout too.

Bahama Breeze *Caribbean*   18 | 20 | 18 | $27

Cherry Hill | Cherry Hill Mall | 2000 Rte. 38 (Haddonfield Rd.) | 856-317-8317 | www.bahamabreeze.com

This "casual" Caribbean with an "island atmosphere" in the Cherry Hill Mall pleases with "giant" portions of "decent" "quasi-

Bahamian" fare; "it's a chain, yes" (this is the only NJ branch), but "you can convince yourself you're in the tropics", espeically after a few of its "excellent" tropical cocktails; P.S. "just be prepared to wait."

Bahrs Landing *Seafood*

| 16 | 15 | 16 | $39 |

Highlands | 2 Bay Ave. (Highland Ave.) | 732-872-1245 | www.bahrs.com
A "tranquil" waterside setting overlooking Sandy Hook Bay and "nostalgia" keep 'em coming back to this "Jersey Shore tradition" in Highlands, which has been dishing out "no-frills" seafood since 1917; some suggest it "needs a face-lift" in menu and milieu, but admirers count on this "landmark" for "good, basic" affordable food.

Baja *Mexican*

| 19 | 15 | 17 | $26 |

Hoboken | 104 14th St. (Washington St.) | 201-653-0610
Jersey City | 117 Montgomery St. (bet. Marin Blvd. & Warren St.) | 201-915-0062
www.bajamexicancuisine.com
"The Jersey City location is much larger" than its "cramped" Hoboken *hermano,* but both offer "substantial portions" of "solid" Mexican *comidas,* "killer margaritas" and "tequila lists that alone are worth the visit"; service can falter "when crowded" and they're often "festive" and "noisy" – "but that's appropriate for this type of restaurant."

Baja Fresh Mexican Grill *Mexican*

| 17 | 10 | 14 | $13 |

East Rutherford | 93 Rt. 17 S. (Paterson Ave.) | 201-507-1644
Wayne | 1600 Rte. 23 N. (Packanack Lake Rd.) | 973-872-2555
East Brunswick | 683 Rte. 18 (Kendall Rd.) | 732-967-0505
East Hanover | 136 Rte. 10 W. (Ridgedale Ave.) | 973-952-0080
Edison | 561 Rte. 1 S. (Wilson Ave.) | 732-985-3555
South Plainfield | 6400 Hadley Rd. (Stelton Rd.) | 908-756-4141
Watchung | 1595 Rte. 22 W. (Raymond Ave.) | 908-322-0202
Middletown | 500 Rte. 35 S. (Oak Hill Rd.) | 732-758-0058
Union Township | 2311 Rte. 66 W. (bet. Rte. 18 & Seaview Sq. Dr.) | 732-493-5300
Mount Laurel | 10A Centerton Rd. (Marter Ave.) | 856-802-0892
www.bajafresh.com
Additional locations throughout New Jersey
You'll receive a "decent value for your peso" at these Shore and North Jersey outposts of the "casual", "quick-service" Mexican chain reputed for "healthier, low-fat" takes on typical eats "complemented by an ample fixings bar"; still, some assert they "can't compare to authentic outfits" and note that "locations tend to vary a bit."

Bamboo Leaf Ⓜ *Thai/Vietnamese*

| 22 | 17 | 18 | $27 |

Bradley Beach | 724 Main St. (bet. Lareine & McCabe Aves.) | 732-774-1661
Howell | Howell Ctr. | 2450 Rte. 9 S. (White Rd.) | 732-761-3939
"Carnivore, herbivore, omnivore?" – "everyone can agree" on the "nice change of pace" offered by the "authentic" fare at this Southeast Asian Shore duo with "pleasant" bamboo-accented decor and "friendly" (if sometimes "spotty") service; while the Bradley Beach locale specializes in "great Thai" and Vietnamese, the Howell outpost concentrates only on Vietnamese – and BYO "adds value" to both.

	FOOD	DECOR	SERVICE	COST

Bangkok Garden *Thai*

| 22 | 14 | 20 | $28 |

Hackensack | 261 Main St. (bet. Camden & Salem Sts.) | 201-487-2620 | www.bangkokgarden-nj.com

The "authentic, spicy" food "is the star" at this neighborhood Thai, an "oasis in Downtown Hackensack" where "the mundane storefront decor is more than offset by the warm, sincere service"; "always consistent", it makes for a "pleasant evening out without spending."

Bank 34 🖼️Ⓜ️ *Pan-Asian/Seafood*

| 23 | 21 | 22 | $38 |

Somerville | 34 Division St. (Main St.) | 908-722-9995 | www.bank34.com

Regulars of this Pan-Asian seafooder in Somerville put their money on its "inventive", "beautifully prepared" dishes (from raw tuna and wasabi pizza to ostrich in green curry); factor in its three-course prix fixe dinner ("an unbelievable deal"), "very attentive service", warm decor and BYO policy and fans ask "what's not to like?", though a few insist its across-the-street sibling, Origin, is "better."

Barnacle Ben's *Seafood*

| 20 | 15 | 18 | $31 |

Moorestown | Moorestown Commons | 300 Young Ave. (Centerton Rd.) | 856-235-5808 | www.barnaclebens.com

At 30 years young, this BYO seafooder "tucked away" in Moorestown Commons is a "good, solid place" with a "strong local following", mainly for its "comprehensive menu" of "fresh fish and seafood" but also for its "earnest" servers, "updated" atmosphere and "good value"; dining on the patio is a fair-weather "plus."

Barnacle Bill's ⚫ *Burgers*

| 21 | 16 | 18 | $28 |

Rumson | 1 First St. (River Rd.) | 732-747-8396

"Burgers still rule" at this "good-time" "shack" overlooking the Navesink River that also purveys "very good" appetizers and "tasty pub grub"; a Rumson "institution", "it's not pretty" – "guests (are encouraged) to throw peanut shells on the floor" – and it's "noisy" to boot, but the fact that "there's always a huge wait" attests to its popularity.

Barnsboro Inn Ⓜ️ *American*

| ▽ 22 | 21 | 22 | $35 |

Sewell | 699 Main St. (Center St.) | 856-468-3557 | www.barnsboroinn.com

"Did George Washington sleep here?" wonder guests of this "charming" Sewell tavern whose history dates back to 1720; these days it serves "delicious" Traditional–New American fare in recently renovated (i.e. less formal) surroundings, including two "lovely" dining rooms, an enclosed sun porch and a "darkly lit" bar; N.B. dinner is served only at the bar on Mondays.

Barone's Tuscan Grille *Italian*

| 20 | 18 | 20 | $32 |

Moorestown | 280 Young Ave. (Main St.) | 856-234-7900

Villa Barone *Italian*

Collingswood | 753 Haddon Ave. (bet. Frazer & Washington Aves.) | 856-858-2999

www.baronerestaurants.com

This pair of "red-gravy" Italian BYOs with a "friendly atmosphere" is "nicely run" by brothers who dish up "good food and lots of it" at prices that "won't break the bank"; just be prepared to put up with the "roar" of the happy but "noisy" South Jersey clientele.

Barrel's *Italian*
17 | 11 | 17 | $30

Linwood | 199 New Rd. (Central Ave.) | 609-926-9900 🛇
Margate | 9 S. Granville Ave. (Ventnor Ave.) | 609-823-4400
www.barrelsfoods.com

These Shore Italian BYOs are "neighborhood" resources offering "good but basic food in a relaxed atmosphere"; fans also tout them for lunch and takeout, and those who felt the decor needed "updating" may be appeased by a 2008 remodeling of the Margate location.

Basilico *Italian*
24 | 21 | 22 | $45

Millburn | 324 Millburn Ave. (Main St.) | 973-379-7020 |
www.basilicomillburn.com

A "solid performer" near Millburn's Paper Mill Playhouse ("go after the theater crowd has rushed out"), this "chic" Northern Italian boasts "inventive versions of traditional fare", "professional" service and a BYO policy that "keeps the cost down"; though a few sniff it's "not what it used to be", most deem it "a safe bet" – "if you can overcome the noise" and score a table: "reserve in advance" as it's "very popular"; P.S. the "pleasant" garden is a "well-kept secret."

Basil T's *American/Italian*
20 | 18 | 20 | $38

Red Bank | 183 Riverside Ave. (Maple Ave.) | 732-842-5990 |
www.basilt.com

"Bodacious" beers handcrafted in-house and "good" pastas and pizzas star at this "upscale" Red Bank brewpub/restaurant with a menu of American and Italian favorites; "friendly" service and a "lively" (read: "noisy") bar crowd add appeal, though some fret that it's "become too expensive."

🌣 Baumgart's Café *American/Pan-Asian*
19 | 14 | 17 | $27

Edgewater | City Pl. | 59 The Promenade (River Rd.) | 201-313-3889
Englewood | 45 E. Palisade Ave. (bet. Dean St. & Grand Ave.) |
201-569-6267
Livingston | Livingston Town Ctr. | 4175 Town Center Way
(Livingston Ave.) | 973-422-0955
Ridgewood | 158 Franklin Ave. (Walnut St.) | 201-612-5688
www.baumgartscafe.com

"Perfect for those who can't agree on what to eat", these "funky little joints" (BYOs except for Edgewater) have built their rep on "an interesting mix" of "tasty" East-West eats ("chow mein followed by a hot fudge sundae – so good!"); though a few are bummed by "inconsistencies", most find it an "enjoyable, eclectic experience."

🌣 Bay Avenue Trattoria Ⓜ *American/Italian*
27 | 12 | 22 | $41

Highlands | 122 Bay Ave. (Cornwell St.) | 732-872-9800 |
www.bayavetrattoria.com

"No decor but who cares?" when Joe Romanowski "still puts out great" American-Italian fare and Maggie Lubcke is "out with the patrons being charming" at this "small" (40-seat), "low-key" BYO

| | FOOD | DECOR | SERVICE | COST |

"gem" in Highlands; "tight tables" and "paper napkins" notwithstanding, reservations are "a must" at this perennial high-scorer.

Bayou Cafe *Cajun/Creole*   ▽ 21 | - | 20 | $28
Freehold | 32 W. Main St. (bet. Court & Throckmorton Sts.) | 732-845-1800 | www.bayoucafe.net
If you "can't get to New Orleans" you'll find "authentic bayou cuisine" (alligator, jambalaya) "jumpin' with flavor and spices" at this Freehold Cajun-Creole BYO that also offers Caribbean dishes (oxtail stew, jerk chicken); a "welcoming staff" adds to the good times; N.B. it recently moved from its Manasquan location.

Bazzarelli *Italian*   21 | 14 | 20 | $32
Moonachie | 117 Moonachie Rd. (Joseph St.) | 201-641-4010 | www.bazzarellirestaurant.com
"Down the road from Giants Stadium", this "casual" Moonachie veteran is the place to go for "good red-sauce Italian" – and pizza "before a game"; although the "seating is a bit close" and "there's no decor to speak of", the portions are "generous" and the service "friendly."

Bazzini at 28 Oak Street 🅉 *American/Italian*   19 | 15 | 19 | $47
Ridgewood | 28 Oak St. (bet. Franklin & Ridgewood Aves.) | 201-689-7313 | www.bazziniusa.com
"The decor is somewhat stale, but the fare is anything but" say admirers of this "underappreciated" Ridgewood BYO serving "inventive – yet nothing crazy" – Italian–New American eats; if some find the food "a bit overpriced"; a "bargain early-bird" prix fixe menu is available nightly, $30 for three courses.

Belford Bistro *American*   ▽ 28 | 19 | 25 | $37
Belford | 870 Main St. (Leonardville Rd.) | 732-495-8151 | www.belfordbistro.com
Fans flock to this American BYO storefront in "sleepy" Belford – a "fantastic find off the beaten path" – for "inspired food prepared to perfection" by husband-wife team Kurt Bomberger and Crista Trovato; the "decor is minimal" but "warm" and the service "knowledgeable" and "caring", but the small room is "loud when full", which is almost always – so make a reservation.

Bella Sogno Ⓜ *Italian*   20 | 16 | 19 | $36
Bradley Beach | 600 Main St. (Brinley Ave.) | 732-869-0700 | www.bellasogno.net
You may need your GPS to find this "small", "family-oriented" storefront BYO in Bradley Beach, but fans say it's worth the hunt for a "decent" Italian meal; "dependable" and "relaxed" sums it up – including the service.

Bell's 🍴 *American/Italian*   21 | 13 | 20 | $28
Lambertville | 183 N. Union St. (bet. Buttonwood & Elm Sts.) | 609-397-2226 | www.bellstavern.com
Still an "unaffected" "real deal", this "convivial" American-Italian "neighborhood favorite" in Lambertville delivers on "fairly priced",

"good red-gravy" specialties served by a "warm and friendly" staff in a "basic dining room"; the popular bar draws a "loud" crowd on weekends; N.B. no reservations, cash only.

Bell's Mansion Ⓜ *American*   17 | 19 | 17 | $39
Stanhope | 11 Main St. (Rte. 183) | 973-426-9977 | www.bellsmansion.com

This "gracious", circa-1840 Stanhope home offers eclectic American eats, from pub grub to beef Wellington, in four "cozy" dining rooms, a taproom and garden patio; service may be "slow" and critics label the food "average", but thanks to a rumored ghost it may provide a "haunting" experience.

Belmont Tavern ⊅ *Italian*   23 | 9 | 15 | $33
Bloomfield | 12 Bloomfield Ave. (Heckel St.) | 973-759-9609

"It's an 'experience' to eat" at this Bloomfield "neighborhood" "throwback in time", an "old-fashioned Italian" "institution" ("ignore the decor") where "only newbies use a menu" to order "homestyle" chicken Savoy and shrimp 'beeps'; "amusingly rude waitresses" add to the charm; N.B. closed Tuesdays.

Benihana *Japanese*   18 | 18 | 19 | $37
Short Hills | 840 Morris Tpke. (South Terrace) | 973-467-9550
Edison | 60 Parsonage Rd. (bet. Mason St. & Oakwood Ave.) | 732-744-0660
NEW **Toms River** | Ocean County Mall | 1201 Hooper Ave. (Oak Ave.) | 732-736-7071
Pennsauken | 5255 Marlton Pike (Lexington Ave.) | 856-665-6320
www.benihana.com

Going strong at 45 years plus, this groundbreaking national Japanese chain's four NJ locations offer "fun" teppanaki shows – "just watch out for flying shrimp!" – plus "remarkably consistent" steakhouse fare (and a "good assortment" of sushi); N.B. the latest location opened in late 2008 at Ocean County Mall in Toms River.

Benito's Ⓜ *Italian*   ▽ 24 | 19 | 22 | $37
Chester | 44 Main St. (Hedges Rd.) | 908-879-1887 | www.benitostrattoria.com

"The dishes are quite delectable and the portions are fair" at this "excellent" Northern Italian BYO in Chester; though some think the "menu needs updating", compensations include a "comfortable" setting and a "friendly" staff that provides "good service when they're not overloaded", making it a "great place to meet friends."

Benny Tudino's ●⊅ *Pizza*   20 | 7 | 14 | $11
Hoboken | 622 Washington St. (bet. 6th & 7th Sts.) | 201-792-4132

"Slices bigger than your head" attract admirers to this "old-school" Hoboken pizza "institution" that "satisfies the urge for a slice of cheesy goodness" at "good-value" prices; there's a "full Italian dinner menu" too, so it's a natural "for a low-budget gathering or quick fill-up."

	FOOD	DECOR	SERVICE	COST

Berkeley Restaurant & Fish Market *Seafood*
▽ 20 | 12 | 18 | $35

South Seaside Park | Central & 24th Aves. (J St.) | 732-793-0400
The "decor is nothing to talk about" at this seasonal South Seaside Park veteran, but the "view overlooking Barnegat Bay" – especially from the 360-degree upstairs windows – "is special", as is seafood "so fresh it should move"; the combo platters get particular raves, and it's touted for takeout too; N.B. the market and bar are open year-round.

☑ Bernards Inn *American*
26 | 26 | 26 | $71

Bernardsville | 27 Mine Brook Rd. (Quimby Ln.) | 908-766-0002 | www.bernardsinn.com
"Outstanding from start to finish", this "gorgeous" Bernardsville New American "exudes elegance" in a "turn-back-the-clock highway inn"; chef Corey W. Heyer's cuisine "changes with the seasons" but remains "consistently fantastic" and is enhanced by "excellent" service and an "impeccable" wine list; if some find it "stuffy", more consider it "one of Jersey's best" – "just be prepared to pay the price"; N.B. jacket suggested.

Berta's Chateau *Italian*
21 | 18 | 21 | $55

Wanaque | 7 Grove St. (Prospect St.) | 973-835-0992 | www.bertaschateau.com
The accent is on Italy's Piedmont region at this "out-of-the-way" "sentimental favorite" in Wanaque with an "expansive menu" and impressive wine list, presented by a "very knowledgeable" and "charming" staff; the "country house setting" is "a splendid place for a romantic dinner", but it's "pricey" and some fret this "grande dame" is "a bit dated."

Beyti Kebab *Turkish*
23 | 10 | 17 | $27

Union City | 4105 Park Ave. (41st St.) | 201-865-6281
This Union City Turkish BYO is known for its butcher storefront and "real thing kebabs", but it attracts vegetarians too with its "wonderful meze" and "exceptional salads"; diners who appreciate "excellent value" don't mind that the "decor could use a lift"; P.S. "it really gets wild" on belly-dancing Saturday nights.

Bienvenue Ⓜ *French*
23 | 20 | 21 | $48

Red Bank | 7 E. Front St. (Wharf Ave.) | 732-936-0640
"Bon appétit!" declare devotees of this "quaint and intimate" French bistro in Red Bank run by a Gallic couple who delivers "authentic", "spectacularly delicious" food that's "pricey – but at least it's a BYO" (wine lovers advise you to "bring lots so you can linger over every bite"); N.B. there's a three-course dinner prix fixe ($35) and a four-course tasting menu ($65).

Big Ed's BBQ *BBQ*
19 | 11 | 16 | $27

Matawan | 305 Rte. 34 N. (Amboy Rd.) | 732-583-2626 | www.bigedsbbq.com
"Prepare to chow down" at this "all-you-can-eat ribfest" in a "quirky" "ol' country barn" in Matawan where "humongous por-

tions" of "delicious" BBQ make you feel "closer to heaven – and a larger pair of pants"; though the meat "can be a little tough – quantity makes up for it"; N.B. it offers combos, sandwiches and kids' meals too.

Bistro at Red Bank, The *Eclectic*
21 | 18 | 19 | $40

Red Bank | 14 Broad St. (bet. Front & Mechanic Sts.) | 732-530-5553 | www.thebistroatredbank.com

"Laugh if you want", but this "casual", "reliable", "conveniently located" Red Bank Eclectic with "diverse" offerings is praised equally for its "delicious" sushi and its "brick-oven" pizzas; sidewalk dining makes for "great people-watching" and servers "know their stuff"; N.B. only NJ wines are served but BYO is welcome.

Bistro di Marino Ⓜ *Italian*
23 | 19 | 21 | $32

Collingswood | 492 Haddon Ave. (Crestmont Terrace) | 856-858-1700 | www.bistrodimarino.com

"Melt-in-your-mouth" gnocchi and other "excellent" Italian food from "young chef" James Marino is served in a "relaxed, easy" ambiance at this BYO in "trendy" Collingswood; "friendly" service, an "affordable lunch buffet" (Tuesdays–Fridays, $11.95) and a takeout shop help make it a local "favorite."

Bistro 44 Ⓢ Ⓜ *American/French*
24 | 19 | 23 | $39

Toms River | 44 Washington St. (bet. Hooper Ave. & Main St.) | 732-818-7644 | www.bistro-44.com

"A beacon of fine dining" in Downtown Toms River, this family-run American-French BYO is "a fantastic bargain" (the "twilight menu" even more so); besides "well-executed", "inventive" seasonal fare, it boasts a "cozy" setting and a staff that's "dedicated to making customers happy."

Bistro Olé Ⓜ *Portuguese/Spanish*
24 | 18 | 22 | $41

Asbury Park | 230 Main St. (bet. Cookman & Mattison Aves.) | 732-897-0048 | www.ricobistroole.com

"Who doesn't love" Rico Rivera, the "irrepressible" owner-host of this "super-popular" Asbury Park Iberian with a "devoted following" that deems the "fantastic" dishes "all hits and no misses"; if a minority thinks it has "slipped", the "omnipresent lines" in summer caused by the no-rezzie policy proves they're outvoted; P.S. bring wine to this BYO "and watch it magically turn into a great pitcher of sangria."

Blackbird Dining Establishment Ⓜ *American*
26 | 19 | 23 | $42

Collingswood | 619 Collings Ave. (White Horse Pike) | 856-854-3444 | www.blackbirdnj.com

Chef-owner Alex Capasso's "first-rate", "creative" seasonal American fare (e.g. housemade pasta, suckling pig) "has what it takes" to "make your taste buds spread their wings and fly" at this "upscale" Collingswood BYO; though "hard-surfaced decor makes it noisy", the "dining room is sunny, airy and beautifully decorated" and service is "prompt and friendly."

Menus, photos, voting and more – free at ZAGAT.com

	FOOD	DECOR	SERVICE	COST

Black Duck on Sunset *Eclectic*
24 | 21 | 23 | $47

West Cape May | 1 Sunset Blvd. (B'way) | 609-898-0100 |
www.blackduckonsunset.com

With "out-of-the-ordinary" Eclectic offerings (e.g. honey rose duck)
ferried by a "friendly" staff, this "homey" Victorian BYO "away from
the hustle and bustle of Downtown Cape May" "is a sure thing" –
and "a must in summer" for sunsets; N.B. hours vary by season.

Black Forest Inn *Continental/German*
22 | 20 | 20 | $45

Stanhope | 249 Rte. 206 N. (I-80, exit 25) | 973-347-3344 |
www.blackforestinn.com

"*Wunderbar!*" is the consensus on the German-Continental dishes
(sauerbraten in red wine, pan-roasted sea scallops) with "no concession to calories" served at this Stanhope veteran, one of the "few re-
maining" Bavarian "bastions" in the area; the servers are "jovial" if "not
always the quickest", and there's a "kitschy quaintness" about it all.

Black Horse Tavern & Pub *Pub Food*
19 | 20 | 19 | $38

Mendham | 1 W. Main St. (Hilltop Rd.) | 973-543-7300 |
www.blackhorsenj.com

Set in a converted 1742 farmhouse, this "lively" Mendham "watering
hole" is "like an old saddle – worn but comfortable"; new owners recently came on board but "American classics" are still served in the
"casual" pub and the "charming", formal tavern (closed Mondays);
still, some whinny the food doesn't "live up to the lofty prices."

Black Trumpet *American*
25 | 18 | 23 | $51

Spring Lake | Sandpiper Inn | 7 Atlantic Ave. (Ocean Ave.) | 732-449-4700 |
www.theblacktrumpet.com

"Savvy foodies" trumpet the "imagination" and "culinary skill" of
chefs/co-owners Mark Mikolajczyk and Dave McCleery, who use
"top-flight" ingredients for their "well-prepared", "creative" American
menu at this Spring Lake BYO "tucked" in the cellar of the Sandpiper
Inn; it's a "low-key" place where service comes "with a smile", so
most don't mind if the tab can climb.

Blu Ⓜ *American*
24 | 17 | 20 | $47

Montclair | 554 Bloomfield Ave. (Maple Plaza) | 973-509-2202 |
www.restaurantblu.com

"Being 'blu' ain't so bad" at this "tiny but inviting" Montclair BYO
storefront where chef-owner Zod Arifai turns out "exceptionally inventive" New American fare at prices that fans consider a "bargain,
considering the quality"; despite the "noise", it's a "really good
neighborhood place in a neighborhood with lots of strong contend-
ers"; N.B. his more casual sibling, Next Door is . . . next door.

Blue *American/Eclectic*
24 | 20 | 21 | $48

Surf City | 1016 Long Beach Blvd. (11th St.) | 609-494-7556 |
www.bluelbi.com

The "adventurous", "jaw-droppingly good" American-Eclectic combinations at this seasonal Surf City BYO have some thinking "New York
City", but the "laid-back", "airy atmosphere" is pure LBI; while "service

can be iffy" and it can get "loud", it's still one of the better places for gourmet dining" in these parts; N.B. closed October to mid-April.

ⓩ Blue Bottle Cafe ⊠Ⓜ *American*   27 | 18 | 22 | $47

Hopewell | 101 E. Broad St. (Elm St.) | 609-333-1710 | www.thebluebottlecafe.com

"Reserve early and often" advise admirers of this "excellent" New American BYO in "charming" Hopewell, where "getting a table is half the battle"; husband-wife team Aaron and Rory Philipson make "delightfully delicious use of local ingredients", while "friendly" servers work three "tight" but "cute" dining rooms.

Blue Danube *E European*   ▽ 23 | 15 | 18 | $32

Trenton | 538 Adeline St. (Elm St.) | 609-393-6133 | www.bluedanuberestaurant.com

"Step back in time – if your arteries dare" – to this "unpretentious", "family-run" Trenton spot for "authentic", "stick-to-the-ribs" Eastern European "ethnic cooking" (e.g. stuffed cabbage, chicken paprikas); it's "a bit cramped and stuffy" and service can be "slow", but it's likely to please "if you know what to expect."

Blue Eyes · *Steak*   20 | 22 | 21 | $41

Sewell | 139 Egg Harbor Rd. (County House Rd.) | 856-227-5656 | www.blueeyesrestaurant.com

"Ring-a-ding-ding" – with "more martinis than Frank had fedoras", this "swell" steak place in Sewell pleases with "relaxed" dining amid "sleek" "Rat Pack" surroundings that make the "good" food "go down a little easier;" N.B. there's a vocalist on weekends.

Blue Fish Grill Ⓜ *Seafood*   21 | 15 | 18 | $29

Flemington | 9 Central Ave. (Mine St.) | 908-237-4528 | www.thebluefishgrill.com

For "a taste of the beach" in Hunterdon County, "check out" the "extremely fresh", "uncomplicated" fish and other wood-fire grilled dishes at this "cheap", "kid-friendly" Flemington BYO; with an "accommodating" staff and "casual atmosphere", it's perfect "for a quick nosh" – once you get past the "wait for a table" (no rezzies).

Blue Pig Tavern *American*   21 | 21 | 20 | $42

Cape May | Congress Hall Hotel | 251 Beach Ave. (bet. Congress & Perry Sts.) | 609-884-8421 | www.congresshall.com

"Nestled inside Cape May's classic" Congress Hotel, this "family-friendly" tavern with a "country farmhouse" setting dishes up "solid" American "comfort food" (plus "interesting" items too) that makes it "worth a visit" for breakfast, lunch or dinner; in warm weather, the patio offers "nice water breezes", and there are wine dinners off-season.

ⓩ Blue Point Grill *Seafood*   25 | 16 | 21 | $42

Princeton | 258 Nassau St. (Pine St.) | 609-921-1211 | www.bluepointgrill.com

"If it swims, they have it" affirm aficionados of this über-popular Princeton BYO "storefront seafooder" serving "the freshest fish, unless you catch it yourself", that's "simply but expertly prepared" and ferried by "pleasant" servers in "modest" surroundings; most find it "worthy every penny" – and every minute spent in the "long lines" occasioned by "no reservations."

Bobby Chez 🅼 *Seafood* | 24 | 10 | 16 | $23 |

Margate | 8007 Ventnor Ave. (Gladstone Ave.) | 609-487-1922
NEW **Mays Landing** | Shoppes at English Creek | 6041 Black Horse Pike (Cape May Ave.) | 609-646-4555
Cherry Hill | Village Walk Shopping Ctr. | 1990 Rte. 70 E. (Old Orchard Rd.) | 856-751-7575 🅱
Collingswood | 33 W. Collings Ave. (Haddon Ave.) | 856-869-8000 🅱
Mount Laurel | Centerton Sq. | Marter Ave. & Rte. 38 (Centeron Rd.) | 856-234-4146
Sewell | 100 Hurffville Cross Keys Rd. (Tuckahoe Rd.) | 856-262-1001
www.bobbychezcrabcakes.com

"Unbelievable" crab cakes "second to none" are "the calling card" at these mostly-for-take-out BYO South Jersey "institutions" also admired for "quality" roast chickens and lobster-mashed potatoes; the "simple decor", "lacking service" and not-exactly-cheap prices "don't matter" because after eating here "you can die happy!"

🅩 Bobby Flay Steak 🅼 *Steak* | 25 | 25 | 24 | $70 |

Atlantic City | Borgata Hotel, Casino & Spa | 1 Borgata Way (Huron Ave.) | 866-692-6742 | www.bobbyflaysteak.com

"A winner – even if you don't win in the casino" brag boosters of this "Borgata babe of beef" that's "worth every penny" for its "perfectly cooked" steaks with "Southwest flair"; this AC "namesake" of the celeb chef gets further flay-re from an "impressive" wine selection, "super" service and "high-energy decor" by David Rockwell.

NEW Bobby's Burger Palace *Burgers* | ▽ 20 | 15 | 17 | $19 |

Eatontown | Monmouth Mall | 180 Rte. 35 (Rte. 36) | 732-544-0200

Famed chef Bobby Flay opened this newcomer adjacent to Monmouth Mall, the second in his intended national chain of casual burger-and-shake joints, each featuring 10 burgers with regional flavors; a few early samplers deem it just "ok", but chalk it up to his not having "worked out all the kinks yet"; N.B. specifying 'crunchi-fied' when placing your order gets you free potato chips piled on top.

Bombay Curry & Grill *Indian* | ▽ 18 | 16 | 19 | $28 |

Basking Ridge | Lyons Mall | 973 S. Finley Ave. (Thomson Pl.) | 908-953-9400 | www.bombaycurryandgrill.com

Though "easy to miss", this Basking Ridge Indian BYO has curried "a great reputation with locals" for its "authentic", "succulent" and "inexpensive" fare, including an "awesome" all-you-can-eat lunch buffet; "very friendly" service and a "nice, casual atmosphere" are also A+.

Bombay Gardens 🅼 *Indian* | ▽ 23 | 15 | 22 | $31 |

East Brunswick | Center 18 Mall | 1020 Rte. 18 N. (bet. Gunia St. & Hillsdale Rd.) | 732-613-9500 | www.bombaygardens.com

"Whether mild or spicy, the food is always well prepared" at this East Brunswick strip-mall Indian BYO with a "vast menu" of "consistently good" multiregional dishes; "courteous service", "affordable prices" and a "large daily buffet" add to the value.

Bosphorus *Turkish* | 21 | 9 | 19 | $23 |

Lake Hiawatha | 32 N. Beverwyck Rd. (bet. Lakeshore Dr. & Vail Rd.) | 973-335-9690

"You're in a strip mall" but the "authentic" food "makes you feel like you're in a Turkish palace" at this "unassuming" Lake Hiawatha BYO that gets extra points for its "large portions" and staff that "treats you like family"; overall, it's a "nice change of pace."

NEW Boulevard Five 72 *American* ▽ 27 | 27 | 25 | $50 |

Kenilworth | 572 Boulevard (bet. 23rd & 24th Sts.) | 908-709-1200 | www.boulevardfive72.com

"Surprising twists on popular favorites" paired with "a top-notch wine list" "attract a crowd" to this Kenilworth New American arrival (in the former Tosca Ristorante space); "lovely decor" and "attentive service" make it "very inviting" – and try "Snyder's homemade chips."

Bourbon County BBQ Smokehouse ⑤Ⓜ *BBQ* | 19 | 10 | 14 | $20 |

Wyckoff | 529 Goffle Rd. (bet. Braen & Ravine Aves.) | 201-444-6661 | www.bourbonbbq.com

Fans of this Wyckoff BBQ "roadhouse" with a "casual, fast-food atmosphere" brag about the "best" 'cue "north of the Mason-Dixon line", citing "superb pulled pork and brisket" and "good sides to back up the main dish"; the less impressed proclaim it's "not real down-home", though it's still "a pretty good deal."

Braddock's *American* | 21 | 21 | 21 | $44 |

Medford | 39 S. Main St. (Coates St.) | 609-654-1604 | www.braddocks.com

Medford's "Main Street USA" pub/restaurant features Traditional Americana fare on two floors of a "cozy" clapboard dating to 1844; the casual lower level offers the likes of homemade chili with cornbread, while the more formal upper dining menu steers toward babyback ribs in raspberry sauce, all served with a "friendly smile"; N.B. the "old tavern ambiance" was freshened up in 2008.

Brandl. Ⓜ *American* | 24 | 17 | 19 | $54 |

Belmar | 703 Belmar Plaza (8th Ave.) | 732-280-7501 | www.brandlrestaurant.com

"Talented" chef-owner Chris Brandl's "difficult to find" Shore "storefront" BYO is a "down-to-earth-gourmand's" destination praised for its "exceptional" New American cooking and presentation; though some question cost that's "a bit too dear" "for the location" and cite "tight" seating and vacillating service, most say it's a "hidden delight."

Brasilia Grill *Brazilian* | 21 | 14 | 19 | $33 |

Newark | 99 Monroe St. (bet. Ferry & Lafayette Sts.) | 973-589-8682 | www.brasiliagrill.com

"Step out of the ordinary" via this "informal", "cavernous" Ironbound Brazilian churrascaria (sibling of the nearby Brasilia

Restaurant) accented with dark-wood booths and palm trees, offering "a beef orgy" of "all-you-want-to-eat, skewered, grilled meats"; throw in a hot food buffet, salad bar and liquor license and most agree "it's a great value" (as well as a "fun place to meet friends and watch sports").

Brasilia Restaurant *Brazilian* 21 | 16 | 19 | $34

Newark | 132 Ferry St. (bet. Madison & Monroe Sts.) | 973-465-1227 | www.brasiliagrill.com

Fans affirm "the best Brazilian in the Ironbound" can be found at this "classic" "carnivore's heaven" (and sibling to Brasilia Grill) – an "all-the-meat-you-can-eat" Newark churrascaria boasting a "lively atmosphere" (decorated with murals) and spot-on service; the accompanying "salad bar is a meal in itself"; N.B. it's BYO.

Brass Rail, The *American* 19 | 18 | 19 | $38

Hoboken | 135 Washington St. (2nd St.) | 201-659-7074 | www.thebrassrailnj.com

A "Hoboken stalwart" serving "generous quantities" of New American fare (including brunch) at "reasonable prices", this pub-cum-restaurant sports a "lively bar downstairs" and "romantic seating upstairs"; still, the doubtful declare the "ambitious menu has so much potential, but always seems to just fall short."

Brennen's Steakhouse *Steak* 23 | 20 | 20 | $49

Neptune City | 62 W. Sylvania Ave. (Morris Ave.) | 732-774-5040 | www.brennenssteakhouse.com

"Very good", "consistent" steak "in a real steakhouse setting" (lots of wood, marble floors, granite bar) is "still the main draw" at this Neptune "local favorite" where "they parade the cuts of meat out so you can see them before ordering"; regulars also appreciate the piano music offered Wednesdays–Sundays.

Brickwall Tavern & Dining Room ● *Pub Food* 18 | 18 | 18 | $27

Asbury Park | 522 Cookman Ave. (Bangs Ave.) | 732-774-1264 | www.brickwalltavern.com

This "casual 'go-to'" in Asbury Park serves an "eclectic mix of pub grub" and Americana (from pulled pork to steak) in a "comfortable" setting with, yes, a "brick wall that's rather neat"; it's "simple, cheap" and works for anything from a meal to drinks or just "screaming at one of the TVs" over the "happening bar" – to "avoid the noise" you can dine outdoors.

Brioso *Italian* 22 | 18 | 18 | $42

Marlboro | Willow Pointe Shopping Ctr. | 184 Hwy. 9 (Union Hill Rd.) | 732-617-1700 | www.briosoristorante.com

"Delicious", "authentic" Italian fare is "amply" served at this "always bustling" "hidden delight" in a Marlboro strip mall; service is generally "pleasant", though some suggest "it helps to be a frequent customer" as "newcomers might not feel quite as welcome" as regulars; P.S. "reasonable prices" are a plus and it's BYO to boot.

	FOOD	DECOR	SERVICE	COST

Brio Tuscan Grille *Italian*   19 | 21 | 20 | $37

Cherry Hill | Town Place at Garden State | 901 Haddonfield Rd.
(Chapel Ave.) | 856-910-8166 | www.brioitalian.com
A "Tuscan atmosphere" reigns at this chain Italian at the Town Place
in Cherry Hill's Garden State mall; most appreciate its "nice-sized
portions" of "above-average" vittles, but a few find it kinda "pricey"
for what it is; P.S. the kids' pizza is "a great deal" and the young ones
get to "play with the dough", which "keeps them busy."

Brix 67 *Eclectic*   18 | 19 | 18 | $41

Summit | 67 Union Pl. (Summit Ave.) | 908-273-4448 |
www.brix-67.com
The Eclectic selections are "quite broad" at this "trendy" neighborhood "standby" whose menu – from shumai and Cajun calamari to
brick-oven pizza and filet mignon – is mostly "satisfying" and works
especially well "for a group or with kids"; the wine bar pours only NJ
vintages, "but you can bring your own too."

Brooklyn's Coal-Burning   23 | 11 | 15 | $20
Brick-Oven Pizzeria ⊄ *Pizza*

Edgewater | Edgewater Commons Shopping Ctr. | 443 River Rd.
(Old River Rd.) | 201-945-9096
Hackensack | 161 Hackensack Ave. (Rte. 4) | 201-342-2727
Ridgewood | 15 Oak St. (Ridgewood Ave.) | 201-493-7600
"No slices served"– and no plastic accepted – at these family-
friendly Bergen County pizzerias where "fresh mozzarella" tops
"crisp-crusty" pies that are so "consistently delicious" most put up
with the "simple" decor and "mediocre" service; N.B. unlike its BYO
siblings, the Hackensack location serves beer and wine.

Brothers Moon Ⓜ *American*   22 | 17 | 21 | $43

Hopewell | 7 W. Broad St. (Greenwood Ave.) | 609-333-1330 |
www.brothersmoon.com
A "seasonal menu" employing "fresh", "locally sourced ingredients"
leads to "great-tasting, beautifully presented dishes" in the hands of
chef-proprietor Will Mooney at this "fun and somewhat funky" BYO
New American on Hopewell's "quaint" main drag; the staff is "accommodating" if "a bit slow" at times; N.B. there's an on-site retail shop.

Buca di Beppo *Italian*   16 | 18 | 18 | $29

Cherry Hill | 2301 Rte. 38 (Haddonfield Rd.) | 856-779-3288 |
www.bucadibeppo.com
"Expect kitsch with a capital K" at the "extravaganza" that is this
lone Jersey outpost of the national Italian chain; "it's hardly fine dining" with its "heaping portions" of "average" food served "family-
style", but its "raucous" "party atmosphere" is well suited for groups
and "the kids" – just "go hungry" ("and bring antacids").

Ⓩ Buddakan *Pan-Asian*   25 | 27 | 23 | $58

Atlantic City | Pier at Caesars | 1 Atlantic Ocean (Arkansas Ave.) |
609-674-0100 | www.buddakanac.com
Stephen Starr "has done it again" with this "sumptuous" third incar-
nation of his Philly and NYC Pan-Asian "experience" at The Pier at

Caesars; "belly up" to the 10-ft. golden Buddha at the "beautiful" communal table, dine in a curtained nook or "celebrate" at a regular table, enjoying "food just adventurous enough to be innovative", topped off by "above-average service"; P.S. "your wallet will know you've been there."

Busch's Seafood Ⓜ *Seafood* | 20 | 14 | 18 | $42 |

Sea Isle City | 8700 Landis Ave. (87th St.) | 609-263-8626 | www.buschsseafood.com

Crabnoscenti still "drive two hours" in season for the she-crab soup (served Sundays and Tuesdays) at this "old-time", "family-run" Sea Isle City seafooder; some bemoan the "faded", "dark" decor, while others "hope they don't update", but either way it's been a "tradition" since 1882; P.S. don't miss the "great desserts – one is large enough for the entire table."

Buttonwood Manor *American* | 14 | 17 | 17 | $37 |

Matawan | 845 Rte. 34 (Edgewater Dr.) | 732-566-6220 | www.buttonwoodmanor.net

Go for the "picturesque" views of Matawan's Lake Lefferts at this "somewhat old-fashioned" American that's popular with a "mature" crowd; while critics cite "average" fare and say "it's really better off as a banquet facility" (its popular alter ego), pragmatists advise "stick with the basics (salad, prime rib, etc.) and you'll be fine."

Cabin, The *American* | 16 | 13 | 17 | $27 |

Howell | 984 Rte. 33 E. (Fairfield Rd.) | 732-462-3090 | www.thecabinrestaurant.net

"Courteous" servers purvey "plentiful" portions of "typical" American "roadside food" at this "popular local hangout" set in a rustic log cabin in a "rural" area of Monmouth County; "thin-crust pizza" stands out among the seafood, steaks and chops on the menu, and the bar "is always hoppin'."

Cafe Arugula Ⓜ *Italian* | 21 | 17 | 20 | $38 |

South Orange | 59 S. Orange Ave. (Scotland Rd.) | 973-378-9099 | www.cafearugula.net

Within walking distance of Seton Hall University in South Orange, this "unassuming" Italian BYO is called an "underappreciated standout" by fans of its "consistently good, imaginative food"– including bison, ostrich and fish dishes – that delivers "good value for the money"; the "excellent gelato" is another plus, but some say "service swings on a giant pendulum."

Cafe at Rosemont, The Ⓜ *American* | 20 | 16 | 20 | $31 |

Rosemont | 88 Kingwood-Stockton Rd. (Rte. 604) | 609-397-4097 | www.cafeatrosemont.com

Take "a delightful step back in time" at this "homey" "find" in Rosemont, a BYO American set in an 1865 general store; the food's "good, while the "shabby-chic clutter" and "friendly service" add to its "special country charm"; N.B. check out the Wednesday night global-themed prix fixe dinners (three courses, $24).

Café Azzurro *Italian* — 24 | 21 | 23 | $42

Peapack | 141 Main St. (bet. Todd & Willow Aves.) | 908-470-1470 |
www.cafeazzurroonline.com

"Great-looking waiters make the food taste even better" at this "up-scale" yet "casual" Peapack BYO storefront Italian renowned for "well-prepared pastas and fresh fish"; it attracts crowds "by 6 PM, even on a Wednesday", so be prepared to wait, "even with reservations"; N.B. "a lovely patio" adds to its charm.

Cafe Bello *Italian* — ▽ 24 | 19 | 22 | $42

Bayonne | 1044 Ave. C (50th St.) | 201-437-7538

"Arrive early or it's very difficult to get a table" at this "beautiful little" Bayonne neighborhood favorite where the Italian food is "first-rate" and the staff is "friendly"; just "be prepared to circle the street to park" – though the "brick-oven pizza", "hot antipasto and seafood salad are worth the trip."

Cafe Coloré Ⓜ *Italian* — 21 | 18 | 21 | $35

Freehold Township | Chadwick Sq. | 3333 Rte. 9 N. (Jackson Mills Rd.) | 732-462-2233 | www.cafecolorenj.com

New owners have maintained the integrity of this "pretty" Freehold strip-mall BYO where you "can't go wrong with a good, basic Italian meal" ferried by a "knowledgeable, friendly and efficient" staff; N.B. a four-course prix fixe dinner ($49) makes it even more "affordable."

Cafe Cucina Ⓧ *Italian* — 21 | 20 | 20 | $41

Branchburg | 3366 Rte. 22 W. (bet. County Line & Readington Rds.) | 908-526-4907 | www.cafecucina.com

"Good, solid Italian food" in a "homey" (if sometimes "noisy") setting complemented by "a nice martini menu" and "a terrific staff" makes for a "delightful surprise on Route 22" in Branchburg; given the "reasonably priced", ample menu and "surprising specials", "the hard part is narrowing down" your options.

Cafe Emilia *Italian* — 21 | 19 | 21 | $48

Bridgewater | 705 Rte. 202 N. (Allen Rd.) | 908-429-1410 |
www.cafeemilia.com

Offering "classic Italian with a wine list to die for" at prices "that won't burn your wallet", this "welcoming" Bridgewater highway Italian "is worth the stop" for "good, solid food prepared to your taste" and "served with flair"; P.S. it's "very convenient after a day of pounding the mall at Bridgewater Commons."

Café Gallery *Continental* — 23 | 22 | 22 | $38

Burlington | 219 High St. (Pearl St.) | 609-386-6150 |
www.cafegalleryburlington.com

Do the Continental – foodwise that is – on Burlington City's High Street at this "nice surprise" that "never disappoints" thanks to "dependably good" food, "delightful views" of the Delaware River from the second floor and an "art gallery" featuring local talent; special mentions go to the "attentive service" and "outstanding" Sunday brunch ($19.75).

	FOOD	DECOR	SERVICE	COST

Cafe Graziella *Italian*
20 | 15 | 19 | $36

Hillsborough | Cost Cutters Shopping Ctr. | 390 Rte. 206 (Andria Ave.) |
908-281-0700 | www.cafegraziella.com

This "low-key, family-style" neighborhood Italian BYO is "easy to
pass by" "in a strip mall on a stretch of Route 206", but it nonetheless
has a "loyal" following that says *grazie* for its "fine, generous" fare
and "interesting specials" "like your *nonna* used to make"; "warm,
attentive service" also helps make it a "solid, reliable" "standby."

Cafe Italiano *Italian*
19 | 15 | 18 | $41

Englewood Cliffs | 14 Sylvan Ave. (Irving Ave.) | 201-461-5041 |
www.cafeitaliano.net

Set in onetime NYC mayor Jimmy Walker's former digs, this
Englewood Cliffs Italian "old reliable" is "always a safe bet" thanks to
"very solid middle-of-the-road fare" ferried in a "friendly environment"; the early-bird dinner is arguably "the biggest bargain around",
and there's outdoor dining on the patio ("a rarity in Bergen County").

Cafe Loren Ⓜ *American*
▽ 26 | 21 | 26 | $44

Avalon | 2288 Dune Dr. (23rd St.) | 609-967-8228 | www.cafeloren.com

"Still wonderful" after 30-plus years, this Avalon New American
BYO remains a "fine-dining" "mainstay" offering "phenomenal" cuisine, "friendly, attentive" service ("it's so nice to be greeted with a
bright smile") and "intimacy"; the only grievance is that "it's only
open during the season."

Cafe Madison Ⓢ Ⓜ *American*
▽ 20 | 25 | 20 | $46

Riverside | 33 Lafayette St. (Madison St.) | 856-764-4444 |
www.cafemadison.com

For "a slice of New York City in South Jersey", acolytes applaud this
"showy" and "sophisticated" contemporary American in Riverside
that comes complete with a dramatic "waterfall martini bar" (purveying "great martinis", natch) and "good" (if "pricey") food; P.S. for
added "adventure", "reach it by the River Line rail."

❷ Cafe Matisse *Eclectic*
27 | 25 | 26 | $66

Rutherford | 167 Park Ave. (bet. Highland Cross & Park Pl.) |
201-935-2995 | www.cafematisse.com

A "wow in all aspects", this "transcendent", "romantic" Rutherford
BYO "hidden" behind a wine shop (where you can purchase *le vin*)
"dazzles and delights" with its seasonally inspired Eclectic cuisine
offered in grazing portions (aka 'Matisse Plates') that come in three,
four or five courses that are "worth the very expensive price tags"; a
"consistently attentive" staff, "tastefully appointed" interior (with
handblown Murano glass chandeliers) and "plush" outdoor dining
complete this "outstanding" oeuvre.

Cafe Metro *Eclectic*
21 | 16 | 19 | $28

Denville | 60 Diamond Spring Rd. (bet. 1st Ave. & Orchard St.) |
973-625-1055 | www.thecafemetro.com

"The food is hip and fresh" at this "charming" Denville Eclectic cafe
serving "amazing vegetarian and vegan fare that omnivores love as

well" (seafood and chicken are on the menu); though it's BYO, the upstairs wine bar serves local vinos, and there's a "cute front porch" for warm weather dining.

☑ Cafe Panache ☒ *Eclectic*   28 | 23 | 25 | $58

Ramsey | 130 E. Main St. (Franklin Tpke.) | 201-934-0030 | www.cafepanachenj.com

Chef-owner Kevin Kohler's "sublime and imaginative" Eclectic fare "continues to impress" and service remains "superb" at this "pricey" Ramsey Eclectic, whose "beautiful redecoration" "makes it even more delightful"; just make sure you "reserve well in advance" to enjoy this "jewel of a space" that's "consistently one of the best BYOs in Bergen County"; N.B. jackets suggested.

Caffe Aldo Lamberti *Italian*   24 | 23 | 22 | $46

Cherry Hill | 2011 Rte. 70 W. (Haddonfield Rd.) | 856-663-1747 | www.lambertis.com

Fans of this "posh" Cherry Hill member of the Lamberti enterprise (with outposts in Delaware and Pennsylvania) applaud its "outstanding" Italian cuisine and wine list, "polished" service and "beautiful" refurb (including an indoor/outdoor bar with a temperature-controlled wine room); it's "pricey", but lovely "for special occasions."

California Grill *Eclectic*   18 | 13 | 15 | $26

Flemington | Kitchen Expo Plaza | 1 Rte. 31 (Hwy. 202) | 908-806-7141 | www.californiagrillnj.com

"Enormous" portions of "fresh, tasty salads", "delicious pizzas" and "creative sandwiches" (with names like 'Femme Fatale' burger) make this "casual" Eclectic BYO a hit for lunch (or dinner) when shopping at the Flemington outlets; "kids love the fish tank" while adults notice the sometimes "slow" service; N.B. a recent change of chef may outdate the above Food score.

Capriccio *Italian*   26 | 23 | 25 | $62

Atlantic City | Resorts Atlantic City Casino & Hotel | 1133 Boardwalk (North Carolina Ave.) | 609-340-6789 | www.resortsac.com

"Still one of Atlantic City's best" declare fanciers of this "high-end" Italian – now in its third decade in Resorts Casino & Hotel – that's like "dining in a villa"; with "ocean views" from window tables and an "experienced, courteous staff" adding to its allure, the "casino prices" can be forgiven.

Capt'n Ed's Place *Seafood/Steak*   18 | 14 | 17 | $35

Point Pleasant | 1001 Arnold Ave. (bet. Maple & Pine Bluff Aves.) | 732-892-4121 | www.captainedsplace.com

"Cooking your own meal on a hot stone" – steaks, shrimp, fish – lures many to this Point Pleasant "staple" that's "cute and entertaining", though some say "the decor could use a redo"; "no reservations" means "a long wait", particularly on weekends and "during the summer"; N.B. it's BYO but a small selection of local wines is available.

| | FOOD | DECOR | SERVICE | COST |

Carmine's ⓞ *Italian* ・ 21 | 19 | 20 | $43
Atlantic City | Quarter at the Tropicana | 2801 Pacific Ave. (Iowa Ave.) |
609-572-9300 | www.carminesnyc.com
For "an abundance" of "big-city, saucy, garlicky Italian comfort food"
served "family-style", throngs head to this sibling of the venerable
NYC institution ensconced in the Quarter at AC's Tropicana; it doles
out "enough food for Caesar's legions" in a "large", "noisy but fun"
room, so for best results "go hungry" and bring a "big group."

Carmine's Asbury Park Ⓜ *Italian* 20 | 19 | 19 | $42
Asbury Park | 162 Main St. (bet. Cookman & Lake Aves.) | 732-774-2222 |
www.carminesnj.com
"Authentic Southern Italian food" complemented by "a great raw bar
and fabulous martinis" receives raves from fans of this Asbury Park
"hangout" with "friendly" service and "cozy" digs (exposed-brick
walls, an open kitchen with a wood-burning pizza oven, a "beautiful"
vintage bar); even so, some dis the "average" food.

Casa Dante *Italian* 23 | 19 | 23 | $50
Jersey City | 737 Newark Ave. (bet. Kennedy Blvd. & Summit Ave.) |
201-795-2750 | www.casadante.com
A "Rat Pack quality" adds to the allure of this Jersey City "institution" serving "classic Italian and newer dishes, well prepared and
professionally served"; weekend entertainment lends a "supper
club atmosphere", but it's also "good for a business dinner"; still,
some nitpick that this "staple" "could use some remodeling."

Casa Giuseppe Ⓜ *Italian* 24 | 19 | 25 | $41
Iselin | 487 Rte. 27 (Talmadge Ave.) | 732-283-9111 |
www.casagiuseppe.com
"Ask for it 'your way' and it shall be done" at this "upscale", "consistently good" Iselin Northern Italian with "a fine wine list" and "grand
and gracious service" that "makes you feel right at home" and helps
justify the "high prices"; in an "unassuming" location among
Metropark's offices, it's "popular with the lunch crowd."

Casa Maya *Mexican* 21 | 14 | 18 | $25
Meyersville | 615 Meyersville Rd. (Hickory Tavern Rd.) |
908-580-0799
High Bridge | 1 Main St. (Bridge St.) | 908-638-4032 Ⓜ
www.casamayamexican.com
The "down-to-earth", "authentic" Sonoran-style Mexican fare
(think subtly spiced) served at these two "hole-in-the-wall" BYO
"cantinas" in High Bridge and Meyersville is *"muy delicioso"* as well
as a "good value" according to appreciative aficionados who come
armed with cerveza and vino; "expect a wait, especially on weekends" (no rezzies), but once seated, service is "friendly" and "quick."

Casa Solar Ⓜ *Pan-Latin* 25 | 19 | 18 | $39
Belmar | 1104 Main St. (11th Ave.) | 732-556-1144 |
www.newjersey-restaurant.com
"Exceptional" is the rave for chef/co-owner Nancy Rios, who puts
"Latin flair" and "her heart into every menu item" at her Downtown

Belmar BYO; while enthusiasts are ok with the "kinda plain interior", service is seen as a "weak" point; P.S. reservations recommended.

Casa Vasca *Spanish*
23 | 16 | 22 | $36

Newark | 141 Elm St. (Prospect St.) | 973-465-1350

Bask in "classic" Basque cuisine at this "welcoming", "established" Ironbound Spanish featuring "huge portions" and "a great wine list"; the digs are "simple" but the "waiters know their food", there's free attended parking next door ("a bonus") and it offers proximity to NJPAC; P.S. dine at the bar for a "more affordable menu."

Casona Ⓜ *Cuban*
22 | 21 | 20 | $35

Collingswood | 563 Haddon Ave. (Knight Ave.) | 856-854-5555 | www.mycasona.com

It's Cuba-in-Collingswood at this "pretty" Victorian BYO where "it's a delight" to dine on "good" "variations of classic fare" on the "wide" wraparound porch in warm weather; while service can be "uneven", you'll "feel like you're down in the islands"; N.B. a coffee bar offers tropical smoothies and pastries.

Catelli *Italian*
25 | 24 | 24 | $54

Voorhees | The Plaza | 1000 Main St. (Evesham Rd.) | 856-751-6069 | www.catellirestaurant.com

This Voorhees "fine-dining" "destination" offers "well-prepared and -presented" Northern Italian fare coupled with "prompt and professional service" in an "elegant", "romantic setting"; it may be "pricey" but it's "worth it for a special night out"; N.B. a budget-conscious prix fixe dinner (four courses for $40) is available Sundays through Fridays.

Cathay 22 *Chinese*
22 | 17 | 19 | $32

Springfield | 124 Rte. 22 W. (Hillside Ave.) | 973-467-8688 | www.cathay22.com

"Fresh and inventive" Sichuan fare is the mainstay of this "upscale" Springfield Chinese that's "more expensive than some", but "worth" the cost as well as "the challenge of driving on Route 22"; the "presentation is impressive", and the "lovely" setting allows for "discreet conversation with ease."

❷ Catherine Lombardi *Italian*
23 | 26 | 25 | $56

New Brunswick | 3 Livingston Ave. (George St.) | 732-296-9463 | www.catherinelombardi.com

"Exquisite" rave respondents who "love" the "beautiful, red-themed decor" at this "upscale" "family-style Italian" in New Brunswick serving "outstanding", "carefully crafted food" "using local ingredients when possible", bolstered by "inventive" drinks and "exemplary" service; those who find this "red-sauce heaven" "overpriced" can sample a late-night snack at the bar (after 10 PM, Fridays–Saturdays).

Cenzino Ⓩ *Italian*
24 | 20 | 23 | $48

Oakland | 589 Ramapo Valley Rd. (Franklin Ave.) | 201-337-6693 | www.cenzinos.com

The "authentic kitchen", "warm atmosphere", and "knowledgeable and competent" staff keep regulars tuned into this Oakland Italian with a "friendly" bar scene; ok, "the dining room can be a bit noisy when crowded", the "decor could use some work" and it's "on the pricey side", but most find it "a pleasure" to dine here.

⚡ Chakra *American*
20 | 26 | 19 | $53

Paramus | 144 W. Rte. 4 E. (Arcadian Ave.) | 201-556-1530 |
www.chakrarestaurant.com

The "big box exterior" of this Paramus New American belies a "romantic interior" akin to "stepping into a dream"– palm trees, silk curtains, candlelight, sculptures – but some say the "nightclub-style" atmosphere "eclipses" the food (though it's still "very good"); the "hip lounge" is a "cool hangout" for a "youngish, singles crowd" that makes for prime "people-watching."

Chand Palace *Indian*
23 | 16 | 19 | $25

Parsippany | 257 Littleton Rd. (Parsippany Rd.) | 973-334-5444
Piscataway | 1296 Centennial Ave. (bet. Stelton Rd. & Washington Ave.) |
732-465-1474
www.chandpalace.com

Though this pair of vegetarian-focused North and Central Jersey Indian BYOs specializes in a lunchtime "bargain buffet" that fans call an "unbelievably satisfying feast", others say that some "menu items are far superior" and "worth the wait"; a "helpful staff" helps make it a "solid" choice; N.B. the Piscataway location is closed Tuesdays.

Chao Phaya *Thai*
24 | 13 | 20 | $27

Somerset | Somerset Village Shopping Ctr. | 900 Easton Ave.
(Foxwood Dr.) | 732-249-0110
Somerville | 9 Davenport St. (Main St.) | 908-231-0655 |
www.chaophayathaicuisine.com

"Always smiling, attentive service" complements the "reasonably priced", "authentic" Thai fare that's prepared "as hot as you can take it (or not)" at these "unassuming" Somerville BYOs; just "don't expect a "charming atmosphere" along with the "amazing value."

Charley's Ocean Grill *American*
18 | 21 | 19 | $36

Long Branch | 29 Avenel Blvd. (Ocean Ave.) | 732-222-4499 |
www.charleysoceangrill.com

Surveyors are split over the merits of a 2008 renovation of this "informal" Long Branch American: while regulars applaud the new, "beautiful" "airy" setting and "second-story ocean views", stalwarts say they "liked the old place better"; and while most are "happy that the food stayed the same", some find it "uneven"; N.B. service is hit-or-miss.

Charrito's *Mexican*
22 | 17 | 17 | $27

Hoboken | 1024 Washington St. (bet. 10th & 11th Sts.) | 201-659-2800
Hoboken | 121 Washington St. (bet. 1st & 2nd Sts.) | 201-418-8600
Jersey City | 395 Central Ave. (bet. Bowers St. & Paterson Plan Rd.) |
201-963-4312
Union City | 4900 Bergenline Ave. (49th St.) | 201-863-0345
www.loscharritos.com

"There's a reason" why this "family-run" quartet of Mexican BYO cantinas have "lines out the door" – "authentic" Oaxacan eats (the "tableside guac rocks", "their burritos are da bomb") at "refreshingly modest prices"; but some say their "small" size makes the "friendly" staff "eager to turn over tables"; P.S. they'll "prepare Mexican-style drinks if you provide the booze", and a fifth location – *con* liquor license – is planned for summer 2009.

NEW Char Steak House Steak — | — | — | M

Raritan | 777 Rte. 202 N. (bet. 1st & Quick Aves.) | 908-707-1777 | www.charsteakhouse.com

This new Raritan steakhouse features floor-to-ceiling, spiraling-flame fireplaces that serve as a bold backdrop to a wall of wines, a raw bar and, the star of the production, steaks; prime and dry-aged, cooked black-and-blue or well-charred, this beef is creating a buzz.

Chart House American 21 | 25 | 20 | $53

Weehawken | Lincoln Harbor | Pier D-T (Harbor Blvd.) | 201-348-6628 | www.chart-house.com

The "breathtaking view of the NY skyline" is guaranteed to "wow" "out-of-town guests", a "romantic date" or "business associates" at this riverside Weehawken American, and if its seafood- and steak-focused menu is "less special", most still find it "consistently good" and made even "better" by the vista; a "cool bar scene" and "friendly" staff also make it "hard to believe this is a chain."

Z Cheesecake Factory American 19 | 18 | 18 | $30

Hackensack | Riverside Square Mall | 197 Riverside Sq. (Hackensack Ave.) | 201-488-0330 ●

Wayne | Willowbrook Mall | 1700 Willowbrook Blvd. (Rte. 46) | 973-890-1400

Edison | Menlo Park Mall | 455 Menlo Park Dr. (Rte. 1) | 732-494-7000

Freehold | Freehold Raceway Mall | 3710 Rte. 9 S. (bet. Rtes. 33 & 537) | 732-462-2872

Cherry Hill | Marketplace at Garden State Park | 931 Haddonfield Rd. (bet. Graham & Severn Aves.) | 856-665-7550
www.thecheesecakefactory.com

Mall crawlers are among those who mob this "busy", "noisy", "crowd-pleaser" chain that doles out "ginormous portions" of Americana from a menu "the size of New Jersey"; predictably, there's "cheesecake to die for" and less predictably, salads earn raves too, and though service can be "slow", that doesn't detract from the "great value" – hence the "crazy long" waits for a table.

Z Chef's Table M French 26 | 19 | 24 | $52

Franklin Lakes | Franklin Square Shopping Ctr. | 754 Franklin Ave. (Pulis Ave.) | 201-891-6644

"Reserve well in advance" to enjoy the "old-world charm and superior dining" at chef/co-owner Claude Baills' French bistro BYO, "tucked in a nondescript shopping center" in Franklin Lakes; despite "staid" decor and "cramped" seating it's a "consistent crowd-pleaser", and if *les malcontents* say it "doesn't live up to its reputation", the happily fed insist if anything it's "getting better."

| | FOOD | DECOR | SERVICE | COST |

Z Chef Vola's Ⓜ🚫 *Italian*   `27` `13` `23` `$53`

Atlantic City | 111 S. Albion Pl. (Pacific Ave.) | 609-345-2022 | www.chefvolas.com

Veterans plead "don't tell anyone", but the word is out – ditto the once-secret reservations number – on this "hard to find, hard to get into and even harder to resist" "ageless" Italian with "superlative" "eats" "like mama's", served in the "cramped", "low-ceiling base-ment" "of a house on a side street in Atlantic City"; P.S. "they don't take walk-ins", and it's "cash only" at this BYO "gem."

NEW Chelsea Prime *Steak*   `–` `–` `–` `E`

Atlantic City | Chelsea Hotel | 111 S. Chelsea Ave., 5th fl. (Pacific Ave.) | 609-428-4545 | www.thechelsea-ac.com

Restaurateur Stephen Starr's version of a '40s supper club comes alive in Atlantic City's Chelsea Hotel via this steakhouse boasting sweeping ocean views and enough dry-aged beef to start a stampede; there's seafood, creamed spinach and classic cocktails too, plus a white grand piano – if you're lucky, maybe Sam will even play it again.

Chengdu 46 Ⓜ *Chinese*   `24` `18` `21` `$41`

Clifton | 1105 Rte. 46 E. (Rock Hill Rd.) | 973-777-8855 | www.chengdu46.com

This venerable "high-end" Clifton Sichuan "isn't your father's take-out place"; the "awesome" "gourmet" cuisine is "fabulously presented" by a "knowledgeable, efficient" "tuxedoed staff", with "a very good wine list" as accompaniment; still, some say the "interior needs updating."

Chez Catherine Ⓢ Ⓜ *French*   `26` `21` `24` `$68`

Westfield | 431 North Ave. W. (bet. Broad & Prospect Sts.) | 908-654-4011 | www.chezcatherine.com

This *très français* taste of Provence in Westfield "never fails to im-press" with its "classical but inventive" menu, "great wine pairings" and "gracious hosts"; it all adds up to "French bliss", but "check your credit line when you reserve", for the "stellar" experience is "incred-ibly pricey"; N.B. dinner is prix fixe only ($59 for three courses, $85 for a six-course tasting menu) with jackets suggested.

Chez Elena Wu *Chinese/Japanese*   `23` `19` `21` `$33`

Voorhees | Ritz Shopping Ctr. | 910 Haddonfield-Berlin Rd. (Laurel Oak Blvd.) | 856-566-3222 | www.chezelenawu.com

With the semi-retirement of matriarch Elena Wu, her family carries on at this "bright, elegant" Asian in Voorhees offering "top-of-the-line Chinese" and "very good" sushi with a French accent; despite its strip-mall locale, "a sophisticated sheen" pervades this BYO with a "reputation for excellence" and "caring" service.

Chickie's & Pete's Cafe ➊ *Pub Food*   `16` `16` `16` `$27`

Egg Harbor Township | 6055 Black Horse Pike (bet. Delilah Rd. & English Creek Ave.) | 609-272-1930
Bordentown | 183 Hwy. 130 (Hwy. 206) | 609-298-9182
www.chickiesandpetes.com

"It's all about the beer" and the "zillion" plasma TVs at these "noisy" but "fun" Jersey outposts of the "famous" Philly sports bars; oh, yes:

the "addictive" "crab fries" with "cheese dipping sauce" ("the best bar food invented" according to many) also rule; otherwise, expect "typical" American pub grub and "casual" service

Chilangos *Mexican* | 21 | 16 | 19 | $27 |

Highlands | 272 Bay Ave. (bet. Marina on the Bay Ct. & Sea Drift Ave.) | 732-708-0505 | www.chilangosnj.com

Aficionados of "above-average" Mexican food and drink head to this "tiny, festive" cantina in Highlands where "affordable" price tags make it easy to sample the likes of "must-try fish tacos", a "killer tequila selection" and "excellent margaritas"; the "friendly" service sometimes slows down on weekends.

China Palace *Taiwanese* | ▽ 24 | 19 | 19 | $30 |

Middletown | Harmony Bowl | 1815 Rte. 35 (Old Country Rd.) | 732-957-0554

"Tasty" Taiwanese "doesn't get any better" than at this authentic spot located within the Harmony Bowl in Middletown; the menu features some "creative items", and though it's located in a bowling alley, the setting is pleasant and includes as "full a bar as you'll find anywhere else" in the area.

Chophouse, The *Seafood/Steak* | 25 | 25 | 24 | $58 |

Gibbsboro | 4 S. Lakeview Dr. (Clementon Rd.) | 856-566-7300 | www.thechophouse.us

"Succulent" steaks and savory seafood share the spotlight at this "consistently delicious", "upscale" steakhouse with "great lake views" "in an unexpected location" – tiny Gibbsboro; an "impressive" wine list and "diligent" servers enhance the "expensive" experience, which is "well worth the price" to most.

Christie's Italian Seafood Grill *Italian* | 23 | 19 | 22 | $37 |

Howell | Howell Ctr. | 2420 Rte. 9 S. (White Rd.) | 732-780-8310 | www.christiesrestaurant.us

This strip-mall Italian BYO in Howell is "a real surprise" for its "large portions" of "well-prepared seafood and pasta", which will "do justice" to any "bottle of wine" you bring; a "wonderful staff" adds to the all-around appeal.

Christopher's Cafe & Restaurant Ⓜ *American* | ▽ 19 | 14 | 18 | $28 |

Colts Neck | Colts Towne Plaza Shopping Ctr. | 317 Rte. 34 (bet. Hwy. 537 & Professional Circle) | 732-308-3668 | www.christopherscafe.com

This Colts Neck BYO Traditional American in a "stylish old farmhouse" "caters to locals" with "good", "reasonably priced" breakfasts, lunches and "casual dinners"; N.B. ratings may not fully reflect recent changes in ownership, chef and decor.

Church Street Kitchen *American* | 14 | 13 | 17 | $34 |

Montclair | 12 Church St. (Bloomfield Ave.) | 973-233-0216 | www.churchstreetkitchen.com

"A touch of SoHo" on a "trendy" Montclair street perfect for people-watching, this BYO New American provides a "nice variety" of "de-

| | FOOD | DECOR | SERVICE | COST |

cent food at a decent price", but some think it "lacks pizzazz" and cite "spotty" service; on the upside, there's live music five nights a week and at Sunday brunch.

Ciao *Italian* | 21 | 20 | 21 | $42 |

Basking Ridge | 665 Martinsville Rd. (bet. Rte. 78 & Valley Rd.) | 908-647-6007 | www.ciaorest.com

"Thoughtful, well-plated bistro food" and "friendly, professional" service keep this rustic Basking Ridge strip-mall Italian (next door to its costlier sibling, 3West) "noisy and crowded on weekends"; diners "can eat outdoors in nice weather" or near "the fireplace in the dining room on cold, rainy days" – either way, it's "always warm and inviting."

Cinnamon *Indian* | 23 | 15 | 18 | $28 |

Morris Plains | 2920 Rte. 10 W. (bet. Parks & Powder Mill Rds.) | 973-734-0040 | www.cinnamonindianrestaurant.com

"The chef makes mixing spices an art form" at this Northern Indian BYO "sleeper" in a Morris Plains strip mall with a "fantastic" lunch buffet – the "price is low but taste is not compromised"; though some feel the "overall ambiance is missing warmth", the "freshly made naan" and "friendly (bordering on cheeky) waiters" compensate.

Cinque Figlie Ⓢ *Italian* | 21 | 19 | 20 | $50 |

Whippany | 302 Whippany Rd. (Park Ave.) | 973-560-0545 | www.fivedaughters.com

One of the owner's *cinque figlie* (five daughters) might serve you at this family-run Whippany Italian "in a lovely old roadhouse"; even those who feel the food "lacks originality" find it "hearty and well meant", and if the "decor could use refreshing", fans insist "you always leave with a smile on your face."

Circa Ⓜ *French* | ▽ 22 | 23 | 21 | $49 |

High Bridge | 37 Main St. (McDonald St.) | 908-638-5560 | www.circa-restaurant.com

"Trendy New York" French brasserie meets High Bridge's "one-block Downtown" at this "great neighborhood restaurant" where banquettes, tin ceilings and mirrors are the backdrop for an "inventive" if "pricey" menu of small plates and creative entrees; the "high-energy" bar and "friendly service" are also *très bien*; N.B. a recent change in chef may outdate the above Food score.

City Bistro *American* | 18 | 18 | 17 | $34 |

Hoboken | 56-58 14th St. (bet. Hudson & Washington Sts.) | 201-963-8200 | www.citybistrohoboken.com

"The food is solid" at this "really hip" New American tri-level brownstone, but the draw is the "happening party scene" on the summertime rooftop bar with its "amazing view" of the "Empire State Building – and the Hoboken females"; the "reasonably priced" menu ranges from "burgers to elaborate entrees", but "service can be spotty."

	FOOD	DECOR	SERVICE	COST

CJ Montana's Pub & Grille *Pub Food*
19 | 20 | 19 | $33

Tinton Falls | 560 Shrewsbury Ave. (bet. Apple & Peach Sts.) | 732-758-0800 | www.cjmontanas.com

"Making a name for itself" in Tinton Falls is this "comfortable" American with a "pretty cool" bar lined in "flat-screen TVs", a more formal dining area and "solid service"; expect a "wide" slate of "well-cooked dishes", from "fantastic firecracker shrimp" to the "best tilapia"; N.B. it was temporarily closed due to a car accident that damaged the building; they hope to reopen shortly.

Clark's Landing *American/Seafood*
17 | 20 | 18 | $41

Point Pleasant | 847 Arnold Ave. (Clarks Landing Dr.) | 732-899-1111 | www.clarksbarandgrill.com

"It's all about the water view" at this seasonal Point Pleasant dock-sider, where an "older" crowd gathers for drinks indoors or at the outdoor "tiki bar on a summer night" – which helps compensate for the "average" American seafood; N.B. the redesigned restaurant and bar were relocated to the lower level.

Claude's *French*
∇ 25 | 21 | 23 | $47

North Wildwood | 100 Olde New Jersey Ave. (1st Ave.) | 609-522-0400 | www.claudesrestaurant.com

"Like Paris plopped down in North Wildwood", this seasonal "Francophile's hideaway" with "delicious", "interesting" food, a new bar, "relaxed" service and "charming" atmosphere is a "delightful escape from the bustle of the Shore"; P.S. despite highish prices, "little fault" is found here.

Clementine's Café ⊠ *Creole*
∇ 23 | 21 | 22 | $43

Avon-by-the-Sea | 306 Main St. (Lincoln Ave.) | 732-988-7979 | www.clementinescafellc.com

Those who know this small Avon BYO report that its New Orleans-style Creole dishes like shrimp and tasso pasta, zydeco gumbo and "the best bread pudding known to man" elevate it to "out of the ordinary"; what's more, the "friendly" owners – who are chef and manager – are said to be "real dolls."

Clydz ● *American*
22 | 18 | 21 | $45

New Brunswick | 55 Paterson St. (Spring St.) | 732-846-6521 | www.clydz.com

The place to get "'martini-ized'" thanks to the "best martini list in the state", this "lively" New Brunswick "underground hideaway" also entices with an "adventurous" New American menu including "exotic" specials like kangaroo and yak to enhance the standard Kobe burgers and veal chops; if some find it "overpriced", others pronounce it "always fun."

CoccoLa *American/Italian*
19 | 23 | 18 | $46

Hillsborough | 150 Rte. 206 S. (bet. Brooks Blvd. & Camplain Rd.) | 908-704-1160 | www.coccolarestaurant.com

"Unexpectedly sophisticated in food, decor – and price", this "hip-looking" Hillsborough New American–Italian works for a "dinner with friends" or a "special occasion"; though some say recent staff changes have resulted in "inconsistencies", they "are trying"; N.B. a new Friday night lounge menu serves food (until 11 PM) and drink specials (10 PM–2 AM).

Coconut Bay Asian Cuisine Ⓜ *Asian* ▽ 20 | 18 | 21 | $26

Voorhees | Echelon Village Plaza | 1120 White Horse Rd. (bet. Echelon Rd. & Executive Dr.) | 856-783-8878 | www.coconutbayasiancuisine.com

There's something for everyone at this Voorhees strip-mall BYO offering a "wide array" of "good", "reasonably priced" dishes on the "multi-Asian" cuisine menu; a "warm", "friendly atmosphere" and "big tables" make it a natural place to "go with a group of friends."

Columbia Inn Ⓜ *Pizza* 21 | 14 | 19 | $33

Montville | 29 Main Rd. (Morris Ave.) | 973-263-1300 | www.thecolumbiainn.com

Though "pizza is the highlight" at this "always reliable" Montville thin-crust specialist, diners also find "great seafood" and "yummy pasta" among its traditional Italian offerings, as well as a "very reasonable wine list"; while the TVs on the bar side have their fans, it can get "too noisy for the elder crowd", and some feel the "friendly" service "can use a pickup."

Conte's *Pizza* 24 | 10 | 17 | $20

Princeton | 339 Witherspoon St. (Guyot Ave.) | 609-921-8041

"Dynamite" pizza with "crust as thin as a butterfly's wing" makes this "proven" "Princeton institution" a "family-friendly" "favorite" despite the "chaotic atmosphere"; service can be "wanting" and it's "tough to win a seat", but it's "worth the wait" to enjoy the food and the "scene"; N.B. it also serves pastas and subs.

Continental *American* 23 | 24 | 22 | $44

Atlantic City | Pier at Caesars | 1 Atlantic Ocean (Arkansas Ave.) | 609-674-8300 | www.continentalac.com

This "fun place to graze" on the Pier at Caesars has Stephen Starr's signature "cool atmosphere" plus "terrific" ocean views that its "Philly cousins" lack; the slate of "consistently good" small plates features "modern takes" on American "classic comfort foods" ("three words: lobster-mashed potatoes"), and the "signature drinks" and sevice earn kudos as well, making it a "satisfying" stop for Atlantic City visitors.

Copeland Restaurant *American* 25 | 24 | 24 | $61

Morristown | Westin Governor Morris | 2 Whippany Rd. (Lindsley Dr.) | 973-451-2619 | www.copelandrestaurant.com

"Well-heeled baby boomers" "don't wait for a special occasion" to enjoy chef Thomas Ciszak's "superior cuisine" and the "utterly gracious service" at this New American in Morristown's Westin Governor Morris; it's "a bit pricey if you're not on an expense account", but given the "beautiful and stylish surroundings" it's "a great place to impress."

	FOOD	DECOR	SERVICE	COST

Copper Canyon *Southwestern*   24 | 21 | 18 | $46

Atlantic Highlands | Blue Bay Inn | 51 First Ave. (bet. Center Ave. & Ocean Blvd.) | 732-291-8444 | www.thecoppercanyon.com

For "mouthwatering" "Southwestern food with a definite twist" and "awesome" margaritas made from an "impressive" tequila selection (150-plus), "look for the horseshoe" "above the door" of this "hidden" Atlantic Highlander with "cute" decor; but "wear earplugs" – it's "noisy" – and be prepared for "rushed service" and "attitude" from management.

Copper Fish *American/Seafood*   ▽ 20 | 18 | 20 | $46

Cape May | 1246 Rte. 109 S. (bet. 6th & 7th Aves.) | 609-898-0354 | www.copperfishrestaurantnj.net

Supporters say "delightful choices abound" at this New American seafooder in Cape May where the "creative chef-owner" uses "only the freshest seafood" ("try the chowder"); but it's not cheap, and while some find the "small" setting "romantic", others deem it "stark", though "attentive" service helps warm it up.

Cork *American*   21 | 18 | 20 | $39

Westmont | 90 Haddon Ave. (bet. Crescent Blvd. & Merion Terrace) | 856-833-9800 | www.corknj.com

A "lively bar scene" brings "distinct hipness" to this Westmont "upscale *Cheers*" featuring an "eclectic" modern American menu that rates "a thumbs-up", especially when you factor in the "great beer selection" (15 on draught) and "personable servers"; since it can get "noisy", quiet-seekers advise go "on weeknights."

Corky's Ribs & BBQ *BBQ*   18 | 13 | 17 | $29

Atlantic City | Marketplace at the Tropicana Casino | 2831 Boardwalk (bet. Iowa & Morris Aves.) | 609-345-4100 | www.corkysbbq.com

It may be "hundreds of miles from its Memphis home", but this chain BBQ spot at the Marketplace in the Tropicana works for AC 'cue fans looking for "a quick, filling meal"; P.S. there's a "nice view of the ocean, but you won't feel like a dip after chowing down."

Corso 98 Ⓜ *Italian*   23 | 19 | 22 | $45

Montclair | 98 Walnut St. (Willow St.) | 973-746-0789

A "great range of food, from pasta to wild boar", prepared by a new chef who adds "twists to old favorites" and "explores flavors without getting too crazy", keeps this family-run Italian storefront BYO in Montclair "vibrant" and "crowded"; the "warm and friendly" ambiance "reflects the owner's hospitality", service is "charming" and insiders whisper "you can get an inexpensive meal if you choose well."

Country Pancake House ⊘ *American*   20 | 9 | 16 | $17

Ridgewood | 140 E. Ridgewood Ave. (Walnut St.) | 201-444-8395 | www.countrypancakehouse.net

"Pancakes the size of hubcaps" and "complimentary cornbread" attract breakfast buffs to this "friendly", "cash-only" Ridgewood "neighborhood joint", "a real gut-buster" also serving lunch and dinner; the wide-ranging menu includes "some interesting ethnic choices", but a few protesters say it's all about "size, no sizzle" and note that the "dinerlike" decor "needs updating."

Court Street *Continental*
| 22 | 18 | 21 | $36 |

Hoboken | 61 Sixth St. (bet. Hudson & Washington Sts.) | 201-795-4515 | www.courtstreet.com

"Consistent" Continental cuisine makes this Hoboken "institution" "a reliable choice", especially given the "restful" setting – in a "pretty dining room" or "comfortable bar area" – with plenty of "elbow room"; a "great-deal" Sunday brunch, "economical lobster night" and "friendly" service are more reasons why it's a local "favorite."

Crab House, The *Seafood*
| 16 | 18 | 15 | $38 |

Edgewater | 541 River Rd. (Gorge Rd.) | 201-840-9311 | www.crabhouseseafood.com

"A variety of seafood for every appetite" is the haul at this "unpretentious" option on the water's edge in Edgewater; though opinions on the food vary ("delicious" vs. "so-so") and some find it "a bit pricey for a chain" operation, the "terrific NYC skyline view, especially from the deck" makes it "worth the visit."

Crab's Claw Inn, The *Seafood*
| 18 | 13 | 17 | $34 |

Lavallette | 601 Grand Central Ave. (President Ave.) | 732-793-4447 | www.thecrabsclaw.com

This Lavallette "mainstay" is "an old favorite" of both "summer visitors and locals", offering "typical Shore seafood" and the "best beer selection" – 100 labels – in the area; its "cottage decor" and service are "alright", but that's just fine with the "over 50 set" and other loyalists; N.B. expect a wait in season.

Crab Trap *Seafood*
| 22 | 17 | 19 | $40 |

Somers Point | 2 Broadway (Somers Point Circle) | 609-927-7377 | www.thecrabtrap.com

"Besides the "great view of the bay", this Somers Point "Jersey Shore tradition" offers a "large selection" of "fresh" seafood (fried, broiled, baked) at "reasonable prices", not to mention "live music for the older crowd" (daily in summer); but the "long waits in season" are a "downer."

Cranbury Inn, The *American*
| 15 | 18 | 18 | $40 |

Cranbury | 21 S. Main St. (bet. Cranbury Station Rd. & Evans Dr.) | 609-655-5595 | www.thecranburyinn.com

The "quaint charm" of this Traditional American housed in a circa-1780 Cranbury lodge "is the best thing about the place" submit surveyors who focus on its "beauty" rather than the food, "which does not live up to the promise of the building"; still, it's an "old standbly and "good for Sunday brunch."

Creole Café Ⓜ *Cajun/Creole*
| ▽ 22 | 16 | 20 | $31 |

Sewell | Harbor Pl. | 288 Egg Harbor Rd. (Huffville Grenloch Rd.) | 856-582-7222 | www.creole-cafe.com

"Is this really in a Jersey strip mall?" ask those who've ventured to this Mardi Gras–themed Cajun-Creole BYO in Sewell that provides a taste "of New Orleans" in an "off-the-beaten-path location"; supporters say "the kitchen knows its stuff", yet a few feel "it's not as good as it used to be."

Crown Palace Chinese
20 | 18 | 18 | $29

Marlboro | 8 N. Main St. (School Rd.) | 732-780-8882
Middletown | 1283 Hwy. 35 (Kings Hwy.) | 732-615-9888

Dim sum is a "very popular" "treat" on weekends and holidays at this Monmouth County duo ("go early" advise regulars), though the rest of the menu strikes some as "standard Chinese", albeit "better than most"; Marlboro's tropical fish tank and outdoor stone garden trump Middletown's "so-so" decor, though "attentive" service crowns both locales.

Cuba Libre Cuban
22 | 25 | 20 | $44

Atlantic City | Quarter at the Tropicana | 2801 Pacific Ave. (Iowa Ave.) | 609-348-6700 | www.cubalibrerestaurant.com

"Awesome mojitos", "a lively Latin dancing scene" and decor that "transports you to a courtyard in Havana" make this a "vibrant" if "noisy" "treat at the Trop" in AC, complete with "delicious" Cuban food; though some contend it's "not as good as" the Philly original, most find it a "welcome break" from "losing your shirt" at the casinos.

Cuban Pete's ● Cuban
18 | 21 | 16 | $31

Montclair | 428 Bloomfield Ave. (Fullerton Ave.) | 973-746-1100 | www.cubanpetesrestaurant.com

The "vibe is almost better than the food" at this "kitschy" Montclair Cuban BYO that's "louder than a Metallica concert"; though some say the *cocina* is "the real deal", to others it's "overrated", but all agree the outdoor courtyard is *perfecto* for "faux Havana fun times" – "if you can brave the long waits."

NEW Cubanu Cuban
∇ 24 | 20 | 22 | $36

Rahway | 1467 Main St. (Lewis St.) | 732-499-7100 | www.cubanu.com

"Fantastic" food paired with a "nice lounge" makes this Cuban in a "gentrified neighborhood" in Rahway a "refreshing" "surprise"; though "parking can be difficult", the "tasty" fare – plus free salsa lessons on Thursdays and live music Fridays–Sundays – is "worth it."

Cubby's BBQ Restaurant BBQ
18 | 9 | 12 | $20

Hackensack | 249 S. River St. (bet. Kennedy & Water Sts.) | 201-488-9389 | www.cubbysbarbeque.com

BBQ buffs in Bergen say you can't go wrong at this Hackensack self-serve, a rollicking "roadhouse" "hidden" beneath Route 80 where die-hard fans get their fill of "sticky-finger" eats – ribs, burgers, chili-dogs and the like; it may not be "a fine-dining experience", but it supplies "very casual, affordable, fun."

Cucharamama Ⓜ S American
25 | 23 | 21 | $44

Hoboken | 233 Clinton St. (3rd St.) | 201-420-1700 | www.cucharamama.com

This "top-tier ethnic restaurant" in Hoboken from celeb-chef (and food historian) Maricel Presilla is a "work of art", with "pricey", "in-

| | FOOD | DECOR | SERVICE | COST |

ventive" South American meals (including "concoctions from a wood-burning oven") as vivid as the "vibrant oil paintings" by her father that are on view; a "sexy bar scene" serving "tremendous drinks" enhances the "unique experience."

Cucina Rosa *Italian*
21 | 17 | 19 | $37

Cape May | Washington Street Mall | 301 Washington St. (bet. Jackson & Perry Sts.) | 609-898-9800 | www.cucinarosa.com

"Solid", "traditional red-sauce Italian" fare is the calling card of this "cozy, comfortable" *cucina* on Cape May's pedestrian mall, and the rosy picture is enhanced by "pleasant" servers and "reasonable prices"; it's BYO but local wines are available; N.B. closed January through mid-February.

Z CulinAriane ⓢⓂ *American*
27 | 19 | 24 | $55

Montclair | 33 Walnut St. (Pine St.) | 973-744-0533 | www.culinariane.com

"Reliably amazing" is the word on the New American cuisine at this "off-the-beaten-path" BYO in Montclair, courtesy of husband-and-wife team Michael and Ariane Duarte (pastry chef and executive chef/*Top Chef* contender, respectively); "warm, friendly" service and a "cozy" if "cramped" setting also attract; P.S. it's "very hard to get a reservation" as it's open for dinner only, Wednesdays–Saturdays, with seasonal outdoor dining.

Dabbawalla Ⓜ *Indian*
18 | 15 | 18 | $30

Summit | 427 Springfield Ave. (Summit Ave.) | 908-918-0330 | www.dabbawalla.com

"An easy entry into Indian food" is offered at this "very reasonable" Summit Indian BYO specializing in "delicately prepared dishes" served in lunch boxes – its name means "lunch box man" – at long "communal tables" (think "high-school cafeteria decor"); N.B. there's an all-you-can-eat lunch buffet and an à la carte menu.

daddy O *American*
19 | 23 | 19 | $45

Long Beach Township | daddy O Hotel | 4401 Long Beach Blvd. (44th St.) | 609-494-1300 | www.daddyohotel.com

This Long Beach "hipster hangout" inside the boutique hotel of the same name brings "the flair of Manhattan" to the Shore – complete with "good" contemporary American food, "slick" decor, "a big bar scene" and, alas, the "noise" and prices too; N.B. a recent change in chef may outdate the above Food score.

da Filippo Autentica Cucina Italiana ⓢ *Italian/Seafood*
23 | 17 | 23 | $45

Somerville | 132 E. Main St. (Meadow St.) | 908-218-0110 | www.dafilippos.com

"Bring a good bottle" because "the food is worthy" at this "lovely little secret" Somerville storefront BYO with the "best Sicilian fish" and osso buco you could "cut with a spoon"; chef-owner Filippo Russo "often adds a musical note on his piano", but some say he "should spend more time in the kitchen" because when Filippo is cooking, "*tutto va bene.*"

	FOOD	DECOR	SERVICE	COST

Dai-Kichi *Japanese* `22` `14` `19` `$30`
Upper Montclair | 608 Valley Rd. (Bellevue Ave.) | 973-744-2954
"Lively every night", this Upper Montclair Japanese BYO attracts "couples and families" who don't mind the "nondescript setting" since it offers "reliable" sushi and "friendly service"; maybe the cooking is "not ambitious", but "the fish is fresh and well prepared"; P.S. there's "a cute heated pavilion out back."

D & L Barbecue *BBQ* ▽ `22` `11` `17` `$26`
Asbury Park | 1206 Main St. (bet. 4th & 5th Aves.) | 732-722-7488 | www.dlbbq.com
"Chow down and enjoy" what fans call "the best BBQ north of the Mason-Dixon line" at this Asbury Park "down-home" joint dishing out "fall-off-the-bone ribs and homemade sides" ("beans and rice, cornbread, great mac 'n' cheese"); it's a "good place to bring the family" for an "affordable", "no-nonsense" feed.

Danny's Steakhouse & Sushi Bar ● *Steak* `20` `17` `20` `$43`
Red Bank | 11 Bridge Ave. (Front St.) | 732-741-6900 | www.dannyssteakhouse.com
"The steaks are fine" and the sushi has its fans too, at Danny Murphy's "been-there-forever" "cozy place" in Red Bank; locals say it's "more neighborhood bar than fine dining", but count on "fair prices" and a staff that's "eager to please."

Dante's Ristorante *Italian* `21` `18` `22` `$38`
Mendham | 100 E. Main St. (Cold Hill Rd.) | 973-543-5401 | www.dantenj.com
The "well-trained", "caring" staff "will bend over backwards" at this "very family-friendly" Mendham Italian BYO, where the "menu always shows some originality" and the pizza is "dependable"; still, some suggest the food, while "tasty", "doesn't live up to the price" and find the quarters "tight."

☑ Daryl Wine Bar Ⓜ *American* `24` `26` `23` `$58`
New Brunswick | Heldrich Hotel | 302 George St. (New St.) | 732-253-7780 | www.darylwinebar.com
"Everything about it is amazing" gush fans of David Drake's "stylish" New Brunswick New American tucked into the "sleek" Heldrich Hotel; his "beyond heavenly" cuisine is offered in "tapas-style small plates" or "traditional-size portions" and coupled with a "mind-boggling menu of wines" in assorted pours, making for "the coolest dining experience"; just "watch the tab" as it can all "add up quickly"; N.B. a late-night menu is served 10:30 PM–1 AM Friday–Saturday.

David Burke Fromagerie Ⓜ *American* `25` `24` `23` `$71`
Rumson | 26 Ridge Rd. (Ave. of Two Rivers) | 732-842-8088 | www.fromagerierestaurant.com
"Renowned" chef-owner David Burke brings his "top-of-the-line" "magic" to this "Rumson landmark", offering "expensive but divine" New American fare distinguished by "intriguing flavor profiles" and

"artistic presentation", as evidenced in "signatures" like "angry lobster" and "cheesecake lollipops"; most applaud the "lighter and brighter" "pretty room", but some note "amateurish" hiccups in the generally "polite" service.

❷ David Drake, Restaurant ⑤ American | 28 | 24 | 26 | $74

Rahway | 1449 Irving St. (Cherry St.) | 732-388-6677 | www.daviddrakes.com

David Drake's near "flawless" "bright spot" in Rahway helps "set the bar" for all other "special-occasion" spots; with "exciting", "seasonal" New American cuisine, "superb" service and a townhouse setting that's as "romantic and intimate" as it gets, it's a "delight for all the senses" and well worth the "splurge"; N.B. there are à la carte options as well as an $79 five-course tasting menu.

DeAnna's Ⓜ Italian | 22 | 20 | 21 | $40

Lambertville | 54 N. Franklin St. (Coryell St.) | 609-397-8957 | www.deannasrestaurant.com

This "good" "little pasta house" gained "sophistication", a bar and weekend entertainment with a move a few years back, but it's still "mainly a local joint" in Lambertville that pleases with a "friendly atmosphere", "efficient" service and a three-course dinner special (Tuesdays–Wednesdays) that's "an excellent value" at $20.

NEW Delicious Heights American | 21 | 23 | 20 | $32

Berkeley Heights | 428 Springfield Ave. (Plainfield Ave.) | 908-464-3287 | www.deliciousheights.com

"Consistency" in food and service and "nicely decorated" rooms hit a high note at this Berkeley Heights New American that was formerly a "tiny take-out" spot; "huge portions" – "one entree is enough for two" – an "awesome new bar" that gives the area "a much-needed nightspot" and "11 flat-screen TVs" are pluses.

DeLorenzo's Pizza ⑤Ⓜ⇆ Pizza | - | - | - | I

Trenton | 1007 Hamilton Ave. (bet. Chambers St. & Olden Ave.) | 609-393-2952 | www.delospizza.com

There are two DeLorenzo's in Trenton (and one in Robbinsville) – relatives but with completely independent businesses – and pizza lovers argue endlessly over who's the top tosser; some say this one's versions are sweeter and cheesier than its Hudson Street neighbor's – and you'd better love pies 'cause it's the only thing on the menu.

❷ DeLorenzo's Tomato Pies Ⓜ Pizza | 27 | 12 | 17 | $17

NEW Robbinsville | Washington Town Ctr. | 2350 Rte. 33 (bet. Lake Dr. & Robbinsville Edinburg Rd.) | 609-341-8480

Trenton | 530 Hudson St. (bet. Hudson Ct. & Swan St.) | 609-695-9534 ⇆ www.delorenzostomatopies.com

"You haven't really eaten pizza" – make that "tomato pie" – until you've tasted "thin-crust, old-fashioned, piping-hot heaven" at this BYO "Central Jersey institution"; some say the original, cash-only Trenton rowhouse ("no decor, no bathroom", "no antipasti") offers "the true experience", while others shout "hooray!" for the new

Robbinsville addition, which boasts appetizers and restrooms and takes credit cards; either way, expect "interminable" weekend waits; N.B. whole pies only; independent from the other Trenton DeLorenzo's.

Delta's 🅼 *Southern* 23 | 23 | 21 | $40

New Brunswick | 19 Dennis St. (bet. Hiram Sq. & Richmond St.) | 732-249-1551 | www.deltasrestaurant.com

"High-end soul food" meets "exquisite decor" at this "always hoppin'" New Brunswick Southern belle serving "amazing" cornbread, crocodile, mac 'n' cheese, ribs and "finger-lickin' good oxtails" to the beat of live entertainment (Tuesdays and Thursdays, Fridays and Saturdays); service can be "spotty", but the "homey" food and the "exquisite" surroundings prevail.

Dimora Ristorante *Italian* 23 | 19 | 20 | $56

Norwood | 100 Piermont Rd. (B'way) | 201-750-5000

"Quite the scene", this residential Norwood Italian gets "ridiculously crowded and noisy" on weekends, but "the pasta is plentiful and sauces artful" (and "they have the branzino down to a science"); still, waits at this "expensive haunt of the country club set" are "way too long" for some and service "a tad rushed."

Dim Sum Dynasty *Chinese* 20 | 15 | 18 | $28

Ridgewood | 75 Franklin Ave. (Oak St.) | 201-652-0686 | www.dimsumdynastynj.com

For "real-deal" "authentic Hong Kong–style dim sum" in NJ, this Cantonese BYO "is not to be missed" – the choice is "modest on weekdays, but dramatic on weekends" when served from carts; if some find prices "steeper than typical", most don't notice since this "family-run" place "tries very hard to please."

Dinallo's *Italian* 22 | 16 | 20 | $44

River Edge | 259 Johnson Ave. (Madison Ave.) | 201-342-1233

"Enjoyable" "old-world" standards rule at this "cozy" (though "a bit cramped" and "noisy") River Edge Italian with a "busy older singles bar scene"; "the food is always consistent and the service friendly", but some think the "decor and staff are stuck in a time warp."

🆕 Dino's Restaurant *Italian* - | - | - | E
(fka Roman Cafe, The)

Harrington Park | 12 Tappan Rd. (Schraalenburgh Rd.) | 201-767-4245 | www.dinoshp.com

It's all in *la famiglia* at this Harrington Park go-to now run by the eponymous chef-owner (and son of the former proprietor); "mom and pop's place" has been "revitalized" with a roster of contemporary and traditional Italian dishes (e.g. sweet potato ravioli) purveyed amid a colorful, cozy ambiance; N.B. closed Tuesdays.

DiPalma Brothers Restaurant 🅼 *Italian* 22 | 17 | 21 | $30

North Bergen | 8728 Kennedy Blvd. (bet. 87th & 88th Sts.) | 201-868-3005

"I'll have the eggplant balls, gnocchi and the chair I'm sitting on" might be overheard at this family-operated North Bergen Italian

BYO in an antique shop – where both the food and surrounding knickknacks are for sale; it may remind some of "eating in an eccentric aunt's house", but the "clutter" is trumped by "sweet" service and "rustic, plentiful" fare.

Dish ⓜ *American* | 24 | 16 | 21 | $43

Red Bank | 13 White St. (Broad St.) | 732-345-7070 | www.dishredbank.com

Fans say the "friendly", "young" staff and the "stellar" seasonal American fare – "fresh", "simple" and "full of flavor" – at this "unpretentious" 45-seat BYO "on a side street" "in hip Red Bank" compensate for "tight quarters" and a "booming noise level"; "don't miss their homemade desserts" – "the chocolate bread pudding is to die for."

Dock's Oyster House *Seafood* | 26 | 21 | 23 | $52

Atlantic City | 2405 Atlantic Ave. (Georgia Ave.) | 609-345-0092 | www.docksoysterhouse.com

"Venture off the boardwalk" and "skip the overpriced casino restaurants" for this "beloved" AC "institution", a "seafood standout" with "fabulous", "fresh" fish, a "pleasing wine list", "excellent" service and "wonderful hosts"; it's been evincing "charm" since 1897 and is "worth the pricey prices" to experience real "old-time class"; N.B. there's piano music almost every night.

Don Pepe *Portuguese/Spanish* | 21 | 16 | 19 | $40

Newark | 844 McCarter Hwy. (Raymond Blvd.) | 973-623-4662
Pine Brook | 18 Old Bloomfield Ave. (Changebridge Rd.) | 973-882-6757
www.donpeperestaurant.com

"Wear loose pants" to these "always packed" Newark and Pine Brook "old-time favorite" Iberians famed for "lobster the size of a small car" and "brontosaurus-size steaks" at "reasonable prices"; some find the "everything is big" experience "fun", others "fail to see the appeal", but most agree the "tired" decor could be freshened up.

Don Pepe's Steakhouse *Steak* | 22 | 18 | 20 | $46

Pine Brook | 58 Rte. 46 W. (bet. Chapin & Van Winkle Rds.) | 973-808-5533 | www.donpepesteakhouse.com

"Count on leftovers" of "excellent steaks and seafood" at this "casual" Pine Brook meatery (an offshoot of the Newark original) where "big crowds" and "appetites" are "welcomed"; while some feel the "ambiance and service leave a lot to be desired", there's "always a fun 'buzz' in the air" and prices are considered "reasonable."

Don Quijote *Spanish* | 17 | 15 | 18 | $37

Fairview | 344 Bergen Blvd. (Jersey Ave.) | 201-943-3133 | www.donquijoterestaurant.net

Diners are split over this Fairview Spaniard: while aficionados assert the "twin lobsters, paella and garlic shrimp" are as good as "any Newark-based restaurant", deriders declare the *comidas* a "disappointment"; likewise, while some find a "very pleasing" atmosphere, others opine it "makes Lawrence Welk seem hip" (despite a weekend mariachi band); however, there are no complaints about the "great early-bird specials" (Monday–Friday).

	FOOD	DECOR	SERVICE	COST

Doris & Ed's Ⓜ *American/Seafood* — 25 | 19 | 22 | $59

Highlands | 348 Shore Dr. (bet. King & Matthews Sts.) | 732-872-1565 |
www.dorisandeds.com

Fish dinners "as fresh as they come" along with Traditional and New
American fare make this Highlands "institution" "tops" with many,
as do the "killer views" of Sandy Hook Bay, "wonderful" service and
"awesome" wine list (all of which trump the few complaints about
"stuffy" decor); prices are "steep" "but worth it" – it's "still the place
to go for seafood"; N.B. a new chef may outdate the Food score.

🅉 Drew's Bayshore Bistro Ⓜ *American* — 26 | 14 | 22 | $39

Keyport | 58 Broad St. (Front St.) | 732-739-9219 |
www.bayshorebistro.com

What this "wonderful surprise" of an American BYO in Keyport "lacks
in decor" and "size" it "more than makes up for" in owner-chef Andrew
Araneo's "inspired" and "creative" cooking with a Cajun-Creole
bent; service is "warm and friendly", and the atmosphere "relaxed."

NEW Due Mari *Italian* — ▽ 26 | 25 | 26 | $54

New Brunswick | 78 Albany St. (Neilson St.) | 732-296-1600 |
www.duemarinj.com

As its Italian name ('Two Seas') suggests, this "wonderful addition"
to Downtown New Brunswick is "strong on seafood" but also delights with "amazing handmade pastas" and "addictive *sfizi* (small-
plate nibbles)"; with a staff that's "genuinely glad to see you, help
you and not bother you", this Due Terre sibling is especially "great
for date night."

Due Terre Enoteca *Italian* — 25 | 22 | 23 | $59

Bernardsville | 107 Morristown Rd. (Finley Ave.) | 908-221-0040 |
www.dueterre.com

This "hip, stylish" strip-mall Italian is a "welcome addition to the
Bernardsville scene", offering "reasonably priced", "inventive" cuisine and "outstanding" service in a "convivial atmosphere"; fans say
the handmade pastas are "luscious" and the steaks "brilliant" – but
"don't plan on talking over the noise."

Dune Restaurant Ⓜ *Seafood* — 25 | 16 | 23 | $45

Margate | 9510 Ventnor Ave. (bet. Jefferson & Madison Aves.) |
609-487-7450 | www.dunerestaurant.com

Despite a change in chef, enthusiasts report there's "no better place
for fish" (or hanger steak) than this "charming" Key West-esque
BYO Margate seafooder, offering "fresh and innovative"
combinations – e.g. black bass in a blueberry beurre blanc; never-
theless, some find the tabs "expensive for the location"; N.B. closed
from December to March.

E & V Ⓜ⫞ *Italian* — 23 | 11 | 19 | $32

Paterson | 320 Chamberlain Ave. (bet. Preakness & Redwood Aves.) |
973-942-8080 | www.evrestaurant.com

"Bring your appetite" say fans of this fortysomething "red-sauce"
Paterson Italian "neighborhood institution" known for "huge por-

tions" of "grandma-style" eats; "the decor has been the same forever" and "the lines and the crowd can be a headache", but "reasonable prices" make it "worth the wait"; P.S. "they don't take plastic", but there's an ATM on-site.

East *Japanese*

19	15	16	$30

Teaneck | 1405 Teaneck Rd. (bet. Rte. 4 & Tryon Ave.) | 201-837-1260
"For a sushi fix that doesn't break the bank", locals head to this "kid-friendly" Teaneck Japanese where the "sushi conveyor belt" is "gimmicky but fun"; there's "a decent cooked menu as well", which helps to compensate for decor that some find "a bit tired."

☑ Ebbitt Room *American*

27	26	26	$63

Cape May | Virginia Hotel | 25 Jackson St. (bet. Beach Ave. & Carpenter Ln.) | 609-884-5700 | www.virginiahotel.com
For "fine dining at its best" in Cape May, "allow yourself to be spoiled" at this "elegant" and "romantic" spot in the Virginia Hotel, a "jewel" that "charms" with "perfectly prepared" New American cuisine and "fantastic" wine "impeccably" served in a "beautiful dining room"; N.B. a change of chefs post-Survey may outdate the above Food score.

Eccola Italian Bistro *Italian*

23	19	20	$41

Parsippany | 1082 Rte. 46 W. (Beverwyck Rd.) | 973-334-8211 | www.eccolarestaurantnj.com
There's "no such thing as 'a quiet table in the corner'" at this "upbeat", "eclectic" Parsippany strip-mall Italian, but "imaginative food" at "fair prices" and an "upscale bar with an interesting mixed crowd" make it "a real find"; N.B. reservations taken only for parties of five or more at dinner.

Edo Sushi *Chinese/Japanese*

19	12	16	$29

Pennington | Pennington Shopping Ctr. | 25 Rte. 31 S. (bet. Delaware & Franklin Aves.) | 609-737-1190
"Solid sushi" and "reliable but not exceptional" Chinese is the take on this "child-friendly" Pennington BYO in a "small shopping center"; service is "fast", but even with a decor redo "it would be nicer if it didn't feel like a high school cafeteria."

Egan & Sons *Irish*

18	20	18	$33

Montclair | 118 Walnut St. (Forest St.) | 973-744-1413 | www.eganandsons.com
The "vibe is alive" at this "warm and friendly", "high-end" Montclair Irish "hot spot" serving "craft-made" brews, "heavenly" burgers and fries, "authentic shepherd's pie" and other "very good pub grub"; though it "can get insanely crowded", that only adds to the festivities.

El Azteca *Mexican*

20	13	19	$22

Mount Laurel | Ramblewood Shopping Ctr. | 1155 Rte. 73 N. (Church Rd.) | 856-914-9302
The "large portions" of "good", "hearty Mexican" fare at this Mount Laurel BYO get points for "authenticity" from some, though a few deem them "standard"; devotees advise "don't let the looks get you down" – just "bring your own tequila and they'll make margaritas."

	FOOD	DECOR	SERVICE	COST

El Cid *Spanish*
21 | 15 | 20 | $43

Paramus | 205 Paramus Rd. (bet. Century Rd. & Rte. 4) | 201-843-0123

Count on "*Flintstone*-size portions" and "a wait for a table" at this Spanish surf 'n' turfer "close to Paramus shopping and the golf course"; although the ambiance is "a little run-down", "the biggest prime rib on the planet" and "the 'twin lobsters' – which are three one-pounders" – keep aficionados coming back for *más*.

NEW elements *American*
– | – | – | E

Princeton | 163 Bayard Ln. (bet. Birch & Leigh Aves.) | 609-924-0078 | www.elementsprinceton.com

Chef-owner Scott Anderson sees food as a canvas, painting plates and exciting palates at this new, soothe-the-senses, fine-dining Princeton beauty; his New American take on worldwide cooking is making him the talk of the tony Princeton restaurant scene for those lucky enough to snag the chef's table for the nightly nine-course tasting menu.

Elements Asia *Pan-Asian*
23 | 20 | 19 | $32

Lawrenceville | Village Commons | 4110 Quakerbridge Rd. (Village Rd.) | 609-275-4988 | www.elementsasia.com

"You can travel throughout Asia without leaving NJ" at this "nirvana in a strip mall", a Lawrenceville BYO with an "inventive" menu of Pan-Asian cuisine; though it "doesn't look like much" from the outside, once inside it's "beautifully appointed", and the service is "friendly and attentive."

Elements Café 🅂Ⓜ *American*
▽ 24 | 18 | 20 | $38

Haddon Heights | 517 Station Ave. (White Horse Pike) | 856-546-8840 | www.elementscafe.com

"Tapas-style" plates showcasing "inventive preparations" are the "concept" behind this "small" Haddon Heights American BYO; fans say chef-owner Fred Kellermann "rocks" and service is "outgoing but not intrusive", though some bemoan the "uncomfortable" chairs.

Elephant & Castle ❶ *Pub Food*
13 | 14 | 14 | $27

Cherry Hill | Clarion Hotel | 1450 Rte. 70 E. (I-295) | 856-427-0427 | www.elephantcastle.com

Though stalwarts insist "it's the perfect place to unwind" with a "good selection of beers on tap", most find the "pub grub" and atmosphere of this "Anglophile"-style national chain link inside Cherry Hill's Clarion Hotel "standard" at best, with "tired" decor and "inattentive" service; N.B. the property was for sale in early spring.

El Familiar *Colombian/Mexican*
▽ 19 | 9 | 15 | $18

Freehold | 3 W. Main St. (Court St.) | 732-303-9400
Toms River Township | Stella Towne Ctr. | 1246 Rte. 166 (Hilltop Rd.) | 732-240-6613 | www.jerseyshorefood.com

Colombian cooking pairs up with Mexican specialties at these Shore BYOs, an uncommon alternative to the area's familiar eateries; the modest decor is handily offset by the interesting – and modestly priced – homestyle fare.

El Meson Cafe *Mexican*

FOOD	DECOR	SERVICE	COST
24	14	21	$25

Freehold | 40 W. Main St. (Court St.) | 732-308-9494

"As close to south of the border" as it gets in Central Jersey, this BYO dishes out "huge" portions of the "very best" Mexican that "generates crowds"; "friendly" service and "attractive" prices are pluses, as is the attached market that's perfect for bodega browsing.

🆕 El Pollo Loco *Chicken*

FOOD	DECOR	SERVICE	COST
–	–	–	I

North Bergen | 2100 88th St. (off Tonnelle Ave.) | 201-868-0500 | www.elpolloloco.com

The first El Pollo Loco in Jersey, located in North Bergen – 15 more are planned – offers citrus-marinated, flame-grilled chicken served alone or in salads, burritos or tacos in an Aztec-influenced building; there are four fresh choices on the self-serve salsa bar, kids get their own menus and you can BYO.

Elysian Cafe *French*

FOOD	DECOR	SERVICE	COST
20	21	20	$35

Hoboken | 1001 Washington St. (10th St.) | 201-798-5898 | www.elysiancafe.com

"Nobody does bistro better" than this French charmer in a restored 1895 saloon, the oldest continually operated bar/restaurant in Hoboken (across the street from its sister, Amanda's); expect "amazing" steak frites, a "mouthwatering" bar menu (half-price on Mondays), "inventive cocktails" and "a heavenly brunch"; P.S. "the great patio seating" is choice for people-watching.

🆕 Eno Terra *Italian*

FOOD	DECOR	SERVICE	COST
–	–	–	E

Kingston | 4484 Nassau St./Rte. 27 (Lakeview Ave.) | 609-497-1777 | www.enoterra.com

Chef Christopher Albrecht brings this newcomer to the cultured Kingston/Princeton neighborhood, offering an Italian-inspired menu featuring local ingredients; devotees line up to enjoy the contemporary cuisine in a historic, certified-green kitchen with a wood-burning grill, fireplace and outstanding wine list.

Epernay Ⓜ *French*

FOOD	DECOR	SERVICE	COST
20	18	20	$44

Montclair | 6 Park St. (Bloomfield Ave.) | 973-783-0447 | www.epernaynj.com

"Dependable French bistro" fare "at reasonable prices", a "romantic atmosphere" and a "warm staff" make this Montclair BYO "a Gallic delight"; though some say a "change of ownership has dented the consistency", the majority maintains it's like "a little trip to France."

Eppes Essen *Deli*

FOOD	DECOR	SERVICE	COST
19	10	14	$22

Livingston | 105 E. Mt. Pleasant Ave. (Livingston Ave.) | 973-994-1120 | www.eppesessen.com

For more than half a century this "classic" Livingston kosher-style deli has been "the place to stuff yourself" on "Jewish comfort food"; it's not about the "dinerlike" surroundings ("who cares about the decor?") or the "brusque" staff ("who said there's service at a Jewish deli, isn't that part of the experience?") – "it's only about the food."

	FOOD	DECOR	SERVICE	COST

Equus *American*   21 | 25 | 21 | $60
Bernardsville | 1 Mill St. (Anderson Rd.) | 908-766-3737 |
www.equustavern.com
With its "magical" "hunt-country decor", this Bernardsville New
American, set in a "fabulous renovation" of the 19th-century Stone
Tavern landmark, offers "pricey though well-thought-out dishes" via
"upscale" restaurant and bar menus; even if some contend service
can be "spotty", most agree this place has "class"; P.S. patio dining
comes "complete with heat lamps to take off the chill."

Espo's ⊘ *Italian*   21 | 11 | 19 | $27
Raritan | 10 Second St. (bet. Anderson & Thompson Sts.) | 908-685-9552
"No surprises, no innovation, who cares?" admit admirers of this
"real down-home", "modestly priced" Raritan traditional Italian
"standby" that's been attracting "a huge local following" with the
"same delicious dinners for years"; its "quirky", "dark tavern setting" is "not a place for a romantic evening", but it's "fun for families
or groups"; P.S. "no credit cards."

Esty Street ⊠ *American*   24 | - | 22 | $53
Park Ridge | 86 Spring Valley Rd. (Fremont Ave.) | 201-307-1515 |
www.estystreet.com
"An excellent dining experience" awaits at this "inventive" Park
Ridge New American where the "seasonal menu" produces "fabulous", if "kind of pricey", food; thanks to a recent redo, the once
"dated" decor has a fresh cozy look replicating a library.

Eurasian Eatery 🅜 *Eclectic*   22 | 13 | 20 | $23
Red Bank | 110 Monmouth St. (bet. Maple Ave. & Pearl St.) |
732-741-7071 | www.eurasianeatery.com
For over 20 years, this "casual" BYO Red Bank Eclectic has kept 'em
happy with "imaginative food" that's "a blend of ethnic cuisines"
and includes "creative vegetarian-vegan options"; the cooking is
abetted by "generous portions", "great prices" and "knowledgeable
service", while its close proximity to the Count Basie Theater
is another plus.

Europa at Monroe 🅜 *Mediterranean*   16 | 18 | 19 | $38
Monroe Township | 146 Applegarth Rd. (Old Church Rd.) | 609-490-9500 |
www.europanj.com
This Monroe Mediterranean "hideaway" gets a thumbs-up from
fans for the Italian and Spanish specialties ("great paella and
tapas") on its "eclectic European menu"; while others report "hit-or-
miss" food, the "friendly service" and weekend entertainment work
in its favor.

Europa South *Portuguese/Spanish*   19 | 15 | 20 | $41
Point Pleasant Beach | 521 Arnold Ave. (Rte. 35) | 732-295-1500 |
www.europasouth.com
With "servings big enough to feed the Spanish armada", this Point
Pleasant Beach veteran is considered a "good" bet "if you're looking
for Iberian cuisine on the Shore"; "great sangria" and "fine service"

also earn applause, yet despite a "sprucing-up", the "dark" "'70s decor" strikes some as "dated."

	FOOD	DECOR	SERVICE	COST

Far East Taste ⓂChinese/Thai

23 | 5 | 20 | $21

Eatontown | 19 Main St. (Broad St.) | 732-389-9866
The kitchen "still has the chops" – courtesy of Frank Qui, nephew of former toque Richard Wang – say fans of the "artful" Chinese-Thai fare at this Eatontown BYO; forget about decor ("there's decor?"), but the servers "could not be more helpful" and it's an "extraordinary value."

NEW Farm 2 Bistro American

- | - | - | I

Nutley | 177 Franklin Ave. (bet. Centre & Stager Sts.) | 973-667-3276 | www.farmtobistro.com
There's no keeping 'em down on the farm when crops go directly to this Nutley American for the day's meals – making use of fresh, local produce is the philosophy behind this new BYO charmer; no wonder fans are plowing their way here in everything but tractors.

Farnsworth House, The Continental

23 | 18 | 21 | $40

Bordentown | 135 Farnsworth Ave. (Railroad Ave.) | 609-291-9232 | www.thefarnsworthhouse.com
A perennial "favorite of locals" for its "twists on classic Italian and Continental dishes", this bi-level representative of "old-time Bordentown", set inside a circa-1682 brick building, remains the place for "a good family meal", particularly upstairs, which is more modern and fashionable than the first floor, boasting a bustling bar.

☑ Fascino ⓈItalian

26 | 22 | 24 | $57

Montclair | 331 Bloomfield Ave. (bet. Grove & Willow Sts.) | 973-233-0350 | www.fascinorestaurant.com
"Unbeatable", "soulful" cucina plus "gracious service" make this family-run Montclair BYO Italian storefront a "primo" place "for a special night out"; chef Ryan DePersio deftly blends "traditional" cooking with "modern updates" and mom Cynthia's desserts justify the caloric "splurge"; it's "expensive", "parking isn't easy" and "getting a reservation is a challenge", but it's ultimately "worth it."

Federici's ⱷ Pizza

22 | 11 | 18 | $25

Freehold | 14 E. Main St. (South St.) | 732-462-1312 | www.federicis.com
Since 1921, "legendary" thin-crust pizza has ruled at this "family-run" Freehold "hometown favorite" (beyond that, the Italian fare strikes some as "average"); regulars like to dine "alfresco on Main Street" "on a nice evening", rather than indoors amid "dated" decor; N.B. son Frankie heads up Frankie Fed's in Freehold Township.

Fedora Cafe Ⓜ Eclectic

18 | 15 | 13 | $22

Lawrenceville | 2633 Main St. (bet. Craven Ln. & Phillips Ave.) | 609-895-0844
"Chill out" at this "funky and fun" Lawrenceville Eclectic BYO "right off the set of Friends" (with "benches and cushions" in addition to table seating), where "blue jeans would be considered

dressed-up"; it dispenses "good" "cafe-style" food ("sandwiches, soups, salads, decadent desserts"), though the "young, bored" staff "could be friendlier."

Fernandes Steakhouse II *Portuguese/Spanish* | 23 | 19 | 20 | $40 |

Newark | 152-158 Fleming Ave. (Chapel St.) | 973-589-4099 | www.fernandessteakhouse.com

"Incredible" rodizio plus "excellent steaks" make this Iberian-Brazilian on the outskirts of Newark's Ironbound "good for a boys' night out"; the "friendly and accommodating" staff and "festive atmosphere with strolling musicians on weekends" add to the "very good value for the money."

Ferrari's Ocean Grill Ⓜ *Italian* | 22 | 19 | 22 | $40 |

Freehold Township | A&M Plaza | 3475 Rte. 9 N. (Three Brooks Rd.) | 732-294-7400 | www.ferrarisrestaurantnj.com

You "wouldn't know it to look at" this storefront BYO in a shopping center on Route 9 in Freehold, but the "Italian staples" are "surprisingly good", as is the "friendly atmosphere and attentive service"; it's "comfortable and accommodating" – and "always crowded."

Ferry House, The *American/French* | 25 | 20 | 23 | $51 |

Princeton | 32 Witherspoon St. (Spring St.) | 609-924-2488 | www.theferryhouse.com

"Every time's as good as the first" rave fans of Bobby Trigg's American-French fare – especially "first-tier" seafood – at this "wonderful", "busy" "fine-dining" spot in Downtown Princeton that also garners "consistently high marks" for its "well-trained" staff; some find the decor "a little dark" and lament "New York prices", but BYO helps.

Fiddleheads Ⓜ *American* | 22 | 15 | 22 | $36 |

Jamesburg | 27 E. Railroad Ave. (Forsgate Dr.) | 732-521-0878 | www.fiddleheadsjamesburg.com

"This is the kind of restaurant you root for" rave proponents of this New American BYO storefront in Downtown Jamesburg, "graciously" purveying "sophisticated yet relaxed" staples (rack of lamb, smoked tomato bisque) and "the occasional surprise" like antelope; it's "small", so "reservations are a must."

55 Main Ⓢ *American* | 20 | 17 | 20 | $41 |

Flemington | 55 Main St. (Bloomfield Ave.) | 908-284-1551 | www.55main.com

There's "always something original" on the "stylish" American menu of this Downtown Flemington BYO where the service "sparkles" and chef-owner Jonas Gold is "free to do his own thing" (crisp green curry puffs, anyone?); though the "minimalist" decor may be in need of "soundproofing", for fans it's a "relaxing evening out."

Filomena Cucina Italiana *Italian* | ▽ 23 | 20 | 22 | $40 |

Clementon | 1380 Blackwood-Clementon Rd. (Millbridge Rd.) | 856-784-6166 | www.filomenascucina.com

This "nice place for a family dinner" in Clementon "constantly delivers" on "authentic" Italian fare – "nothing exciting or innovative", but "delicious" nonetheless and served in "generous portions" by a "friendly" staff; N.B. there's live music Wednesdays–Saturdays.

Filomena Cucina Rustica *Italian* ▽ 23 | 20 | 22 | $40

West Berlin | 13 Cross Keys Rd. (White Horse Pike) | 856-753-3540 | www.filomenasberlin.com

For "a taste of Italy" in West Berlin's "own backyard", eager eaters head to this "favorite" that "knows how to please" with its "big portions" and "attentive" staff; some enjoy dining in the "walled garden", others go for the "live entertainment", though it "can be loud."

Filomena Lakeview *Italian* ▽ 24 | 25 | 24 | $41

Deptford | 1738 Cooper St. (Almonesson Rd.) | 856-228-4235 | www.filomenalakeview.com

"Fantastic" Italian fare, "top-notch" service and a "beautiful", "upscale" setting – including three fireplaces and a banquet room – combine to make this a Deptford favorite for parties and group celebrations; there's a "lively bar scene on weekends", and entertainment Tuesdays–Sundays that can reach "din" level.

Fiorino 🗷 *Italian* 23 | 21 | 23 | $53

Summit | 38 Maple St. (Springfield Ave.) | 908-277-1900 | www.fiorinoristorante.com

This Summit Northern Italian "holds its own in a restaurant-rich area" by way of its "excellent food served in an elegant atmosphere"; it may be "crowded, loud" and "more expensive than necessary", but the "reliable" fare, "upscale atmosphere" and "old-world service" "never fail"; N.B. rent the wine cellar for 30 or more.

NEW Fire & Oak *American* - | - | - | M
(fka South City Prime)

Little Falls | 1 Rte. 23 S. (bet. Hobson Ave. & Muller Pl.) | 973-785-4225 | www.southcitygroup.net

There's something for everyone – from sushi to surf 'n' turf to salad and seafood – at this wallet- and family-friendly American in Little Falls; N.B. two other branches are in the works – one in the Courtyard by Marriott in Montvale and another in the Newport Westin in Jersey City slated for a spring '09 debut.

Fishery, The *Seafood* - | - | - | I
(fka Morgan Fishery)

South Amboy | 1812 Rte. 35 N. (Midland Ave.) | 732-721-9100

Offering seafood by the pound or platter – fried, broiled, grilled or baked – this little BYO South Amboy standard (formerly known as Morgan's Fishery) cooks up fish 'n' chips, clam strips, steamers and soft-shells; it's everything you'd expect from a local take-out/eat-in place that's reeled in generations of satisfied locals.

Five Guys Famous Burgers & Fries *Burgers* 21 | 9 | 15 | $11

Hackensack | Home Depot Shopping Ctr. | 450 Hackensack Ave. (Grand Ave.) | 201-343-5489
Millburn | Milburn Mall | 2933 Vauxhall Rd. (Valley St.) | 908-688-8877
(continued)

(continued)

Five Guys Famous Burgers & Fries

Edison | Wick Shopping Plaza | 561 Rte. 1 (bet. Dey Pl. & Fulton St.) |
732-985-5977

Parsippany | Troy Hills Shopping Ctr. | 1105 Rte. 46 (bet. Intervale Rd. &
Waterview Blvd.) | 973-335-5454

Watchung | Blue Star Shopping Ctr. | 1701 Rte. 22 (Terrill Rd.) |
908-490-0370

Woodbridge | Woodbridge Mall | 344 Woodbridge Center Dr.
(Woodbridge Terrace) | 732-636-1377

Brick | Habitat Plaza | 588 Rte. 70 (Cedar Bridge Ave.) |
732-262-4040

Toms River | Orchards at Dover | 1311 Rte. 37 W. (bet. Bimini Rd. &
St. Catherine Blvd.) | 732-349-3600

Cherry Hill | 1650 Kings Hwy. N. (Rte. 70) | 856-795-1455

Mount Ephraim | Audubon Shopping Ctr. | 130 Black Horse Pike
(bet. Kennedy Dr. & Pershing Ave.) | 856-672-0442
www.fiveguys.com
Additional locations throughout New Jersey

"It's all about" the "amazing burgers" and "plentiful" fries (cooked
in peanut oil) at the NJ franchises of this "no-frills" national chain
that also rates as NJ's Best Bang for the Buck; boosters rate it "a cut
above" the competition thanks to "fresh ground beef" piled high
with "unbeatable" toppings – "what more can you hope for?";
N.B. coming soon – locations in Howell and Westfield.

Fleming's Prime Steakhouse *Steak*   23 | 23 | 23 | $64

Edgewater | City Pl. | 90 The Promenade (River Rd.) | 201-313-9463

NEW Marlton | 500 Rte. 73 N. (bet. Baker Blvd. & Lincoln Dr.) |
856-988-1351
www.flemingssteakhouse.com

You can count on an "excellent steak" at this "top-tier expense-
account" chophouse in Edgewater with "a water view that's just as
delicious" – though "the windows are too high" to "see it from the
tables"; "forget that it's a chain" and focus on the "prime" meat,
"delightful seafood", "splendid wine list" and "impeccable" service;
N.B. another branch recently debuted in Marlton.

Forno Pizzeria & Grille *Pizza*   - | - | - | I

Maple Shade | 28 Church Rd. (bet. I-295 & Kings Hwy.) | 856-608-7711 |
www.lambertis.com

Take the kids to watch 'zas fly high as they're tossed in the open
kitchen at this child-friendly Maple Shade mainstay where pizza is
king but pasta is tradition; low prices will make even the most cost-
conscious put an extra topping on pies and add another seat for
long-lost relatives at the family-style Sunday dinners.

Fornos of Spain *Spanish*   23 | 18 | 21 | $41

Newark | 47 Ferry St. (Union St.) | 973-589-4767 |
www.fornosrestaurant.com

"Still the gold standard in the Ironbound", this Newark Spaniard has
been pleasing patrons with "plentiful helpings" of "consistently
good" seafood, steak, paella and suckling pig plus "old-world ser-

vice" for two decades; the "partylike atmosphere" makes it "good for large groups", and there's free on-site parking.

410 Bank Street *Creole* | 26 | 21 | 24 | $52 |

Cape May | 410 Bank St. (bet. Broad & Lafayette Sts.) | 609-884-2127
"Chef Henry Sing Cheng's song is as beautiful as ever" at this veteran Cape May Creole in a "rambling" Victorian, where the "consistently amazing" dinners are "so good you can take them to the bank"; "top-tier" service helps temper "long waits" and "special-occasion" prices; N.B. it serves NJ wines but you can also BYO.

Frankie Fed's Ⓜ *Italian* | 22 | 11 | 19 | $23 |

Freehold Township | 831 Rte. 33 E. (Kozloski Rd.) | 732-294-1333 | www.frankiefeds.com
Son Frankie of the Federici clan famed for its thin-crust pizza in Freehold upholds the family tradition (partisan *paesani* posit he "goes one better") at his Freehold Township BYO serving 'zas "just as good as at the main place", plus other "good home-cooked Italian" eats; little atmosphere takes a back seat to "attentive" service.

Frenchtown Inn, The Ⓜ *Eclectic/French* | 25 | 23 | 24 | $52 |

Frenchtown | 7 Bridge St. (Rte. 29) | 908-996-3300 | www.frenchtowninn.com
Andrew Tomko's "beautifully prepared" Eclectic-French fare remains a "standard for fine dining" at this "romantic" "destination eatery" tucked in an 1805 brick inn "nestled" beside the Delaware River in "increasingly charming" Frenchtown; N.B. the adjacent grill room affords a more casual dining option.

Frescos *Italian/Mediterranean* | 24 | 21 | 21 | $45 |

Cape May | 412 Bank St. (Lafayette St.) | 609-884-0366
Patrons approve of the "refreshingly light menu" at this "friendly, trattoria-style" seasonal Italian-Med in Cape May (sister to next-door 410 Bank Street) that includes "lots of fresh seafood"; expect a wait – despite reservations, which are "a must" – and focus on the "energetic and entertaining staff"; N.B. local wines are available but it's BYO.

Fresco Steak & Seafood Grill *Seafood/Steak* | 25 | 21 | 22 | $42 |

Milltown | Heritage Shopping Plaza | 210 Ryders Ln. (Blueberry Dr.) | 732-246-7616 | www.restaurantfresco.com
Impressive "all the way around", this Milltown strip-mall BYO surf 'n' turfer serves "generous, well-prepared portions" of "big-city food" bolstered by "exceptional" service and a "festive atmosphere" – not to mention "great-value" prices; though "excellent" for date night, keep in mind it's "noisy on weekends."

Freshwater's Southern Cuisine Ⓜ *Southern* | ▽ 21 | 17 | 23 | $33 |

Plainfield | 1442 South Ave. (Terrill Rd.) | 908-561-9099 | www.myfreshwaters.com
"Upscale Southern food" plus "true Southern hospitality" reign at this "reasonable and friendly" Plainfield BYO whose fans "can't get enough of the cornbread" but know to "save room for authentic pe-

can or sweet potato pie"; "the husband-wife owners are very charming", and "service is always spot-on" and "with a smile";
N.B. weekends are crowded, so get there early.

☑ Frog and the Peach *American*

FOOD	DECOR	SERVICE	COST
26	24	24	$62

New Brunswick | 29 Dennis St. (Hiram Sq.) | 732-846-3216 |
www.frogandpeach.com
Still "one of the tops" after 25 years, this "venerable" New
Brunswick New American "keeps getting better" thanks to chef
Bruce Lefebvre's "inventive and surprising" food that "looks and
tastes like a dream"; "polished, friendly service", an "excellent" wine
list and "gorgeous surroundings" add to its aura, and while it's "expensive", the lunch and dinner prix fixe options make it "more affordable."

Fuji Ⓜ *Japanese*

FOOD	DECOR	SERVICE	COST
24	21	21	$38

Haddonfield | Shops at 116 | 116 Kings Hwy. E. (Tanner St.) |
856-354-8200 | www.fujirestaurant.com
Citing "the best sushi in South Jersey", acolytes ask "will someone
please just canonize Matt Ito?", the chef-owner of this Haddonfield
shopping-center BYO Japanese, which also offers kaiseki meals (a formal lineup of seven or eight dishes) and the more casual five-course
omakase; the decor is "sleek and spare", and as for cost it's $$$.

Full Moon *Eclectic*

FOOD	DECOR	SERVICE	COST
21	15	19	$27

Lambertville | 23 Bridge St. (Union St.) | 609-397-1096 |
www.cafefullmoon.com
A "groovy" '70s feel and "pleasant staff" make this "extremely casual"
Eclectic BYO cafe just right for a "very good" breakfast, brunch or
lunch when you're "strolling in Lambertville"; the solo monthly dinner
is offered only during – you guessed it – the eponymous full moon.

Fusion *Asian Fusion*

FOOD	DECOR	SERVICE	COST
22	21	20	$38

Flemington | 123 Main St. (Mine St.) | 908-788-7772 |
www.fusiononmain.com
An "interesting menu" of "flavorful Asian-fusion" cuisine draws din-
ers to this "beautifully restored Victorian" BYO in Downtown
Flemington; service is "professional" and "outdoor dining on the
front porch" can't be beat "in season."

☑ Gables, The *Eclectic*

FOOD	DECOR	SERVICE	COST
25	26	24	$72

Beach Haven | Gables Inn | 212 Centre St. (bet. Bay & Beach Aves.) |
609-492-3553 | www.gableslbi.com
For a "delightful" "gourmet meal", admirers tout this "lovely" LBI
BYO Eclectic (closed January to mid-February) housed in a "romantic"
Victorian B & B; "nonintrusive" service is part of the charm, and if din-
ner is too "expensive", try lunch or high tea in "the spectacular gar-
den"; N.B. a post-Survey change of chef may outdate the Food score.

Gaetano's *Italian*

FOOD	DECOR	SERVICE	COST
20	15	18	$36

Red Bank | 10 Wallace St. (Broad St.) | 732-741-1321 |
www.gaetanosredbank.com
The aromas "take you in" to this "steady", "homestyle" Italian serv-
ing "comfort food" in a "comfortable", "family-friendly" setting in

Downtown Red Bank; selections from a NJ winery are on tap but you can BYO; N.B. a new on-premises market selling housemade cookies, sauces, pastas and the like is another draw.

Gallagher's Steak House *Steak* | 22 | 20 | 20 | $60 |

Newark | Newark Int'l | Terminal C | 973-286-0034
Atlantic City | Resorts Atlantic City Casino & Hotel | 1133 Boardwalk (North Carolina Ave.) | 609-340-6555 | www.resortsac.com

Expect "a great steak" plus "old-school stylings and service" at this chophouse at AC's Resorts Casino Hotel that most find "solid all-around" (even if a few claim it's "not as good as the NYC original"); typical for the genre, it's best enjoyed "on someone else's check"; N.B. some swear by the outpost in Newark Airport's Terminal C.

Garlic Rose Bistro *Eclectic* | 20 | 16 | 20 | $35 |

Cranford | 28 North Ave. W. (bet. Eastman St. & Union Ave.) | 908-276-5749
Madison | 41 Main St. (bet. Green Village Rd. & Waverly Pl.) | 973-822-1178
www.garlicrose.com

"If you're a garlic lover" ("or hard of smelling"), check out this "garlic-lovers' paradise" purveying "big portions of priced-right" Eclectic "comfort food" spiked with the 'stinking rose' (including garlic ice cream); while some find the pungency "satisfying", others say "they overdo it"; P.S. Madison is BYO, Cranford serves alcohol – and both have "mouthwash in the bathroom."

Gaslight *American/Italian* | 19 | 17 | 18 | $31 |

Hoboken | 400 Adams St. (4th St.) | 201-217-1400 | www.gaslightnj.com

This Hoboken "go-to place" is appreciated for its front bar offering "good food and great brews on tap", as well as for its "cozy" "draped back room" serving Italian-American favorites; though the *ciao* garners mixed reviews ("consistently solid" vs. "lackluster"), it's hard to argue with the "reasonable prices", and brunch is "a deal" – $15 for one course and two drinks.

Gazelle Café & Grille 🗷 *American* | 24 | 18 | 23 | $32 |

Ridgewood | 11 Godwin Ave. (Franklin Ave.) | 201-689-9689 | www.gazellecafe.com

"Innovative dishes for the health conscious" are the order of the day at this "warm", "unpretentious" Ridgewood American BYO, where the "open kitchen allows diners to watch the chefs cook their hearts out"; though "sometimes noisy", it's a "tasty", "reasonably priced" "change of pace"; N.B. it's decorated with figurines of the namesake.

GG's 🗷 *American* | ▽ 24 | 20 | 22 | $47 |

Mount Laurel | DoubleTree Guest Suites Mount Laurel | 515 Fellowship Rd. (Rte. 73) | 856-222-0335 | www.ggsrestaurant.com

"Surprise, you're in a hotel and the food is great!" praise proponents of this New American "oasis in a culinary desert" located in the Mount Laurel DoubleTree; the "food and service are well worth the professional pricing", and a nightly "piano bar" can be a "delight with the right crowd."

Ginger Thai   Thai

▽ | 16 | 16 | 17 | $28

Freehold Township | A&M Plaza | 3475 Rte. 9 N. (Three Brooks Rd.) | 732-761-2900

Though there's some debate about the merits of the Thai cooking at this Freehold Township BYO ("never a disappointment" vs. "just ok"), the fact that it shares a kitchen with adjacent sibling Aangan means you can "order from either menu", which ups your chances of satisfaction; "service can be slow", but at least prices are modest.

Girasole   Italian

25 | 22 | 21 | $57

Atlantic City | Ocean Club Condos | 3108 Pacific Ave. (bet. Chelsea & Montpelier Aves.) | 609-345-5554 | www.girasoleac.com

Escape the AC casino "glitz" and "crowds" at this "comfy and classy" Versace-designed Southern Italian located between the Tropicana and the Hilton; supporters cite "high-quality food served with old-world charm" – "if you can afford it" and need "a break" from gambling, check it out.

Girasole   Italian

26 | 19 | 24 | $43

Bound Brook | 502 W. Union Ave. (Thompson Ave.) | 732-469-1080 | www.girasoleboundbrook.com

You "can't go wrong" at this "quaint" Bound Brook BYO Italian where the "consistently outstanding" entrees include "exceptional seafood and pasta" purveyed by "professional and gracious" servers; though dissenters say it's "overrated by locals", the fact that it's "hard to get a table" because it's "always crowded" proves they're in the minority.

Giumarello's 🗷 Ⓜ Italian

24 | 23 | 23 | $49

Westmont | 329 Haddon Ave. (bet. Cuthbert Blvd. & Kings Hwy.) | 856-858-9400 | www.giumarellos.com

"Well-prepared and -presented" Northern Italian fare combined with "delish" martinis, "traditional atmosphere" and the staff's "positive attitude" explain why this "upscale" family-run Westmont spot is a local "favorite"; N.B. the restaurant's new GBar Lounge offers the same food in a more relaxed atmosphere.

Gladstone Tavern   American

21 | 22 | 21 | $45

Gladstone | 273 Main St. (Pottersville Rd.) | 908-234-9055 | www.gladstonetavern.com

Look for the life-size horse on the porch of this "absolutely charming" Gladstone American in a "rustic" mid-19th-century landmark farmhouse; with "solid" food that's "creative but not over the top", it doubles as "both a destination restaurant and a local hub"; P.S. the "country-meets-modern atmosphere" includes "nice patio seating for summer."

GoodFellas Ristorante 🗷 Italian

20 | 16 | 20 | $38

Garfield | 661 Midland Ave. (Plauderville Ave.) | 973-478-4000 | www.goodfellasnj.com

Dine on "family-style" scampi and Caesar salad at this Garfield Italian, which admirers insist is "better and more upscale than its name implies"; while "pricey for the genre, the food is good overall" according to most, though a few deem it somewhat "ordinary" and perhaps "best for lunch."

Gotham City ● *Diner* | 18 | 18 | 16 | $21 |

Fair Lawn | 39-10 Broadway (Tunbridge Rd.) | 201-398-9700
Ridgefield | 550 Bergen Blvd. (Greenmount Ave.) | 201-943-5664
www.gothamcitydiner.com

"Much nicer" than your typical diner, thanks to "interesting decor" evocative of NYC subways and neighborhoods, this North Jersey diner-amic duo offers "big portions" of "solid food" with "slight variances" on traditional items (e.g. custom chopped salads); though "noisy at times", they're "reliable" and won't break the bank.

☒ Grand Cafe, The ☒ *French* | 26 | 26 | 26 | $67 |

Morristown | 42 Washington St. (Rte. 24) | 973-540-9444 |
www.thegrandcafe.com

This "classic" Morristown French – "one of the last outposts of civility", "where the waiters still wear tuxedos" and "make you feel like royalty" – has, "believe it or not, gotten better over the years"; though "not for the weak of spending", it's "a great place to celebrate a merger – "personal or business" – over "always excellent" food in an atmosphere of "old-world elegance."

Grand Colonial, The ☒Ⓜ *Eclectic* ∇ | 23 | 25 | 21 | $54 |

Union Township | 86 Rte. 173 W. (Van Syckels Rd.) | 908-735-7889 |
www.grandcolonialnj.com

"A grand place" for "an outstanding dining experience" in Hunterdon County report those who've discovered this Eclectic set in a "beautifully restored" 1685 Colonial manor house, where seating options include "romantic" "smaller rooms", an ice bar, cheese cave, grill room (a former walk-in fireplace) and patio; still, with a grand ballroom for private events, some grumble that it's "more about catering than à la carte."

Grand Shanghai *Pan-Asian* ∇ | 19 | 15 | 15 | $29 |

Edison | 700 Hwy. 1 (Old Post Rd.) | 732-819-8830

"This is the real deal" say fans of this casual Pan-Asian in Edison that offers "sushi, authentic Chinese and Chinese-American food" including specialties "you don't see in many places" (*hong sao* or red pork, "outstanding soup buns"); the "weekend Shanghai-style dim sum" gets high praise too.

Greek Taverna *Greek* | - | - | - | M |

Edgewater | City Pl. | 55 Promenade (River Rd.) | 201-945-8998
NEW **Montclair** | 292 Bloomfield Ave. (Gates Ave.) | 973-746-2280
www.greektavernausa.com

Bring your ouzo and watch fish grilled whole and lamb chops sizzle in the open kitchen at these moderately priced Greek tavernas in Edgewater (the original) and Monclair (recently opened), cooking all the traditional favorites and a few modern-day dishes; try an appetizer platter to get your fingers snapping – and you'll be dancing by dessert.

	FOOD	DECOR	SERVICE	COST

Grenville, The Ⓜ *American* — 21 | 24 | 21 | $49

Bay Head | Grenville Hotel | 345 Main Ave. (bet. Harris & Karge Sts.) | 732-892-3100 | www.thegrenville.com

For most, this "sweet spot" of an American inside Bay Head's "wonderful old Victorian" Grenville Hotel is a "quaint", "elegant throwback" esteemed especially for its "economical" Sunday brunch; still, others say it's "hit-or-miss", noting frequent changes in chef – the latest of which may outdate the above Food score.

Grill 73 Ⓜ *American* — 21 | 14 | 20 | $38

Bernardsville | 73 Mine Brook Rd. (Woodland Rd.) | 908-630-0700 | www.grill73.com

There's "something for everyone" at this New American Bernardsville BYO with a "groovy menu" offering "surprisingly delicious choices" – including "great kids'" options and an "excellent Sunday brunch"; the "spartan", "almost dinerlike setting" can get "noisy and crowded", but overall it's an "excellent blend between upscale and casual."

Grimaldi's Pizza *Pizza* — 24 | 12 | 16 | $20

Hoboken | 133 Clinton St. (2nd St.) | 201-792-0800 | www.grimaldis.com

"Go no further – you've come to the right spot" for "thin-crust deliciousness" (no slices here) with "fresh mozzarella" at this "quaint" Hoboken coal-fired brick-oven pizzeria; though some find the room "stale", there's "great outdoor seating" to make amends; N.B. no relation to the Brooklyn original.

Grissini Restaurant *Italian* — 22 | 20 | 19 | $59

Englewood Cliffs | 484 Sylvan Ave. (Palisade Ave.) | 201-568-3535 | www.grissinirestaurant.com

"The people-watching is worth the price" at this "high-end" Englewood Cliffs Italian that's "always jumping late at night" with "singles club action"; an "outstanding variety" of "classic" choices, including "excellent homemade pasta", attracts a "flashy" crowd of "Mercedes owners" who don't seem to mind if service can be "distracted."

GRUB Hut Ⓜ *BBQ* — 21 | 10 | 17 | $24

Manville | 307 N. Main St. (Knopf St.) | 908-203-8003 | www.grubhutbbq.com

"Pig out for a night" on an "interesting mix" of barbecue, Southwestern and Mexican food at this "hole-in-the-wall" Manville BYO where the "tables are so close you end up wearing someone else's cologne" and "the staff is very chummy"; P.S. you can always take out the "enormous portions" of grub.

Gusto Grill ❶ *American* — ▽ 17 | 18 | 18 | $28

East Brunswick | 1050 Rte. 18 N. (Rues Ln.) | 732-651-2737 | www.gustogrill.com

Fine "for a quick bite" at a "fair price", this East Brunswick American "local hangout" is appreciated for its "fun" if "noisy" atmosphere (including live entertainment on Wednesday, Friday and Saturday nights); still, veterans advise it's best to "stick to the basics rather than trying the more adventurous (and pricey) options."

	FOOD	DECOR	SERVICE	COST

Hale & Hearty Soups *Sandwiches/Soup* | 18 | 10 | 13 | $12 |

Jersey City | Newport Centre Mall | 30 Mall Dr. W. (Thomas Gangemi Dr.) | 201-217-4400
Livingston | 464 W. Mount Pleasant Ave. (Walnut St.) | 973-597-0200
www.haleandhearty.com

These soup/salad/sandwich franchises of a New York–based chain let you "sample your choice before committing" and "make your own salads"; some say the "tasty" "fast food that's good for you" "doesn't kill the wallet", while others think prices "are a bit steep", but either way it's "good for a quick bite" despite the "assembly-line atmosphere."

Hamilton's Grill Room *Mediterranean* | 25 | 22 | 23 | $51 |

Lambertville | 8 Coryell St. (Union St.) | 609-397-4343 | www.hamiltonsgrillroom.com

This "best in class" Lambertville Med "hideaway" near the Delaware River Canal "continues to distinguish itself" thanks to chef Mark Miller's "marvelous talents" at the wood-fire grill; "if you can secure a reservation", the "knowledgeable" staff will help compensate for "being on top of other diners" in the "crowded" but "utterly charming" rooms; P.S. it's BYO but sage sippers "love" the Boat House "across the alley" for a pre-dinner drink.

Hard Grove Cafe ● *American/Cuban* | 15 | 12 | 13 | $24 |

Jersey City | 319 Grove St. (Christopher Columbus Dr.) | 201-451-1853 | www.hardgrovecafe.com

Fans of this "quirky" Jersey City American-Cuban say it serves "real working-class food with no pretense", including what boosters call "the best pot roast this side of Havana"; it's a "big after-work happy-hour place" near the PATH station, and though the less enchanted say it dishes out "pretty average diner" fare that's "variable in quality", there's no arguing that it's "affordable."

Harrison, The *American* | ∇ 22 | 20 | 21 | $42 |

Asbury Park | 716 Cookman Ave. (Bond St.) | 732-774-2200

"Trendy" Asbury Park "does it again" with this "intimate" American that's a "favorite hangout for locals" (especially the bar) thanks to "solid offerings", a "staff that treats you like a friend" and "modern", yet "comfortable" surroundings; still, some "wonder if it has lost some of its charm [since its move] from the smaller place."

Harry's Lobster House *Seafood* | ∇ 21 | 13 | 19 | $65 |

Sea Bright | 1124 Ocean Ave. (New St.) | 732-842-0205

The "decor may be dated" (it's been around since 1933) but "you don't go for the ambiance" – it's the "excellent stuffed lobster" and "steak cooked the way it should be" that make it "worth the trip" to Sea Bright; though "very expensive", the upside is "you never need a reservation."

Harvest Bistro Ⓜ *French* | 21 | 24 | 19 | $54 |

Closter | 252 Schraalenburgh Rd. (Bergenline Ave.) | 201-750-9966 | www.harvestbistro.com

With its "fabulous interior, happenin' bar and deck, and roaring fireplace", this "warm and inviting" "stone home–turned–French bistro"

| | FOOD | DECOR | SERVICE | COST |

(complete "with copper accents" and a "huge gabled ceiling") in Closter is "romantic without trying too hard"; chef Denis Whitton "is ingenious when using seasonal ingredients", but some say "too bad" the "pricey" food and service "can't keep up with the decor."

Harvest Moon Inn M *American* — 23 | 22 | 21 | $50

Ringoes | 1039 Old York Rd. (Rte. 202) | 908-806-6020 | www.harvestmooninn.com

Choose between "fine dining" in the more "formal" area or pub fare in the "charming tavern" of this "warm" and "inviting" New American set in a "great old" stone house in Ringoes; the chef utilizes "local farm fresh ingredients, unsurprising since farms are right there", and the dishes are backed up by "a wine list second to none"; a few find performance "uneven", but the consensus is "worth the trip" and cost.

Harvey Cedars Shellfish Co. ⊘ *Seafood* — 22 | 11 | 16 | $33

Beach Haven | 506 Centre St. (Pennsylvania Ave.) | 609-492-2459
Harvey Cedars | 7904 Long Beach Blvd. (79th St.) | 609-494-7112
www.harveycedarsshellfishco.com

"They still line up" for tables in summer at these two "extremely casual" LBI "seafood shack" BYOs because the fish and shellfish are "same-day fresh" and "worth the wait"; some opt for takeout, but all pay cash at these simple "staples."

Havana *Cuban* — ▽ 16 | 19 | 15 | $34

Highlands | 409 Bay Ave. (Central Ave.) | 732-708-0000 | www.havanatropicalcafe.com

In warm weather, dining on the patio – mojito in hand – overlooking a koi pond amps up the "vacation-in-the-tropics vibe" of this "kitschy, fun" Highlands Cuban (indoors, colorful murals and palm trees substitute); while the "food is ok" and the "aim-to-please" service is "uneven", fans are "rooting for this place to succeed."

Z Highlawn Pavilion *American* — 25 | 28 | 25 | $65

West Orange | Eagle Rock Reservation | Eagle Rock Ave. (Crest Dr.) | 973-731-3463 | www.highlawn.com

"Proof that a spectacular view and extraordinary food can coexist", this "special-occasion" New American perched on a West Orange mountaintop boasts "first-class decor and a warm atmosphere" along with an "exceptional view of NYC" that "brings out the romance in everyone" – and enhances its "beautifully presented" cuisine; a "wonderful wine list" and "grand, gracious service" also help make it worth the elevated tabs; N.B. the dress code is business casual.

High Street Grill *American* — ▽ 23 | 18 | 22 | $33

Mount Holly | 64 High St. (bet. Brainerd & Garden Sts.) | 609-265-9199 | www.highstreetgrill.net

Picture "your hometown pub with great food" and you've got this Mount Holly American purveying "updated, hearty American fare", a notable selection of microbrews and a "good wine list" for pairing with dishes; the bi-level setting includes "romantic", white-tablecloth dining quarters (with piano music) upstairs and a more casual tavern downstairs.

Menus, photos, voting and more – free at ZAGAT.com

	FOOD	DECOR	SERVICE	COST

Hiram's Roadstand ♥ *Hot Dogs*
| | 20 | 6 | 13 | $11 |

Fort Lee | 1345 Palisade Ave. (Harmon Ave.) | 201-592-9602
"*Happy Days* lives" at this Fort Lee wiener "throwback" renowned for its "deep-fried dogs that deliver", decor that's "original from the '50s" and "no-frills service"; "the restrooms are outside near the dumpster", but fans insist that the atmosphere at this "dive" is "priceless."

Hobby's Deli ⊠ *Deli*
| | 23 | 10 | 18 | $19 |

Newark | 32 Branford Pl. (Halsey St.) | 973-623-0410 | www.hobbysdeli.com
For "truly sensational deli" eats fans say look no further than this "raucous", "super-friendly" 97-year-old Newark "institution" where the "pastrami melts in your mouth" and the "soups warm the soul"; it's breakfast and lunch only, though it's also open for dinner before Devils games at the Rock (where it operates a concession); the "only problem is the decor . . . but is that really a problem or part of the charm?"

Holsten's ● *American*
| | 17 | 13 | 17 | $15 |

Bloomfield | 1063 Broad St. (Watchung Ave.) | 973-338-7091 | www.holstens.com
"A Bloomfield mainstay way before *The Sopranos* made it famous" (it was the setting for the series' last scene), this "archetypal" "old-fashioned ice cream/candy parlor" serving "easy" American "comfort food" and "homemade ice cream that can't be beat" is un-deniably "charming and warm"; still, service can be "maddeningly slow" and even fans think "it could use a little sprucing up."

Homestead Inn ♥ *Italian*
| | 24 | 14 | 22 | $49 |

Trenton | 800 Kuser Rd. (bet. Barbara Dr. & Nottinghill Ln.) | 609-890-9851
Still called Chick & Nello's by locals – since 1939 – this unchanged, "unpretentious" family-run "Prohibition-era roadhouse" in Trenton is a keeper for its homey Italian menu "that never changes" – just know that it's "spoken" rather than printed, and devoted regulars say if you "want to see a menu or ask for prices, you shouldn't go."

⬇ Hotoke *Pan-Asian*
| | 21 | 27 | 19 | $55 |

New Brunswick | 350 George St. (Bayard St.) | 732-246-8999 | www.hotokerestaurant.com
This "swanky" bi-level New Brunswick Pan-Asian serves a "good mix of sushi, small plates and regular entrees" to go with its "super-chic" vibe and "beautiful decor" (including a "big Buddha in the dining room"); it's "expensive" and views on the food vary ("delicious" vs. "doesn't live up to" the setting), but that doesn't put a damper on the "singles' scene" that "gets loud", so "get there before the disco dancing starts."

House of Blues ● *Southern*
| | 16 | 20 | 17 | $33 |

Atlantic City | Showboat Casino | 801 Boardwalk (New Jersey Ave.) | 609-236-2583 | www.hob.com
Showboat Casino is the Atlantic City home for this link of the na-tional Southern-themed chain known for its "festive" atmosphere, "pretty cool" blues acts and Sunday gospel brunch; while some find the vittles "surprisingly good", others deem "the music better than

the food", but it'll do the trick for "a quick burger while waiting for the slot machines to cool off."

Hunan Chinese Room *Chinese* 22 | 19 | 20 | $27

Morris Plains | 255 Speedwell Ave. (Hanover Ave.) | 973-285-1117
Acolytes applaud the "cut-above typical Chinese" – Cantonese, Hunan and Sichuan – at this Morris Plains Asian offering "dishes you won't find outside Chinatown" in a "Zen-like setting"; it's suitable for "a nice night" out but is also "family-friendly, with a room for kids" so others aren't "disturbed"; still, some find the victuals a tad "Americanized."

Hunan Spring *Chinese* 20 | 12 | 18 | $25

Springfield | 288 Morris Ave. (Caldwell Pl.) | 973-379-4994 | www.hunanspringnj.com
There's "nothing flashy or unique" about this "always reliable" BYO Chinese "staple" in Springfield that's been attracting a "very local crowd" for over 20 years; for "great egg foo yong" in an "old diner setting", look no further, though some say a "face-lift" is in order; N.B. new ownership may outdate the above scores.

Hunan Taste *Chinese* 24 | 24 | 22 | $34

Denville | 67 Bloomfield Ave. (B'way) | 973-625-2782 | www.hunantaste.com
This "white-tablecloth" Chinese in Denville dazzles with "beautiful presentations" of "authentic" Hunan, Mandarin and Sichuan specialties served amid "Hong Kong–style" "pagoda" decor and "multiple fish tanks"; the "attentive staff in formalwear" can sometimes "rush the meal" and it's "a little pricey", but it's still a "favorite."

Hunt Club Grill *Seafood/Steak* 21 | 20 | 21 | $43

Summit | Grand Summit Hotel | 570 Springfield Ave. (Morris Ave.) | 908-273-7656 | www.grandsummit.com
At age 80, this Summit hotel beef 'n' reefer is still going strong, offering "pleasant dining and good food" along with "a terrific Sunday brunch that will keep you going until Tuesday"; some say it's "on the stuffy side" while others advocate it's "unpretentious" and "expensive."

Huntley Taverne *American* 22 | 24 | 20 | $50

Summit | 3 Morris Ave. (Springfield Ave.) | 908-273-3166 | www.harvestrestaurants.com
"Pricey and crowded", this "hip, happening" Summit New American "turns out a menu of winners" in its "buzzing" bar and "upscale-ski-lodge"–style dining room that's "suitable for business entertaining" or "pleasure"; "there's a great porch" for outdoor dining, but "try to get a seat by the fireplace" in winter.

Iberia Peninsula ● *Portuguese/Spanish* 19 | 15 | 18 | $36

Newark | 63-69 Ferry St. (bet. Prospect & Union Sts.) | 973-344-5611

Iberia Tavern ●Ⓜ *Portuguese/Spanish*

Newark | 80-84 Ferry St. (bet. Congress & Prospect Sts.) | 973-344-7603
www.iberiarestaurants.com
These "clamorous", "crowded, big-platter" Ironbound Iberian sisters entice with "tasty and abundant" rodizio, seafood and paella –

not to mention "amazing" sangria – all "at moderate prices"; though "the decor is rough around the edges" and some sniff there are "better choices", they're "close to Penn Station and the Rock" and have free parking to boot.

I Cavallini *Italian*

| | | 23 | 21 | 19 | $54 |

Colts Neck | 29 Rte. 34 S. (Hwy. 537) | 732-431-2934

Italian food "prepared with care" is what's for dinner at this "elegant" Colts Neck spot where "you can't go wrong" with "any pasta dish"; just be aware that the prices match the "high-scale" neighborhood, putting it in the "special-occasion" category for some, and even admirers acknowledge that it can be "loud" – "the acoustics need to be addressed."

Ichiban *Japanese*

| | | 18 | 13 | 18 | $36 |

Princeton | 66 Witherspoon St. (bet. Hulfish St. & Paul Robeson Pl.) | 609-683-8323

A portion of Princetonians praise this "small", "plain" Japanese BYO for its "plentiful vegetarian options", "good, basic sushi" and alfresco dining on the patio in warm weather, while others rate the fare "standard" and say the decor needs "a major face-lift"; still, it can be "fun with the kids."

Ikko *Japanese*

| | | ▽ 25 | 19 | 24 | $32 |

Brick | Brick Plaza Mall | 107 Brick Plaza (Chambers Bridge Ave.) | 732-477-6077 | www.ikkosteakhouse.com

Brick's own "small-scale Benihana" is "deservedly popular" thanks to its "fresh, creative" sushi and sashimi, the "great show" put on by the hibachi chefs and the "excellent" service, including a "wonderful" owner who makes every diner "feel special" – so what if the decor at this BYO is "nondescript"?

❷ Il Capriccio Ⓢ *Italian*

| | | 26 | 25 | 25 | $63 |

Whippany | 633 Rte. 10 (Whippany Rd.) | 973-884-9175 | www.ilcapriccio.com

Expect "high-quality" cuisine – and a "hefty check at the end of the meal"– at this "richly atmospheric Italian showplace" in Whippany with "superb service" that's "perfect for a special occasion"; though its "old-world charm" is lost on those who find it "overdecorated", most think it's "like dining in an Italian villa"; N.B. jacket suggested.

NEW Il Fiore *Italian*

| | | ▽ 26 | 18 | 24 | $28 |

Collingswood | 693-695 Haddon Ave. (Collings Ave.) | 856-833-0808

Fans don't know which they like more: the "top-quality", "freshly prepared" Italian bistro fare or the "amazing", "low, low prices" that make this BYO on Collingswood's "Restaurant Row" an "excellent value"; capping off the experience is "attentive", "high-energy" service.

Il Michelangelo *Italian*

| | | 21 | 21 | 21 | $45 |

Boonton | 91 Elcock Ave. (Highwood Terrace) | 973-316-1111 | www.ilmichelangelo.com

"First-timers are treated like longtime regulars" at this "charming" Boonton Italian located "a bit off the main drag" in a 19th-century former stagecoach inn; reactions to the "hearty" fare range from "outstanding" to "run-of-the-mill", but it's generally "dependable", as is the "wonderful attitiude" of the "inviting" owner and "attentive" servers.

Z Il Mondo Vecchio ⊠ *Italian* 25 | 20 | 22 | $50

Madison | 72 Main St. (Central Ave.) | 973-301-0024 | www.ilmondovecchio.com

The "less formal, more affordable cousin" of Michael Cetrulo's Scalini Fedeli, this "top-flight", "reliable old-world" Italian BYO storefront in Madison offers "lots of food for the $$$"; service can be "iffy" at times, seating is so "tight" it's "like flying coach" and "the big room can be extremely loud", but "the extensive menu holds up" so "be prepared to wait" given all its fans.

Z NEW Il Mulino New York *Italian* 26 | 22 | 24 | $68

Atlantic City | Trump Taj Mahal | 1000 Boardwalk at Virginia Ave. (Pennsylvania Ave.) | 609-449-6006 | www.ilmulino.com

"Ahhh, Italia" sigh those enamored by this AC Taj Mahal outpost of the famed NYC original; so what if it's "pricey" – the food is "magnificent" ("portions are large" so "be prepared to eat big"), the decor "elegant yet fun" and "courteous" servers "treat you like royalty"; N.B. the adjacent Marketplace vends signature sauces, extra-virgin olive oils, coffee and more.

Il Villaggio ⊠ *Italian* 23 | 21 | 22 | $50

Carlstadt | 651 Rte. 17 N. (Passaic Ave.) | 201-935-7733 | www.ilvillaggio.com

The "extensive selection of specials makes the menu almost unnecessary" at this "expense-account", "old-school" Carlstadt Italian that recently had a "long overdue renovation"; "excellent" food and "service above reproach" make this "one of the better restaurants near the Meadowlands", whether before or after the game.

India on the Hudson *Indian* 20 | 15 | 18 | $29

Hoboken | 1210 Washington St. (bet. 12th & 13th Sts.) | 201-222-0101 | www.indiaonthehudson.com

Expect "solid", "well-prepared" Indian fare at this recently renovated, smallish Hoboken storefront "with waiters who still dish out your food at the table"; though "not inexpensive", there's an "affordable lunch buffet" as well as dinner buffets on Monday and Tuesday nights – just "arrive early or be prepared to wait."

Indigo Smoke *BBQ/Southern* 21 | 16 | 17 | $30

Montclair | 387 Bloomfield Ave. (Willow St.) | 973-744-3440 | www.indigosmoke.com

Kansas City BBQ meets Southern soul food at this "funky and fun" but "sneaky expensive" Montclair BYO dishing out "divine" fried chicken, "amazing" mac 'n' cheese, "fantastic" brisket and sides and "huge biscuits that are a meal in themselves"; a new "counter-service" format "makes for quicker meal service", but some think it "cheapens the experience."

	FOOD	DECOR	SERVICE	COST

Inlet, The *American*

19 | 24 | 19 | $47

Somers Point | 998 Bay Ave. (Goll Ave.) | 609-926-9611 |
www.inletrestaurantnj.com

The "stunning" views of Great Egg Harbor Bay "can't be beat" at this
"large" and "flashy-but-elegant" New American from the same
team behind daddy O, Plantation and Philly's Moshulu; some insist
the "good" modern American fare "tastes better" out on the deck,
where live "loud" music is added to the mix.

Inlet Café *Seafood*

20 | 17 | 19 | $35

Highlands | 3 Cornwall St. (Shrewsbury Ave.) | 732-872-9764 |
www.inletcafe.com

"Breathtaking" views of Sandy Hook Bay and "the city" from the outdoor deck of this "relaxed" Highlands docksider make it "a perfect
place" "on a summer day" (or night) to enjoy "consistently good" –
if "pricey" – seafood; expect "pleasant" service and a "long wait" in
high season if you show up without a reservation.

In Napoli *Italian*

17 | 14 | 18 | $38

Fort Lee | 116 Main St. (Linwood Ave.) | 201-947-2500 | www.inapoli.com
Offering "a good deal for the money", though "not much in the way
of decor", this Fort Lee Italian "local" "staple" near the GW Bridge
includes family-style salad and antipasto in the price of its dinner
entrees and attracts "lots of regulars for the reasonable early-bird";
still, some find the menu "too diverse to be good."

Inn at Millrace Pond *American/Continental*

21 | 25 | 21 | $49

Hope | 313 Hope Johnsonburg Rd. (Rte. 611) | 908-459-4884 |
www.innatmillracepond.com

"Twisting country lanes" lead to the "charming surroundings" of this
converted 1769 gristmill in Hope, where enthusiasts enjoy "dependably good" Traditional American–Continental fare and "leisurely,
quiet conversation" by candlelight; the downstairs tavern offers a
"nice alternative" to the pricier main dining room.

Inn at Sugar Hill Ⓜ *American*

▽ 23 | 25 | 22 | $43

Mays Landing | 5704 Mays Landing-Summers Point Rd. (River Rd.) |
609-625-2226 | www.innatsugarhill.com

A "lovely atmosphere" pervades the Victorian B&B in Mays Landing
that houses this "romantic" Traditional American; besides "good
food and service", it offers "great" river views from an enclosed veranda and, in summer, from the Dockside Grill, a tented casual area
near the water's edge featuring fresh-cooked seafood, cocktails
and live entertainment.

Inn of the Hawke *American*

18 | 17 | 19 | $31

Lambertville | 74 S. Union St. (Mt. Hope St.) | 609-397-9555
This "unpretentious" Lambertville pub is an "informal" "hangout"
boasting "comfortable surroundings, comfortable prices and comfortable food" in the form of "sturdy and dependable" American bar
fare plus "great" beers on tap; the staff is "friendly", and when the
weather suits, "patio dining is a plus."

Irish Pub & Inn ●◐⇗ Pub Food
| | 18 | 18 | 19 | $22 |

Atlantic City | 164 St. James Pl. (Pacific Ave.) | 609-344-9063 | www.theirishpub.com

"A touch of the old sod lingers" at this "authentic" AC "classic" that "never closes" (food is served until 4 AM); expect "decent" Irish pub grub that's "downright cheap", an atmosphere that "makes you feel comfortable" and an "eclectic" crowd; N.B. credit cards accepted in the hotel and gift shop.

Isabella's American Bistro Ⓜ American
| | 18 | 16 | 18 | $37 |

Westfield | 39 Elm St. (bet. Broad St. & North Ave.) | 908-233-8830 | www.isabellasbistro.com

Serving "new twists on Traditional American comfort food" – "meatloaf, anybody?"– this Westfield BYO is a "solid" choice for "a quick dinner" and "good for brunch with kids"; but some think "the cuisine is less interesting than Theresa's and Mojave Grill" nearby.

Island Palm Grill Ⓜ American
| | 19 | 16 | 19 | $38 |

Spring Lake | 1321 Third Ave. (bet. Jersey & Washington Aves.) | 732-449-1909 | www.islandpalmgrill.com

A "cozy atmosphere" and a "unique" American menu with "an island bent" as well as some Italian options make this Spring Lake BYO a "good" choice for locals; benefiting from a "great Shore location", it also pleases with its "responsive" staff and "restful" "storefront setting", even if some feel it's in need of "a bit of freshening."

It's Greek To Me Greek
| | 17 | 12 | 16 | $24 |

Cliffside Park | Vitos Plaza | 352 Anderson Ave. (bet. Jersey & Morningside Aves.) | 201-945-5447
Englewood | 36 E. Palisade Ave. (bet. Dean & Engle Sts.) | 201-568-0440
Fort Lee | 1636 Palisade Ave. (Main St.) | 201-947-2050
Hoboken | 538 Washington St. (6th St.) | 201-216-1888
Jersey City | 194 Newark Ave. (Jersey Ave.) | 201-222-0844
Livingston | 6230 Town Center Way (bet. Livingston Ave. & Rte. 10) | 973-992-8999
Ridgewood | 21 E. Ridgewood Ave. (bet. Broad & Chestnut Sts.) | 201-612-2600
Westwood | 487 Broadway (bet. Irvington St. & Washington Ave.) | 201-722-3511
Holmdel | 2128 Hwy. 35 (Laurel Ave.) | 732-275-0036
Long Branch | 44 Centennial Dr. (Chelsea Ave.) | 732-571-0222
www.itsgreektome.com

"If you're craving the basics", fans tout this "bustling" chain of Hellenic "workhorse" BYOs for "consistent" fare served in a "friendly" manner at "reasonable" prices – so who cares if the "ambiance could be a littler nicer"?; dissenters say these "pseudo-Greeks" serve up "short-order taste", but word is "some locations are better than others."

Ivy Inn American
| | 20 | 23 | 20 | $47 |

Hasbrouck Heights | 268 Terrace Ave. (bet. Kipp Ave. & Washington Pl.) | 201-393-7699 | www.ivyinn.com

This former 19th-century stagecoach inn has been refurbished into a "sweet" Hasbrouck Heights Traditional American with "quality food and a friendly staff"; the "cozy", "romantic ambiance" evokes "a small European cafe", complete with fireplaces, cherry beams and a re-veneered horseshoe bar, and "live piano music" (Thursdays–Saturdays) "adds a nice touch."

izakaya *Japanese* ▽ 26 | 25 | 25 | $62
Atlantic City | Borgata Hotel, Casino & Spa | 1 Borgata Way (Huron Ave.) | 609-317-1000 | www.theborgata.com
Celeb chef Michael Schulson's new solo debut – a "sleek" Japanese "gastropub" – is an "excellent addition to the Borgata" say AC casino denizens; the "exceptional" sushi and robatayaki (from an open-hearth grill) are "to die for" (though portions "are small"), and the room and staff are equally "beautiful"; N.B. there's a late-night DJ.

Jack Cooper's Celebrity Deli *Deli* 18 | 10 | 16 | $21
Edison | Tano Mall | 1199 Amboy Ave. (Rte. 1) | 732-549-4580 | www.jackcoopersdeli.com
"It's so good it's almost kosher" kvell advocates of this "old-world" Edison deli where the "obscenely delicious" food is always "plentiful" and "sharing is a must" – the "piled-high sandwiches" could "feed an army" (at a "moderate cost") and service is "quick and professional"; N.B. regulars are relieved the newest owner has "kept the spirit" intact.

Java Moon *American* 18 | 14 | 17 | $22
Jackson | 1022 Anderson Rd. (Rte. 537) | 732-928-3633 | www.javamooncafe.com
A "casual" menu with "innovative spins" and "always fresh" fare makes for "trusty", "light family meals" at this "pleasant" American coffeehouse BYO in Jackson where a "friendly" crew dispenses "inventive" salads and "not-your-usual" sandwich choices; N.B. three other branches in NJ have closed in the past year.

JD's Steak Pit *Steak* 18 | 13 | 17 | $42
Fort Lee | 124 Main St. (Central Rd.) | 201-461-0444 | www.jdsteak.com
For three decades this Fort Lee steakhouse near the GW Bridge has attracted "a good drinking crowd as well as regular dinner patrons" with its "specialty" ribs and "reasonably priced", "tasty" steaks; but faultfinders say the service is just "ok" and the "tired" "paper place mat" ambiance "needs a face-lift."

Jerry & Harvey's Noshery *Deli* 18 | 8 | 15 | $19
Marlboro | Marlboro Plaza | 96 Rte. 9 (Rte. 520) | 732-972-1122 | www.jerryandharveys.com
"Nothing has changed" in the last quarter century at this kosher-style deli in Marlboro that mavens applaud for touchstones like the "best" pastrami, corned beef, smoked fish and the like doled out by countermen who are "pros"; but many maintain "this place really needs" to "update" its "run-down" decor.

Je's Ⓜ *Soul Food* ▽ 24 | 10 | 21 | $19
Newark | 34 William St. (Halsey St.) | 973-623-8848
For three decades, this Newark "soul food institution" with a "nice family feeling" has been serving "amazing" Southern favorites – "the

next best thing to mom's home cooking" at breakfast ("a great way to start your day"), lunch and diner; it may be in a "run-down area", but it's "packed on Sundays" and kids eat for half price.

Jimmy's *Italian*
23 | **14** | **19** | **$43**

Asbury Park | 1405 Asbury Ave. (Prospect Ave.) | 732-774-5051 | www.jimmysitalianrestaurant.com

This "old-time" Italian "in the heart of" Asbury Park "has endured" for good reason – it's an "outstanding family-style restaurant" that's "always a surefire bet for copious portions served by knowledgeable waitresses"; the decor may be "very tired", but this "joint" is the "one-and-only."

NEW JL Ivy *French/Japanese*
19 | **22** | **20** | **$49**

Princeton | 378 Alexander St. (Faculty Rd.) | 609-921-1113 | www.jlivy.com

"Lots of cozy spaces" and patio dining in fair weather attract locals to this Princeton East-West hybrid that fuses "reliable" French bistro cooking and "surprising" sushi in "nicely appointed" quarters; soaring hand-painted murals, lush banquettes, natural-stone walls and a lounge help make it a "worthy addition" to the neighborhood.

Joe Pesce *Italian/Seafood*
23 | **18** | **21** | **$41**

Collingswood | 833 Haddon Ave. (bet. Collings Ave. & Cuthbert Blvd.) | 856-833-9888

For "fish-focused" fare "with an Italian flair", locals say look no further than this "addition to the Collingswood restaurant scene", a "creative" BYO with a "companion" restaurant in Philly; it may be "small" and "crowded", but the staff "makes you feel right at home" and overall most consider it "a find."

Joe's Peking Duck House Ⓜ ⊄ *Chinese*
23 | **12** | **20** | **$25**

Marlton | Marlton Crossing Shopping Ctr. | 145 Rte. 73 S. (Rte. 70) | 856-985-1551

"Go for the duck, not the surroundings" say respondents who opine that some of the "best inexpensive" Chinese food can be had at this "modest", cash-only Marlton BYO where even the won ton soup rates raves and the staff "treats you like family" – and word is that a recent redecoration upgraded the decor to a "passable level"; N.B. dim sum is served at lunch on weekends.

John Henry's Seafood Ⓜ *Seafood*
∇ **24** | **17** | **22** | **$41**

Trenton | 2 Mifflin St. (bet. Franklin & Washington Sts.) | 609-396-3083 | www.johnhenrysseafood.com

This family-owned "Trenton standby" in the Chambersburg section may be "getting long in the tooth" but it's "worth every penny" for its "always wonderful", "well-prepared seafood and Italian cuisine", backed up with "equally good" service; reservations are "a must" on weekends, but you can always opt to shop at the on-premises retail market and get your food to-go.

Johnny Rockets *Burgers*
15 | **16** | **15** | **$16**

Elizabeth | Jersey Gardens Mall | 651 Kapkowski Rd. (Jersey Gardens Blvd.) | 908-994-0110

(continued)

Johnny Rockets

Hoboken | 134 Washington St. (bet. 1st & 2nd Sts.) | 201-659-2620 ◐

Paramus | Garden State Plaza | 1 Garden State Plaza (Roosevelt Ave.) | 201-291-1700

Short Hills | Short Hills Mall | 1200 Morris Tpke. (Canoe Brook Rd.) | 973-258-9338

Woodbridge | Woodbridge Center Mall | 250 Woodbridge Center Dr. (Maple Hill Dr.) | 732-326-1500

Eatontown | Monmouth Mall | 180 Hwy. 35 (Rte. 36) | 732-389-1120

Freehold | 3710 Rte. 9 (Raceway Mall Dr.) | 732-294-7995

Jackson | Six Flags New Jersey | 1 Six Flags Blvd. (Monmouth Rd.) | 732-928-2000

Atlantic City | Bally's Casino | Boardwalk (Park Pl.) | 609-340-0099 ◐

Mays Landing | Hamilton Mall | 4403 Black Horse Pike (Wrangleboro Rd.) | 609-569-1500

www.johnnyrockets.com

"Decent" shakes, burgers, and fries plus a "singing staff" that shakes, rattles and rolls to golden oldies make this "cheap eats" '50s malt shop–theme chain "a fun" "family" place; "wear a poodle skirt and saddle shoes", pop a nickel in the jukebox and you may feel like you're at "Arnold's from *Happy Days*"; still, party-poopers say "only if your kids force you."

Jose's *Mexican*   ▽ 24 | 8 | 18 | $19

Spring Lake Heights | 101 Rte. 71 (Jersey Ave.) | 732-974-8080

"Come hungry" and "forget" the "early garage" atmosphere say aficionados of this "excellent" Spring Lake Heights Mexican BYO that proves "good things come in small packages"; it offers "quick, authentic", "amazing" meals "for the price", with "great service" to up the ante.

Jose's Mexican Cantina *Mexican*   20 | 17 | 19 | $26

New Providence | 24 South St. (Springfield Ave.) | 908-464-4360

Warren | Quail Run Ctr. | 125 Washington Valley Rd. (Morning Glory Rd.) | 732-563-0480

www.josescantina.com

"Good for family night", this pair of "kid-friendly" Mexican BYOs in Warren and New Providence provokes a bit of debate over the food ("full of flavor" vs. "nothing special"), but on the plus side portions are "big", prices "reasonable" and the ambiance "festive" – though the downside is a predictably "long wait during prime time."

Juanito's *Mexican*   22 | 16 | 19 | $27

Howell | 3830 Rte. 9 S. (Aldrich Rd.) | 732-370-1717

Red Bank | 159 Monmouth St. (West St.) | 732-747-9118

"Fancy schmancy" they are not, but these "comfortable", "relaxed" Monmouth County Mexican BYOs are appreciated for "simple", "well-prepared" fare served by a "friendly staff"; whether you side with those who consider the *comidas* "Americanized" or "authentic", you'll agree that portions are "gigantic" and come "at great prices."

	FOOD	DECOR	SERVICE	COST

Kanji Steakhouse & Sushi Bar *Japanese/Steak*
25 | 23 | 23 | $34

Tinton Falls | 980 Shrewsbury Ave. (Rte. 35) | 732-544-1600 | www.kanjisteakhouse.com

Followers of chef-owner Roger Yang (ex SAWA) say the "master" has created "sushi heaven" in a Tinton Falls strip mall, as well as one of the "best hibachi bars around", complete with a "fun" "show" – all in a "beautifully decorated" space that's "surprisingly hip" and "comfortable"; "super-friendly" servers seal the deal; N.B. it's BYO.

☒ Karen & Rei's ⊘ *American*
26 | 23 | 25 | $49

Clermont | 1882 Rte. 9 N. (bet. Avalon Blvd. & Rte. 83) | 609-624-8205 | www.karenandrei.com

"Exquisite", "ever-changing" New American fare from "super" chef-owner Karen Nelson paired with co-owner Rei Prabhakar's "great" hosting skills keep "discriminating diners" coming back to this "beautiful" Clermont BYO; add "knowledgeable" servers and you have a "fabulous Shore" option that feels like "a private dinner party"; N.B. reservations are required, and it's cash-only.

Karma Kafe *Indian*
24 | 17 | 18 | $27

Hoboken | 505 Washington St. (bet. 5th & 6th Sts.) | 201-610-0900 | www.karmakafe.com

"Exotic flavors and wonderful naan at a reasonable price" make this one of "the best Indians" in the Hoboken area (it's sibling to India on the Hudson); fans are also impressed with the "good-value" lunch buffet ($9.99), but delivery that's "insanely slow" has diners wishing this 50-seater were "larger."

Kaya's Kitchen Ⓜ *Vegetarian*
▽ 20 | 12 | 15 | $28

Belmar | Belmar Plaza | 817 Belmar Plaza (bet. 8th & 10th Aves.) | 732-280-1141 | www.kayaskitchennj.com

"Where a vegan like me can eat like 'a regular person'" typifies reaction to this small Belmar BYO that appeals with a "huge" and "creative" menu of "healthy", "good-tasting" fare (e.g. spicy tofu Buffalo wings); "well-informed" servers and "friendly" surroundings complete the "cozy" picture; N.B. Sunday dinner buffet costs $19.95.

Khun Thai Restaurant *Thai*
23 | 19 | 20 | $31

Short Hills | 504 Millburn Ave. (Campbell Rd.) | 973-258-0586 | www.khunthainj.com

"Delicious, authentic" fare is the draw at this "semi-casual" Thai BYO "on a quiet commercial stretch" in Short Hills, where specialties include "awesome" boar and "flavorful" fish – but "they accommodate vegetarians easily" too; though the "interior needs some work" and it "can be loud", "remarkably friendly" service helps makes it a "winner."

Kibitz Room *Deli*
22 | 9 | 14 | $19

Cherry Hill | Shoppes at Holly Ravine | 100 Springdale Rd. (Evesham Rd.) | 856-428-7878 | www.thekibitzroom.com

The cholesterol crowd kvells over the "great" Jewish "soul food" found in this Cherry Hill deli issuing "really big" corned beef and pastrami sandwiches, matzo ball soup and whatnot; slightly "surly servers" notwithstanding, it's still "the closest thing to the Carnegie in South Jersey."

Kinchley's Tavern ●🍴 *Pizza* | 23 | 9 | 16 | $21 |

Ramsey | 586 N. Franklin Tpke. (Orchard St.) | 201-934-7777
"The decor hasn't changed" for decades "but who cares?" cheer fans of this "longtime favorite" Ramsey tavern dishing out "thin-crust" "pizza that rocks"; "they do take reservations", but "no credit cards are accepted" so make sure you bring enough cash.

Kitchen 233 *American* | 20 | 22 | 20 | $43 |

Westmont | 233 Haddon Ave. (Glenwood Ave.) | 856-833-9233 | www.kitchen233.com
Diners choose between a "cozy" front room and a "sophisticated" back room that opens to the outdoors at this Westmont American purveying an "outstanding mix of meat, seafood and pasta dishes"; while all laud the "exemplary" wine list and "hip bar", some find the "varied menu" somewhat uneven.

Klein's Fish Market & Waterside Cafe *Seafood* | 19 | 12 | 16 | $36 |

Belmar | 708 River Rd. (bet. 7th & 8th Aves.) | 732-681-1177 | www.kleinsfish.com
Paper plates have been banished and a highly regarded Sunday brunch added at this "bustling" Belmar seafood "treasure", where most prefer to down "ocean fresh" Jersey seafood and sushi on the waterside deck on the Shark River Inlet; regulars advise "stick with the simple stuff" and tolerate the "collegiate" service – or patronize the attached fish market to circumvent "long waits."

K.O.B.E. Ⓜ *Japanese* | 22 | 19 | 18 | $37 |

Holmdel | Commons at Holmdel | 2132 Rte. 35 (Commons Way) | 732-275-0025 | www.kobecuisine.com
"A large selection of innovative rolls" "rules" at this "class-act" Japanese BYO in a Holmdel strip mall proffering a "seemingly endless" selection of "fresh", "interesting and tasty" sushi, sashimi and, to a lesser extent, cooked fare; the decor is "minimalist", but the staff (including the sushi chef) is "helpful."

Komegashi *Japanese* | 23 | 18 | 20 | $36 |

Jersey City | 103 Montgomery St. (Warren St.) | 201-433-4567
Komegashi Too *Japanese*
Jersey City | 99 Town Square Pl. (Washington Blvd.) | 201-533-8888 www.komegashi.com
"Outstanding sushi" that's "tasty but pricey" is the common denominator at these "inventive" and "reliable" Jersey City Japanese; while the original Montgomery Street spot near Exchange Place follows a "more traditional style", its "waterfront" sibling offers "fusion" cuisine – perhaps because it "has to compete with the to-die-for view of the NYC skyline."

	FOOD	DECOR	SERVICE	COST

Konbu ⓜ Japanese
▽ 25 | 16 | 20 | $34

Manalapan | Design Ctr. | 345 Rte. 9 S. (Union Hill Rd.) | 732-462-6886
Regulars at chef-owner James Tran's Manalapan BYO gush it's "great sushi for our area" – "pricey but innovative" and as "fresh as can be"; if some find the decor "uninspiring", at least the staff is "attentive", "friendly and helpful."

Krave Café Ⓢ American
▽ 23 | 16 | 21 | $39

Newton | 15 E. Clinton St. (Water St.) | 973-383-2600
This "remarkably interesting", "wonderfully inventive" and "very reasonably priced" eclectic American BYO "tucked away" in a side-street strip mall in Newton is worth "searching out" if you're in the area; the atmosphere may be "simple", but service "with a smile" helps compensate.

Kunkel's Seafood &
Steakhouse ⓜ Seafood/Steak
24 | 21 | 24 | $44

Haddon Heights | 920 W. Kings Hwy. (bet. Black Horse & White Horse Pikes) | 856-547-1225 | www.kunkelsrestaurant.com
Locals consider this family-run Haddon Heights chophouse "a small-town treasure" for its "wonderful" offerings from "both sea and land", enhanced by "reasonable prices", "friendly, pleasant" service and handsome mahogany decor; N.B. it's BYO, but management maintains a wine closet to store customers' bottles.

Kuzina by Sofia Greek
▽ 20 | 13 | 18 | $26

Cherry Hill | Sawmill Vill. | 404 Rte. 70 W. (Sawmill Rd.) | 856-429-1061 | www.kuzinabysofia.com
There's "good variety" on the "ambitious" menu at this "slightly upscale" BYO Greek taverna in a Cherry Hill shopping center, and if some say the "awesome appetizers" outshine the entrees ("a bit bland"), most think it all "hits the spot"; a Greek band is on hand Saturday evenings, and though service can be "slow", at least "they're trying."

Labrador Lounge Eclectic
23 | 16 | 19 | $38

Normandy Beach | 3581 Rte. 35 N. (Peterson Ln.) | 732-830-5770 | www.kitschens.com
"Offbeat" for the Shore, this "funky" Normandy Beach BYO offers something other than the area's standard eats, with a "tasty" Eclectic slate including Thai coconut shrimp served by a "good" staff; P.S. it's even more "worthwhile if you sit outside."

La Campagna Italian
22 | 19 | 20 | $44

Millburn | 194 Essex St. (Main St.) | 973-379-8989
Morristown | 5 Elm St. (South St.) | 973-644-4943
www.lacampagnaristorante.com
"A solid dining experience" awaits at these "authentic" Italians in Millburn and Morristown that are "always a good choice" for "well-prepared, interesting meals"; the "knowledgeable staff" adds to the enjoyment, and the BYO policy "keeps the cost in check"; P.S. "the Millburn location is less cramped and noisy than Morristown."

	FOOD	DECOR	SERVICE	COST

La Campagne ☒ *French* | 24 | 23 | 23 | $55

Cherry Hill | 312 Kresson Rd. (bet. Brace & Marlkress Rds.) |
856-429-7647 | www.lacampagne.com

Tucked into an 1841 farmhouse, the "small, intimate" dining rooms
with "multiple fireplaces" are a fitting backdrop for the "wonderful"
country French fare at this "charming" Cherry Hill BYO; it's a tad
"pricey for the area", but service is "impeccable" and the chef offers
cooking classes; N.B. "eat on the terrace" for a "romantic interlude."

Laceno Italian Grill *Italian/Seafood* | 26 | 16 | 21 | $43

Voorhees | Echelon Village Plaza | 1118 White Horse Rd.
(Haddonfield-Berlin Rd.) | 856-627-3700

This "solid and well-run" Voorhees BYO Italian is considered a strip-
mall "gem" thanks to its "superb" cuisine, including seafood "worthy" of your "good wine"; the "minimal" decor "isn't pretty" but
service is "very attentive."

La Cipollina · *Italian* | 21 | 20 | 21 | $43

Freehold | 16A W. Main St. (South St.) | 732-308-3830 |
www.lacipollina.com

After 20 years, this "warm and caring" Italian BYO is "still delivering
excellent, inventive dishes" and "attentive service" to "the Freehold
faithful"; "tucked down an alley" off the beaten path, it's "one of the
better local" options, and while prices make it "a special meal" for
some, the prix fixe dinners are considered "a great value."

La Esperanza ☒ *Mexican* | ▽ 22 | 17 | 22 | $24

Lindenwold | 40 E. Gibbsboro Rd. (Arthur Ave.) | 856-782-7114 |
www.mexicanhope.com

"If you are going to eat Mexican food, do it right and eat here" say
partisans of this "friendly", family-run Lindenwold spot dishing out
the traditional fare like cactus tamales; assets include a "large"
menu, "fair" prices and "reasonable drinks" – including a selection
of 100 tequilas.

La Focaccia *Italian* | 24 | 19 | 21 | $43

Summit | 523 Morris Ave. (Aubrey St.) | 908-277-4006 |
www.lafocaccianj.com

"Better than your typical neighborhood Italian", this Summit BYO is
"always difficult to get into and always terrific"; "despite an expan-
sion that changed everything for the better", the "friendly" service
"can be slow" and the "waits tedious" on the weekend, so some advise "stick to lunch" when the "dining room is most appealing."

Lahiere's ☒ *Continental/French* | 22 | 20 | 21 | $58

Princeton | 11 Witherspoon St. (Nassau St.) | 609-921-2798 |
www.lahieres.com

A "nicely updated" menu at this "icon" of "old Princeton" pairs
Continental-French fare (veal cheeks and polenta, oysters mignon-
ette) with New American dishes to mostly favorable reviews; but it's
"not cheap", and some think this 90-year-old "could use a face-lift" –
after all, "Einstein still dines here" via a photo over his favorite table.

	FOOD	DECOR	SERVICE	COST

La Isla *Cuban*
26 | 9 | 18 | $23

Hoboken | 104 Washington St. (bet. 1st & 2nd Sts.) | 201-659-8197 |
www.laislarestaurant.com

"Havana comes to Hoboken" at this BYO Cuban luncheonette
known for its "cheap", "awesome" and "authentic" *comida* that's
"worth the sometimes long lines" and "incredibly cramped" "cafeteria environment"; the sometimes "rushed" service, however, leads
some to savor the "fantastic" fare in their own *casas*.

Lalezar *Turkish*
18 | 17 | 19 | $35

Montclair | 720 Bloomfield Ave. (St. Luke's Pl.) | 973-233-1984 |
www.lalezarcuisine.com

Portions "generous" enough "to share" are part of the deal at this
"lovely", "welcoming" Montclair Turkish BYO whose "wonderful
couscous dishes" and "great grilled meats" come via an "attentive"
crew; on weekends the "place rocks" with a "provocative" belly
dance show that lets you "leave your troubles at the door."

Lambertville Station *American*
17 | 20 | 19 | $39

Lambertville | 11 Bridge St. (Delaware River) | 609-397-8300 |
www.lambertvillestation.com

This Lambertville American with a "grand" setting in a restored
19th-century railway station is considered a "must-do" "at least
once" for visitors to the area; alas, the "basic" fare and "adequate"
service varies, although the winter wild game menu garners praise
and just about everyone likes "the inventive Sunday brunch."

NEW Langosta Lounge 🅢🅜 *Eclectic*
- | - | - | M

Asbury Park | Asbury Park Boardwalk | 1000 Ocean Ave. (2nd Ave.) |
732-455-3275 | www.kitschens.com

Fans of Shore restaurateur Marilyn Schlossbach (Labrador Lounge,
Pop's Garage) applaud her latest Eclectic BYO on the Asbury Park
boardwalk ("a brave debut, in winter") serving breakfast, lunch, dinner and snacks (chilaquiles, Mexican pho, tomato-feta-rum tart);
there's a full bar too, complete with an ocean view.

La Pastaria *Italian*
19 | 16 | 19 | $34

Summit | 327 Springfield Ave. (Summit Ave.) | 908-522-9088
Red Bank | 30 Linden Pl. (Broad St.) | 732-224-8699
www.lapastaria.com

These "reliable", "neighborhood" BYO Italians in Summit and Red
Bank purvey "generous portions" of "affordable, solid" "comfort food"
in "noisy" environs; the "price is right" and the staff "friendly", so even
if it's "ordinary", for regulars it's "awesome for the entire family."

NEW LaPrete's *Italian*
∇ 22 | 25 | 23 | $44

Belleville | 369 Washington Ave. (Joralemon St.) | 973-450-1555 |
www.lapretes.com

"You'll think that grandma is in the kitchen" at this "gorgeous"
Belleville Italian with a "great family atmosphere"; though selections are "limited", "homemade" favorites like chicken roulade and
Italian meatloaf make it "simply delightful."

	FOOD	DECOR	SERVICE	COST

La Scala 🅼 *Italian* — 22 | 16 | 20 | $41

Somerville | 117 N. Gaston Ave. (bet. Bartine & William Sts.) |
908-218-9300 | www.lascalafineitalian.com

"Divine!" applaud admirers of chef-owner Omar Aly's "flavorful"
"contemporary" Italian cuisine, including "wild game", that hits all
the high notes at this "bustling" Somerville BYO; however, even
those who "love" this "strip-mall" "find" concede the bi-level interior can be a little "too bright" and "somewhat noisy."

La Sorrentina *Italian* — ▽ 26 | 14 | 18 | $27

North Bergen | 7831 Bergenline Ave. (79th St.) | 201-869-8100

"A surprisingly good wine list" complements the "excellent Southern
Italian food" and "great brick-oven pizza" at this modest "family-
run" North Bergen "neighborhood" Italian across the street from
North Hudson Park; "cheap but reliable eats" and a "friendly atmosphere" make it "a must go!"

La Spiaggia *Italian* — 24 | 20 | 24 | $50

Ship Bottom | 357 W. Eighth St. (Barnegat Ave.) | 609-494-4343 |
www.laspiaggialbi.com

"Elegance without pretense" is the name of the game at this "excellent" Northern Italian BYO "oasis" on LBI's North Shore, where "the
chef is not afraid to be creative", the service is "top notch" and
"quiet" prevails; there's valet parking – oh, and the "best" Bolognese
sauce on the island.

La Strada 🅼 *Italian* — 22 | 19 | 21 | $42

Randolph | 1105 Rte. 10 E. (bet. Canfield & Eyland Aves.) | 973-584-4607 |
www.lastradarestaurant.com

"Don't let the waiters in tuxedoes scare you away" from this "classy"
but "relaxing" Randolph Italian where the food's "wonderful" and
the chef is even known to "make dishes to order for regulars"; its
"old-world" "romantic" atmosphere (enhanced by live piano music
on weekends) and "attentive" staff make it ideal for "celebrations."

Latitude 40N *Seafood* — 23 | 15 | 21 | $42

Point Pleasant Beach | 816 Arnold Ave. (bet. Lincoln Ave. &
Woodland Rd.) | 732-892-8553 | www.latitude40n.com

Set your coordinates to Downtown Point Pleasant Beach for "nicely
done", "simple yet elegant" seafood at this "warm" chef-owned BYO
"hidden" in a "nondescript" strip mall; the nautically appointed room
is "a little crowded" but "they take care of you like a long lost relative."

🆉 Latour 🅼 *French* — 26 | 22 | 25 | $56

Ridgewood | 6 E. Ridgewood Ave. (Broad St.) | 201-445-5056 |
www.latourridgewood.com

"Ooh-la-la!" sigh devotees of the "exquisite" Classic French cuisine
at this "classy" Ridgewood BYO, where "gracious" chef-owner
Michael Latour "makes a point of getting around the dining room";
"seating is a little cramped" and the "very rich" fare is "expensive", but
service is "solicitous", there's "no rush to get you out" and "the prix
fixe dinners are the best buy in town"; P.S. "good luck getting a table."

	FOOD	DECOR	SERVICE	COST

Le Fandy ⓈⓂ *French*
25 | 18 | 24 | $54

Fair Haven | 609 River Rd. (Cedar Ave.) | 732-530-3338 |
www.lefandybistro.com

Those who favor this "cute little BYO" in Fair Haven deem the "adventurous" French bistro fare of chef-owner Luke Peter Ong "fantastic in every way" – with "impeccable" service to match; though some find "the restaurant too small", the food keeps bringing them back.

ⓩ Legal Sea Foods *Seafood*
21 | 18 | 19 | $42

Paramus | Garden State Plaza | 1 Garden State Plaza (Rte. 17) |
201-843-8483
Short Hills | Short Hills Mall | 1200 Morris Tpke. (John F. Kennedy Pkwy.) |
973-467-0089
www.legalseafoods.com

"If it swims, they have it" at these "energetic" chain seafooders anchored in high-profile Short Hills and Paramus malls, offering "promptly served" "delicious fresh fish" that'll "even please the kiddies"; "weekend waits can be long", the decor's "nothing special" and they're "a tad pricey", but it sure "beats going to the food court."

Le Jardin *French*
18 | 22 | 19 | $55

Edgewater | 1257 River Rd. (North St.) | 201-224-9898 |
www.lejardinnj.com

There's "no location more breathtaking" than at this Edgewater French overlooking the Hudson, where "the open terrace is one of the best spots" in the area "to while away a steamy summer night"; "wines are reasonably priced" but the consensus is the food, though "well prepared", and decor "take a back seat to the views."

Le Petit Chateau Ⓜ *French*
25 | 22 | 25 | $70

Bernardsville | 121 Claremont Rd. (Rte. 202) | 908-766-4544 |
www.thelepetitchateau.com

"Feel like royalty" at this "chic", "romantic" and "expensive" Bernardsville Classic French, where a "spectacular" wine list, "knowledgeable" staff and "personalized attention" from chef-owner Scott Cutaneo add up to "a memorable experience"; if the tab seems a bit much, "the prix fixe menu is a good choice"; N.B. jacket suggested.

Le Rendez-Vous Ⓜ *French*
26 | 17 | 23 | $53

Kenilworth | 520 Boulevard (21st St.) | 908-931-0888 |
www.lerendez-vousnj.com

This "romantic" French BYO storefront in Kenilworth is "the real Gallic deal" for devotees who delight in "superb Provençal cuisine" and "classic bistro fare"; it's "a bit pricey", but "you'll never feel rushed" – though the "surroundings are so cramped you have to protect your meal from your neighbors"; P.S. remember to "book ahead" for this "little slice of Paris."

Liberty House Restaurant Ⓜ *American*
20 | 23 | 19 | $52

Jersey City | Liberty State Park | 76 Audrey Zapp Dr. (Freedom Way) |
201-395-0300 | www.libertyhouserestaurant.com

With "unobstructed views" of Lady Liberty and lower Manhattan, this Jersey City Traditional American in Liberty State Park is a "great place to impress out-of-town visitors or a special date"; though the "pricey" food draws mixed reviews ("wonderful" vs. "hit-or-miss"), most agree on the "great Sunday brunch"; N.B. Valiant, a 97-ft. yacht moored next to the restaurant, is used for private parties.

Light Horse Tavern, The *American* | 23 | 23 | 21 | $44 |

Jersey City | 199 Washington St. (Morris St.) | 201-946-2028 | www.lighthorsetavern.com

This "quintessential tavern" in Downtown Jersey City "stands out" thanks to "an unbeatable beer selection", a "top-flight" (and rather "expensive") New American menu featuring a "combination of pub standards and gourmet inventions", a "rustic", bi-level setting in a circa-1850 brick building and a generally "attentive" staff; N.B. the Food score may not reflect the recent addition of a new chef.

Lilly's on the Canal *Eclectic* | 21 | 21 | 21 | $39 |

Lambertville | 2 Canal St. (Bridge St.) | 609-397-6242 | www.lillysonthecanal.com

An Eclectic menu of "excellent food" at "reasonable prices" makes this industrial-chic bi-level cafe in Lambertville suitable for "a casual lunch or dinner" in several venues – the first floor's "open kitchen lets you see the action", while the upper deck is quieter, and there's "very nice outside seating" along the canal in summer too; N.B. it's BYO, but local wines are available.

NEW Limani *Greek* | 22 | 18 | 20 | $43 |

Westfield | 235 North Ave. W. (Lenox Ave.) | 908-233-0052 | www.limaniwestfieldnj.com

True to its name (which means seaport), this young Greek BYO storefront harbors "an ambitious menu" with an "excellent selection of fish dishes" served by a "willing" staff; fans call it "attractive" and a "welcome addition to the Westfield restaurant scene", even if it can be "loud when crowded" and some feel it's "still trying to find its niche."

Limestone Cafe Ⓜ *American* | 21 | 16 | 17 | $44 |

Peapack | 89 Main St. (Blair Rd.) | 908-234-1475

"Traditional American food is homey yet creative" at this "cozy" BYO in a "quaint" Peapack Victorian; faultfinders might fret the service is "spotty" and it's "getting a little tired", but boosters still consider it a "solid, reliable", "family-friendly" choice with "something for everyone."

Lincroft Inn *Continental* | 18 | 18 | 19 | $42 |

Lincroft | 700 Newman Springs Rd. (Middletown Lincroft Rd.) | 732-747-0890 | www.lincroftinn.com

The "extensive" wine list is "off the charts" at this "historic old" Lincroft inn (in business since 1697) where diners choose between "reliable" Continental cuisine in the recently renovated, "very elegant" dining room or the likes of "massive homemade burgers" in the "cozy" wood-paneled bar; still, doubters say it "wants to be gourmet, but doesn't make it."

	FOOD	DECOR	SERVICE	COST

Little Café, A 🖐M *Eclectic*
25 | 18 | 23 | $40

Voorhees | Plaza Shoppes | 118 White Horse Rd. E. (Burnt Mill Rd.) | 856-784-3344 | www.alittlecafenj.com

The room is "indeed little" at this Voorhees strip-mall BYO, but when chef-owner Marianne Cuneo Powell cooks her "rich" and "inventive" Eclectic fare, the flavors and plates are "big" – and "you'll leave full"; fans add that the "attentive" staff also makes this "pound for pound one of the best around."

Little Food Café *Sandwiches*
▽ 25 | 14 | 16 | $15

Bayonne | 330 Kennedy Blvd. (10th St.) | 201-436-6800 ⊘
Pompton Plains | 585 Newark Pompton Tpke. (bet. Jackson & Poplar Aves.) | 973-616-8600

Good "food is always prepared to perfection" at this "small", "friendly" Bayonne "neighborhood" sandwich shop that offers wraps, soups and salads too and is also "great for breakfast"; "use the take-out menu to call ahead to pick up your order" if you want to "avoid waiting on the long line in the little waiting room"; N.B. no credit cards for purchases under $50.

Little Saigon *Vietnamese*
25 | 10 | 17 | $29

Atlantic City | 2801 Arctic Ave. (Iowa Ave.) | 609-347-9119

The "spartan" appearance of this small Atlantic City BYO belies the "authentic" Vietnamese cuisine served within – "priced right and always fresh", it's "a treat" for those who step away from the casinos; since the "nice" owner and his wife "are the staff", service can be "slow", so "sit back, relax and enjoy."

Little Tuna, The *Seafood*
21 | 18 | 20 | $38

Haddonfield | 141 Kings Hwy. E. (Haddon Ave.) | 856-795-0888 | www.thelittletuna.com

"First-rate fish in a comfortable, classy space" is what admirers find at this "solid" Haddonfield seafood-and-more BYO with a sprawling menu, "fair prices" and "a fun staff"; consider dining on the second floor to avoid the "extremely noisy" downstairs.

Lobster House *Seafood*
21 | 18 | 19 | $40

Cape May | Fisherman's Wharf | 906 Schellenger Landing Rd. (Rte. 109) | 609-884-8296 | www.thelobsterhouse.com

For decades this "mega-sized" Cape May "tourist mecca" has provided "the quintessential Shore lobster-house experience" with "simple", "fresh" seafood, a "rustic wharf setting and "rushed" but "well-meaning" servers; there's "always a long wait", so the outdoor raw bar (or takeout) is an "excellent" option.

Lodos M *Mediterranean/Turkish*
23 | 16 | 22 | $28

New Milford | 690 River Rd. (Henley Ave.) | 201-265-0004

"Graze to your heart's content" on "creative dishes" at this "tasty" Mediterranean-Turkish BYO, "an unexpected pleasure" in New Milford, where "service is friendly" and the owners "attentive"; though "it's very small", there's room for a first-Friday-of-the-month "bonus" – belly dancing.

	FOOD	DECOR	SERVICE	COST

Lola's *Spanish*
21 | 20 | 18 | $42

Hoboken | 153 14th St. (Bloomfield St.) | 201-420-6062

"¡Magnifico!" cry aficionados of the "myriad amazing tapas" at this sometimes "loud" Hoboken Spanish with an outdoor "plaza"-cum-"wine cellar" look on its main level – and a real wine cellar below; there's "friendly service" all-around, and if the "small bites" cost "big money", at least they're "large enough to share."

⚡ Lorena's ℳ *French*
28 | 22 | 27 | $57

Maplewood | 168 Maplewood Ave. (Highland Pl.) | 973-763-4460 | www.restaurantlorena.com

Set "in the heart" of Maplewood, this French BYO is "a real gem, albeit a small one"; "sublime" food from chef Humberto Campos Jr., a "warm welcome" from his partner – the "courteous and efficient" host Lorena Perez – and "impeccable" service "make up for the inconvenience" of the "cramped" but "perfectly appointed oasis."

Los Amigos *Mexican/Southwestern*
22 | 20 | 21 | $29

Atlantic City | 1926 Atlantic Ave. (bet. Michigan & Ohio Aves.) | 609-344-2293
West Berlin | 461 Rte. 73 N. (Franklin Ave.) | 856-767-5216 ℳ
www.losamigosrest.com

Go for the "must-have" margaritas, but stay for the "seriously good", "not-your-typical" Mexican-Southwestern fare is the consensus on this pair of "comfortable" veterans in Atlantic City and West Berlin; "adorable" decor and a "friendly" staff add to the pleasure.

Lotus Cafe *Chinese*
24 | 12 | 19 | $27

Hackensack | Home Depot Shopping Ctr. | 450 Hackensack Ave. (Grand Ave.) | 201-488-7070

"Constant quality" and "cool prices" keep the "crowds" coming to this Hackensack Chinese BYO; the atmosphere in a "nondescript suburban strip mall" (near the upscale Riverside Square Mall) "leaves something to be desired", but the "owners try hard", the "staff is happy to accommodate" and the "large menu has tons of yummy choices."

LouCás *Italian*
23 | 18 | 20 | $40

Edison | Colonial Village Shopping Ctr. | 9 Lincoln Hwy. (Parsonage Rd.) | 732-549-8580 | www.loucasrestaurant.com

Chef and co-owner Loucás Sofocli offers "consistently excellent" Italian cuisine on his "extensive menu" (lots of "fresh seafood") at this "family-oriented" bi-level BYO strip-maller in Edison that "still packs them in"; though it's "very loud on weekends", prices are "fairly reasonable" and you can "eat with abandon and still take home leftovers."

Lua *Pan-Latin*
22 | 24 | 20 | $46

Hoboken | 1300 Sinatra Dr. N. (14th St.) | 201-876-1900 | www.luarestaurant.com

"Spectacular city views, awesome food and sublime service" draw crowds to this "elegant yet fun and lively" Hoboken "hot spot" along the Hudson that gets "clubby at night"; the "awesome Latin-fusion" menu includes "spins on Tex-Mex staples" but it's *muy* "expensive."

	FOOD	DECOR	SERVICE	COST

Luca's Ristorante *Italian* — — — M

Somerset | 2019 Rte. 27 (Schmidt Ln.) | 732-297-7676 |
www.lucasristorante.com

With faux greenery covering the ceiling, bright earthenware dishes,
statues and an abundance of amusing art, this Somerset spot resembles a movie set of an Italian restaurant; but the Di Meglio
brothers serve up serious old-world recipes with new-world twists,
luring loyalists who line up to *mangia* homemade gnocchi and ravioli, all at moderate prices.

Luce 🅂 🅼 *Italian* — 21 | 20 | 21 | $45

Caldwell | 115 Bloomfield Ave. (Elm Rd.) | 973-403-8500 |
www.lucerestaurant.com

"Large portions of very good traditional Italian food", including
"homemade pastas" and "very unusual" specials, have fans of this
Caldwell BYO Eclectic-Italian proclaiming it's the "real deal"; though
it's "noisy on weekends", the "pleasant" decor and "very attentive"
service make fans "feel at home."

Luchento's 🅼 *Italian* — — — M

Millstone Township | 520 Hwy. 33 W. (Dugans Grove Rd.) | 732-446-8500 |
www.luchentos.com

Recent changes at this sprawling, barnlike BYO in Millstone
Township include new owners, a new chef, an all-Italian menu (with
occasional Cajun-Creole specials) and a decor redo (it's brighter
and airier); what remains are "reasonable" prices and the "basic"
flavors that make it "good" for a "casual family outing."

NEW **Luciano's** *Italian* — — — M

Rahway | 1579 Main St. (Monroe St.) | 732-815-1200 |
www.lucianosristorante.com

Savor the *ciao* and welcome the warmth of the staff at this
Tuscan-style Italian newcomer in Rahway that proves you can
find surprises in unlikely places; though politicos and celebs have
been spotted in the crowd, it's the moderately priced food –
inventive, contemporary twists on traditional recipes – that keeps
this place hot and happening.

Lucky Bones Backwater Grille ● *American* — 21 | 17 | 19 | $32

Cape May | 1200 Rte. 109 S. (3rd Ave.) | 609-884-2663 |
www.luckybonesgrille.com

This "relaxed", "family-friendly" spot in Cape May "does what it
does well" – visitors adore the "crackling, thin-crust pizzas" and
other American "pub-style" fare at "reasonable" prices; live music
Wednesdays through Saturdays, a "fun and friendly bar" and "decent" service add appeal.

Luigi's *Italian* — 23 | 17 | 22 | $42

East Hanover | Berkeley Plaza | 434 Ridgedale Ave. (McKinley Ave.) |
973-887-8408 | www.luigisitalianrestaurant.com

"Outstanding food and attentive service" are the calling cards of this
East Hanover strip-mall storefront purveying "consistently excel-

lent", "authentic Italian fare" (with some new, more upscale dishes); the "romantic atmosphere" in the "comfortable dining room and bar area" supplemented by "outdoor seating" helps make it "a place to go back to again and again."

Luka's ⓩ *Italian* — 22 | 14 | 20 | $34

Ridgefield Park | 238 Main St. (Park St.) | 201-440-2996 | www.lukasitaliancuisine.com

"Great warmth and great food" emanate from this "dependable" Ridgefield Park BYO Italian storefront that "feels like home", thanks to the "accommodating kitchen" that dishes out "big portions" of "authentic food"; though "crowded and noisy", the "friendly" atmosphere and "reasonable prices" offset the "little discomforts."

Luke's Kitchen ⓩ Ⓜ *American* — ▽ 21 | 14 | 19 | $44

Maplewood | 175 Maplewood Ave. (bet. Baker St. & Highland Pl.) | 973-763-4005 | www.lukeskitchen.com

"Simple but welcoming", this "intimate" BYO New American set in a Maplewood storefront is considered a solid "local" choice for an "upscale dinner" in "relaxed" environs; the kitchen's "great execution" yields "delicious" results, while the "excellent prix fixe deal" is the answer to kinda "pricey" rates.

Lu Nello ⓩ *Italian* — 25 | 22 | 22 | $62

Cedar Grove | 182 Stevens Ave. (Lindsley Rd.) | 973-837-1660 | www.lunello.com

This "upscale", "romantic" Cedar Grove Italian is "outstanding in every way", with "classy and experienced waiters" who ferry food that's "out of this world" – "with prices to match"; though nitpickers note "too many choices on the menu" and say "the wait can be long" (it "helps to be a regular"), it remains a primo place to "see and be seen."

Madame Claude Cafe Ⓜ⇟ *French* — 23 | 15 | 19 | $28

Jersey City | 364½ Fourth St. (Brunswick St.) | 201-876-8800 | www.madameclaudecafe.com

"Pretend you're in a cafe in Paris" at this "delightful", "casual", cash-only BYO in an "unlikely section" of Downtown Jersey City that's "worth seeking out" for bistro "classics" that are equally "wonderful" for brunch or "a full dinner" and come at prices that "won't burn a hole in the wallet"; you may be "cheek by jowl with your neighbor" at this "tiny treasure", but it leaves most exclaiming "c'est fantastique!"

Mad Batter *American* — 23 | 19 | 20 | $33

Cape May | Carroll Villa Hotel | 19 Jackson St. (bet. Beach Ave. & Carpenter Ln.) | 609-884-5970 | www.madbatter.com

You'll think you "died and went to breakfast" declare those devoted to that meal as well as brunch and lunch at this "friendly" American inside a national landmark B&B in Cape May; "eat outdoors" or in the 'greenhouse' in the rear and let the light shine on some of NJ's best pancakes, Benedicts and omelets.

	FOOD	DECOR	SERVICE	COST

Madeleine's Petit Paris Ⓜ *Continental/French* — 25 | 20 | 23 | $54

Northvale | 416 Tappan Rd. (Paris Ave.) | 201-767-0063 | www.madeleinespetitparis.com

"You can never go wrong" at this "upscale", "cozy" Northvale Continental French where "cordial" chef Gaspard Caloz and his wife, Madeleine, "still weave their magic" for a loyal "older, quiet crowd"; the "graciously served", "top-notch" fare is as "French as Northern NJ can get" – and though it's "pricey", the prix fixe is an "excellent value"; N.B. it's BYO on Tuesday nights.

Madison Bar & Grill *American* — 20 | 19 | 19 | $36

Hoboken | 1316 Washington St. (14th St.) | 201-386-0300 | www.madisonbarandgrill.com

Catering mostly to "twenty- and thirtysomething dudes and dudettes", this Hoboken New American is a "neighborhood favorite" thanks to its "classic barroom" and "comfortable" dining room dispensing "quality" "casual" bites; its "fantastic" buffet-brunch is ideal for "young families", and prices are generally "reasonable for the area"; N.B. parking is validated if you spend $60 or more.

Magic Pot Ⓜ *Fondue* — 18 | 15 | 17 | $36

Edgewater | 934 River Rd. (bet. Dempsey & Hilliard Aves.) | 201-969-8005 | www.magicpotfondue.com

"Who doesn't love a place where you can eat from the pot?" muse mavens of this Edgewater BYO offering a "tasty, interesting" range of fondue dishes with Caribbean, Asian, Italian and French flavors; maybe the decor "could use a pick-me-up" and the tab can be "expensive for what you get", but it's considered a safe bet for a "fun time."

Mahogany Grille *American* — 23 | 22 | 22 | $54

Manasquan | 142 Main St. (Parker Ave.) | 732-292-1300 | www.themahoganygrille.com

This American serving "consistent", "high-quality" fare amid "formal decor" is appreciated for bringing a "little bit of NYC sophistication" to Downtown Manasquan with its "clubby feel", "nice bar" and "lovely" staff; it may be "very expensive" but it's "romantic."

Mahzu *Japanese* — 21 | 15 | 18 | $33

NEW **East Windsor** | 761 Rte. 33 W. (bet. Hickory Corner & Wyeth Rds.) | 609-371-2888

Aberdeen | Aberdeen Plaza | 1077 Rte. 34 (Lloyd Rd.) | 732-583-8985

Freehold | 430 Mounts Corner Dr. (Soloman Way) | 732-866-9668 www.mahzu.net

A "fresh, creative" assortment of "well-prepared" sushi (including "many interesting rolls") and "entertaining" hibachi high jinks "for the family" ("kids love it") plus "friendly" service keep these Central NJ Japanese BYOs "a cut above others in the area"; a third location recently debuted in East Windsor.

Main Street Bistro *American* — 21 | 18 | 20 | $38

Freehold | 30 E. Main St. (Spring St.) | 732-294-1112 | www.bistro1.com

This bi-level BYO New American in Freehold attracts a "young crowd" with creative bistro fare distinguished by "consistency" and "imagination"; service is "friendly" if "occasionally a little harried", and dining alfresco in warm weather is a plus; P.S. "go early or it will be a long wait", and be aware that it can be "noisy" when crowded.

Main Street Euro-American
Bistro & Bar *American/Continental*

19 | 17 | 19 | $36

Princeton | Princeton Shopping Ctr. | 301 N. Harrison St. (Valley Rd.) | 609-921-2779 | www.mainstreetprinceton.com

A "big part of the Princeton" dining "scene" is this "solid neighborhood restaurant" offering "reliable" American-Continental cuisine and service that "usually stacks up"; the "comfortable" "bistro ambiance pleases", while the courtyard patio is "fine" for alfresco; N.B. an outdoor bar is expected to open in summer 2009.

Maize ⓧ *American*

18 | 22 | 17 | $46

Newark | Best Western Robert Treat Hotel | 50 Park Pl. (bet. Center & Park Sts.) | 973-733-2202 | www.maizerestaurant.com

Choicely situated "across the street from NJPAC", this Newark standby's New American fare with a Portuguese accent "makes for the perfect pre-concert meal" – and "the bar mixes a good drink to boot"; critics who claim the "food and service aren't up to the prices" or the "beautiful room" say it's "riding on location", but to most the overall experience is a "treat"; N.B. there's a $45 pretheater prix fixe on performance nights.

Makeda *Ethiopian*

25 | 23 | 21 | $38

New Brunswick | 338 George St. (bet. Bayard St. & Livingston Ave.) | 732-545-5115 | www.makedas.com

"Everything pops with flavor" and is "finger-licking good" – literally – at this "utensils-optional" New Brunswick Ethiopian whose "sumptuous", "exotic" dishes, "sopped up with spongelike" injera bread, and pleasantly "dark", moody atmosphere add up to an enjoyable "adventure in eating"; given its "cool, fashionable crowd", happening bar and live music on weekends, it's an "interesting nightlife" option as well.

Manhattan Steakhouse *Steak*

19 | 17 | 18 | $55

Oakhurst | 2105 Rte. 35 N. (Park Ave.) | 732-695-6009 | www.mshsteaks.com

Oakhurst denizens call this carnivorium "our local Ruth's Chris" (some say "wannabe") with "solid" but "pricey" cuts and other "classic" steakhouse fare; detractors find the decor "dated" and say service could use a boost, but a recent change in ownership might change the picture.

Manna ⓧ Ⓜ *American*

▽ 24 | 20 | 23 | $44

Margate | 8409 Ventnor Ave. (Jerome Ave.) | 609-822-7722 | www.mannaattheshore.com

Chef-owner John Merlino's "beautifully presented" modern American fare is "perfection" according to those who have discovered this "intimate" and "relaxing" BYO in Margate; paella and risotto are standouts and it's all served up by a "young", competent staff; N.B. it's open year-round but with reduced hours in winter.

| | | FOOD | DECOR | SERVICE | COST |

Manon ⓂⒹ French
25 | 20 | 22 | $51

Lambertville | 19 N. Union St. (Bridge St.) | 609-397-2596

"Provence on the Delaware" is how partisans describe this "great little find", a "romantic" Lambertville BYO from chef-owner Jean-Michel Dumas; expect "beautifully presented" French cuisine (bouillabaisse, rack of lamb) enhanced by "attentive" service in a "unique" room famously featuring a rendition of 'Starry Night' on the ceiling; N.B. dinner only, Wednesdays–Sundays.

Ⓩ Manor, The Ⓜ American
24 | 25 | 24 | $65

West Orange | 111 Prospect Ave. (Woodland Ave.) | 973-731-2360 | www.themanorrestaurant.com

"Stands the test of time" say admirers of this circa-1956 West Orange Traditional American "grande dame", a "wow" of a "dress-up place" that delivers "opulence in all its glory", complete with "textbook service"; regulars rave about the seafood buffet, Sunday brunch and Le Dome lounge with its "beautiful view of the grounds", and if some find it bigger on "glitz" than substance, it's still a "community treasure" that hosts "special occasions and weddings galore"; N.B. BYO with no corkage is a plus, as are Tuesday night wine specials in the Terrace Lounge.

Mantra Indian
24 | 24 | 22 | $42

Paramus | 275 Rte. 4 W. (bet. Bogert Rd. & Forest Ave.) | 201-342-8868 | www.mantranj.com

"What a find" exult fans of this "upscale" Paramus strip-mall subcontinental "with flair", which combines "classic Raj-era Indian food" with a "chic", "romantic" setting; the happening "bar scene" and "personable" service are two more reasons it has many declaring it "nirvana" – "pricey"-for-the-genre tabs notwithstanding; N.B. a new chef may outdate the above Food score.

Marco & Pepe Ⓜ American
22 | 16 | 19 | $36

Jersey City | 289 Grove St. (Mercer St.) | 201-860-9688 | www.marcoandpepe.com

The "creative takes on mac 'n' cheese" and other New American "cool comfort" dishes "really hit the mark" at this "funky" Jersey City standout boasting a "hip", "mellow" feel; it's prized for its "lovely brunch" and "reasonable" prices (not to mention half-portion options that really "keep costs down"), but faulted for "tight" seating – though you can always "sit outside when it's warm."

Margherita's Ⓜ Italian
21 | 12 | 17 | $28

Hoboken | 740 Washington St. (8th St.) | 201-222-2400

"Huge portions" of "awesome" Italian basics – pasta, pizza, chicken parm – at "inexpensive" prices have folks lining up "out the door" of this "small, stark" Hoboken BYO; that it's "super-popular" and "doesn't take reservations" ensures it's "notoriously crowded" and "mind-numbingly loud" at prime times, but there's a reason "people keep coming back for more."

| | FOOD | DECOR | SERVICE | COST |

Marie Nicole's *American*   ▽ 24 | 23 | 24 | $50

Wildwood | 9510 Pacific Ave. (bet. Jefferson & Richmond Aves.) |
609-522-5425 | www.marienicoles.com
Pro service "the way it should be" and "delicious" seasonal New
American fare served in "cozy" quarters have many ranking this
Wildwood "surprise" "several steps above the expected shore restaurant"; it boasts a "comfortable" bar and patio dining in warm
weather, and, considering its "tourist-destination" locale, most find
the prices "fair."

Market in the Middle *Eclectic*   21 | 19 | 19 | $35

Asbury Park | 516 Cookman Ave. (Bangs Ave.) | 732-776-8886 |
www.themarketinthemiddle.com
Tucking an "interesting" restaurant into a gourmet food market/
wine shop strikes admirers as a "unique concept", and this small
Asbury Park Eclectic BYO makes the most of its setting by offering
"creative fare that changes constantly", a "happy" vibe and "wonderfully friendly" staff; this "different dining experience" also features alfresco seating choices and a "full bar."

Market Roost Ⓜ *Eclectic*   ▽ 21 | 12 | 14 | $21

Flemington | 65 Main St. (Bloomfield Ave.) | 908-788-4949 |
www.marketroost.com
Though reminiscent of "an old-fashioned luncheonette", you're
more likely to find Kahlua French toast than eggs-over-easy at
this veteran Eclectic Flemington eatery-cum-gift-gallery; the
scoop is that the food at this breakfast/lunch/brunch spot is
"always fresh and tasty" and the desserts "delicious"; P.S. it
takes a while for the "very pleasant" folks behind the counter to
get the grub.

Marmara Ⓜ *Turkish*   ▽ 19 | 18 | 18 | $30

Manalapan | Summerton Plaza | 339 Rte. 9 S. (Union Hill Rd.) |
732-780-9990 | www.marmararestaurant.com
Turkish cuisine isn't easy to come by in western Monmouth County,
so this "friendly" storefront BYO on Route 9 in Manalapan is appreciated for its "authentic", "tasty" and "plentiful" vittles; the belly
dancer on weekend nights makes it "upbeat and fun."

Marra's *Italian*   20 | 16 | 18 | $38

Ridgewood | 16 S. Broad St. (Ridgewood Ave.) | 201-444-1332
Yes, the "romantic" quarters are "cramped" and "noisy", but the
"Southern Italian comfort food" is "solid" at this "longtime neighborhood" "mainstay" in Ridgewood; "abundant portions" and a BYO
policy attract those who "seek good value" and don't mind much if
the menu "could use updating."

Martini Bistro & Bar *American*   18 | 19 | 18 | $43

Millburn | 40 Main St. (Milburn Ave.) | 973-376-4444 |
www.martinibistro.com
A "reliable" bistro with a "busy bar scene", this "pricey" Downtown
Millburn New American packs in the "Gucci-and-Mercedes set"

with its "extensive" martini list and "upscale", "wholesome" cooking; the "over-40s single scene" "occasionally overwhelms", but there's always the option to dine "early or very late" – or come at lunchtime.

Martino's Ⓜ Cuban
22 | 11 | 19 | $24

Somerville | 212 W. Main St. (Doughty Ave.) | 908-722-8602 | www.martinoscubanrestaurant.com

The chicken is "melt-in-your-mouth juicy", the oxtails "tender" and the plantains "yummy" at this "tiny" but "comfortable" and "engaging" Somerville Cuban BYO beloved for its "simple, satisfying", "modestly priced" fare and "welcoming" service; if you show up at the right time you may even "catch Martino dancing with one of the waitresses."

Mastoris ◖ Diner
20 | 13 | 19 | $24

Bordentown | 144 Hwy. 130 (Rte. 206) | 609-298-4650 | www.mastoris.com

To many, this "landmark" Central Jersey diner situated at the Bordentown "crossroads" between Philly and NYC epitomizes the diner experience: "outsized" portions of "good" homey fare, multiple rooms that regularly handle tour busloads, a menu "the size of a short story" and "waitresses who call you 'hon'"; P.S. "don't miss" the "legendary" complimentary cinnamon and cheese breads.

Matisse American
21 | 22 | 21 | $51

Belmar | 1300 Ocean Ave. (13th Ave.) | 732-681-7680 | www.matissecatering.com

You "can't beat the view" of the Atlantic or the "signature" short ribs at this oceanside American BYO in Belmar, whether you're "outside on the deck", at a table "by a window at sunset" or really anywhere in its "bright" interior; service is reliably "professional" year-round, but meals served (such as brunch) vary with the season.

Mattar's Bistro ◖ American
- | - | - | M

Allamuchy | 1115 Rte. 517 (Ridge Rd.) | 908-852-2300 | www.mattars.com
A post-Survey switch to a bistro format – as well as extensive renovations – mean the formality has been ditched and a new cost-consciousness now prevails at this "gracious" Allamuchy New American; with the same owners and staff, it may well retain its "first-rate" status; N.B. a change in menu and decor may outdate the above scores.

Matt's Red Rooster Grill Ⓜ American
25 | 21 | 23 | $52

Flemington | 22 Bloomfield Ave. (Main St.) | 908-788-7050 | www.mattsredroostergrill.com

Emphasis is on the "excellent wood-grilled" dishes at this "lively", "comfortable" bi-level New American in an updated Flemington Victorian, but then everything coming from owner-chef Matt McPherson's open kitchen is rated "fabulous" – and the "friendly" service is of "the same caliber"; upstairs is "more sedate", and outdoor seating is a fair-weather option; N.B. it's BYO.

| | FOOD | DECOR | SERVICE | COST |

Z McCormick & Schmick's *Seafood*   `20` `18` `19` `$44`

Hackensack | Shops at Riverside | 175 Riverside Sq. (Hackensack Ave.) | 201-968-9410
Bridgewater | Bridgewater Commons | 400 Commons Way (Prince Rodgers Ave.) | 908-707-9996
Atlantic City | Harrah's | 777 Harrah's Blvd. (Brigantine Blvd.) | 609-441-5000
Cherry Hill | 941 Haddonfield Rd. (bet. Graham & Severn Aves.) | 856-317-1711
www.mccormickandschmicks.com

This chain seafood quartet "gets it right" with "consistent" quality – fish "doesn't get much fresher than this" – and also "breaks the mold" by offering "fine service and atmosphere", all of which makes it "definitely worth the cost"; the AC outpost is a "good alternative to the steakhouse standards."

McLoone's *American*   `17` `21` `18` `$43`

NEW **Fords** | 3 Lafayette Rd. (Ford Ave.) | 732-512-5025
Long Branch | 1 Ocean Ave. (Seaview Ave.) | 732-923-1006
Sea Bright | 816 Ocean Ave. (Rumson Rd.) | 732-842-2894
www.mcloones.com

"It's all about" the "marvelous" views, both indoors and out, at two of these "casual" Americans – in Sea Bright overlooking the Shrewsbury River and at Pier Village in Long Branch overlooking the ocean; sure, the service can be "slow", the food is "nothing special" and the prices are kind of "steep" but the view more than "trumps it"; N.B. the newest Fords location is inland, but fans can enjoy the same menu.

Mediterra *Mediterranean*   `21` `21` `20` `$47`

Princeton | 29 Hulfish St. (bet. Chambers & Witherspoon Sts.) | 609-252-9680 | www.terramomo.com

Its "terrific location" and patio dining on Palmer Square help explain why Princetonians who appreciate this "bustling", "upscale" Mediterranean "consistent performer" willingly overlook the "crowded and noisy" conditions; N.B. the recent hiring of noted Spanish chef Luis Bollo and a post-Survey retooling of the menu and Decor may outdate the above scores.

Meemah M *Chinese/Malaysian*   `22` `9` `17` `$23`

Edison | Colonial Village Shopping Ctr. | 9 Lincoln Hwy. (Parsonage Rd.) | 732-906-2223 | www.meemah.com

"Creative" Chinese-Malaysian dishes – including some "seldom-seen" specialties – "more than make up for" the "lacking decor" at this "tiny" strip-mall BYO in Edison; it's "reasonable" too, so "just block out the surroundings" and focus on the "delicious" flavors – or consider getting it "for takeout."

Megu Sushi *Japanese*   ▽ `24` `16` `21` `$36`

Cherry Hill | Village Walk Shopping Ctr. | 1990 Rte. 70 E. (Old Orchard Rd.) | 856-489-6228 | www.megusushi.com

Fans of this funky, colorful Cherry Hill strip-mall Japanese say it's worth seeking out its BYO "can't-see-it-from-the-street location" because the "imaginative" sushi is "above average", as are the tuna dumplings, teppanyaki and other fare; its "something-for-everyone" menu offers "enjoyable hibachi" items too.

Mehndi ⓜ Indian — 24 | 25 | 22 | $48

Morristown | 88 Headquarters Plaza | 3 Speedwell Ave. (Park Pl.) | 973-871-2323 | www.mehtanirestaurantgroup.com

There's "a fancy vibe" – and prices to match – at this "modern", "elegant" Morristown Indian from the Mehtani Restaurant Group, where the "creative", "gourmet" Mughlai and Punjab fare is complemented by "innovative cocktails", and "outstanding" service adds to the "fantastic experience" (as do the henna tattoos on Friday and Saturday nights); P.S. the lunch buffet is a locals' "cheap office favorite."

Meil's ⊉ American — 22 | 13 | 18 | $28

Stockton | Bridge & Main Sts. | 609-397-8033 | www.meilsrestaurant.com

Those in need of "down-home" American "comfort food" – and "ample" portions of it – pack cash and go to this "highly informal" BYO cafe in a former gas station in "quaint" Stockton; "lines form" on weekends, especially for "awesome" breakfasts showcasing its "lovely" baked goods, while the lunch and dinner menus offer more Eclectic options.

Mélange @ Haddonfield Creole/Southern — 25 | 18 | 24 | $39

NEW **Haddonfield** | 18 Tanner St. (Kings Hwy.) | 856-354-1333

Mélange Cafe ⓜ Creole/Southern

Cherry Hill | 1601 Chapel Ave. (Woodland Ave.) | 856-663-7339
www.melangerestaurants.com

Joe Brown – the "talented" and "creative" chef-owner behind these casual BYOs – "is an artist" when it comes to his "delicious and unusual menu" that offers takes on Creole and Southern fare (with some Italian accents) served in "good quantity"; while some remain loyal to the Cherry Hill original and others delight in the newer, more "upscale" Haddonfield addition, both offer "wonderful" service.

Melting Pot Fondue — 18 | 19 | 19 | $48

Hoboken | 100 Sinatra Dr. (1st St.) | 201-222-1440
Westwood | 250 Center Ave. (Westwood Ave.) | 201-664-8877
Somerville | 190 W. Main St. (Doughty Ave.) | 908-575-8010
Whippany | Pine Plaza Shopping Ctr. | 831 Rte. 10 (Jefferson Rd.) | 973-428-5400
Red Bank | The Galleria | 2 Bridge Ave. (Front St.) | 732-219-0090
Atlantic City | 2112 Atlantic Ave. (Arkansas Ave.) | 609-441-1100
www.meltingpot.com

This "kitschy but fun" chain is a "fondue lover's dream" where "all the food is prepared for dipping into oil, broths, cheeses and chocolate"; it's ideal for "large groups" or "a romantic date", and many opt for the 'Big Night Out', a four-course prix fixe extravaganza that averages $42 per person; à la carte is also available.

Memphis Pig Out ⊉ BBQ — 21 | 14 | 19 | $29

Atlantic Highlands | 67 First Ave. (Center Ave.) | 732-291-5533 | www.memphispigout.com

"If you're a vegan, this place is not for you" (though there is a salad bar), but if you ever want to "pig out" on "barbecue" or "great ribs" head to this "funky, fun and filling" Atlantic Highlands "neighborhood eatery" with "oddball" "pig-inspired" decor "that has not changed in 25 years" – "everywhere you look, little piggies look back at you"; P.S. the staff is "friendly" too.

Merion Inn, The *American*

23	23	25	$52

Cape May | 106 Decatur St. (Columbia Ave.) | 609-884-8363 | www.merioninn.com

A "beautiful, very Cape May house" provides the "traditional setting" for this "gorgeous little" "favorite" that's "perfect" for dining on "well-prepared" American "classics" whose prices offer relative "good value" for the location; a "beautiful old bar" with a nightly piano player adds "another nice touch", as does downright "excellent" service.

Meson Madrid *Spanish*

18	13	17	$38

Palisades Park | 343 Bergen Blvd. (Palisades Blvd.) | 201-947-1038 | www.mesonmadridrestaurant.com

Maybe "the menu and decor haven't changed since the Inquisition", but "quality" fare in "large portions" "priced fairly" ensure this "loud, family-style" Palisades Park Spaniard is "still kicking"; regulars note the "lobster dishes especially" are a "good value", and when the sangria flows, it's "fun for large groups" – never mind if it "badly needs a makeover."

Metropolitan Cafe *Pacific Rim*

21	22	19	$42

Freehold | 8 E. Main St. (South St.) | 732-780-9400 | www.greatrestaurantsnj.com

"Looks mahvelous" say surveyors of this "upscale" Freehold standout – and the "trendy" clientele that kicks up a "happening scene" in its "cool lounge area" complete with "extensive" martini menu; maybe most "don't go for the food", but those who can focus on it say the Pacific Rim fare is "pretty good", if "predictable", noting that it tastes even better in the "outdoor seating in summer" that circumvents the "noise" and "crowds."

Metuchen Inn *American*

21	20	20	$52

Metuchen | 424 Middlesex Ave. (Linden Ave.) | 732-494-6444 | www.themetucheninn.com

"Fine" cuisine "presented with elegance" vies for attention with the "romantic" "old-world atmosphere" at this "pricey" Metuchen New American whose "historic inn" building dating from 1843 boasts "multiple fireplaces"; maybe service "can be slow" and the decor "could use sprucing up", but overall the effect is "charming and rustic."

Mexican Food Factory *Mexican*

20	15	18	$25

Marlton | 601 Rte. 70 W. (Cropwell Rd.) | 856-983-9222

Maybe it "doesn't look great from the outside", but this "relaxed", "conveniently located" Marlton "cantina" has been dishing out "decent" Mexican "favorites" for three decades now; just watch out for those margaritas – the "dark" room's multitude of Frida Kahlo paintings can "start to blink at you if you drink too many."

Mexico Lindo ⓜ *Mexican*   ▽ 23 | 11 | 20 | $22

Brick | 1135 Burnt Tavern Rd. (Lanes Mill Rd.) | 732-202-1930
This "little treasure" of a Mexican BYO in Brick "stands out" for the "authentic" fare served up by the "nice" family who runs it, not for its "no-frills" atmosphere; N.B. open Tuesdays–Sundays in summer.

Meyersville Inn, The ⓜ *Eclectic*   17 | 18 | 19 | $41

Gillette | 632 Meyersville Rd. (New Vernon Rd.) | 908-647-6302 | www.meyersvilleinn.com
Service is "friendly" and prices "reasonable" at this Gillette tavern that makes a "great date spot" in a "country setting"; if a few fear it has "lost its way" in recent times, the return of a former chef – who has restored "a bit of Cajun" to the Eclectic menu studded with Italian and American favorites – and the addition of a new bargain prix fixe are signs of promise.

Mia ⓩⓜ *Italian*   25 | 24 | 24 | $68

Atlantic City | Caesars on the Boardwalk | 2100 Pacific Ave. (Arkansas Ave.) | 609-441-2345 | www.miaac.com
"Thank you, Georges Perrier" (and Chris Scarduzio) extol fans of Philly's favorite restaurant team and their "high-quality", high-price venue in the "cavernous" former Temple Bar at Caesars on the Boardwalk, whose "wonderful", "classy" Italian fare comes in "over-the-top" quarters complete with "impressive" "Roman-style columns"; a "well-trained" staff adds to the overall appeal, leaving only the "noise" from its "open-area" locale near the casino floor to detract; P.S. check out the "value"-oriented midweek prix fixe dinner.

Mi Bandera *Cuban*   23 | 14 | 16 | $32

Union City | 518 32nd St. (bet. Central & Summit Aves.) | 201-348-2828 | www.mibanderanj.com
"Fresh, flavorful" Cuban food at a "price we all can appreciate" is the selling point at this "big, bold, family-style" Union City mainstay atop a Latin American supermarket of the same name; maybe "there really isn't too much to the decor", but most don't mind much given that the "authentic cooking" comes in "huge" portions and "there's a great lunch special" too.

Michael's Cucina Italia ⓜ *Italian*   19 | 11 | 18 | $30

Manalapan | Alexander Plaza | 333 Rte. 9 S. (Union Hill Rd.) | 732-409-4777 | www.michaelscucinaitalia.com
Thin-crust pizzas and Southern Italian standards in "huge portions" present "good value" – especially since they're "meant to be shared" – at this "solid", "family-style" Manalapan BYO; service can be "erratic" and the strip-mall location "doesn't help the ambiance", but most are too busy chowing down to notice.

Midori *Japanese*   22 | 14 | 20 | $32

Denville | Denville Commons Mall | 3130 Rte. 10 W. (bet. Franklin & Hill Rds.) | 973-537-8588 | www.midorirestaurant.com
The setup "isn't fancy, but the food is" at this "reliable and popular" Japanese BYO in a Denville strip mall; the "delicious" sushi and

cooked dishes are presented by "attentive waitresses wearing traditional dress" and "the karaoke wall projection is a nice touch", but most agree the decor – "an old diner, with booths and all" – could use a "revamp."

Mie Thai *Thai*

24 | 13 | 20 | $26

North Brunswick | Ryan Plaza | 2800 Rte. 27 N. (Finnegan Ln.) | 718-297-3066 Ⓜ
Woodbridge | 34 Main St. (Berry St.) | 732-596-9400
www.miethai.com

These North Brunswick and Woodbridge Thai BYOs have heat-lovers fired up about the "amazing bold flavors" of their "imaginative", "mouthwatering" and "plentiful" fare; an "eager, friendly" staff adds to the "true-value" experience.

Mignon Steakhouse *Steak*

22 | 17 | 20 | $48

Rutherford | 72 Park Ave. (Franklin Pl.) | 201-896-0202 |
www.villagerestaurantgroup.com

There's no beef about the "excellent steaks" and "professional" service at this "reasonably priced" Rutherford BYO chophouse that also lands "excellent fish"; the "small, intimate" space "does get noisy" and street parking is a "drag", but nonetheless to most this "neighborhood" spot is "a find."

Mikado *Japanese*

23 | 17 | 20 | $30

Cherry Hill | 2320 Rte. 70 W. (Union Ave.) | 856-665-4411
Maple Shade | 468 S. Lenola Rd. (Kings Hwy.) | 856-638-1801
Marlton | Elmwood Shopping Ctr. | 793 Rte. 70 E. (Troth Rd.) |
856-797-8581
www.mikado-us.com

"Fresh" and "first-rate" sushi and sashimi at this trio of "family-friendly" Japanese South Jerseyans are given an assist by "good" service and "reasonable prices"; cooked fare and "fun" hibachi presentations "keep the pace" in all but sushi-only Cherry Hill; N.B. only the Marlton location has a liquor license.

Milford Oyster House *Seafood*

▽ 23 | 20 | 23 | $43

Milford | 92 Rte. 519 (York St.) | 908-995-9411 |
www.milfordoysterhouse.com

Although oysters are no longer its focus following a move a few years back to "charming" 1830s-former-stone-mill digs, brother-sister team Amy and Edwin Coss' seafooder-and-more remains a "hidden treasure" in the Delaware River town of Milford; given the kitchen's "outstanding" output and the general "homey" vibe abetted by "warm, efficient" service, it's no wonder most rate it a "don't-miss."

Mill at
Spring Lake Heights, The Ⓜ *American*

21 | 23 | 22 | $49

Spring Lake Heights | 101 Old Mill Rd. (Ocean Rd.) | 732-449-1800 |
www.themillatslh.com

This lakeside phoenix in Spring Lake Heights rose from the ashes of a fire years ago, then made a switch to an almost all catering venue and now (post-Survey) has reinstituted regular restaurant hours under new management (but the same owner); a new chef and a "classic" American steak-and-seafood menu indicate it has "rebounded nicely."

Minado *Japanese* `19` `12` `14` `$34`

Little Ferry | 1 Valley Rd. (Waterside Dr.) | 201-931-1522
Morris Plains | 2888 Rte. 10 W. (bet. Powder Mill Rd. & Yacenda Dr.) | 973-734-4900
www.minado.com

You need an "extra stomach" to best take advantage of these Japanese "megaplex buffets" in Morris Plains and Little Ferry, whose "bewildering assortment" of sushi, hibachi items and other Asian specialties is served up in "noisy", "cavernous" settings; all appreciate that the "high-volume" business ensures offerings are "constantly replenished", though a few parental types complain that the pricing-by-height policy for kids is "not family-friendly."

Ming 🅼 *Pan-Asian* `21` `22` `20` `$38`

Edison | Oak Tree Shopping Ctr. | 1655-185 Oak Tree Rd. (bet. Grove & Wood Aves.) | 732-549-5051 | www.mingrestaurants.com

Edison locals "pack" this "inviting" strip-mall BYO serving up "fancy", "spicy-as-anything" Pan-Asian cuisine; tabs are "a little high" for the genre, but enthusiasts declare the "delicious" "smells that greet you" here "alone are worth the price."

Ming II 🅂 *Pan-Asian* `▽ 24` `26` `21` `$56`

Morristown | 88 Headquarters Plaza | 3 Speedwell Ave. (Park Pl.) | 973-871-2323 | www.ming2morristown.com

A perfect "place to impress", this "upscale" Morristown Pan-Asian (an offshoot of the Edison original) excels at "creative" cuisine and "off-the-charts" cocktails; however, it's the "really neat" red-and-black, banquette-bedecked decor that seals its standing as a "surefire hit"; N.B. there's validated parking in the adjacent Hyatt garage.

Mirabella Cafe *Italian* `▽ 20` `19` `20` `$35`

Cherry Hill | Barclay Farms Shopping Ctr. | 210 Rte. 70 E. (Kings Hwy.) | 856-354-1888 | www.mirabellacafe.com

This "strip-mall" Cherry Hill Italian BYO on Route 70 comes via South Jersey's popular chef-owner Joe Palumbo, known for his "humble" "housemade pastas" and more; his "attractive" Tuscan-style "spaghetti house" is most appreciated for its Sunday all-you-can-eat fusilli with mama's 'gravy.'

Moghul 🅼 *Indian* `25` `20` `21` `$34`

Edison | Oak Tree Shopping Ctr. | 1655-195 Oak Tree Rd. (bet. Grove & Wood Aves.) | 732-549-5050 | www.moghul.com

"Prepare to leave stuffed" from this Edison BYO "standout" specializing in "delicious" Northern Indian cuisine and offering a lunch buffet that regulars tout as "the best value" around; its "upscale setting" is "newly redecorated" and service is "helpful and prompt" – no wonder there's "often a wait" without a reservation; N.B. the latest look may outdate the above Decor score.

	FOOD	DECOR	SERVICE	COST

Mohawk House *American*
19 | 24 | 19 | $47

Sparta | 3 Sparta Jct. (Rte. 15) | 973-729-6464 | www.mohawkhouse.com
Loyalists "love the decor" of this "rustic lodge" in Sparta specializing in "inventive" New American fare, though many opt for the "bar food, especially the pizzas", over the "offerings in the dining room"; it's a real crowd-pleaser in summer thanks to "outdoor service and a bocce court"; N.B. live entertainment on weekends.

Mojave Grille *Southwestern*
23 | 19 | 20 | $39

Westfield | 35 Elm St. (North Ave.) | 908-233-7772 | www.mojavegrille.com
"Creative food extraordinaire" that's "served with flair" has admirers calling this Westfield Southwestern BYO "a good splurge in a nice town"; it's a solid "family favorite" even though it's "a bit cramped", leading many to lament it's a "shame they don't take reservations" – "if you don't like to wait" just wave it *adiós* on weekend nights."

Moksha *Indian*
∇ 22 | 22 | 20 | $33

Edison | Oak Tree Shopping Ctr. | 1655-200 Oak Tree Rd. (bet. Grove & Wood Aves.) | 732-947-3010 | www.moksharestaurants.com
The "terrific" South Indian specialties on the "vast menu" at this "classy", casual Edison strip-mall "standout" (yes, another from the Mehtani family) are "a rich revelation" – as are the "reasonable prices"; the "serene setting" and solid service also win approval; N.B. no dinner on Tuesdays.

Molly Pitcher Inn *American*
23 | 25 | 24 | $49

Red Bank | Molly Pitcher Inn | 88 Riverside Ave. (Front St.) | 732-747-2500 | www.mollypitcher-oysterpoint.com
"No aspect of the dining experience is overlooked" at this "grande dame" in an "upscale hotel" in Red Bank, where "exceptional" views of the Navesink River form the backdrop for "delightful", "elegantly presented" Traditional American fare deemed "worth every penny"; it's "especially known" for its "real treat" of a Sunday brunch; P.S. "gentlemen must wear jackets" in the evening.

Mompou *Spanish*
21 | 21 | 19 | $33

Newark | 77 Ferry St. (Congress St.) | 973-578-8114 | www.mompoutapas.com
Named for the Catalan composer, this "cool", "upbeat" Ironbound Spanish near the Rock and NJPAC hits high notes with its "sophisticated", "tantalizing" tapas and "quietly swinging feel"; the service is "efficient" enough, but it's the "beautiful outdoor courtyard", musical entertainment and "bargain" wine tastings that make for "a great escape" here.

Monster Sushi *Japanese*
20 | 15 | 17 | $32

Summit | 395 Springfield Ave. (Maple St.) | 908-598-1100 | www.monstersushi.com
"True to its name", the rolls are "Godzilla-size" at this "noisy, kid-friendly" Summit spawn of the Manhattan Japanese eateries characterized by "cute monster-themed decor"; the "convivial at-

mosphere", "reasonable" rates and "get-you-in-and-out" service ensures it's a solid "starter sushi" joint for "your little monsters."

Montville Inn, The M *American*   21 | 21 | 19 | $48

Montville | 167 Rte. 202 (River Rd.) | 973-541-1234 |
www.montvilleinn.com

"Dare-to-be-different" New American cuisine (think fried devilled eggs) attracts a "good-looking crowd" to this "upscale" and "inviting" Montville "find" on the site of a pre-Revolutionary inn; the tabs can induce "sticker shock" and the acoustics are on the "noisy" side during prime time, but all appreciate the "cheerful" vibe.

Moonfish Grill *Seafood*   - | - | - | E

Cape May | 416 S. Broadway (Sunset Blvd.) | 609-898-1600 |
www.moonfishgrill.com

Opened post-Survey and run by the folks behind Cape May's Tisha's Fine Dining, this Cape May American features a menu of meat and seafood accented by the chef's special sauces along with more creative fare; N.B. it's BYO and open year-round.

Z Moonstruck M *American/Mediterranean*   25 | 24 | 24 | $51

Asbury Park | 517 Lake Ave. (bet. Main St. & Ocean Ave.) | 732-988-0123 |
www.moonstrucknj.com

This Asbury Park "winner" in a "delightful", "lovingly restored" Victorian with wraparound porches and lakeside views impresses with its "delicious" American-Mediterranean "food with flair" and "A-plus" service; but the no-rezzie policy is "a pain", so "enjoy a drink and an appetizer" at one of the "fun, lively" bars "while you wait."

Mo' Pho M *Vietnamese*   24 | 12 | 19 | $27

Fort Lee | 212 Main St. (Lemoine Ave.) | 201-363-8886

Saigon R. M *Vietnamese*

Englewood | 58 W. Palisade Ave. (William St.) | 201-871-4777
www.saigonmopho.com

"Outstanding" Vietnamese specialties – notably the "best" "big bowls" of pho noodle soup "this side of the Hudson" – at "bargain" rates draw "locals and those in-the-know" to these Vietnamese BYOs in Fort Lee and Englewood; the "tight" quarters and "minimal" decor don't deter the masses, so "reservations are essential."

Z Morton's The Steakhouse *Steak*   25 | 22 | 24 | $68

Hackensack | Shops at Riverside | 274 Riverside Sq. (Hackensack Ave.) |
201-487-1303 | www.mortons.com

"Magnificent" steaks at "over-the-top" prices lure meat lovers looking to "show off" at this Hackensack link of the "classic" "carnivorium" chain manned by a "superb" staff; a few find its tradition of "bringing raw, plastic-wrapped" cuts to the table "a useless exercise", but to most it's all part of the "old-fashioned steakhouse experience."

Mr. Chu *Chinese*   21 | 13 | 18 | $24

East Hanover | 44 Rte. 10 W. (Ridgedale Ave.) | 973-887-7555
"Convenient to shopping and movies", this "reliable", "unpretentious" East Hanover Chinese BYO in a "converted diner" supple-

ments "solid favorites" with "innovative specials", all at "affordable" prices"; the "efficient" staff can be almost "too quick" – though parents appreciate that they're "accommodating to kids."

Mr. C's Beach Bistro Restaurant *Seafood* 19 | 21 | 18 | $43

Allenhurst | 1 Allen Ave. (Ocean Pl.) | 732-531-3665 | www.mistercsbeachbistro.com

The view from the bar's "wall of windows" looking out onto the ocean "right atop the beach" is "fantastic" at this Allenhurst seafooder, where you can have "a vino", dine on small plates or choose from the menu of "freshly prepared meals" served in the rear dining room or outside; N.B. the place has recently been freshened up.

Mud City Crab House *Seafood* 24 | 13 | 18 | $32

Manahawkin | 1185 E. Bay Ave. (bet. Heron St. & Marsha Dr.) | 609-978-3660 | www.mudcitycrabhouse.com

This seasonal Manahawkin BYO "crab shack" has "so little atmosphere it has atmosphere" as well as what some call the "best" jumbo lump crab cakes "this side of Baltimore" – even with a "one- to two-hour wait" (no rezzies); it's "worth it" even if "it's in a swamp" – just "bring tons of bug spray", "board games" and "a cooler."

Mundo Latino *Cuban/Spanish* ▽ 21 | 13 | 20 | $36

North Bergen | 8619 Bergenline Ave. (bet. 85th & 87th Sts.) | 201-861-6902 | www.mundolatinorestaurant.net

An "abundant menu" at this "down-to-earth" North Bergen Cuban-Spaniard features "tasty", "traditional" "arteries-be-damned" dishes "from Spain and the Caribbean" in "huge portions"; the service is "gracious" and the prices "reasonable", and though it "doesn't look like much", verdant Hudson County Park is right across the street.

My Little Fat Greek Restaurant Ⓜ *Greek* 18 | 9 | 19 | $23

Freehold | 3430 Rte. 9 S. (Elton Adelphia Rd.) | 732-683-1304 | www.mylittlefatgreekrestaurant.com

"Your Greek *yia yia* would approve" of this "tiny", "unassuming" family-run BYO along Route 9 in Freehold that hits the spot with its "homestyle" Hellenic "staples"; "reasonable" prices and "friendly" service are pluses, and for those put off by the seriously "unassuming bungalow" digs, takeout is an option.

Nag's Head ⌘ *American* ▽ 23 | 9 | 18 | $26

Ocean City | 801 Asbury Ave. (8th St.) | 609-391-9080 | www.nagsheadoc.net

The dining room of this "very informal" American located inside an old bank building in the "heart" of Downtown Ocean City "isn't much to look at", but the kitchen delivers "excellent" "quality for the price"; N.B. no alcohol is allowed, and neither are credit cards.

Nana's Deli Ⓢ *Deli* 22 | 11 | 17 | $18

Livingston | 127 S. Livingston Ave. (Wilson Terrace) | 973-740-1940 | www.nanasdeli.com

"Tuna is an art form", the soups are "incredible" and the sloppy joes "top-notch" at this "casual, cute" Jewish-style Livingston deli that's also known for its Italian specialties; it may be "a little on the pricey side", but to most it's a longtime "storefront haven" nonetheless.

Napa Valley Grille *American*　21 | 21 | 21 | $47

Paramus | Garden State Plaza | 1146 Garden State Plaza (Rtes. 4 & 17) | 201-845-5555 | www.napavalleygrille.com

The "inventive" New American fare and "extensive wine list" at this "comfortable, welcoming" "oasis" in Paramus bear the imprint of chef Giacomo Mistretta (formerly of Esty Street), so "don't expect a food-court experience"; private rooms make it "good for business luncheons and small groups", and there's also afternoon tea, but navigating the parking lot can be a "hassle."

Nauvoo Grill Club *American*　16 | 25 | 16 | $42

Fair Haven | 121 Fair Haven Rd. (River Rd.) | 732-747-8777 | www.nauvoogrillclub.com

"Winning" ambiance created by "fantastic" Mission-style decor that looks "as if Frank Lloyd Wright designed it himself" "makes up for" "mediocre" fare at this Fair Haven American ("stick to the "solid" burgers) where "chefs come and go" and servers can seem "uninterested"; N.B. they are in the process of getting a new chef.

Navesink Fishery Ⓜ *Seafood*　24 | 10 | 19 | $35

Navesink | A&P Shopping Ctr. | 1004 Rte. 36 S. (Valley Dr.) | 732-291-8017

"Fresh fish", "consistently well prepared" with no frills" is the drill at this "unpretentious" strip-mall Navesink BYO in the rear of a retail fish market; that it's open all year is a plus, as is the "friendly" service, but its "zero atmosphere" is a minus.

Neelam *Indian*　20 | 14 | 18 | $27

Berkeley Heights | 295 Springfield Ave. (Snyder Ave.) | 908-665-2212
South Orange | 115 S. Orange Ave. (Irvington Ave.) | 973-762-1100
Middletown | Village Mall | 1178 Rte. 35 S. (New Monmouth Rd.) | 732-671-8900 Ⓜ

"Accommodating to both the adventurous and cautious diner", this trio of separately owned Jersey BYOs satisfies a taste for "soothing" "old-fashioned" Indian cuisine at "reasonable" prices; "the decor is nothing special", but the "bargain" buffets "offset that just fine" and many "just order" takeout.

Nero's Grille *Steak*　17 | 15 | 17 | $47

Livingston | 618 S. Livingston Ave. (Hobart Gap Rd.) | 973-994-1410 | www.neros.com

There's "something-for-everyone" at this 40-year-old Livingston "diamond-in-the-rough" steakhouse that maintains a "loyal following" for its "decent" beef and "super" chopped salads; most agree the "dated" digs "need an overhaul", but a "fairly vibrant bar scene" flourishes here nonetheless.

New Main Taste *Thai*　23 | 15 | 16 | $36

Chatham | 225 Main St. (bet. Hillside & Passaic Aves.) | 973-635-7333

"Fantastic satays and curries" are among the Thai-lights at this Chatham BYO, where fans "put up with" the "painfully slow" service and "dated decor" in order to enjoy that "unbelievable" – though "strongly seasoned and not for the faint-hearted" – "made-to-order" fare; aesthetes note "takeout" is an option.

Next Door ⓂAmerican
21 | 11 | 19 | $29

Montclair | 556 Bloomfield Ave. (bet. Midland Ave. & Park St.) | 973-744-3600

"Affordable prices" make the "enjoyable" "down-home comfort food" at this "friendly" Montclair American BYO sibling of the adjacent Blu an "excellent bargain"; the staff can seem "overtaxed" and the "informal" setup goes "beyond minimalist" ("virtually no decorations"), but still most agree "for price, portion size and quality, you can't do better."

Nha Trang Place Vietnamese
24 | 7 | 15 | $19

Jersey City | 249 Newark Ave. (bet. Cole & 2nd Sts.) | 201-239-1988

"The decor has all the charm of a cafeteria", but the kitchen at this Jersey City BYO cranks out "nothing but the best" Vietnamese classics (including "perfect pho" noodle soups) at seriously "inexpensive prices"; its "loud, bustling" room "always seems to be filled", but service is "fast", and it's also a "terrific choice for takeout."

🆉 Nicholas Ⓜ American
28 | 27 | 29 | $86

Middletown | 160 Rte. 35 S. (bet. Navesink River Rd. & Pine St.) | 732-345-9977 | www.restaurantnicholas.com

"Still the gold standard", this New American on the Middletown-Red Bank border is again ranked NJ's Most Popular as well as No. 1 for Food and Service; run by chef/co-owner Nicholas Harary and wife Melissa, it's "near perfect" all around, from the "stellar" cuisine" and "deep", "well-researched" wine list to the "polished but not pretentious" service and "contemporary", "understated elegant ambiance", enhanced by the "brilliant addition" of a "more casual" bar for small-plates dining and a four-seat chef's table; yes it's "expensive", but the $59 three-course dinner (one of several prix fixe options) is "a great value"; N.B. jacket suggested.

Nicky's Firehouse American
19 | 14 | 16 | $21

Madison | 15 Central Ave. (Main St.) | 973-765-0565 | www.nickysfirehousenj.com

Brick-oven pizzas plus "some pretty inventive high-end dishes" make this Madison American BYO a "prized neighborhood spot" for "quick, inexpensive family dinners"; the atmosphere "can get a little hectic" and "overrun with kids" who "love" the firefighting-themed decor, but those overwhelmed can beat a retreat to the "nice outdoor patio."

Nifty Fifty's Diner
18 | 20 | 20 | $18

Clementon | 1310 Blackwood-Clementon Rd. (Millbridge Rd.) | 856-346-1950
Turnersville | 4670 Black Horse Pike (Fries Mill Rd.) | 856-875-1950
www.niftyfiftys.com

"Feel like you just stepped back into the '50s" at these two "cute" South Jersey outposts of a small "fun diner" chain; the milkshakes are "heavenly", the hamburgers "commendable" and it "will not cost a fortune"; N.B. Clementon has a drive-thru.

	FOOD	DECOR	SERVICE	COST

Nikko *Japanese* | 24 | 16 | 21 | $38

Whippany | 881 Rte. 10 E. (Rte. 287) | 973-428-0787 | www.nikkonj.com
The sushi tastes like it's "right out of the water" and "the specials board is not to be missed" at this Whippany Japanese, "a tranquil respite in the middle of strip-mall heaven" with "friendly service" from kimono-clad waitresses; though it's "a little tired", the decor includes "tatami rooms . . . if your back can take it."

NEW 9 North Ⓜ *American* | - | - | - | M

Wayne | Cider Mill Ctr. | 37 Berdan Ave. (bet. Alps Dr. & Paterson Hamburg Tpke.) | 973-832-4284 | www.9northrestaurant.com
This simple yet elegant BYO newcomer in Wayne offers updated American food in a family-friendly setting; chef-owner Joshua Bernstein's prix fixe menus are seasonal, sassy and bold, from the whimsical amuse-bouche to the signature chocolate hazelnut cake – and a good value too.

NEW Nisi Estiatorio *Greek* | - | - | - | E

Englewood | 90 Grand Ave. (bet. Chester & Tracey Pls.) | 201-567-4700 | www.nisirestaurant.com
Chef John Piliouras (ex Manhattan's Molyvos) moors classic Aegean specialties to French techniques at this elegant Englewood Greek newcomer; evocative of Mediterranean grottoes, the nautically inspired interior complements his deft treatment of whole fish, which diners can select from an artistic display; N.B. dinner served daily, lunch Mondays–Saturdays.

Nobi *Japanese* | ▽ 25 | 15 | 22 | $31

Toms River Township | T.J. Maxx Plaza | 1338 Hooper Ave. (Bey Lea Rd.) | 732-244-7888 | www.nobicuisine.com
For over a decade this "small" but "standout" strip-mall BYO in Toms River has been cranking out "great" sushi and Japanese fare (bento box lunches are "really great deals"); while the "average" decor may be "a bit run-down", the service is "warm" and "careful."

No. 9 Ⓜ *American* | 26 | 15 | 23 | $46

Lambertville | 9 Klines Ct. (Bridge St.) | 609-397-6380
"In a town filled" with good restaurants, this "rather plain" and "noisy" BYO storefront in Lambertville rates a '10' for its "short" but "excellent" Contemporary American slate (e.g. braised short ribs with horseradish sauce) executed by chef-owner Matthew Kane using "high quality ingredients"; "friendly and competent" servers enhance the experience.

Noodle House, The *Asian* | 18 | 16 | 17 | $28

North Brunswick | 2313 Rte. 1 S. (bet. Aaron Rd. & Commerce Blvd.) | 732-951-0141
A "soothing atmosphere" including "hot towels before dinner" completes the "culinary-trip-through-Asia" experience at this "mod"-

looking North Brunswick BYO noodle specialist; given its "friendly" vibe and "terrific-value" prices, most happily overlook the "strip-mall" milieu; P.S. "Sunday dim sum is a blast!"

Nori *Pan-Asian* | 23 | 14 | 19 | $33 |

Caldwell | 406 Bloomfield Ave. (Academy Rd.) | 973-403-2400
Montclair | 561 Bloomfield Ave. (Maple Plaza) | 973-655-8805
www.nori-sushi.com

"Creative and yummy" sushi rolls are among the favorites at this pair of "family-friendly" Pan-Asian BYOs in Caldwell and Montclair also offering "fusion selections"; though "a great place for a mid-week sushi fix", "decor is sadly lacking", so some "stick to takeout or delivery"; P.S. "the lunch specials are a good value too."

Norma's Eastern | 21 | 15 | 21 | $23 |
Mediterranean Restaurant *Mideastern*

Cherry Hill | Barclay Farms Shopping Ctr. | 132-145 Rte. 70 E. (Kings Hwy.) | 856-795-1373 | www.normasrestaurant.com

This three-fold Middle Eastern BYO in a Cherry Hill strip mall combines a "falafel stop" cafe offering "reasonably priced" fare and "nice size portions", a "cute" ethnic grocery store and, in the back, Cous Cous, a Moroccan restaurant and hookah lounge complete with weekend belly dancers; expect "good food" and service throughout.

Nouveau Sushi *Pan-Asian* | 24 | 18 | 19 | $48 |

Montclair | 635 Bloomfield Ave. (Valley Rd.) | 973-746-9608

"Saves the schlep to Nobu" say "sushi gourmands" who appreciate the "craziest, most creative" rolls at this "trendy" Montclair Japanese-Asian, which also offers "fantastic hot dishes"; the BYO policy "helps ease the pain" of "high prices", but a few wish they'd refresh the slightly "faded" decor and boost the "slow" service.

Nunzio Ristorante Rustico *Italian* | 24 | 22 | 21 | $43 |

Collingswood | 706 Haddon Ave. (Collings Ave.) | 856-858-9840 | www.nunzios.net

The "quality" Italian fare at Nunzio Patruno's BYO in Collingswood – including veal "so tender" it should be "illegal" – and a "bright and beautiful atmosphere" mostly trump the "loud" acoustics and close tables; N.B. chef-owner Nunzio also offers cooking classes.

Oceanos *Seafood* | 23 | 21 | 22 | $50 |

Fair Lawn | 2-27 Saddle River Rd. (Meadow View Terrace) | 201-796-0546 | www.oceanosrestaurant.com

The accent is Greek at this "expensive" Fair Lawn seafooder where "the fish is always fresh", the bread is "housemade" and "they know how to cook a steak" too; "weekends are hectic", but the "servers are knowledgeable" and the setting, complete with a "delightful courtyard" in warm weather, is reliably "romantic."

Octopus's Garden *Seafood* | 23 | 21 | 22 | $39 |

Stafford | 771 S. Main St. (Mayetta Landing Rd.) | 609-597-8828

"Care in the preparation" of the seafood at this BYO in the Mayetta part of Stafford Township is evident to regulars who followed it from its previous location on LBI; a "something-for-everyone" menu, an "attractive", "somewhat upscale" interior and "courteous" service are pluses; N.B. hours vary by season.

Oddfellows *Cajun/Creole* | 18 | 15 | 16 | $29 |

Hoboken | 80 River St. (bet. Hudson Pl. & Newark St.) | 201-656-9009 | www.oddfellowsrest.com

Named for a New Orleans cemetery, this "laid-back" Hoboken Cajun-Creole "near the PATH" train is a "festive" foothold for "solid" "Louisiana cooking"; the "hopping bar scene", "darts and two pool tables" ensure it's a "frat-boy" "favorite", especially "on weekends", but there's always the "pleasant outdoor garden."

Old Bay Restaurant, The ⓩ *Cajun/Creole* | 19 | 17 | 18 | $35 |

New Brunswick | 61-63 Church St. (Neilson St.) | 732-246-3111 | www.oldbayrest.com

Popular with Scarlet Knights, this "reasonable", "divey" New Brunswick "watering hole" hosts live bands on weekends and satisfies those "ravin' for Cajun" with "decent" "New Orleans food" enjoyed in a "Mardi Gras atmosphere"; in short, it's a "fun", "noisy", "raucous" scene "built for a young crowd."

Old Homestead *Steak* | 26 | 24 | 24 | $72 |

Atlantic City | Borgata Hotel, Casino & Spa | 1 Borgata Way (Huron Ave.) | 609-317-1000 | www.theoldhomesteadsteakhouse.com

A "paradise for the steak lover", this Borgata Hotel, Casino & Spa chophouse is a "close copy" of the legendary NYC original, complete with "handsome" setting, "professional, polished" servers and "epic", "easily shared" portions that entail a tab that's "heavy" but for most, "worth the splurge."

Old Man Rafferty's *American* | 18 | 17 | 17 | $29 |

Hillsborough | 284 Rte. 206 (Triangle Rd.) | 908-904-9731
New Brunswick | 106 Albany St. (George St.) | 732-846-6153
Asbury Park | 541 Cookman Ave. (bet. Bangs & Mattison Aves.) | 732-774-1600
www.oldmanraffertys.com

"Save room for dessert" say supporters of this American threesome, where everything from "pub fare to gourmet delights" (plus "sinful cakes and pies") comes in "copious quantities" and at "fair prices"; just keep in mind that one diner's "franchise-esque" is another's "relaxed, friendly and hip"; P.S. "popular with the Rutgers crowd", the New Brunswick location includes a gourmet shop.

ⓩ Ombra Ⓜ *Italian* | 26 | 26 | 24 | $59 |

Atlantic City | Borgata Hotel, Casino & Spa | 1 Borgata Way (Huron Ave.) | 866-692-6742 | www.theborgata.com

This "beautiful" Italian wine bar and trattoria in the Borgata is appreciated equally for its "authentic", "rustic" fare executed by chef James Hennessy and for its "beautiful" wine-cellar ambiance, with "vaulted ceilings and wine racks along the walls" (it offers some 14,000 bottles of vino); "first class" service completes the picture.

	FOOD	DECOR	SERVICE	COST

One 53 *American*
23 | 20 | 20 | $49

Rocky Hill | 153 Washington St. (Princeton Ave.) | 609-924-1019 |
www.restaurantone53.com

"Imaginative cookery" comes "beautifully presented" in "airy, modern, inviting" environs at this "trendy" Rocky Hill New American; the "friendly" servers "seem to be enjoying themselves" despite the "cramped" quarters that really get "crowded on weekends" ("book early"); P.S. "save room for the amazing cookies on the house."

Onieal's *American*
18 | 15 | 18 | $31

Hoboken | 343 Park Ave. (4th St.) | 201-653-1492 |
www.oniealshoboken.com

You may have to "fight through the bar crowd" to find the "relatively tranquil dining area" at this "boisterous" Hoboken New American off Church Square Park; once there, regulars insist you'll find a "solid", "simple" meal delivered by some of the city's "friendliest staffers."

NEW Orange Squirrel ⊠ *American*
– | – | – | M

Bloomfield | 412 Bloomfield Ave. (bet. Hill & Orange Sts.) | 973-337-6421 |
www.theorangesquirrel.com

The setting looks like chic, Downtown Manhattan and so does the crowd at this hot Bloomfield New American entry from chef-owner Francesco Palmieri; dishes include comfort food like homemade pasta and a bar menu for grazers that has locals and travelers alike heading here to meet, eat and relax.

Orbis Bistro Ⓜ *American*
20 | 14 | 18 | $45

Upper Montclair | 128 Watchung Ave. (Fullerton Ave.) | 973-746-7641 |
www.orbisbistro.com

"Simple, honest food prepared with care and taste" – and "occasionally a stroke of genius" – is the deal at chef-owner Nancy Caballes' "intimate" Upper Montclair New American BYO; though lunch is no longer served and some find the decor "a bit too spare", for most it's "the kind of place you go back to over and over."

☑ Origin *French/Thai*
26 | 20 | 21 | $39

Basking Ridge | 25 Mountainview Blvd. (Liberty Corner Rd.) |
908-647-7781
Morristown | 10 South St. (Dehart St.) | 973-971-9933 Ⓜ
Somerville | 25 Division St. (Main St.) | 908-685-1344
www.originthai.com

"Always buzzing", this "hip", "reasonable" trio of Thai-French BYOs "wow" with a "sublime" "symphony of flavors" for meat lovers and vegetarians alike; the "upscale" ambiance may be slightly "diminished by the close tables and noise", but all's forgiven when the "friendly" staff performs "one of the most hilarious" (or "dreadful", depending on your point of view) birthday song celebrations.

Osteria Giotto *Italian*
25 | 18 | 20 | $44

Montclair | 21-23 Midland Ave. (Bloomfield Ave.) | 973-746-0111 |
www.osteria-giotto.com

"Securing a reservation" for this "casual", "fairly priced" Montclair BYO is "brutal", but "once you do", you're in for a "terrific" treat featuring "creative fresh pastas, hearty meats, flavorful fish" and other "stellar" Italian fare; the brick-and-arches interior is "overcrowded" and "crazy loud", but "dining outside in good weather" is "pleasant"; N.B. closed Tuesdays.

Ota-Ya Ⓜ Japanese   22 | 15 | 19 | $36

Lambertville | 21 Ferry St. (Union St.) | 609-397-9228 | www.ota-ya.com
This Lambertville Japanese BYO with "longevity" is admired as much for what it is not – "self-conscious, overly creative" – as for what it offers: "consistent", "high-quality" sushi and "authentic" cooked fare; the surroundings are "drab", but service is "friendly."

Ox American   23 | 19 | 23 | $44

Jersey City | 176 Newark Ave. (bet. Erie St. & Jersey Ave.) | 201-860-4000 | www.oxrestaurant.com
A "chic" "jewel" in a "transitioning neighborhood" in Jersey City, this "noisy" New American with a "minimalist" "gallery feel" "impresses" with "fabulous" fare, "unique cocktails" and "attentive service"; the portions may be "too small" for the "upscale prices", but "real deals" can be found during happy hour.

Oyako Tso's Japanese   ▽ 23 | 18 | 19 | $31

Freehold | 6 W. Main St. (bet. South & Throckmorton Sts.) | 732-866-1988 | www.oyakotsos.com
This "friendly" Japanese BYO in Downtown Freehold suits families who enjoy the "varied menu" that includes "beautifully" presented sushi and sashimi and "good" hibachi, all served in a "comfortable" setting that offers tatami, regular dining and sushi bar seating.

Pad Thai Thai   21 | 13 | 17 | $25

Highland Park | 217 Raritan Ave. (bet. 2nd & 3rd Aves.) | 732-247-9636 | www.pad-thai.com
Highland Parkers posit you "can't go wrong with any dish" off the huge menu at this "inexpensive" Thai – just remember that "'mild' is quite hot" and 'hot' is "burn-your-mouth-off" "fiery" ("your server will guide you to the right degree of spiciness" in an "efficient", possibly "abrupt" manner); the decor's "nothing to get excited about", but that doesn't prevent a daily "packed house."

Palm, The Steak   25 | 21 | 24 | $70

Atlantic City | Quarter at the Tropicana | 2801 Pacific Ave. (Iowa Ave.) | 609-344-7256 | www.thepalm.com
"Reliable as the sun rising", this "representative of the classic steak tradition" at The Quarter at the Tropicana in AC is home to "succulent", "dinosaur-sized" steaks and lobsters as well as the chain's signature celeb-caricature decor; it's "bustling" and "energetic", with "pro" service that helps soften the "big bucks" expended.

Pamir Afghan   21 | 15 | 20 | $31

Morristown | 85 Washington St. (bet. Cobb Pl. & Phoenix Ave.) | 973-605-1095 | www.pamirrestaurant.com
Named for the mountainous Central Asian region known as 'the roof of the world', this Morristown BYO scales "exotic" heights with "de-

licious Afghan" cuisine, which is "served with a smile" by "warm", "attentive" staffers; the decor is "a bit dated", but it's still "worth a visit" for a "reasonably priced" "change of pace."

Panico's *Italian*   23 | 20 | 23 | $51

New Brunswick | 103 Church St. (Neilson St.) | 732-545-6100 | www.panicosrestaurant.com

"When you want to feel taken care of", book this "elegant" Italian in New Brunswick's Theater District, which is as revered for "superior service" as it is for "delectable", "robust" fare (starring "incredible osso buco"); the tabs are "fairly expensive", but across the street there's a brick-oven pizza sibling that's "reasonable and fun as well."

Papa Razzi *Italian*   17 | 17 | 18 | $31

Paramus | Garden State Plaza | 298 Garden State Plaza (off Passaic St.) | 201-843-0990
Short Hills | Short Hills Mall | 1200 Morris Tpke. (John F. Kennedy Pkwy.) | 973-467-5544
www.paparazzitrattoria.com

"After a long day of shopping", these Garden State Plaza and Short Hills Mall outposts of the Boston-based chain are "workmanlike" options for "reasonably priced" "classic Italian" fare (there are some "unexpected" options, but best to "keep it simple"); a "fairly nice wine selection" and "friendly" staff help to keep things "lively."

⊠ Park & Orchard *Eclectic*   22 | 15 | 20 | $40

East Rutherford | 240 Hackensack St. (Union Ave.) | 201-939-9292 | www.parkandorchard.com

"You name it", it's on the "huge" Eclectic menu at this East Rutherford "crowd-pleaser" doling out "huge portions" of "reasonably priced" fare, including "great gluten-free", veggie, vegan and organic options; the "friendly" staffers trump the "cold", "cavernous", "machine shop"–like setting and are adept at suggesting pairings from the "world-class wine list", one of the "deepest" to be found in these parts.

Park Avenue
Bar & Grill ◐ *American/Pan-Latin*   ▽ 18 | 25 | 19 | $44

Union City | 3417 Park Ave. (34th St.) | 201-617-7274 | www.parkavenuebarandgrill.com

The "hot, young" crowd that frequents this Pan-Latin–New American pegs it as a real "up-and-comer", as the multilevel, "beautifully renovated building" – including a "fine-dining" room, "lovely" zebra-striped lounge, weekend dance club and "amazing" outdoor spaces (topped by a rooftop patio) – makes for one-stop evenings of eating and "partying"; if "the decor outshines the food" and the staff vacillates between "receptive" and "aloof", still it's "a pleasure to have a place" so "hip" in Union City.

Park Steakhouse, The *Seafood/Steak*   25 | 19 | 22 | $60

Park Ridge | 151 Kinderkamack Rd. (bet. Grand & Park Aves.) | 201-930-1300 | www.theparksteakhouse.com

"Fantastic steaks" "cooked perfectly", "innovative" seafood and "amazing sides and sauces" drive fans to this Park Ridge surf 'n' turf specialist that looks like it "was designed for men" ("dark wood, dim lighting"); yes, it's "expensive", but "you get what you pay for": "solid" victuals, an "extensive wine list" and "attentive service."

Passage to India Ⓜ *Indian*

21	17	19	$30

Lawrenceville | Lawrence Shopping Ctr. | 2495 Brunswick Pike (bet. Colonial Lake Dr. & Texas Ave.) | 609-637-0800 | www.mypassagetoindia.info

Partisans plug the "quality Indian" food proffered at this "unlikely" location "in a Lawrenceville shopping center", particularly the "bargain" lunch buffet with "plenty of vegetarian options" that's really worth a try"; the room, while "spacious", is "a little austere", but the staff is "efficient" and "great with kids."

Passionne Ⓜ *French*

23	18	21	$50

Montclair | 77 Walnut St. (Grove St.) | 973-233-1006 | www.restaurantpassionne.com

A chef that "delivers" on his "serious aspirations" generates passionate accolades at this "cozy", "romantic" Montclair spot where the "delicious, refined French cuisine" comes in both "traditional" and "creative" permutations; everything's "served graciously" by "true professionals", and though it's a bit pricey, the BYO policy abets in "keeping costs down."

Pasta Fresca Café and Market *American*

▽ 19	12	15	$31

Shrewsbury | Grove Shopping Ctr. | 637 Broad St. (Shadow Brook Rd.) | 732-747-5616 | www.pastafresca-nj.com

"Fresh" is the key word for the "light", "easy" American fare dished up at this casual BYO cafe with a to-go market and patio seating; since it's just "steps" from "upscale" shopping at Shrewsbury's Grove mall, it's a favorite of the "stroller-pushing" lunch crowd.

Paula at Rigoletto Ⓜ *Italian*

▽ 21	16	22	$40

Weehawken | 3706 Park Ave. (bet. 37th & 38th Sts.) | 201-422-9500 | www.paulaatrigoletto.com

The "yummy", "authentic Italian" staples and "homemade specials" will "knock your socks off" promise pros of this "pricey" Weehawken BYO where chef-owner Paula Frazier (formerly Bruce Springsteen's personal chef) and her "professional" staff offer the "family treatment"; though some appreciate the "intimate", "old-fashioned storefront's" "simple elegance", some say "don't look for atmosphere."

Penang *Malaysian/Thai*

21	16	17	$27

Lodi | 334 N. Main St. (bet. Saddle River Rd. & Terrace Ave.) | 973-779-1128
East Hanover | 200 Rte. 10 W. (bet. Ridgedale Ave. & River Rd.) | 973-887-6989
Edison | 505 Old Post Rd. (bet. Rte. 1 & Vineyard Rd.) | 732-287-3038
Princeton | Nassau Park Pavilion | 635 Nassau Park Blvd. (Brunswick Pike) | 609-897-9088
Maple Shade | 480 Rte. 38 E. (Cutler Ave.) | 856-755-0188
www.penangnj.com

"Serving exotic fare that makes taste buds sing", these Malaysian-Thai chain BYOs with "contemporary" (some say "austere") decor offer "the curious diner" "a change of pace" for "reasonable" rates; though the "big menu" can be "confusing" to first-timers , "amiable" servers can assist, especially with "customizing the level of spice" – when they're not "distracted", that is.

Perryville Inn ⓜ *American* | 23 | 23 | 22 | $57

Union Township | 167 Perryville Rd. (Frontage Rd.) | 908-730-9500 | www.theperryvilleinn.com

Admirers applaud "highly skilled" chef-owner Paul Ingenito's "mouthwatering" American fare at this "enchanting" 1813 Federal-style Hunterdon County country inn with a "cavernous" main dining room; "it's not cheap but it's worth the trip" for food that "consistently" "hits the mark", plus "no-attitude" service; P.S. there's a new "affordable" tavern menu.

Pete & Elda's ◑ *Pizza* | 22 | 9 | 18 | $22

Neptune City | 96 Woodland Ave. (Laurel Ave.) | 732-774-6010 | www.peteandeldas.com

"Pie-hungry" hordes don't mind the "huge lines" – "even on a Monday night in January" – at this Neptune "joint" that's been purveying some of "the best thin-crust pizza" "and a pint" (or a pitcher) for more than half a century; it's "tight, crowded, loud", "run-down" – and "fun"; N.B. also serving Italian entrees and pub grub.

🅩 Peter Shields Inn ⓜ *American* | 26 | 26 | 25 | $57

Cape May | 1301 Beach Ave. (Trenton Ave.) | 609-884-9090 | www.petershieldsinn.com

For many, the "superbly prepared" "gourmet" American fare at this "romantic" BYO makes it a Cape May "top contender", as do "excellent" service and a "dreamlike" setting in a "gorgeous" 1907 Georgian Revival B&B with a "beautiful" view of the ocean from the veranda; P.S. a piano player a few nights a week adds to the "relaxed" atmosphere.

🅩 P.F. Chang's China Bistro *Chinese* | 20 | 21 | 19 | $34

Hackensack | The Shops at Riverside | 50 Riverside Square (Hackensack Ave.) | 201-646-1565

West New York | 10 Port Imperial Blvd. (Riverbend Dr.) | 201-866-7790

Freehold | Freehold Raceway Mall | 3710 Rte. 9 S. (bet. Rtes. 33 & 537) | 732-308-1840

Atlantic City | Quarter at the Tropicana | 2801 Pacific Ave. (Iowa Ave.) | 609-348-4600 ◑

Princeton | Marketfair Mall | 3545 Rte. 1 (Meadow Run) | 609-799-5163

Marlton | Promenade at Sagemore | 500 Rte. 73 S. (Rte. 70) | 856-396-0818

www.pfchangs.com

"It may be a chain", but it's a "well-oiled" one and "always busy" thanks to its "tasty", "reliable", "modern" Chinese fare ("check out the lettuce wraps") served in a relatively "upscale" environment that's "loud" but "fun"; just be aware that service "varies", and the wise advise "make reservations or you will wait."

Pheasants Landing ☐ *American/Continental* 19 | 17 | 20 | $41

Hillsborough | 311 Amwell Rd. (Willow Rd.) | 908-281-1288 |
www.pheasantslanding.com

The "most interesting" fare at this American-Continental "farmhouse"
in Hillsborough is the stuff "no one else does", namely "Swiss-
influenced game" and "real fondue", plus "Austrian and German
specialties" (some gourmands deem the American supplements
just "average"); though it's "a bit pricey", "good portion sizes" and an
"attentive", "child-friendly" staff have helped to earn it "a following."

Phillips Seafood *Seafood* 19 | 18 | 18 | $47

Atlantic City | Pier at Caesars | 1 Atlantic Ocean (Arkansas Ave.) |
609-348-2273 | www.phillipsseafood.com

"A good bet when you don't want a surprise" describes this "decent"
member of a family of classic American seafood restaurants noted
for its "great" crab cakes and crab soup; its glassed-in dining room
at AC's Pier at Caesars overlooks the ocean, which helps distract
from "high" prices and "spotty" service.

☑ Piccola Italia *Italian* 27 | 23 | 24 | $48

Ocean Township | 837 W. Park Ave. (bet. Rtes. 18 & 35) | 732-493-3090 |
www.piccolaitalianj.com

"Phenomenal", "decadent" Italian fine dining at the hands of "talented" chef-owner Brian Gualtieri affords "the cachet of NYC" to a
"quiet suburban" strip mall in Monmouth County; the "exceptional
quality" extends to the "unbeatable" service", "superb" wine list,
"comfortable" atmosphere and "top-notch" bar – all affordable.

Pic-Nic *Portuguese/Spanish* ∇ 24 | 14 | 22 | $30

East Newark | 224 Grant Ave. (Central Ave.) | 973-481-3646 |
www.picnicrestaurant.com

"Authentic Portuguese cuisine" with a focus on "excellent seafood"
is the main draw at this moderately priced, casual East Newark
venue that also doles out a fair share of Spanish fare; "friendly service" helps ensure that the cozy, rustic, brick-and-tile setting remains "festive even on weekdays."

Piero's Restaurant ☐ *Italian* ∇ 21 | 16 | 21 | $43

Union Beach | 1411 Rte. 36 W. (Patterson Ave.) | 732-264-5222 |
www.pierosrestaurant.com

This "upscale" Italian is a Union Beach go-to for its "solid offerings"
of "red-sauce" and more "eclectic" fare, enhanced by a "wide selection of wines", "romantic decor" and "entertainment on weekends";
supporters say it's "worth a try."

Pietro's Coal Oven Pizzeria *Pizza* 20 | 14 | 17 | $24

Marlton | 140 Rte. 70 W. (Rte. 73) | 856-596-5500 | www.pietrospizza.com
The "crispy" thin-crust pizzas "rock" at this Marlton pizzeria/
"basic" Italian, which has two sisters in Philly; it may be "more expensive than the local slice" but it's "a winner" report advocates,
who also appreciate the "decent" wine and beer list – if not the
sometimes "sloppy" service.

	FOOD	DECOR	SERVICE	COST

Pine Tavern *American*
| | 18 | 14 | 18 | $37 |

Old Bridge | 151 Rte. 34 (Cottrell Rd.) | 732-727-5060 | www.pinetavern.net

Supporters say the "solid, reasonably priced" fare served at this Old Bridge New American "is better than" the "pedestrian", "old-fashioned-tavern" decor suggests; but a dissenting faction contends the newish owners' "updated menu" displays "less creativity" – perhaps they're "more concerned with the bar trade"?

Pino's La Forchetta *Italian*
| | ▽ 19 | 19 | 20 | $48 |

Marlboro | 448 Rte. 9 N. (Union Hill Rd.) | 732-972-6933 | www.famouspinos.com

A "friendly staff" ferries the "great" brick-oven pizza and "good" Italian offerings at this "noisy", "popular" Route 9 spot in Marlboro; while some feel "it's a bit overpriced", "plenty" of parking and frequent live entertainment add to its appeal.

Pithari Taverna *Greek*
| | 23 | 16 | 19 | $33 |

Highland Park | 28 Woodbridge Ave. (Raritan Ave.) | 732-572-0616 | www.thepithari.com

Highland Park Hellenic fans deem the "melt-in-your-mouth delicious" Greek fare served at this "casual", "reasonably priced" spot "as authentic as it gets outside of *yia yia*'s kitchen"; if the interior is pure "NJ diner", the "recently expanded" outdoor area is quite "pleasant"; P.S. it's BYO, so grab a bottle of retsina at "the deli next door."

Pizzicato *Italian*
| | ▽ 20 | 19 | 18 | $32 |

Marlton | Promenade at Sagemore | 500 Rte. 73 S. (Rte. 70) | 856-396-0880

A menu featuring "good" and even "surprising" choices served in a "pretty" setting means this Italian BYO trattoria in a Route 73 shopping center in Marlton is "always packed"; "wonderful" outdoor seating and "friendly" service make it "well worth a visit."

P.J. Whelihan's ◑ *Pub Food*
| | 16 | 16 | 17 | $24 |

Cherry Hill | 1854 E. Marlton Pike (Greentree Rd.) | 856-424-8844
Haddonfield | 700 Haddon Ave. (Ardmore Ave.) | 856-427-7888
Maple Shade | 396 S. Lenola Rd. (Kings Hwy.) | 856-234-2345
Medford Lakes | 61 Stokes Rd. (Hampshire Rd.) | 609-714-7900
Sewell | 425 Hurffville-Cross Keys Rd. (Regulus Dr.) | 856-582-7774
www.pjspub.com

These "fun, loud", "above-average" South Jersey "local bars" are "fit for families" or "a night out with friends"; expect "good" brews, "solid" pub grub ("best wings in NJ") and "many" plasma TVs for "when you're in the mood for sports."

Plan B Ⓜ *American*
| | - | - | - | M |

Asbury Park | 705 Cookman Ave. (Bond St.) | 732-807-4710 | www.restaurantplanb.com

Plan B is usually a backup idea, but this original is no one's understudy; a trendy BYO New American that's SoHo hip, with an urban vibe and adventurous food from a young chef with flair and whimsy, it's become Asbury Park's Restaurant Row's hottest place to meet and greet locals.

Plantation *American* | **20** | **20** | **18** | **$45** |

Harvey Cedars | 7908 Long Beach Blvd. (79th St.) | 609-494-8191 | www.plantationrestaurant.com

One of the "more upscale" restaurants on the lighthouse side of LBI, this "always hopping" eclectic American with a "very comfortable Key West atmosphere" can be counted on for "good", "dependable" fare year-round; P.S. "the bar area is where the fun really is."

Z Pluckemin Inn *American* | **26** | **27** | **26** | **$74** |

Bedminster | 359 Rte. 206 S. (Pluckemin Way) | 908-658-9292 | www.pluckemininn.com

Delivering an "awesome experience from start to finish", this "high-class" Bedminster New American is set in a "stunning" re-creation of a 19th-century farmhouse that has as its "centerpiece" a "unique" three-story wine tower (the "magical" sommelier can "please even the most esoteric tastes"); chef David C. Felton's "splendid" fare is conveyed by "impeccable" servers – just "make sure your charge card has plenty of room on it"; P.S. the attached Plucky bar is "action"-packed and "more affordable."

NEW Pollo Campero *Chicken* | **-** | **-** | **-** | **I** |

West New York | 6425 Bergenline Ave. (65th St.) | 201-662-6190 | www.campero.com

The Latin American spirit is evident in this West New York link in a chain specializing in chicken – marinated, breaded, rotisseried or baked; it's family-friendly too – kids play, while parents save money on dinner.

Pollo Tropical *Chicken* | **-** | **-** | **-** | **I** |

Clifton | 374 Rte. 3 W. (bet. Main Ave. & River Rd.) | 973-745-0242
NEW Little Ferry | 146 Hwy. 46 E. (Frederick St.) ●
NEW North Bergen | 3013 Kennedy Blvd. N. (32nd St.) | 201-864-4060 ●
NEW Metuchen | 77 Rte. 1 (bet. Menlo Ave. & Parsonage Rd.) | 732-494-1645 ●
www.pollotropical.com

For grilled Caribbean-style chicken, ribs or roast pork, these outposts of a Florida-and-Jersey-based chain are island-cool and "secret" mojo sauce hot; rice and beans come on the side, your family can eat cheap with value meals and if you'd rather settle for a salad, that's here too – whether you take out or eat in.

Ponzio's ● *Diner* | **18** | **13** | **18** | **$22** |

Cherry Hill | 7 Rte. 70 W. (Kings Hwy.) | 856-428-4808 | www.ponzios.com

"How do they stay so consistent?" ask dedicated denizens of this "large", "plain" Cherry Hill diner "fixture" that's "utterly dependable" if you "stick to the standards" and the "wonderful" baked goods; even though some say it's "a little long in the tooth" (at 45 years), this "classic" is still the place "to be seen" in the area.

Pop's Garage *Mexican* | ∇ **22** | **16** | **16** | **$19** |

NEW Asbury Park | Asbury Park Boardwalk | 1000 Ocean Ave. (2nd Ave.) | 732-455-3275

(continued)

Pop's Garage

Normandy Beach | 560 Rte. 35 N. (7th Ave.) | 732-830-5700 | www.kitschens.com

Listen up "true surfers, wannabes and those with wrinkles around their knees": Shore restaurateur Marilyn Schlossbach's artfully "divey" seasonal Mexican BYO with an adjacent surfer art gallery in Normandy Beach has a newer, liquor-serving sib on the boardwalk in Asbury Park (open year-round with hours that vary by season); at either, expect "not your typical *comidas* in a very beachy setting."

Pop Shop *American*   20 | 18 | 19 | $18

Collingswood | 729 Haddon Ave. (Collings Ave.) | 856-869-0111 | www.thepopshopusa.com

Kids are encouraged to wear their PJs to Collingswood's "feel-good" "soda fountain" "throwback", a "fun", "inexpensive" and "loud" "family magnet" serving burgers, shakes, sundaes and other "'50s" fare; the "brilliant" grilled cheese sandwich menu with some 30 varieties earns special raves.

Portobello *Italian*   19 | 20 | 16 | $40

Oakland | 175 Ramapo Valley Rd. (Long Hill Rd.) | 201-337-8990 | www.portobellonj.com

"Completely renovated", this freshly "lovely" Oakland Italian offers several rooms ranging from rustic farmhouse to cozy library plus a "new something-for-everyone approach" in its various menus, with more steak and raw bar options; maybe the "staff won't win any prizes", but the eats are "filling" and the "prices are on the mark."

Portofino Ⓜ *Italian*   23 | 19 | 20 | $48

Tinton Falls | 720 Tinton Ave. (Sycamore Ave.) | 732-542-6068 | www.portofino-ristorante.com

Loyalists of this Tinton Falls Italian laud its "charm" and "kitchen competence" that yields "thoughtful food combinations, well-prepared with fresh ingredients" and a "killer wine list" of some 400 labels focused on Italy; despite reports of "high prices" and "spotty service", most would return "because the food is so good."

Porto Leggero Ⓩ *Italian*   22 | 24 | 21 | $54

Jersey City | Harborside Financial Plaza 5 (Pearl St.) | 201-434-3200 | www.portoleggero.net

"Classic preparations" are juxtaposed with "gourmet" "innovations" on the "intricate" "split menu" of this Jersey City Harborside Italian where the "terrific" staff also proffers a "nice selection of wines" from The Boot and "out-of-this-world desserts"; the "gorgeous", "upscale" space studded with "stunning chandeliers" further "justifies" the "large costs" (ostensibly "geared toward business" dining).

Portuguese Manor *Portuguese*   20 | 15 | 20 | $35

Perth Amboy | 310 Elm St. (bet. Fayette & Smith Sts.) | 732-826-2233

"Where else" in Perth Amboy can you get "surf 'n' turf for [about] 30 clams?" but at this "humble" Portuguese venue whose "generous portions" of "flavorful" fare make the prices seem that much more "reasonable"; no wonder it's "always crowded" with folks enjoying the "great sangria" and "weekend entertainment."

Posillipo Ⓜ *Italian* ▽ 22 | 14 | 20 | $44

Asbury Park | 715 Second Ave. (Bond St.) | 732-774-5819 | www.posilliporestaurant.com

"Your Italian grandmother couldn't spoil you any better" than this "old-world-style" Asbury Park "classic", a "comfortable", "consistent bright light" that's been around for 80 years and is as beloved for its Wednesday night opera/classic Broadway entertainment as for its "perfect" pasta, "proper portions" and "accommodating" service.

NEW Prairie Ⓜ *American* - | - | - | M

Monmouth Beach | 36 Beach Rd. (Riverdale Ave.) | 732-263-0019

The Midwestern-style New American menu at this charming, warmly lit BYO newcomer in Monmouth Beach features the cooking of chef Kevin Morrall, who's home on the range with organic ingredients – and a mortar and pestle instead of a microwave; from cinnamon rolls at breakfast to trout at supper, it's a cost-conscious concept that's perking up interest.

Primavera *Italian* 21 | 18 | 21 | $47

West Orange | 350 Pleasant Valley Way (bet. Marmon Terrace & Sullivan Dr.) | 973-731-4779 | www.primaverawestorange.com

For a "fancy yet not stuffy night out", fans of "old-style" Italian dining spring over to this West Orange spot that's also "excellent for a business lunch"; the fare is "reliable" and "plentiful", while "well-paced" service is offered by the "professional" staffers – just make sure you "ask them the price" before ordering off the "long list of specials" (they "tend to be expensive").

Pub, The *Steak* 19 | 14 | 19 | $35

Pennsauken | Airport Circle | 7600 Kaighns Ave. (Crescent Blvd.) | 856-665-6440 | www.thepubnj.com

This 500-seat "oldie but goodie" in Pennsauken "brings back nice memories" for "loyal customers" who have been chomping down its "decent" steaks, all-you-can-eat salad bar and other Americana "at reasonable prices" for "over half a century"; however, the "barn-meets–The Tudors" surroundings have "seen better days" report those immune to the "nostalgia."

Queen Victoria
Tea Room Ⓜ *Tearoom* ▽ 23 | 23 | 22 | $22

Toms River | Victoria on Main | 600 Main St. (Broad St.) | 732-818-7580 | www.victoriaonmain.com

An "absolutely stunning" landmark Victorian B&B in Toms River provides two settings (indoors or on the porch) for two seatings (Wednesdays–Sundays) of a traditional afternoon tea of sandwiches, scones and sweets; N.B. reservations are required for the $17 prix fixe fare.

Quiet Man, The *Pub Food*

Dover | 64 E. McFarlan St. (Hudson St.) | 973-366-6333 |
www.quietmanpub.com

"Filled with pictures from its namesake movie", this "convivial" Dover address with an Irish soul is "like eating in a John Wayne museum"; the "terrific pub food" (best "enjoyed with a pint of Guinness") is "fairly priced", and "while the bar area is typically crowded" and "noisy" with "locals" and occasional live musicians, the "large side dining room" is generally, well, "quiet."

Raagini *Indian*

Mountainside | 1085 Rte. 22 E. (Mill Ln.) | 908-789-9777 |
www.raagini.com

"Regional specialties" and "innovative twists on tradition" are all the rage at this "stylish", "upscale" Mountainside Indian; a "warm, helpful staff" and "sitar music on Saturday nights" are two more "delights", and while prices are for the most part "reasonable", the "special-treat lunch buffet" is a flat-out "bargain."

Radicchio *Italian*

Ridgewood | 32 Franklin Ave. (Chestnut St.) | 201-670-7311 |
www.radicchiorestnj.com

A "seemingly endless list" of "contemporary", "outstanding specials" accompanies "wonderful" "homemade pastas" and other "Italian classics" at this "small", "crowded and noisy" Ridgewood trattoria; though some suspect service is "attentive" only if "you're 'someone'", and it's "expensive for a BYO", you can "never complain about" the "flavors."

Raimondo's *Italian*

Ship Bottom | 1101 Long Beach Blvd. (Emilie Ln.) | 609-494-5391 |
www.raimondoslbi.com

This Ship Bottom BYO is a "perennial favorite" on LBI given its "always excellent" Italian fare (the Bolognese sauce is "heaven on a plate") and "wonderful" service, which both trump its "very average setting"; "terrible acoustics" leads some to prefer this extremely "popular" place in the off-season.

⚡ Ram's Head Inn Ⓜ *American*

Galloway | 9 W. White Horse Pike (bet. Ash & Taylor Aves.) |
609-652-1700 | www.ramsheadinn.com

"Refinement and elegance live" at this "old-school" Traditional American in Galloway, part of the Knowles family of "special-occasion" establishments (The Manor, Highlawn Pavilion); "superb" cuisine, "polished" service and "beautiful" decor add up to an "awesome" place to "spend your Atlantic City winnings"; N.B. jacket suggested.

Rare, The Steak House *Steak*

Little Falls | 440 Main St. (bet. Fairfield & Zeliff Aves.) | 973-256-6699 |
www.rarestk.com

Champions of this "lively", "trendy", relatively new Little Falls chophouse call it a "truly rare" find thanks to "solid" steaks, a "comfortable" setting and "attentive" service; critics, however, deem the decor too "ordinary" and the fare and staff too "hit-or-miss" for such "expensive" tabs; P.S. check out the "great bar" for "light" bites.

Z Rat's M *French*

| | 25 | 28 | 25 | $64 |

Hamilton | Grounds for Sculpture | 16 Fairgrounds Rd. (Sculptors Way) | 609-584-7800 | www.ratsrestaurant.org

Nestled inside Hamilton's "near mystical" Grounds for Sculpture park – inspired by Monet's fabled Giverny – is this New French "gastronomic feast" with an "enchanting", "magical" ambiance that once again earns it the No. 1 rating for Decor; be sure to walk the grounds before or after your "exquisite", "expensive-but-worth-it" meal because admission is included, as is "five-star" service; P.S. the equally "amazing" cafe/lounge offers casual dining at reasonable prices.

Rattlesnake Ranch Café *Southwestern*

| | 15 | 13 | 16 | $27 |

Denville | Foodtown Shopping Ctr. | 559 E. Main St. (bet. Fox Hill Rd. & Front St.) | 973-586-3800 | www.rattlesnakeranchcafe.com

"If you're curious" about alligator, buffalo, ostrich or other "wild game" served up Southwest-style, hit this "quirky", "crowded and noisy" Denville strip-maller where the interior's "kind of tacky", the "large outdoor dining area is festive" and the Wednesday karaoke and weekend cover bands can be "enjoyable"; the "food is inconsistent" and "service could be better", but "the prices aren't bad."

Raven and the Peach *American*

| | 25 | 25 | 23 | $60 |

Fair Haven | 740 River Rd. (Fair Haven Rd.) | 732-747-4666 | www.ravenandthepeach.net

"Drop-dead gorgeous" *Casablanca* ambiance ("you'll love the palm trees") combined with "first rate", "imaginative" New American cuisine and "seamless" service has respondents ravin' about this "upscale" Fair Haven "place to be seen"; just "bring your wallet" to this "special-occasion" spot.

Raymond's *American*

| | 21 | 18 | 20 | $28 |

Montclair | 28 Church St. (bet. Fullerton Ave. & Park St.) | 973-744-9263 | www.raymondsnj.com

"Ordinary meals are unusually delicious" at this "cool", "reasonably priced" all-day New American BYO "institution" that resembles a "delightful old soda parlor" with a "hopping" patio attached; it's practically "the center of social life in Montclair", which translates to "loud noise" inside and "long lines outside", "especially on summer weekends" – but that's part of the "fun."

Ray's Little Silver Seafood ⊄ *Seafood*

| | 22 | 11 | 19 | $36 |

Little Silver | Markham Place Plaza | 125 Markham Pl. (Prospect Ave.) | 732-758-8166

"Fantastic seafood" without the "frills" is the calling card at this Little Silver "local" "favorite", a cash-only BYO storefront where "simple yet delicious" "local" fish keeps it a "sure bet" despite the "bland" interior; it's an "excellent value" "worth waiting" for (no reservations).

	FOOD	DECOR	SERVICE	COST

Rebecca's Ⓜ *Cuban* 25 | 20 | 22 | $47

Edgewater | 236 Old River Rd. (River Rd.) | 201-943-8808 |
www.rebeccasedgewater.com

At this "intimate, charming" "hideaway in Edgewater", the "addictive", "well-prepared Cuban" fare comes via a "delightful staff"; "it's a bit small, so reserve in advance", especially if you want to be seated in the "secluded backyard" (just "made for lovers"); P.S. BYO helps "reduce the expense."

Red *American* 20 | 21 | 19 | $49

Red Bank | 3 Broad St. (Front St.) | 732-741-3232 | www.rednj.com
"Disco-meets-downtown" at this "stylish", "trendy" Red Bank "hangout" boasting an "interesting", "lively" bar scene in the upstairs lounge and "reliably good" New American fare – steaks, sandwiches, sushi – on the lower level; "pricey" drinks and "a bit of attitude" accompany nightly entertainment.

Red Hot & Blue *BBQ* 19 | 13 | 17 | $27

Cherry Hill | Holiday Inn | 2175 Old Marlton Pike (Conestoga St.) |
856-665-7427 | www.redhotanblue.com

This "not bad" barbecue-and-blues chain inside the Cherry Hill Holiday Inn is a "good place to relax with the family" over "tender ribs", "reliably good" fried catfish and live blues on weekends; it's "very affordable" and has a "friendly" staff to boot.

Red's Lobster Pot *Seafood* 23 | 13 | 19 | $38

Point Pleasant Beach | 57 Inlet Dr. (B'way) | 732-295-6622 |
www.redslobsterpot.com

"Lobsters that taste like they just walked out of the ocean" are part of the draw at this seafood "shack" "on the water" in Point Pleasant Beach; the "small", "close" quarters indoors offer "more inventive cooking" while the dockside menu pleases with an "excellent" raw bar, more casual fare and the "best" view of the fishing boats.

☒ Red Square *Eclectic/Russian* 21 | 26 | 22 | $62

Atlantic City | Quarter at the Tropicana | 2801 Pacific Ave. (Iowa Ave.) |
609-344-9100 | www.chinagrillmgt.com

With "more vodka than you can shake a stick at", this opulent "Russian-themed" extravaganza in The Quarter at the Tropicana evinces "great style", including a "must-see" ice bar and "romantic private, velvet-curtained" tables; the Eclectic-Russian fare is "wonderful" too, so "prepare to be indulged . . . and to pay for it."

Redstone American Grill *American* 22 | 21 | 20 | $38

Marlton | Promenade at Sagemore | 500 Rte. 73 S. (Rte. 70) |
856-396-0332 | www.redstonegrill.com

Offering "high-end casual dining" on American grilled meats and more, this NJ outpost of a small Midwestern chain in Marlton's "upscale" "shopping mecca" boasts "consistent", "well-made" food, a "well-trained" staff and a bar that's "a huge scene"; it's "cozy" in the winter with fireside dining and "excellent" in the summer on the patio.

Redwood's *American*

16 | 16 | 17 | $34

Chester | 459 Main St. (bet. Main St. & Sentry Ln.) | 908-879-7909 |
www.redwoodsgrillandbar.com

Parents appreciate that the "simple" fare, much of which is
cooked on a wood-burning grill, is "kid-friendly" and that the
"helpful staff" gets everyone "in and out quickly" at this "casual"
Chester American; though some numbers-crunchers feel it's "a
tad overpriced" for being "uneven in quality", there are always
"lots of promos" to be found, plus "lunch prices are cheaper", and
that makes everybody happy.

Renault Winery
Gourmet Restaurant M *American*

23 | 23 | 23 | $47

Egg Harbor | 72 N. Bremen Ave. (Moss Mill Rd.) | 609-965-2111 |
www.renaultwinery.com

"Romantic with a capital 'R'" registers with respondents who enjoy the "beautiful setting" at this Egg Harbor winery that dates
back to 1864; expect "perfectly paced" multicourse New
American meals paired with "excellent" service (and wine) in a
"quiet, relaxing atmosphere"; N.B. dinner served Fridays–Saturdays,
brunch on Sundays.

Reservoir Tavern Ø M *Italian*

22 | 8 | 15 | $25

Boonton | 92 Parsippany Blvd. (Intervale Rd.) | 973-334-5708 |
www.mypizza-store.com

"Get past" the "insufferable waits" for a table "pretty much any
night" of the week, the "disorganized" service and "shabby" setting
("wear a blindfold") and you're in for "pizza to die for" and "wonderful" "Italian homestyle cooking" at this Boonton "family place";
"huge portions" and "reasonable prices" help to keep it the "great
value" it's been since 1936.

Restaurant, The M *Italian*

19 | 22 | 20 | $54

Hackensack | 160 Prospect Ave. (bet. American Legion Dr. & Beech St.) |
201-678-1100 | www.therestaurant.net

On the ground floor of a Hackensack high-rise, this "lovely", "upscale" Italian is known for attracting "a mature bar crowd looking to
make social connections" to the strains of DJ-supplied or live music;
as for the fare, past "inconsistencies" have made it seem "overpriced", but a new post-Survey chef may change that (and outdate
the above Food score).

Restaurant L *Continental*

20 | 20 | 20 | $51

Allendale | 9 Franklin Tpke. (bet. Mackay Ave. & Waibel Dr.) |
201-785-1112 | www.go2l.com

This "cozy" Continental "hideaway" in Allendale promises
"something for everyone", and although the fare "sometimes
misses", there are many dishes "worth" their "expensive" price
tags; surveyors are split on service ("fabulous" vs. "harried") and
the manly, leather-bedecked dining room ("comfortable" vs.
"cramped"), but all agree that the "bar is happening" and the "patio is
a great experience."

	FOOD	DECOR	SERVICE	COST

Restaurant Latour ✉ American

25 | 24 | 24 | $76

Hamburg | Crystal Springs Resort | 1 Wild Turkey Way
(Crystal Springs Rd.) | 973-827-0548 | www.crystalgolfresort.com

This "small and special" contemporary American with "quiet elegance" in Hamburg's Crystal Springs Resort is an "exquisite find" for its "first-class" fare by chef Michael Weisshaupt (ex The Manor), "unhurried", "white glove" service, and "awesome" wine list (3,600 labels); overall, it's "worth selling your firstborn for."

restaurant.mc American/Eclectic

23 | 21 | 19 | $56

Millburn | 57 Main St. (Millburn Ave.) | 973-921-0888 |
www.restaurantmc.com

Consulting chef David Burke's "inventive, exciting" Eclectic–New American fare, an "intelligent wine list" and a "trendy" backdrop of "mood lighting and modern architecture" make this "lively" "place" feel like a bit of "Manhattan" in Millburn; still, some call it just an "overpriced" "wannabe" with service that can seem "a bit pompous."

NEW Resto French

∇ 21 | 19 | 23 | $46

Madison | 77 Main St. (bet. Central & Greenwood Aves.) | 973-377-0066 |
www.restonj.com

The name is slang for restaurant in French, but you won't find any shortcuts at this tiny, 26-seat BYO in Downtown Madison, where diners are "overwhelmed by sublime meals prepared by the friendly and talented chef-owner", and service that can be almost "too attentive"; N.B. seats are prized, so call ahead.

Richard's ✐ Deli

21 | 10 | 19 | $20

Long Branch | 155 Brighton Ave. (Sairs Ave.) | 732-870-9133 |
www.richardsdeli.com

For "a nosh at the Shore", "go enjoy" say supporters of this "old-fashioned" "kosher-style" Long Branch deli that "knows how to make a sandwich" ("very good corned beef, pastrami") and sets down "yummy" pickles, coleslaw and macaroni salad "as soon as you are seated"; just "close your eyes" to the basic interior and "bring cash."

Richie Cecere's
Restaurant & Supperclub Italian

20 | 24 | 21 | $74

Montclair | 2 Erie St. (Label St.) | 973-746-7811 | www.richiececere.com

You'll feel "as if you were dropped into a Bogie movie" at this "swanky", "nostalgic" tri-level Montclair supper club where a "fantastic" live 18-piece "big band" with "showgirls" and Richie himself on vocals (weekends only) are presented alongside "solid" Italian eats and "excellent drinks"; though some find it a bit "corny", everyone else is thoroughly "entertained" – but because it's "really, really expensive", it's a "once-in-a-while place."

Rick's ✉ Italian

∇ 20 | 12 | 17 | $30

Lambertville | 19 S. Main St. (Ferry St.) | 609-397-0051 |
www.ricksitalian.com

This "cozy", "kitschy" "neighborhood" BYO in Lambertville is touted for its "decent" "homemade" Italian food served "with no pretenses" by a "very friendly" staff; it's a "great place to have in the neighborhood" – "loud but fun" and "good for a crowd."

Rio 22 *Brazilian* 19 | 21 | 19 | $45

Union | 2185 Rte. 22 W. (Chestnut St.) | 908-206-0060 | www.rio22.net

"Show up starving" at this "pricey" Union Brazilian where "all-you-can-eat" "meat on swords" sliced by "lovely men" is augmented by "amazing sushi" (what a "surprise!") and a "giant salad bar" that "has everything you could want – except earplugs"; indeed, it's "quite a scene", especially Thursdays–Saturdays when there's a "glitzy" "show with gyrating dancers in skimpy carnival costumes."

Risotto House *Italian* 23 | 14 | 19 | $32

Rutherford | 88 Park Ave. (bet. Pasaic Ave. & Ridge Rd.) | 201-438-5344

"If you like risotto", this "casual", "small" yet "comfortable" Rutherford BYO does a "super" job, while the rest of the Italian fare is just as "fresh and delicious"; "good portions", "fair prices" and "efficient" staffers make it a "pleasant" "neighborhood trattoria."

Ristorante da Benito *Italian* 24 | 20 | 23 | $58

Union | 222 Galloping Hill Rd. (Walton Ave.) | 908-964-5850 | www.dabenito.com

"Superlative Italian" cuisine plus "superior service" add up to one "superb" experience at this "pricey" Union "power haunt"; there's "wonderful ambiance" throughout, but for a truly "memorable" experience, "book a table in the wine room", select a bottle from the "extensive" vino collection and toast to the "romantic" evening ahead.

Ritz Seafood *Pan-Asian/Seafood* 24 | 15 | 21 | $35

Voorhees | Ritz Shopping Ctr. | 910 Haddonfield-Berlin Rd. (Laurel Oak Blvd.) | 856-566-6650 | www.ritzseafood.com

Reservations are "a must" on weekends at this "cramped" "diamond-in-the-rough" BYO storefront in Voorhees on account of chef-owner Dan Hober's "dynamite" Pan-Asian and "superb" seafood; he and co-owner Gloria Cho are "always on site" so service is "attentive", making it a "favorite" when attending a movie nearby.

⊿ River Palm Terrace *Steak* 24 | 19 | 22 | $63

Edgewater | 1416 River Rd. (Palisade Terrace) | 201-224-2013
Fair Lawn | 41-11 Rte. 4 W. (Saddle River Rd.) | 201-703-3500
Mahwah | 209 Ramapo Valley Rd. (bet. Ramapo Ave. & Rte. 17) | 201-529-1111
www.riverpalm.com

"Well-aged beef given proper respect", "fish as good as the steaks" and other "reliable" selections served in "huge portions" keep these North Jersey chophouses so "packed" that a reservation merely "grants you the right to be on the waiting list"; "each location has its own personality and service varies", but "all are loud" and offer "extensive wine lists" (have a few glasses to numb the "sticker shock").

	FOOD	DECOR	SERVICE	COST

Roberto's Dolce Vita *Italian*   22 | 19 | 21 | $44

Beach Haven | 12907 Long Beach Blvd. (bet. 129th & 130th Sts.) | 609-492-1001

They "actually take reservations" at this "little" Beach Haven BYO Italian, "a big plus" on LBI "where restaurants are packed"; it's also "a hit" for its "consistently" "well-done" traditional dishes and service "that makes you feel welcome"; N.B. hours vary by season.

Roberto's II Ⓜ *Italian*   19 | 12 | 19 | $46

Edgewater | 936 River Rd. (bet. Dempsey & Hilliard Aves.) | 201-224-2524 | www.robertos2.com

"Sinatra songs" and an "old-world" vibe await at this somewhat pricey Edgewater Italian "institution", overseen by "congenial hosts" and a "tuxedo-clad staff"; the "high-quality" "traditional" fare and "market-tuned specials" are served in "ample portions" and "brim with fresh flavors" – the decor, on the other hand, is "older than Methuselah."

Robin's Nest *American*   22 | 21 | 21 | $31

Mount Holly | 2 Washington St. (White St.) | 609-261-6149 | www.robinsnestmountholly.com

This "quaint" cafe inside a historic 1800 building with "fitting" decor is a Downtown Mount Holly "fave" for its "pleasant" slate of "inventive" "homestyle" Americana that's "served with a smile"; of particular note are Sunday brunch and "to-die-for" "homemade" desserts; P.S. "outside dining is nice" at the newly renovated bar area, with music on Fridays.

Robongi *Japanese*   24 | 16 | 20 | $30

Hoboken | 520 Washington St. (bet. 5th & 6th Sts.) | 201-222-8388

"Creative, delicious" sushi of such "high quality" it "practically swims onto your plate" lures afishionados to this Hoboken Japanese BYO that also serves "flavorful" veggie and teriyaki dishes, all at "fantastic" prices; service is "efficient", but there's one catch: the "cramped" "bait shack–esque" setting.

RoCCA *Italian*   23 | 17 | 21 | $40

Glen Rock | 203 Rock Rd. (bet. Glen Ave. & Main St.) | 201-670-4945 | www.roccaitalianrestaurant.com

"Superb, inventive" fare, "wonderful" desserts and "reasonable prices" make this Glen Rock BYO Italian rock, and while the staff may be "a little young", it's "efficient" and "eager to please"; the "tables are properly spaced", which helps on weekends when it can get "crowded and noisy"; P.S. fans on the run recommend the newly expanded Market at RoCCA for "high-level takeout."

Rod's Olde Irish Tavern *Pub Food*   18 | 15 | 18 | $31

Sea Girt | 507 Washington Blvd. (5th Ave.) | 732-449-2020 | www.rodstavern.com

This "favorite" of both Sea Girt "locals" and the "summer crowd" is a "family-friendly" "Shore staple" with "reliable" pub fare and "lots of Irish hospitality"; it "fits like a comfortable sweater" – "it hasn't changed in 20 years", including its "friendly" "longtime" staff – and the "price" is right too; P.S. "expect a wait" in summer.

Rod's Steak & Seafood Grille *Seafood/Steak* 22 | 23 | 22 | $52

Morristown | Madison Hotel | 1 Convent Rd. (Madison Ave.) | 973-539-6666 | www.rodssteak.com

Whether in the "elegant" main dining room or in one of the two restored antique Pullman cars, "dining is a wonderful experience" at this "romantic" (though "pricey") Morristown hotel surf 'n' turf specialist where "old-school glamour" reigns; you "can't go wrong with any selection" on the menu, which includes an "incredible" Sunday brunch, and the "professional" staff delivers "top-notch service."

Rooney's Oceanfront *Seafood* 18 | 21 | 18 | $47

Long Branch | 100 Ocean Ave. N. (Cooper Ave.) | 732-870-1200 | www.rooneysocean.com

This "popular" Long Branch seafooder's "killer location" "overlooking" the Atlantic Ocean is "spectacular", whether dining "indoors, outdoors, or halfway in between", but for many, the "decent", "somewhat pricey" food "doesn't match the view" (though there's a "great" raw bar); no matter, it's a "sentimental" favorite that "seems to get better with age."

Roots Steakhouse *Steak* 25 | 24 | 24 | $69

Summit | 401 Springfield Ave. (Maple St.) | 908-273-0027 | www.rootssteakhouse.com

Housed in a "beautiful" "turn-of-the-century bank building", this Summit chophouse is a "stylish beef-lovers' lair" where "scrumptious" steaks and "top-shelf" seafood are served in a "clubby", "upscale" setting; "impeccable" service is another plus, but the "eye-popping" prices limit it to "special nights out", unless you have a "handsome expense account."

Rosa Luca's Italian Bistro Ⓜ *Italian* ▽ 24 | 18 | 20 | $49

Asbury | 1114 Rte. 173 (bet. Mine & Stortz Rds.) | 908-238-0018 | www.rosalucas.com

"A real find" "out in the boondocks" of Hunterdon County, this "small and simple" Italian in Asbury purveys "incredible" homemade pastas and sauces with ingredients from owners Jill and Carmine Castaldo's garden; service that "treats you like family" and a "great" martini list are more reasons that it's "worth the trip."

Rosemary and Sage Ⓢ Ⓜ *American* 26 | 19 | 24 | $52

Riverdale | 26 Hamburg Tpke. (bet. Haycock & Morris Aves.) | 973-616-0606 | www.rosemaryandsage.com

Run by a "dedicated family", this "hidden gem" in Riverdale showcases chef/co-owner Brooks Nicklas' "imaginative" New American seasonal menus that are "always on the mark"; "engaging, informed" service adds to the experience, and though it's "a bit crowded at times", the "cozy", "unpretentious surroundings" are usually "quiet" enough so that "you can actually have a conversation"; N.B. open Wednesdays–Saturdays for dinner only.

	FOOD	DECOR	SERVICE	COST

Rosie's Trattoria *Italian* | 21 | 19 | 22 | $38 |

Randolph | 1181 Sussex Tpke. (Brookside Rd.) | 973-895-3434 |
www.rosiestrattoria.com

The "friendly staff makes you feel at home" at this Randolph trattoria where "classic" Southern Italian dishes and "interesting specials" are "prepared well and reasonably priced"; the "cozy" bar makes it a popular "local gathering spot", and while some fashionistas think the "decor needs updating", others take a rosier view, noting the "outdoor deck is great in warm weather."

Royal Warsaw ●Ⓜ *Polish* | 23 | 19 | 21 | $33 |

Elmwood Park | 871 River Dr. (bet. Garden Dr. & Roosevelt Ave.) |
201-794-9277 | www.royalwarsaw.com

It's like "dining in Poland on grandma's cooking" at this Elmwood Park Pole where "reasonably priced" potato pancakes, pickle soup and pierogi aplenty are the "ultimate in comfort food", which can be washed down with an "excellent imported beer selection"; "fantastic" service from the Polish (and English) -speaking staff and a "terrific" bar pouring "great drink specials" also help make it one of the "best values in the state" according to fans.

⛋ Ruth's Chris Steak House *Steak* | 25 | 22 | 23 | $64 |

Weehawken | Lincoln Harbor | 1000 Harbor Blvd. (19th St.) | 201-863-5100
Parsippany | Hilton Hotel | 1 Hilton Ct. (Campus Dr.) | 973-889-1400
Atlantic City | The Walk | 2020 Atlantic Ave. (bet. Arkansas &
Michigan Aves.) | 609-344-5833
NEW Princeton | Forrestal Village Shopping Ctr. | 2 Village Blvd.
(College Rd.) | 609-452-0041
www.ruthschris.com

It "might be a chain", but the "sizzling" butter-topped steaks and "white-linen" service at these "classic" chophouses offer "pure bliss" to carnivores who also appreciate the "huge" sides – and say the similarly sized tabs are "worth the splurge"; P.S. decor is "polished, if standardized", but the window seats at the Weehawken location offer a "great" view of NYC.

Rutt's Hut ⊘ *Hot Dogs* | 21 | 6 | 14 | $12 |

Clifton | 417 River Rd. (bet. Delawanna Ave. & Peekay Dr.) | 973-779-8615

Fans of this "legendary" 81-year-old Clifton landmark relish the "abso-frickin-amazing" hot dogs known as "rippers" that are "deep fried until they split" and best taken with "relish to-die-for" and "excellent", "greasy" onion rings; while the "no-frills" dining room has "table service and blue-plate specials", regulars prefer "standing up at a counter" and "sinking into a '50s state of mind."

Sabor *Nuevo Latino* | 22 | 21 | 19 | $46 |

Hawthorne | 1060 Goffle Rd. (Rte. 208) | 973-238-0800 | Ⓢ
North Bergen | 8809 River Rd. (bet. Churchill & Old River Rds.) |
201-943-6366
www.saborlatinbistro.com

The scene's "alive and jumping" at these "hot, hot, hot" Nuevo Latino twins in Hawthorne and North Bergen, where "beautiful people" savor "decadent cocktails" and "sophisticated" fusion fare served up by a "well-informed" staff; a few find the *alimento* "overpriced" and say the "dark", "noisy" setting is suited "more for dancing than eating", but all agree it's "very romantic and sexy."

☒ Saddle River Inn ⑤Ⓜ *American/French* | 28 | 26 | 26 | $65 |

Saddle River | 2 Barnstable Ct. (Saddle River Rd.) | 201-825-4016 | www.saddleriverinn.com

"Phenomenal" French-American cuisine, "first-class" service and a "romantic", "casually elegant" setting in a restored 19th-century barn make this Saddle River BYO a "treasure"; though some think the menu could "vary a bit more" and complain that "if you aren't a regular, you're invisible", most agree this "charming" spot is "as close to heaven as it gets in NJ" – but like heaven, it's tough to get into ("good luck getting a reservation").

Saffron Indian Cuisine *Indian* | 22 | 20 | 21 | $30 |

East Hanover | 249 Rte. 10 (New Murray Rd.) | 973-599-0700 | www.saffronnj.com

Enthusiasts exhort "don't be fooled by the exterior" of this "solid" East Hanover strip-mall Indian BYO, for the "authentic" fare, "friendly, attentive" service and "comfortable" ambiance in the "traditional"-looking space make for a "soothing and tasty experience"; what's more, the "extensive, satisfying" lunch buffet is a "steal."

☒ Sagami Ⓜ *Japanese* | 27 | 15 | 22 | $36 |

Collingswood | 37 Crescent Blvd. (bet. Haddon & Park Aves.) | 856-854-9773

For devotees of this long-lived Collingswood BYO – aka "sushi heaven in South Jersey" – there is "no place better" for "seriously authentic" rolls, sashimi and even tempura – "except for going to Japan"; the "low-ceilinged" "subpar" decor and "cramped" waiting area where "crowds" converge are offset by "friendly" service.

Sage Ⓜ⇄ *Mediterranean* | 24 | 17 | 22 | $45 |

Ventnor | 5206 Atlantic Ave. (Weymouth Ave.) | 609-823-2110

"Sagacious diners" applaud this "vibrant" addition to the Ventnor scene where chef-owner Lisa Savage's "imaginative" Mediterranean fare employs the "finest" ingredients – and keeps her BYO "crowded"– though the chef's specialties can be purchased at an adjacent market, which she also owns; N.B. pros "highly recommend calling in advance to reserve" in the summer.

Sakura-Bana Ⓜ *Japanese* | 25 | 16 | 21 | $38 |

Ridgewood | 43 Franklin Ave. (bet. Chestnut & Oak Sts.) | 201-447-6525 | www.sakurabana.com

"Outstanding" sushi and sashimi and "skillfully prepared" tempura entice foodies to overlook "long waits" at this "sometimes noisy" Ridgewood Japanese BYO; though "the quality and selection come at a pretty steep price", a "quirky", "friendly" staff and newly renovated quarters help cushion the cost.

| | FOOD | DECOR | SERVICE | COST |

Sakura Spring *Chinese/Japanese* ▽ 22 | 21 | 21 | $30

Cherry Hill | 1871 Marlton Pike E. (Greentree Rd.) | 856-489-8018 | www.sakuraspring.com

Among the numerous restaurants "hidden away in strip malls" in Cherry Hill, this BYO "gem" stands out for the "unique" mix of "consistently" executed Japanese and Chinese offerings on its "expansive" menu and for its "pleasant" service; it's also a "great place for lunch" thanks to daily specials.

Sallee Tee's Grille *American/Eclectic* 19 | 17 | 18 | $36

Monmouth Beach | 33 West St. (Channel Dr.) | 732-870-8999 | www.salleeteesgrille.com

Expect "NY-style deli by day" (corned beef, turkey, roast beef triple-deckers and such) and by night, the works – sushi, salads, steaks, seafood, pasta; "every mood is engaged" at this "loud", "fun" and "comfortable" American-Eclectic "institution" "right on the water" at the Channel Club Marina in Monmouth Beach; "it's all good", and it's served up "friendly and quick."

Sally Ling *Chinese* 18 | 14 | 17 | $30

Fort Lee | 1636 Palisade Ave. (bet. Main & Whiteman Sts.) | 201-346-1282 | www.sallylingsonline.com

Fans of this "attractive" Fort Lee strip-mall Chinese claim its "upscale" cuisine "never fails to hit the spot" and praise the lunch and early-bird specials as "fabulous"; however, a "disappointed" contingent cites "slightly standoffish" service and "Americanized" fare that seems "overpriced for what you get."

Salt Creek Grille *American* 19 | 23 | 20 | $45

Rumson | 4 Bingham Ave. (River Rd.) | 732-933-9272
Princeton | Forrestal Village Shopping Ctr. | 1 Rockingham Row (bet. Lionsgate Dr. & Village Blvd.) | 609-419-4200
www.saltcreekgrille.com

The "relaxing" Craftsman-style architecture at this Traditional American duo with a "solid" "meat lover's menu" conjures "a lodge in Aspen or California" to those who also enjoy the "cool", "high-octane" happy-hour scene; while Rumson features a "picturesque" view of the Navesink River and an all-you-can-eat Sunday brunch, the larger Princeton locale offers jazz with its Sunday fixings.

Salt Water Beach Café *American* ▽ 18 | 21 | 17 | $41

Asbury Park | 1200 Ocean Ave. (bet. 4th & 5th Aves.) | 732-774-1400 | www.saltwaterbeachcafenj.com

"Location, location, location" in a "fantastic" oceanside setting makes Shore restaurateur Tim McLoone's "great newcomer" to the Asbury Park boardwalk a "beautiful" go-to; a circular dining room with wraparound windows is where casual, "pricey" New American vittles ("truffled Parmesan fries – oh my!") are served, while upstairs is the slightly more upscale Tim McLoone's Supper Club; N.B. a change of chef post-Survey may outdate the above Food score.

	FOOD	DECOR	SERVICE	COST

Samdan *Turkish* — 23 | 16 | 19 | $35

Cresskill | 178 Piermont Rd. (Union Ave.) | 201-816-7343 |
www.samdanrestaurant.com

The grilled seafood and meats are "outstanding" and come in "easy-to-share large portions" at this "welcoming", "value"-oriented Cresskill Turk that's the most "fun with a group" or "the entire family"; a complete post-Survey renovation (new furniture, new bar) should dispel thoughts about "uninspiring" decor.

Sammy's Ye Old Cider Mill *Steak* — 21 | 9 | 16 | $63

Mendham | 353 Mendham Rd. W. (Oak Knoll Rd.) | 973-543-7675 |
www.sammyscidermill.com

There's "no sign out front" and the dining room "resembles a VFW hall", but this "peerless" Mendham "former speakeasy", known for its "terrific", "pricey" steak and lobster, is "packed almost every night"; you "order on arrival, then wait downstairs at the bar/game room" – it's a "unique experience" that folks either "love or hate."

San Remo *Italian* — 23 | 16 | 23 | $39

Shrewsbury | 37 E. Newman Springs Rd. (Rte. 35) | 732-345-8200 |
www.sanremoitaliana.com

"It's worth finding" this "local favorite", a Shrewsbury BYO Italian that's "not your usual", given its "outstanding menu" and "excellent" service; the seasoned say that though the "outside" could use a "facelift" the "inside is charming"; N.B. make sure you have a rezzie.

Sanzari's New Bridge Inn *Italian* — 20 | 20 | 20 | $55

New Milford | 105 Old New Bridge Rd. (New Bridge Rd.) | 201-692-7700 |
www.sanzarisnewbridgeinn.com

Near the spot where Washington retreated across the Hackensack, this "quiet", "spacious" New Milford Italian (not far from the Shops at Riverside) is just "the ticket for traditionalists"; the "attentive" staff won't "rush [you] out the door", and though the "decent", "predictable" fare "can be steep", more budget-friendly dishes have been added to the menu lately.

Sapori *Italian* — ∇ 24 | 18 | 23 | $39

Collingswood | 601 Haddon Ave. (Harvard Ave.) | 856-858-2288 |
www.sapori.info

The Southern Italian fare at this "wonderful" Collingswood BYO manages to be "truly authentic" yet "full of surprises" at the same time; the secret is owner-chef Franco Lombardo, a Palermo native who designed and built the "cozy", rustic, stone-walled-trattoria interior himself and is seemingly "always there" to "greet you like family" – as does the "friendly" staff; N.B. closed Tuesdays.

SAWA Steakhouse & Sushi Bar *Japanese* — 22 | 21 | 20 | $38

Eatontown | 42 Rte. 36 (Rte. 35) | 732-544-8885
Long Branch | Pier Vill. | 68 Ocean Ave. (Centennial Dr.) | 732-229-0600
www.sawasteakhouse.com

A "lively atmosphere" prevails at these two "family-friendly" Japanese houses offering "excellent" sushi and "inventive" sashimi, as well as grilled fare that's "priced right" from "entertaining" hibachi tables; the giant fish tanks are "worth a visit" to Eatontown, whereas the Long Branch spot is more "upscale" and, some say, "more relaxing."

Z Scalini Fedeli ⧄ *Italian* `27` `25` `26` `$73`
Chatham | 63 Main St. (bet. Parrott Mill Rd. & Tallmadge Ave.) | 973-701-9200 | www.scalinifedeli.com
"Prepare to be transported" to "gastronomy heaven" via Michael Cetrulo's "exceptional" Chatham Italian, offering a $54 four-course prix fixe at dinner with "loads of options" (lunch is à la carte); though a few claim "the chef is spread too thin" and find his flagship "overpriced" and "stuffy", given the "impeccable" cuisine, "elegant atmosphere" and "fantastic" staff, the faithful majority declares it a "first-class operation."

Scarborough Fair Ⓜ *American* `21` `23` `20` `$43`
Sea Girt | 1414 Meetinghouse Rd. (Rte. 35) | 732-223-6658 | www.scarboroughfairrestaurant.com
The "enchanting" decor and layout of the "beautiful" circa-1900 wood-and-brick farmhouse this Sea Girt New American calls home "make you feel like you're in a fairy tale"; "relax and forget about the outside world" in "romantic" nooks along the staircase, while a "friendly" staff delivers "unique" and "pleasant" dishes from an "extensive seasonal menu."

Z SeaBlue *Seafood* `27` `26` `26` `$77`
Atlantic City | Borgata Hotel, Casino & Spa | 1 Borgata Way (Huron Ave.) | 609-317-8220 | www.theborgata.com
Michael Mina is "the man", and his "beautiful" Tihany-designed AC seafooder in the Borgata "has few equals", what with its "amazing" "world-class" fare ("art that dances in your mouth"), "superb" wine list, "well-versed", "friendly" staff and "soothing" multiple-screened virtual aquarium; although a few carp over the "noise from the casino floor", to most it's a "magical eating experience" and "so worth" the "pricey" tabs.

Sea Shack ⧄ *Seafood* `21` `17` `21` `$52`
Hackensack | 293 Polifly Rd. (Rte. 17) | 201-489-7232 | www.seashack.com
It's been around "forever, and deservedly so" declare devotees of this "expensive" Hackensack seafooder that remains a "local favorite" after more than 30 years thanks to its "fresh" fish and "old-school" service; "dated" decor and "long waits on weekends" are "turnoffs" for some but all appreciate that its "calm atmosphere" ensures "you can always hear your companions."

Segovia *Portuguese/Spanish* `22` `14` `20` `$41`
Moonachie | 150 Moonachie Rd. (Garden St.) | 201-641-4266 | www.segoviarestaurant.com
The portions are "huge, prices aren't" at this "loud and crowded" Moonachie Iberian that's a "favorite" for seafood and steaks "before any game at the stadium or arena"; maybe the "traditional" decor

"needs to be updated" and the "no-reservations" policy (except for six or more any day but Saturday) means there "can be a wait", but once you're in you can count on "attentive" service.

Senorita's Mexican Grill *Mexican*   20 | 18 | 18 | $28

Bloomfield | 285 Glenwood Ave. (Conger St.) | 973-743-0099 | www.senoritasmexicangrill.com

"Good, inexpensive" fare that "beats any chain hands down" has fans cheering "*olé!*" for this "colorful" Bloomfield Mexican that also boasts "responsive" service and "cozy, saucy" decor ; its "wide assortment of options outside the usual combo picks" includes "lots of veggies and fish", and the margaritas are "potent" – but just "don't come here for a quiet meal."

Z Serenade *French*   28 | 25 | 26 | $72

Chatham | 6 Roosevelt Ave. (Main St.) | 973-701-0303 | www.restaurantserenade.com

Paeans resound for James Laird and Nancy Sheridan Laird's "serene oasis" in Chatham, where the "exceptional" French cuisine with a locally grown bent is "smart and sexy" and the ambiance "refined" – though you may need "a chest of gold bullion to settle the bill"; some say the "excellent" staff's occasional "haughty" attitude can strike a flat note, but they're drowned out by the chorus of devotees singing "top shelf in every way"; N.B. jacket suggested.

Sergeantsville Inn, The M *American*   23 | 25 | 23 | $49

Sergeantsville | 601 Rosemont-Ringoes Rd. (Rtes. 523 & 604) | 609-397-3700 | www.sergeantsvilleinn.com

It's a "real treat" to drive through "bucolic" Hunterdon County to this "wonderfully" restored 18th-century stone inn in "quaint" Sergeantsville, where "delicious" American fare is served by an "attentive, but not fussy" staff in one of its "charming", "romantic" fireplace-equipped rooms; carnivores crow "if you like game, this is the place", though the menus – including the "more informal" one offered in the "warming" tavern – include "seafood and vegetarian options" too.

Settebello Cafe Z *Italian*   21 | 18 | 20 | $41

Morristown | 2 Cattano Ave. (Speedwell Ave.) | 973-267-3355 | www.settebellocafe.com

"Always busy but always welcoming", this "charming", "dependable" Italian BYO "tucked away on a side street in Downtown Morristown" is appreciated for its "wonderful" homemade pastas dressed with "sauce like grandma used to make"; its "popularity" adds up to "noisy, crowded" conditions at prime times, but there's always "the patio."

Seven Hills of Istanbul *Turkish*   22 | 17 | 19 | $34

Highland Park | 441 Raritan Ave. (5th Ave.) | 732-777-9711 | www.7hillsofistanbul.com

"Terrific flavors" are in store at this "reliable" Highland Park Turkish BYO "staple", where the "grilled meats", "trimmings and salads" are "authentic", "tasty and satisfying"; it takes "no reservations for parties less than six", meaning "waits can be long on busy weekend nights", but "quality and charm" make it "well worth" it for most.

	FOOD	DECOR	SERVICE	COST

Shanghai Jazz Ⓜ *Chinese*
21 | **20** | **22** | **$44**

Madison | 24 Main St. (Green Village Rd.) | 973-822-2899 | www.shanghaijazz.com

"Cool" live jazz goes down well with "innovative interpretations of Chinese classics" at this "one-of-a-kind" Madison supper club beloved for its "lively cosmopolitan vibe"; some find it "expensive", but there's "no cover" for the nightly entertainment and "the service keeps the beat" too; N.B. don't miss the bento box lunch specials (Tuesday–Thursday) as well as Friday's all-you-can-eat lunch buffet.

Ship Inn, The *Pub Food*
15 | **17** | **17** | **$29**

Milford | 61 Bridge St. (Rte. 519) | 908-995-0188 | www.shipinn.com

"Hang and have a pint" of one of the "tasty" beers brewed on-site at this "relaxed" "British-style brewpub" in Milford near the Delaware River, dishing up "filling", "traditional English" tavern fare in a "homey" setting with a nautical theme; although an increased use of organic ingredients will please green and health-conscious diners, some sniff the victuals "could be better."

Shipwreck Grill *American*
25 | **18** | **20** | **$50**

Brielle | 720 Ashley Ave. (Higgins Ave.) | 732-292-9380 | www.shipwreckgrill.com

A "step above the usual Shore seafood" spots, this "place to be seen" in Brielle offers an "ambitious", "eye-catching" menu of "wonderful" "gourmet" New American fin fare and "excellent grill items"; while some describe it as an "expensive" "noise box" (especially the "frenetic" bar scene) with "less-than-impressive" decor and "iffy" service, others insist the "top-notch" cuisine more than compensates.

Shogun *Japanese/Steak*
22 | **20** | **21** | **$36**

East Brunswick | Center 18 Mall | 1020 Rte. 18 N. (bet. Gunia St. & Hillsdale Rd.) | 732-390-1922 | www.shogun18.net

Green Brook | 166 Rte. 22 (Washington Ave.) | 732-968-3330 | www.shogun22.net

Kendall Park | 3376 Rte. 27 (Sand Hills Rd.) | 732-422-1117 | www.shogun27.com

Toms River Township | Bey Lea Golf Course | 1536 N. Bay Ave. (Oak Ave.) | 732-286-9888 | www.shogunbeylea.com

Shogun Legends *Japanese/Steak*

Wall | 1969 Rte. 34 S. (Allenwood Rd.) | 732-449-6696 | www.shogunlegends.com

"Kids love the cook-in-front-of-you" experience at these "entertaining" Japanese hibachi specialists that also offer "unusual and delicious sushi"; a few find some of the offerings kinda "pricey" and the decor varies with the location, but the trademark "friendly" service ensures a "fun atmosphere" at whichever branch you visit.

Shumi Ⓜ *Japanese*
25 | **13** | **21** | **$44**

Somerville | 30 S. Doughty Ave. (Veterans Memorial Dr.) | 908-526-8596 | www.shumirestaurant.com

"Exceptional" rolls are "your reward" for tracking down this "hard-to-find" Somerville Japanese BYO, where "friendly sushi master" Ike has a "genius" touch with "warm rice and cool fish"; "delightful" service "makes up" for what it "lacks in decor", and though "prices aren't cheap – quality never is."

Siam Ⓜ⇪ *Thai*
20 | 12 | 18 | $26

Lambertville | 61 N. Main St. (bet. Coryell & York Sts.) | 609-397-8128
"Inexpensive" "down-home" Thai keeps this "little" cash-only stalwart in Lambertville "busy, busy, busy", even though some complain the "ambiance leaves a lot to be desired" and the service vacillates between "friendly" and "crotchety"; still, thanks to the "tasty" fare and a BYO policy that "helps keep the tab down", it "remains a must-go" for many.

Siam Garden *Thai*
24 | 20 | 21 | $35

Red Bank | The Galleria | 2 Bridge Ave. (Front St.) | 732-224-1233 |
www.siamgardenrestaurant.com
An "extensive" menu of "deliciously distinctive", "beautifully presented" Thai cuisine, including "wonderful curry dishes" and "superb whole fish", makes this "popular" BYO in Red Bank's Galleria a "keeper" for many; "helpful" service and "colorful, peaceful" decor featuring antiques, silks and woodcarvings from Thailand enhance its status as "an all-around pleasure."

Silver Spring Farm Ⓜ *French*
▽ 26 | 21 | 24 | $53

Flanders | 60 Flanders Drakestown Rd. (bet. Old Township Rd. & Theresa Dr.) | 973-584-0202 | www.silverspringfarm.com
"Off the beaten path" in Flanders, this "longtime favorite" set in a "cozy" circa-1870 farmhouse provides "very French, very creamy, very rich" fare "as authentic as it gets", presented with "no haughty attitude"; some say the "charming" "old-world" decor may "need a little updating", but to most the overall experience is a "romantic step back in time"; N.B. open Wednesday–Sunday for dinner only.

Simply Radishing Ⓩ *American*
▽ 19 | 8 | 15 | $21

Lawrenceville | Lawrence Shopping Ctr. | 2495 Brunswick Pike/Rte. 1 (bet. Colonial Lake Dr. & Texas Ave.) | 609-882-3760 |
www.simplyradishing.com
"Dependable salads and sandwiches" and "feel-good" American dishes are all "well prepared" at this Lawrenceville BYO, which also features a popular "fresh bread bar"; the "ambiance isn't much" and service can be "inattentive" according to critics, who conclude that while it may be a "good value", it's "not a dining experience."

Sirena *Italian*
22 | 25 | 18 | $54

Long Branch | Pier Vill. | 27 Ocean Ave. (Cooper Ave.) | 732-222-1119 |
www.sirenaristorante.com
"At last, a good choice with an ocean view" cheer fans of this Pier Village Italian in Long Branch (*fratello* of Chatham's Scalini Fedeli) serving "consistently good", "upscale" cuisine in "beautiful" environs with "fantastic" vistas and outdoor dining; though the vibe is "casual", it's "not for the poor of wallet" warn budget-watchers, while others wish the "slow" and "too-cool-for-school" service would "catch up with the rest of the restaurant."

| | FOOD | DECOR | SERVICE | COST |

Sirin *Thai* ▽ 24 | 22 | 22 | $36

Morristown | 3 Pine St. (South St.) | 973-993-9122 |
www.sirinthairestaurant.com

This Morristown BYO Thai is just right for "an adventure into delicious ethnic food", purveying "traditional" as well as "interesting flavors" ("outstanding duck"); the husband (chef) and wife (hostess) team are "very cordial", and "attentive service" comes with the "intimate surroundings."

Siri's Thai French Cuisine *French/Thai* 24 | 20 | 22 | $38

Cherry Hill | 2117 Rte. 70 W. (bet. Haddonfield Rd. & Penn Ave.) |
856-663-6781 | www.siris-nj.com

"Siri-ously fine" and "interesting" fare that's a "wondrous" "balance" of French and Thai with a dash of "doting" service makes "every meal special" at this 15-year-old "white-tablecloth" "delight" in a strip mall off busy Route 70 in Cherry Hill; P.S. "it's an excellent value because it's BYO."

Sister Sue's *Caribbean* ▽ 21 | 13 | 16 | $24

Asbury Park | 311 Bond St. (Mattison Ave.) | 732-502-8383 |
www.sistersuesroti.com

A "treat for jaded palates", this small, family-run Asbury Park BYO specializes in Trinidadian and island fare like oxtail stew and curried goat, with plenty of choices for vegetarians and vegans too; "service with the widest of smiles" "will keep you coming back", even if it is "slow."

Skylark Fine Diner & Lounge ● *American* 20 | 20 | 19 | $26

Edison | 17 Wooding Ave. (bet. Old Post Rd. & Rte. 1) | 732-777-7878 |
www.skylarkdiner.com

Comfort food with "upscale gourmet" leanings ensures this "sophisticated" Edison New American with a "'50s" "retro-future" look is "not your typical diner"; "friendly" service and a general "fun and exciting" feel are other endearments, not to mention the attached "old-fashioned cocktail lounge" mixing "interesting drinks" to the tune of a DJ (Wednesday–Saturday nights).

Smithville Inn *American* 21 | 23 | 21 | $41

Smithville | 1 N. New York Rd. (Old New York Rd.) | 609-652-7777 |
www.smithvilleinn.com

This "beautifully appointed" 1787 inn with a "Colonial feel" is nestled among the shops at Historic Smithville and is chock-full of "cozy" warmth from six fireplaces and a "very friendly staff"; while the "consistently good" Traditional American fare is "nothing fancy", that's "ok" with longtime visitors.

Smoke Chophouse & Cigar Emporium *Seafood/Steak* 23 | 19 | 21 | $65

Englewood | 36 Engle St. (Palisade Ave.) | 201-541-8530 |
www.smokechophouse.com

"Red meat, drinks and a cigar" mean "life is good" at this "sophisticated", "pricey" Englewood surf 'n' turfer that's "one of the last places in NJ where you can have a stogie with your meal" (though the downstairs room is "smoke-free"); "top-quality" steaks and "snappy service" in "clubby" environs have "masculine" types calling it "great for a guy's night out."

	FOOD	DECOR	SERVICE	COST

Sogno *Italian*

22	18	20	$44

Red Bank | 69 Broad St. (bet. Monmouth & Wallace Sts.) | 732-747-6969 | www.sognoredbank.com

"Delicious" Italian food prepared "with a wonderful flair" trumps the "tight quarters" and "terrible acoustics" at this "popular" BYO in Red Bank – plus the owner, host and servers are all "friendly", so even though the decor is "nothing special", it conjures a "seductive atmosphere when not crowded."

SoHo on George *American*

23	22	21	$49

New Brunswick | 335 George St. (bet. Bayard & Liberty Sts.) | 732-296-0533 | www.sohoongeorge.com

"Convenient to the Theater District", this "metro-style" New Brunswick New American lets you "order light fare or a full meal" in "chic, casual, unpretentious" environs – and the "big bar" also has its own menu; though it can get "a bit loud" and "pricey", the "interesting" cuisine is "top-notch" and is delivered by a "friendly" crew.

Soho 33 *Eclectic*

19	15	19	$33

Madison | 33 Main St. (bet. Green Village Rd. & Waverly Pl.) | 973-822-2600 | www.soho33.com

When you "don't want fancy", just "casual" dining with "a bit of kitchen flair", head for this Eclectic Madison BYO that some consider "better for lunch" than dinner – though the "bar scene" is an evening draw; maybe it's "nothing to jump up and down about", but the "pricing is good" and the "outdoor dining in summer is a treat."

Solaia Restaurant *Italian*

18	19	18	$55

Englewood | 22 N. Van Brunt St. (Palisade Ave.) | 201-871-7155 | www.solaiarestaurant.com

"Right next to Bergen PAC", this "trendy" Englewood Italian bustles with theatergoers and "Euro-chic" types supping on "upscale" seafood-centric cuisine in spacious quarters complete with a "nice bar" and a "pleasant outdoor area"; however, those who feel the overall package "should be better" given the "pricey" tab declare the "convenient" location as its prime virtue.

Solari's ⊠ *Italian*

20	17	21	$46

Hackensack | 61 River St. (Bridge St.) | 201-487-1969 | www.solarisrestaurant.com

Matching "traditional" Southern Italian fare with "old-world" service, this "pricey" "third-generation" Hackensack "throwback" is "the trough and watering hole of most of the movers and shakers of Bergen County", particularly at lunch; the "active bar" and live big-band music and dancing on weekends and selected nights keep it "swinging" in the evenings.

| | FOOD | DECOR | SERVICE | COST |

Solo Bella *Italian* ▽ 21 | 19 | 21 | $30
Jackson | 426 Chandler Rd. (Jackson Mills Rd.) | 732-961-0951 | www.solobella.com

There is a Bella in the kitchen here, and "she goes out of her way" to provide "big portions" of "well-prepared", "Brooklyn-style" Italian meals at her Jackson BYO, which also pleases with its "good" service and "reasonable" prices.

So Moon Nan Jip ● *Korean* ▽ 25 | 12 | 16 | $32
Palisades Park | 238 Broad Ave. (Brinkerhoff Ave.) | 201-944-3998

For "true Korean BBQ, including the coals placed in the middle of the table", carnivores crowd into this "noisy" Palisades Park practitioner that also slices sushi and sashimi; the "clientele is mostly Korean", but the "staff is helpful" with novices as well – though in any language, some say the "prices can add up fast."

Somsak *Thai* ▽ 23 | 14 | 23 | $24
Voorhees | Echo Shops | 200 White Horse Rd. (bet. Lucas Ln. & Burnt Mill Rd.) | 856-782-1771

Surveyors consider this Voorhees Thai BYO storefront "the best in the area", in part for "perfect" pad Thai that will leave you "tongue-Thai-ed", and also for the "reasonable" prices and a "wonderful" staff that "remembers their regular customers"; don't forget to order the homemade ice creams – "blueberry or pumpkin . . . yum!"

Sono Sushi *Japanese* 25 | 13 | 20 | $33
Middletown | Village Mall | 1098 Rte. 35 S. (New Monmouth Rd.) | 732-706-3588 | www.sonosushi.com

"Startlingly good" sushi "elevates" this Japanese BYO from its "tucked-away-in-a-strip-mall locale" in Middletown, as do the "fresher than fresh" sashimi and cooked dishes; "always crowded and always tasty", it's been "delighting" denizens for more than two decades – and its "warm" and "friendly" service helps make up for "decor that needs sprucing."

Sonsie *American* 21 | 23 | 21 | $42
Atlantic City | Pier at Caesars | 1 Atlantic Ocean (Arkansas Ave.) | 609-345-6300 | www.sonsieac.com

"Outstanding looks" and views of the ocean at this Piers at Caesars New American bistro/cafe (an offshoot of Boston's Sonsie) make it a "nice alternative to the overpriced casino restaurants"; AC gamblers amble by for breakfast, lunch and dinner featuring "good" (some say "decent") chow.

Sophie's Bistro Ⓜ *French* 22 | 18 | 22 | $42
Somerset | 700 Hamilton St. (Baier Ave.) | 732-545-7778 | www.sophiesbistro.net

The "terrific" "bistro classics" from this Somerset Gallic "treasure" fill the bill when you can't take that "trip to the French countryside"; the decor's "a little stark", but the "charming owner", "attentive" staff, "extensive wine list, even by the glass" and "reasonable prices" ensure this "neighborhood find" is a "popular" choice nonetheless.

		FOOD	DECOR	SERVICE	COST

Soufflé ⓜ *French*
22 | 21 | 23 | $49

Summit | 7 Union Pl. (Summit Ave.) | 908-598-0717 |
www.soufflerestaurant.com

"Gracious low-key service" complements the "classic" French cuisine at this "romantic" Summit storefront BYO where the "transcendent" dessert soufflés alone are "worth the trip"; "parking is the only problem", but happily this "quiet", "sweet little place" is "across from the train station"; N.B. reservations required for weekday lunch and weekend dinner.

South City Grill *American*
22 | 22 | 19 | $50

Jersey City | 70 Town Square Pl. (Washington Blvd.) |
201-610-9225
Rochelle Park | 55 Rte. 17 S. (Passaic St.) | 201-845-3737
Mountain Lakes | 60 Rte. 46 E. (Crane Rd.) | 973-335-8585
www.southcitygrill.com

The vibe is "upbeat, sexy and chic" at this "swanky", "trendy" American trio where "both sea and land" dishes are "tasty and interesting", but "earplugs should be supplied" when the "singles scene" heats up at the bar on weekends; "attractive, modern" decor helps justify "expensive" tabs; P.S. the Jersey City locale "validates parking in the lot next door."

Spain *Portuguese/Spanish*
22 | 16 | 21 | $38

Newark | 419 Market St. (Raymond Blvd.) | 973-344-0994 |
www.spainrestaurant.com

The "quality matches the quantity" insist fans of this "unassuming", "inviting" Ironbound Iberian "institution" known for "big portions" of steak and seafood "at a fair price"; "interesting Spanish wines", "gracious old-world" service and "proximity to Penn Station" make up for the nothing-fancy atmosphere.

Spanish Tavern *Spanish*
22 | 17 | 21 | $40

Mountainside | 1239 Rte. 22 E. (Locust Ave.) | 908-232-2171
Newark | 103 McWhorter St. (Green St.) | 973-589-4959
www.spanishtavern.com

"Enormous, delicious portions" of paella, stuffed lobsters and the like make these "consistently excellent" Ironbound-Mountainside Spaniards "darn good for the $$$"; they're on the "crowded and loud" side, but "attentive, accommodating" servers "work hard to give you an experience worthy of shouting '*olé!*'"; N.B. the Mountainside branch offers a prix fixe on Tuesdays and game in season.

Spargo's Grille ⓜ *American*
24 | 18 | 22 | $45

Manalapan | Andee Plaza | 130 Rte. 33 W. (Millhurst Rd.) | 732-294-9921 |
www.spargosgrille.com

This Manalapan BYO may be tucked into a "none too attractive strip mall", but the seasonal, highly eclectic New American menu of chef-owner Tim Murphy delivers a "creative", "savory" "surprise"; it offers "cordial" service and a spruced-up setting that may appease fans who plead, "atmosphere please!"; P.S. the four-course prix fixe menu is a "wonderful" bargain at $44.

	FOOD	DECOR	SERVICE	COST

Spike's *Seafood*
23 | 9 | 17 | $30

Point Pleasant Beach | 415 Broadway (St. Louis Ave.) | 732-295-9400

"Get in line before you are starving" at this "real casual" Point Pleasant BYO "fish market with tables" because the waits "go on forever" in high season, due to "fresh-off-the-boat" seafood that's "inexpensive" and "good", if "nothing fancy"; the authentic "old Shore atmosphere" extends to a "salty" staff and "uncomfortable" bench seating.

Squan Tavern Ⓜ *Italian*
21 | 14 | 19 | $29

Manasquan | 15 Broad St. (Main St.) | 732-223-3324 | www.squantavern.com

An "old favorite" of Manasquan "locals", this "homey", "family-run" traditional Southern Italian restaurant/bar/pizzeria has the "typical" "solid" and "filling" offerings, although the "very good" pizza is "the thing"; it's also "kid-friendly" and "reasonably priced", but some say "long waits in summer can make you lose your appetite."

Sri Thai *Thai*
23 | 9 | 17 | $21

Hoboken | 234 Bloomfield St. (bet. 2nd & 3rd Sts.) | 201-798-4822

"Some of the most delicious and flavorful food this side of Bangkok" awaits at this "hole-in-the-wall" Hoboken Thai BYO; insiders advise "forget" the "not-so-appetizing environment" and focus on the "affordable" "mouthwatering" fare delivered by a "friendly" crew.

Stage House Restaurant & Wine Bar *American*
22 | 21 | 21 | $51

Scotch Plains | 366 Park Ave. (Front St.) | 908-322-4224 | www.stagehouserestaurant.com

A "charming" Colonial-era barn is the backdrop for this Scotch Plains New American comprising an "expensive" "formal" restaurant and a "well-priced" "informal" tavern with "lovely outdoor dining" and a "lively bar scene"; though a few fret the jackets-suggested "fine-dining" room has "suffered from the attention to the tavern", for fans it remains a "favorite" for "intimate" "celebratory" meals; N.B. check out the various prix fixe options.

Stage Left *American*
26 | 24 | 24 | $69

New Brunswick | 5 Livingston Ave. (George St.) | 732-828-4444 | www.stageleft.com

It's "food heaven" "right next door to the State Theater" at this "upscale" New Brunswick "destination", where the "creative" New American cuisine is "never anything but amazing" – and is matched with an "impeccable" 1,000-strong wine list; "quietly elegant" decor and "polished" service completes the "top-shelf", "business credit card–essential" experience (jacket suggested); N.B. gourmet homemade chocolates are served après dinner.

NEW Stamna Greek Taverna *Greek*
23 | 16 | 20 | $33

Bloomfield | 1045 Broad St. (bet. Johnson & Watchung Aves.) | 973-338-5151 | www.stamnataverna.com

This year-old, "family-run" Bloomfield Greek BYO stays "packed" thanks to its "totally delicious", "authentic down-home" fare at "rock-

| | FOOD | DECOR | SERVICE | COST |

bottom prices"; the setup can feel "cramped", but its "positive energy" abetted by a "friendly" staff helps make it a "welcome addition."

NEW Steakhouse 85 Steak — | — | — | M

New Brunswick | 85 Church St. (George St.) | 732-247-8585 | www.steakhouse85.com

While serious steak lovers appreciate the all-natural, Black Angus beef at this New Brunswick chophouse, fish fans welcome right-off-the-boat seafood; brew tastings keep the bar busy, while the deep, rich wood surroundings with live jazz in the background measure up to the sophisticated menu of chef Brian Karluk.

NEW Stella Marina Italian — | — | — | M

Asbury Park | 800 Ocean Ave. (Asbury Ave.) | 732-775-7776

With ocean views on two floors, including a balcony, this upscale trattoria on Asbury Park's boardwalk is the newest Italian entry by the Cetrulo restaurant team (Scalini Fedeli, Sirena, to name two); a wine list that's 75% Italian complements the moderately priced menu.

Steve & Cookie's By the Bay American 25 | 22 | 22 | $53

Margate | 9700 Amherst Ave. (Monroe Ave.) | 609-823-1163 | www.steveandcookies.com

"Impressively well-done" New American fare – especially seafood – has made Caroline 'Cookie' Till's "busy" but "excellent" year-rounder a Margate "tradition"; "each room is a gem" – there are "lovely" views of the bay, nightly live jazz and an "attentive" crew to set the mood for an "outstanding" experience.

☒ Stonehouse at Stirling Ridge Ⓜ American 22 | 26 | 21 | $56

Warren | 50 Stirling Rd. (Stiles Rd.) | 908-754-1222 | www.stirlingridgeevents.com

A "mix of lighter fare and hearty" dishes, all "done with style and attention to detail", competes for attention with the "dramatic, modern, lodgelike" environs at this "gorgeous" Warren New American, the restaurant section of a Watchung Mountain catering facility; it can get "noisy" and the prices are a bit steep (especially for the "terrific cocktails"), but to most the overall experience is "enjoyable" nonetheless.

☒ Stony Hill Inn Continental/Italian 23 | 26 | 23 | $59

Hackensack | 231 Polifly Rd. (Mary St.) | 201-342-4085 | www.stonyhillinn.com

It's "fine dining at its best" swoon supporters of this "elegant", "multiroom" Hackensack Continental-Italian in a converted 1818 farmstead that exudes "romantic Colonial charm"; the "outstanding" cuisine complemented by an "extensive but pricey wine list", "wonderful, friendly" service and "live music and dancing" Thursday–Saturday ensure it's ideal for "special occasions."

Strip House Steak 23 | 22 | 22 | $64

Livingston | Westminster Hotel | 550 W. Mt. Pleasant Ave. (bet. Daven Ave. & Microlab Rd.) | 973-548-0050 | www.striphouse.net

Promising the "quintessential night-out-with-the-guys" experience, this Livingston link of the burgeoning chophouse chain delivers with "top-quality meats" enjoyed in trademark "old-school" "brothelesque" digs; the "monster portions" are matched by a "humongous bill", but to most it's "worth it for a special occasion."

Sumo *Japanese*   ▽ 25 | 23 | 25 | $31

Wall | Pathmark Shopping Ctr. | 1933 Rte. 35 (Allaire Rd.) | 732-282-1388 | www.sumowalltwp.com

This "nicely decorated" BYO Japanese in a Wall strip mall has it all – some of the "best" sushi rolls "in Monmouth County" ("particularly the chef's selections"), "good" hibachi with "fun" chefs and "prompt", "friendly" servers in "authentic" Japanese dress; P.S. it's "very kid-friendly", with bento boxes or childrens' menus for the little ones.

Sunny Garden *Chinese*   20 | 20 | 20 | $31

Princeton | 15 Farber Rd. (Rte. 1) | 609-520-1881 | www.sunnygarden.net

Most agree this "upscale" BYO is Princeton's "most stylish" restaurant for "standard" Chinese fare and "uncommonly good" sushi; with its location just off busy Route 1, it's a "reliable" lunch spot for the "corporate class", offering a "quiet" experience, but a minority suggests a "decline" in "food quality" since new owners took over in 2007.

Surf Taco *Mexican*   20 | 14 | 15 | $15

Belmar | 1003 Main St. (10th Ave.) | 732-681-3001
NEW **Forked River** | 44 Manchester Ave. (Lacey Rd.) | 609-971-9996
Jackson | 21 Hope Chapel Rd. (Veteran's Hwy.) | 732-364-8226 ◖
NEW **Long Branch** | 94 Brighton Ave. (2nd Ave.) | 732-229-7873
Manasquan | 121 Parker Ave. (Stockton Lake Blvd.) | 732-223-7757
Point Pleasant Beach | 1300 Richmond Ave. (Marcia Ave.) | 732-701-9000
Seaside Park | 212 SE Central Ave. (bet. Franklin & Lincoln Aves.) | 732-830-2111
Toms River | 1887 Hooper Ave. (bet. Church & Moore Rds.) | 732-255-3333
www.surftaco.com

You can count on counter service at this local mini-chain – including the newest locales in Long Branch and Forked River – serving "surfer-Mex" "Shore staples", i.e. "fresh, cheap, quick" and "dependable" Mexican burritos, tacos, salads and the like; N.B. all locations are BYO except for Jackson, which has a lounge.

Sushi by Kazu *Japanese*   ▽ 26 | 13 | 22 | $37

Howell | 2724 Rte. 9 S. (bet. 2nd & 3rd Sts.) | 732-370-2528

Devotees give "thanks" for this Japanese BYO in Howell, chef Kazu Mukai's showcase for "extremely fresh" fish used for his undeniably "great" sushi and other near "perfect" fare; to experience "top quality", arrive early – the "small" space "fills up"; N.B. closed Tuesdays.

Sushi Lounge *Japanese*   22 | 20 | 19 | $41

Hoboken | 200 Hudson St. (2nd St.) | 201-386-1117
Totowa | 235 Rte. 46 W. (bet. Minnisink Rd. & Union Blvd.) | 973-890-0007
Morristown | 12 Schuyler Pl. (Washington St.) | 973-539-1135
www.sushilounge.com

"Creative sushi combinations" come with "thumping music and amazing drinks" at this "swanky" Japanese trio considered a "step above run-of-the-mill joints" – and "priced accordingly"; "always humming" with a "beautiful" crowd, it boasts a "fun, clubby environment", but be advised that "the later you go, the louder it gets."

Swanky Bubbles *Pan-Asian* | 20 | 21 | 18 | $38 |

Cherry Hill | Short Hills Shopping Ctr. | 482 E. Evesham Rd. (Short Hills Dr.) | 856-428-4999 | www.swankybubbles.com

This eclectic Pan-Asian in Cherry Hill (an offshoot of the Philly original) offers a "good selection" of cocktails, sushi, entrees and, of course, bubbly, making it "a much needed hip location" for "young" South Jerseyans to "meet" and "hang out; P.S. fans deem it a "classic stop that lives up to its name."

Sweet Basil's Cafe *American* | 23 | 15 | 21 | $27 |

West Orange | 641 Eagle Rock Ave. (Pleasant Valley Way) | 973-325-3340 | www.sweetbasilscafe.com

"Creative, well-prepared" New American dishes based on "high-quality ingredients" make for an "outstanding" breakfast, "totally tempting" brunch or "wonderful" lunch at this BYO storefront in West Orange's Pleasantdale section; its looks are "simple", but "pleasant" service helps explain why it's a local "favorite."

Table 8 Ⓜ *American* | 23 | 21 | 22 | $48 |

Montclair | 615 Bloomfield Ave. (bet. Midland Ave. & Valley Rd.) | 973-746-2233 | www.table8nj.com

"Delectable fare" that "changes with the seasons" has admirers rating this "trendy" New American BYO storefront "one of Montclair's top tables" for dinner; though the "swanky" setting feels "cramped" and can get "a bit noisy", the "solicitous staff" ensures it's "one to go back to" nonetheless.

Tabor Road Tavern *American* | 21 | 25 | 20 | $47 |

Morris Plains | 510 Tabor Rd. (Rte. 10) | 973-267-7004 | www.harvestrestaurants.com

The "new kid on the block got it right the first time" say fans of this one-year-old "cozy yet bustling" Morris Plains New American from Harvest Restaurants; though the "friendly" staff may still be "working out some kinks" and "the bill tends to be high" for "what you get", the "gorgeous chalet-type" setting and "upscale creative food and wine" make for "a fabulous dining experience"; N.B. there's an abbreviated tavern menu between lunch and dinner.

Tacconelli's Pizzeria Ⓜ⊄ *Pizza* | 22 | 10 | 17 | $19 |

Maple Shade | 450 S. Lenola Rd. (Rte. 38) | 856-638-0338 | www.tacconellispizzerianj.com

"Quality" pizzas with "just right" thin crusts emerge from the brick oven at this BYO pizzeria across from Maple Shade's Moorestown Mall; some say it trumps the legendary Philly original because it also offers salads and desserts and there's no need to call ahead to reserve your dough; P.S. you "gotta bring cash."

	FOOD	DECOR	SERVICE	COST

Taka ⓜ *Japanese*
| | 25 | 23 | 23 | $40 |

Asbury Park | 632 Mattison Ave. (Main St.) | 732-775-1020 |
www.takaapnj.com

The "truly exceptional food made a non-sushi eater into a convert" at
Taka Hirai's "upscale" BYO in Asbury Park, also serving "inventive"
cooked fare; in addition, the "beautiful" decor – including a communal table – is "straight out of SoHo" and service is "top-notch."

Takara *Japanese*
| | ▽ 24 | 20 | 22 | $31 |

Oakhurst | Orchard Plaza | 1610 Rte. 35 S. (Willow Dr.) | 732-663-1899
"Fresh" sushi, a "great" hibachi, four tatami rooms, a large fountain
with a koi pond (a favorite with kids) and a "friendly" staff all add up
to an enjoyable experience at this Japanese in the Oakhurst section
of Ocean Township; if you like Japanese food, "this is the place
you must visit."

Tapas de Espana *Spanish*
| | 21 | 18 | 20 | $38 |

Englewood | 47 N. Dean St. (bet. Palisade Ave. & Park Pl.) | 201-569-9999
North Bergen | 7909 Bergenline Ave. (79th St.) | 201-453-1690
"It's best to go with a large group and explore" "very good Spanish
food" "without the need to go to the Ironbound" at these separately
owned tapas specialists in Englewood and North Bergen; while both
promise an "authentic" "variety" of "small plates" (entrees too) and
a "fun" time, some prefer Englewood's "old-world charm" while others say "they make you feel like an old friend has returned" at the
original North Bergen spot.

Taqueria ⓜ *Mexican*
| | 22 | 12 | 14 | $16 |

Jersey City | 236 Grove St. (Grand St.) | 201-333-3220
There are "no fajitas or nachos", just "truly authentic" Mexican
"street food, freshly made" at this family-run Jersey City BYO, where
you order at the counter and eat in a "funky underground dining
room" or on *el patio*; despite sometimes "cooler-than-thou" service,
the "great cheap eats" keep fans "coming back again and again."

Taro *Asian Fusion*
| | 20 | 21 | 20 | $37 |

Montclair | 32 Church St. (bet. Fullerton Ave. & Park St.) | 973-509-2266 |
www.tarorestaurant.com
"Cool" and "dependable", this BYO "sexy date spot" in Montclair
proffers "tasty" Asian fusion fare, including "weekend dim sum", in
"stylish" "Zen"-like environs; some lament "the menu hasn't varied
in years", but service remains "pleasant" – and "large portions"
"make up for" tabs that wallet-watchers call "a bit high."

Taste of Asia, A ⓜ *Malaysian*
| | 21 | 15 | 19 | $28 |

Chatham | 245 Main St. (Passaic Ave.) | 973-701-8821 |
www.atasteofasianj.com
"Delicious" Malaysian specialties come in "upbeat", "kid-friendly"
quarters at this unpretentious Chatham storefront BYO; it's "always
a good bet for enjoying a less common cuisine", and "the lunch
menu is a bargain", but a less-impressed contingent shrugs "accept-
able" but "nothing to write home about."

Tattoni's Restaurant 🅱 *Italian*
∇ 21 | 12 | 21 | $28

Hamilton Township | 1280 Hwy. 33 (Whitehorse Hamilton Square Rd.) | 609-587-9700

Lou Tattoni, son of the founder, is still using "the old family recipes" for the "peasant-style" Italian fare at this BYO in a Hamilton strip mall, which he relocated to a few years back from the "old-time Chambersburg landmark" in Trenton; though the decor still "leaves something to be desired", the "best-value", "quality" food and "outstanding" service reign supreme.

Teak *Pan-Asian*
20 | 22 | 18 | $45

Red Bank | 64 Monmouth St. (Drummond Pl.) | 732-747-5775 | www.teakrestaurant.com

"Hang with the beautiful people" at this Red Bank "hot spot" whose "creative" cocktails and "upscale" Pan-Asian "mix-and-match" fare "with flair" is served in "chic", "Zen-like" quarters; those who wish to "escape the hubbub" sit in the back, while those looking to dodge "expensive" tabs come Mondays for "half-price" dinner or Sundays for $25 all-you-can-eat sushi.

Ted's on Main 🅱 Ⓜ *American*
∇ 25 | 18 | 23 | $40

Medford | 20 S. Main St. (Bank St.) | 609-654-7011 | www.tedsonmain.net

Medfordites rave about this "great addition to Main Street" due to chef-owner Ted Iwachiw's "original", "exceptionally well-prepared" New American lineup that's an "interesting" reflection of his background in New Orleans, the Caribbean and Philly's Striped Bass; its "little" "storefront" BYO setting is "bare-bones", but service isn't.

Teplitzky's Ⓜ *Diner*
- | - | - | M

Atlantic City | Chelsea Hotel | 111. S. Chelsea Ave. (Pacific Ave.) | 609-428-4550 | www.thechelsea-ac.com

Diner-inspired and retro-chic, this casual Stephen Starr entry in Atlantic City's hot Chelsea Hotel is designed to bring you back to tuna melts, club sandwiches and big, bountiful breakfasts; order a quick corned beef sandwich at the counter or linger in the hideaway cocktail lounge – either way, classic diners were never this hip.

Teresa Caffe *Italian*
22 | 17 | 18 | $33

Princeton | Palmer Sq. | 23 Palmer Sq. E. (Nassau St.) | 609-921-1974 | www.terramomo.com

To Princetonians, this Palmer Square Italian "mainstay" "defines cafe dining: casual, consistent, cheerful and a good value"; it offers "artisan" pizzas, "pretty good" pastas and a "respectable" wine list, but just "don't expect a quiet meal" given its "close-together" tables, and don't be surprised if there's a "wait on busy weekends" (it takes no reservations).

Terrace Restaurant *Mediterranean*
∇ 22 | 23 | 23 | $53

Short Hills | Hilton at Short Hills | 41 JFK Pkwy. (Rte. 24, exit 7C) | 973-912-4757 | www.hiltonshorthills.com

Whether for a "special occasion" or a "cocktail and shellfish" at the bar, this "upscale" Mediterranean-influenced New American at the

Short Hills Hilton "never fails to please" with its "delicious" fare, "soothing ambiance" and "professional" yet "surprisingly friendly" service; sure, it's "pricey", but Sunday brunch is "wonderful."

Tewksbury Inn *American*

22 | 20 | 20 | $51

Oldwick | 55 Main St. (King St.) | 908-439-2641 | www.thetewksburyinn.com

"Very pleasant surroundings" include both the "picture-postcard" town of Oldwick and this "charming old" 1800 stagecoach inn, where the "casual" barroom is "convivial", the dining room more "formal", and the garden terrace a plus; in each, expect "honest" American fare, "friendly" servers and a "pricey" wine list.

Texas Arizona *Tex-Mex*

14 | 12 | 14 | $26

Hoboken | 76 River St. (Hudson Pl.) | 201-420-0304 | www.texasarizona.com

"Great for drinking with the boys", this Hoboken Tex-Mex dispenses "typical" pub grub "across the street" from the PATH station; the "lively" "sports bar atmosphere" can become a "rowdy" "frat-boy scene", but service is "prompt" and sidewalk seating provides "awesome people-watching on a nice day."

Thai Chef *Thai*

21 | 17 | 18 | $35

Hackensack | Riverside Square Mall | 169 Hackensack Ave. (Rte. 4) | 201-342-7257
Montclair | 664 Bloomfield Ave. (bet. Orange & Valley Rds.) | 973-783-4994
www.thaichefusa.com

"Interesting" fare, "decent prices" and "friendly" service distinguish this Thai-French fusion duo; the Montclair BYO's "outside dining patio is a big hit", while the Hackensack mall setting offers a "wine and martini list" along with some "tranquility"; P.S. "don't leave without trying the soufflé."

Thai Kitchen *Thai*

24 | 15 | 22 | $25

Bridgewater | 1351 Prince Rodgers Ave. (I-287, exit 14B) | 908-231-8822
Bridgewater | Somerset Shopping Ctr. | 327 Hwy. 202 (Rte. 22) | 908-722-8983
Hillsborough | Hillsborough Shopping Ctr. | 649 Hwy. 206 (Amwell Rd.) | 908-904-8038
NEW **Warren** | 41 Mountain Blvd. (Mt. Bethel Rd.) | 908-822-1188
www.thaikitchennj.com

You "can't go wrong with any choice" at this "affordable" and "appealing chain" of "fantastic" Thai BYOs – though the "modest digs" can be "crowded and noisy"; "professional" service that's "exceedingly fast during lunch" causes some to "feel rushed" – but clock-watchers find it "efficient."

Thai Thai *Thai*

23 | 15 | 20 | $29

Stirling | 1168 Valley Rd. (bet. Poplar Dr. & Warren Ave.) | 908-903-0790 | www.thaithaifinecuisine.com

"Noodle and duck dishes shine" at this "consistently delicious", "popular" Stirling strip-mall Thai BYO with "charming" servers and a "serene setting" (though when busy, "the noise level can be deafening"); it's "properly priced", with lunch specials a particularly "great value"; N.B. closed Tuesdays.

Theater Square Grill *American*

20	23	18	$53

Newark | New Jersey Performing Arts Ctr. | 1 Center St. (McCarter Hwy.) | 973-642-1226 | www.theatersquaregrill.com

"Convenient for theater-goers", this "pricey" American in Newark's NJPAC serves dinner Monday–Saturday, lunch Monday–Friday (hours vary) and a "terrific" brunch after Sunday events in its "light-filled space" with "service mindful of showtimes"; P.S. the seasonal Calçada outdoor terrace is "very European", while the Theater Square Bistro (Tuesday–Saturday dinner) is a lower-priced option to the Grill.

Theresa's *Italian*

22	17	20	$39

Westfield | 47 Elm St. (bet. Broad St. & North Ave.) | 908-233-9133 | www.theresasrestaurant.com

"Fantastic" "homemade" pastas and "excellent salads" are among the "crowd-pleasers" at this Westfield storefront Italian BYO; though "waits can be long on weekends" and some knock the "bland", "dark" ambiance, prices are "reasonable" and it's "wonderful for lunch"; N.B. a makeover is planned for 2009.

3 Forty Grill *American*

21	21	18	$42

Hoboken | 340 Sinatra Dr. (bet. 3rd & 4th Sts.) | 201-217-3406 | www.3fortygrill.com

Fans of this "trendy" Hoboken New American savor the "great bar scene" (even if it gets "loud") and "good food", best eaten alfresco with "amazing" views of the NYC skyline; P.S. though some find prices "high", the weekend brunch prix fixe is a "deal" – and there's validated parking if you spend more than $50.

3 West *American*

22	24	21	$52

Basking Ridge | 665 Martinsville Rd. (Independence Blvd.) | 908-647-3000 | www.3westrest.com

"NY comes to NJ – with prices to match" at this "classy" New American in Basking Ridge that attracts a "hip crowd"; most find the food and the "boisterous bar scene" "very good", though some cite Ciao, the next-door sibling, as "better value for the money."

Tick Tock Diner ◐ *Diner*

18	13	17	$21

Clifton | 281 Allwood Rd. (bet. Bloomfield & Passaic Aves.) | 973-777-0511 | www.tictockdiner.com

"Whatever you're in the mood for" is on the "tremendous menu" at this "inexpensive" "classic" Clifton diner that's "always open" (and has been since 1948); service is "super fast", and though some ticked-off tasters find just "average fare", fans swear "you never leave hungry."

NEW Tim McLoone's Supper Club Ⓜ *American*

17	24	19	$53

Asbury Park | 1200 Ocean Ave. (5th Ave.) | 732-774-1155 | www.timmcloonessupperclub.com

On Asbury Park's boardwalk is the eponymous Shore restaurateur's "fabulous" upstairs room (above Salt Water Beach Café), boasting "incredible" 360-degree ocean views plus New American fare that's "pretty good" if a bit "steep" in price; overall it's a "fun", "fabulous" "throwback" to a "1940s nightclub" – including live shows.

Tim Schafer's Cuisine *American* | 25 | 18 | 22 | $49 |

Morristown | 82 Speedwell Ave. (bet. Cattano Ave. & Clinton Pl.) | 973-538-3330 | www.timschafersrestaurant.com

"Even without the eponymous Tim Schafer" this "cozy", sunny-colored Morristown New American storefront "still shines" with an "inventive menu" that spotlights game, much of it "made with a variety of beers"; while the tab for the "small portions" is "expensive", "BYO helps."

Tina Louise Ⓜ *Asian* | 24 | 15 | 21 | $30 |

Carlstadt | 403 Hackensack St. (bet. Broad St. & Division Ave.) | 201-933-7133 | www.villagerestaurantgroup.com

"Run by two sisters who really seem to enjoy" it, this "tiny", brick-walled Carlstadt Asian BYO near the Meadowlands offers "unique" fare that's "high on flavor", though some wish for "bigger portions"; service that's "on top of things" adds to the "excellent value."

Ⓩ Tisha's Fine Dining *American* | 26 | 24 | 25 | $47 |

Cape May | 714 Beach Ave. (Stockton Pl.) | 609-884-9119 | www.tishasfinedining.com

"There probably isn't a prettier location" in Cape May than this "tiny", "fine-dining" seasonal BYO; a "phenomenal" ocean view (especially at outdoor "sunset" tables) is matched by the "inventive", "superbly prepared" New American fare and "savvy" servers; N.B. the owners opened Moonfish Grill in West Cape May post-Survey.

Toast *American* | ▽ 20 | 17 | 19 | $23 |

Montclair | 700 Bloomfield Ave. (bet. Orange Rd. & St. Luke's Pl.) | 973-509-8099 | www.toastmontclair.com

"Reliably good breakfast and lunch" washed down with "fabulous coffee" keeps early birds flocking to this "very casual" Montclair American BYO; though crusty critics cry "it's sometimes so crowded that the service suffers", brunch is "great – if you love children."

Tokyo Bleu *Japanese* | ▽ 22 | 18 | 24 | $38 |

Cinnaminson | 602 Rte. 130 N. (Westfield Lees Dr.) | 856-829-8889 | www.tokyobleusushi.com

It may be on a "very busy" stretch of Route 130 in Cinnaminson, but the service at this "simple" Japanese BYO is "so impeccable" that "once inside" "you soon forget"; adding to this pleasant amnesia is "fresh" sushi "lightly enhanced" with "a bit of fresh herbs" and offered at "reasonable" prices, which also extends to the cooked fare.

Tomatoes *Californian/Eclectic* | 24 | 22 | 22 | $53 |

Margate | 9300 Amherst Ave. (Washington Ave.) | 609-822-7535 | www.tomatoesmargate.com

"It's like you've been transported to LA" when you "step inside" this "energetic", "popular" Margate Californian-Eclectic, a "must-go" that draws a "fashionable" crowd to its "great" bar scene; the "delish"

| | FOOD | DECOR | SERVICE | COST |

menu is "expertly conceived and executed", the extensive wine list is "clever" and the service is "professional" if sometimes "cool."

Tomo's Cuisine ▣ *Japanese* ▽ 21 | 8 | 17 | $38

Little Falls | 113 Rte. 23 (bet. 1st & 2nd Sts.) | 973-837-1117

"High-quality sushi" and "pure Japanese cooking" come in a "tight" strip-mall setting at this Little Falls BYO; "skilled" chef-owner Tomo Tanaka's "special sushi is the way to go, but the teriyaki chicken is a must for non-sushi eaters" – that's why "Japanese executives keep coming back" for more of the "yummy" and "affordable" fare.

Tom Sawyer ◗ *Diner* 17 | 17 | 17 | $20

Paramus | 98 E. Ridgewood Ave. (Garden State Pkwy.) | 201-262-0111 | www.tomsawyerdiner.com

"Back from the ashes" after a 2006 fire, this family-run Paramus diner's "upgraded decor" features new booths and a blue-and-yellow scheme; despite "above-average" fare, some note the "courteous" service "needs to be much faster"; but even so, Route 17 shoppers find it a "handy" "go-to."

Tony Da Caneca *Portuguese/Spanish* 23 | 17 | 23 | $41

Newark | 72 Elm Rd. (Houston St.) | 973-589-6882 | www.tonydacanecarestaurant.com

"They know their fish" and present it in "more than satisfying portions" at this "reasonably priced" 40-year-old Iberian "off the beaten track" in Newark's Ironbound; the "charming staff" and "comfortable" space featuring Spanish tiles make for a "delightful experience"; P.S. there's even a "parking lot."

Tony Luke's *Sandwiches* 21 | 12 | 16 | $18

Atlantic City | Borgata Hotel, Casino & Spa | 1 Borgata Way (Huron Ave.) | 609-317-1000 | www.theborgata.com

Some casino denizens consider this "quick-service", food-court-style sandwich stop in the cafeteria area of the Borgata "the best Philly export – bar none", especially for its signature pork or steak rolls topped with "garlicky" broccoli rabe; fans insist "if you love steak sandwiches, you can rarely do better than Tony Luke's – and definitely not in AC."

Tony's Baltimore Grill ◗⊄ *Pizza* 18 | 9 | 17 | $22

Atlantic City | 2800 Atlantic Ave. (Iowa Ave.) | 609-345-5766 | www.baltimoregrill.com

"Step back into the Atlantic City of decades ago" for "good cheap eats" and drinks at this cash-only "basic" pizzeria-pasta-sandwich "joint" where the bar is open 24/7; "grumpy" waitresses are "part of the charm", the decor has changed very little and songs on the "old-time" jukebox may be "older than the restaurant itself."

NEW Torcello ▣ *Italian* - | - | - | I

Red Bank | 91 Broad St. (bet. Canal St. & Linden Pl.) | 732-530-0602 | www.torcellorestaurant.com

Step into romantic Venice at this new BYO in trendy Red Bank, where restaurant competition is fierce, but considering that owner

Mike Bitici's last place was Greenwich Village's The Grand Ticino (the 'star' trattoria in *Moonstruck*), he knows something about showmanship and food; the gnocchi and ravioli are homemade – and proposals are on the house.

Tortilla Press *Mexican*   22 | 19 | 19 | $30

Collingswood | 703 Haddon Ave. (Collings Ave.) | 856-869-3345 | www.thetortillapress.com

In Collingswood, "fresh flavors" make chef/co-owner Mark Smith's "nontraditional" "variations" on Mexican "favorites" "*delicioso*"; fans also give a nod to the "bold, colorful" decor and "really good" setups for margaritas (just BYO tequila); so what if service is "friendly" but "rushed" and the room "loud"?

Tortuga's Mexican Village ⊄ *Mexican*   20 | 9 | 17 | $23

Princeton | 44 Leigh Ave. (bet. John & Witherspoon Sts.) | 609-924-5143 | www.tortugasmv.com

"Don't judge the food by the decor" at this Princeton "no-frills" "hole-in-the-wall" BYO Mexican in a residential neighborhood; its "local following" says it's the place for "good, cheap" south-of-the-border fare that's "tasty and reliable"; though the cash-only policy is "a drag" and the service "could use a little improvement" it remains "a local favorite."

Trap Rock *American*   21 | 22 | 20 | $46

Berkeley Heights | 279 Springfield Ave. (bet. Snyder & Union Aves.) | 908-665-1755 | www.traprockrestaurant.net

"Trendy but not stuck-up", this Berkeley Heights New American pub and microbrewery serves an "extensive menu" of "inventive" cuisine and "first-rate home-brews" in a "convivial and often loud" lodgelike setting (though "more sedate areas are available"); it's "a little pricey" but "friendly" service makes it "always enjoyable."

⑦ Tre Figlio ⊠ *Italian*   27 | 21 | 25 | $51

Egg Harbor | 500 W. White Horse Pike (Mannheim Ave.) | 609-965-3303 | www.trefiglio.com

"In all respects" this "special", "out-of-the-way gem" is "worth the drive" to Egg Harbor for a "stellar", "upscale" Italian "experience" that includes "the best" pasta, a "huge" wine list, a "lovely" setting and "superb" service, all courtesy of the Cordivari family, of which son James is the chef; N.B. there's live entertainment upstairs on weekend nights.

Tre Piani *Italian/Mediterranean*   22 | 22 | 22 | $49

Princeton | Forrestal Village Shopping Ctr. | 120 Rockingham Row (Village Blvd.) | 609-452-1515 | www.trepiani.com

"Fresh" ingredients "shine" at this "upscale" Italian-Mediterranean taking its cue from Slow Food USA; some say it's "out-of-the-way" in Princeton/Plainsboro's Forrestal Village, but its "attractive" three floors (*tre piani*) plus patio sport a "relaxed yet sophisticated atmosphere" and a staff that's "well versed"; N.B. downstairs is a small-plates wine bar, Tre Bar.

	FOOD	DECOR	SERVICE	COST

Trinity *American*
23 | 23 | 21 | $40

Keyport | 84 Broad St. (bet. Front & 3rd Sts.) | 732-888-1998 |
www.trinitykeyport.com

Chef Michael d'Ennery "tends well to his flock" with "sophisti-cated", "top-notch" New American cuisine that soars inside a "beautiful", "romantic" "converted church" in Keyport; considering the "attentive" service, "average" prices and an appealing down-stairs lounge, acolytes wink "not to go here would be sacrilegious."

Triumph Brewing Co. *American/Eclectic*
16 | 18 | 17 | $31

Princeton | 138 Nassau St. (Washington Rd.) | 609-924-7855 |
www.triumphbrewing.com

"Conveniently" located in Downtown Princeton, this "cool", "cav-ernous" two-story "temple of beer" is "going strong" at 15; insiders suggest "go for burgers and beers", because although the seasonal "handcrafted" brews "can't be beat", the rest of the Eclectic-American slate is just "ok"; N.B. live bands Thursday–Saturday.

Trovato's ⓜ *Italian*
∇ 25 | 18 | 22 | $39

Elmwood Park | 206 Hwy. 46 (Mill St.) | 201-797-7552 |
www.trovatosnj.com

Trovato's Due 🅂ⓜ *Italian*
(fka Ruga)

NEW Oakland | 4 Barbara Ln. (Oakland Ave.) | 201-337-0813

Fish, homemade pasta and other "terrific dishes" served in a "cozy, ro-mantic" setting lure a "strong local following" to this Southern Italian duo in Elmwood Park and Oakland; add in a "friendly staff" and "moderate cost", and most contend it's "outstanding in every way."

Tsuki 🅂 *Japanese*
∇ 22 | 14 | 17 | $36

Bernardsville | 23 Mine Brook Rd. (Mt. Airy Rd.) | 908-953-0450

"Handy for a bite before the movies", this Bernardsville Japanese is known for "outstanding sushi rolls", while also offering cooked dishes; though the decor "could use updating" and service can be "erratic", "reasonable prices", BYO and "nightly specials" make it a "staple."

Tuckers Eating &
Drinking Establishment *American*
16 | 16 | 18 | $32

Beach Haven | 101 West Ave. (Engleside Ave.) | 609-492-2300

For Traditional American "comfort food" at the Shore, this "very ca-sual" year-round pub and grill in Beach Haven is a "reliable" "standby"; the bar area is "noisy but fun", the dining room "calmer" and deck dining is "wonderful" with views of Barnegat Bay.

Tun Tavern ◑ *American*
17 | 15 | 16 | $29

Atlantic City | Sheraton Hotel | 2 Miss America Way (Baltic Ave.) |
609-347-7800 | www.tuntavern.com

After shopping the nearby outlets, this "busy", "casual" American brewpub in Atlantic City's Sheraton makes "a good resting place" for a "decent", "reasonable" lunch or dinner, especially if you opt for one of its "interesting" microbrews and a "good" burger; "basic" de-cor and just-"average" service are part of the package.

	FOOD	DECOR	SERVICE	COST

Tuptim *Thai* | 20 | 15 | 18 | $30

Montclair | 600 Bloomfield Ave. (bet. Park St. & Valley Rd.) | 973-783-3800 | www.tuptimthaicuisine.com

"Wonderfully spiced" "honest Thai cuisine" with many vegetarian options makes this "dependable", "family-owned and -run" Montclair BYO a local pick "for a casual night out"; while there can be an "occasional blip in service", it's always a "reasonable value."

Tutto a Modo Mio *Italian*   ▽ 23 | 18 | 23 | $38

Ridgefield | 482 Bergen Blvd. (Edgewater Ave.) | 201-313-9690 | www.trattoriasaporito.com

"The warmest, friendliest people" serve the housemade pastas, pizzas and other "always delicious" Southern Italian specialties at this "reasonably priced" Ridgefield storefront BYO, whose name means 'everything my way'; though nitpickers say "close" seating makes it "noisy", most dub it a "small and cozy" "gem."

Tuzzio's *Italian* | 20 | 9 | 18 | $30

Long Branch | 224 Westwood Ave. (Morris Ave.) | 732-222-9614 | www.tuzzios.com

"Large portions" of "solid", "old-school" Italian "comfort" fare at "low" prices keep Long Branch families happy at this old-timer "hidden away from the Pier Village stiletto set"; "brusque" service is "part of the experience", while, depending on your viewpoint, the decor is either "totally unpretentious" or "dowdy."

2Senza Ristorante Ⓜ *Italian/Mediterranean* | 21 | 19 | 20 | $44

Red Bank | The Galleria | 2 Bridge Ave. (Front St.) | 732-758-0999 | www.2senza.com

"Dependable" Med-Italian fare prepared in a "bustling" open-kitchen setting keeps this "rustic" find in Red Bank's historic Galleria building "a notch above" the competition; somewhat "pricey" tabs are offset by "attentive" service and convenience to the Count Basie Theater; N.B. wine and beer are served but you can BYO.

Ugly Mug ⬤ *Pub Food* | 17 | 14 | 17 | $24

Cape May | 426 Washington St. (Decatur St.) | 609-884-3459

"Informal, unstuffy and satisfying" is how fans describe this "old-time" watering hole on Cape May's Washington Street mall that's open year-round, drawing locals and visitors alike who come for "reliable" American pub staples, including "delicious" crab cakes, and "great" people-watching on the patio; the "bartenders are friendly" and "there's always a game on", plus there's live music weekly in summer.

Underground Café Ⓜ *E European*   ▽ 19 | 17 | 21 | $34

Princeton | 4 Hulfish St. (Witherspoon St.) | 609-924-0666 | www.cafe-underground.com

A menu of "out-of-the-ordinary" Bulgarian specialties supplemented with Italian and French standards is on offer at this underground BYO, a "quirky", "unexpected find" in Princeton; the "space-age" Euro-tech decor strikes some as a bit "strange" but the "friendly, attentive" service wins praise, and most find the "tasty" victuals "very satisfying."

Undici ☒ *Italian* — 21 | 23 | 19 | $55

Rumson | 11 W. River Rd. (Bingham Ave.) | 732-842-3880 |
www.undicirestaurant.com

It "feels just like a Tuscan farmhouse" at this Rumson Italian where aging brick, stone columns and a fireplace create a "stunning" yet "cozy" setting for "fresh, authentic" pastas and other "delectable" dishes, complemented by an "expansive" wine list; while fans praise the service as "attentive", others say it falls "wide of the mark", and even in this "wealthy community", most find the experience "quite costly."

Union Park Dining Room *American* — 25 | 25 | 24 | $53

Cape May | Hotel Macomber | 727 Beach Ave. (Howard St.) |
609-884-8811 | www.unionparkdiningroom.com

Swooners have "not one complaint" about this "elegant" and "romantic" New American in Cape May's Hotel Macomber, offering the epitome of "fine dining" "without the attitude" in a "beautiful" setting; the "polite" staff is as "polished" as the sterling silver, while the wraparound veranda provides "views of the ocean and promenade"; it's BYO (with local wines served).

Vanthia's *Seafood* — ▽ 21 | 16 | 22 | $34

West Cape May | 106 Sunset Blvd. (B'way) | 609-884-4020 |
www.vanthias.com

"Off the beaten path" in West Cape May, this "family-run" BYO seafooder reels in fans with "fabulously fresh" Greek- and Italian-style fin fare and "very good" pasta dishes, as well as "excellent" weekend breakfasts in high season; some sniff the "decor is not the greatest" in the "unpretentious older house", but the atmosphere is "lovely" and the "price is right."

Varka Fish House *Greek/Seafood* — 26 | 23 | 22 | $57

Ramsey | 30 N. Spruce St. (Main St.) | 201-995-9333 |
www.varkarestaurant.com

"Superb" seafood "selected from the menu or by the pound" makes this "classy", "pricey" Ramsey Greek with a "hot bar scene" a "star"; the staff is "attentive", but you may want to "bring earplugs for busy nights" or sit on the "outside patio in summer" "to avoid the noise."

Ventura's Greenhouse *Italian* — 17 | 16 | 18 | $35

Margate | 106 S. Benson Ave. (Atlantic Ave.) | 609-822-0140 |
www.venturasgreenhouse.com

The beach, the ocean and even Margate's "wonder" – Lucy the Elephant – are all in view, especially from the outdoor deck, at this casual Italian that's "decent to good" for pasta and such upstairs and pizza in the downstairs cafe; in summer, things go "a little young and scene-y", which spells "horrendous" lines on weekends.

Verdigre ☒☒ *American* — ▽ 21 | 23 | 20 | $52

New Brunswick | 25 Liberty St. (bet. George & Neilson Sts.) |
732-247-2250 | www.verdigrenb.com

"Interesting", "tasty small plates" are served in an "urban atmosphere" at this "artsy", expensive New Brunswick New American–

Med that "turns into a cool club on weekends"; "go early to enjoy relative quiet"; N.B. closed Sunday–Tuesday.

	FOOD	DECOR	SERVICE	COST

Verjus ☒ French
25 | 20 | 23 | $49

Maplewood | 1790 Springfield Ave. (Rutgers St.) | 973-378-8990 | www.verjusrestaurant.com

"Consistently excellent" "for lunch and dinner" and "superb" for brunch, this Maplewood New French run by a "delightful husband-and-wife team" boasts a "quiet", "unassuming" ambiance; decor featuring the works of local artists, "well-spaced tables" and an "intelligent, moderately priced wine list" also help make it a "hideaway."

Verve ☒ American/French
22 | 19 | 21 | $46

Somerville | 18 E. Main St. (bet. Bridge & Grove Sts.) | 908-707-8655 | www.vervestyle.com

A "hip vibe permeates" this "solid mainstay" in Somerville, a tri-level New American–French purveying "creative", "well-presented" steaks and seafood specials; a "classy" upstairs bar "with live jazz" "adds to a fun (if expensive) night out"; N.B. a new chef may outdate the above Food score.

Vespa's Restaurant Italian
17 | 16 | 18 | $38

Edgewater | 860 River Rd. (Hillard Ave.) | 201-943-9393

For pastas, pizza and "generous" entrees at "a decent price", fans of "straightforward Italian" scoot over to this Edgewater "neighborhood place" decked out in "cool" vintage Vespa decor; though the pace can be "a little rushed", there's "no attitude" from the "hospitable staff."

Vic's ☒ Pizza
20 | 11 | 18 | $24

Bradley Beach | 60 Main St. (Evergreen Ave.) | 732-774-8225 | www.vicspizza.com

Thin-crust pizzas are "in a class by themselves" at this Bradley Beach "mecca" that's "been there forever" (or at least since 1947), with an "old tavern" ambiance and "hit-or-miss" service; but as for the rest of the "red-sauce" menu, "you're on your own"; P.S. "expect waits in summer and on weekends."

Vila Nova do Sol Mar Portuguese
▽ 23 | 22 | 23 | $37

Newark | 267 Ferry St. (Niagara St.) | 973-344-8540

"Quieter" than the "usual" Ironbound Iberians, this midpriced Newark Portuguese connected to a 40-year-old bar is "always a treat" for a "laid-back dinner"; the "typical setting" features cobblestone floors and murals, and there's dining to the beat of live bands outdoors in the summer.

Village Gourmet Eclectic
21 | 16 | 18 | $30

Rutherford | 73-75 Park Ave. (Ridge Rd.) | 201-438-9404 | www.villagerestaurantgroup.com

"Creatively wrapped around a glass-enclosed liquor store", this "cozy" Rutherford Eclectic BYO has "something for everyone" – from "casual" burgers to "exotic" dumplings and "upscale" steak, with "specials priced just right"; though naysayers decry "too many cuisines under one roof", it suits most "for a quick" meal.

	FOOD	DECOR	SERVICE	COST

Village Green *American*
23 | 18 | 21 | $56

Ridgewood | 36 Prospect St. (Dayton St.) | 201-445-2914 |
www.villagegreenrestaurant.com

"Every taste is wonderful" from the prix fixe menu at this "romantic"
Ridgewood New American BYO; though some find the portions
"soooo small" and "costly", others consider the "unique" fare and
"attentive service" a "delightful" "bargain"; N.B. à la carte options
offered Mondays–Thursdays only.

Villa Vittoria *Italian*
22 | 18 | 21 | $39

Brick | 2700 Hooper Ave. (Cedar Bridge Ave.) | 732-920-1550 |
www.villavittoria.com

"Now this is Italian!" proclaim locals about this Brick "staple" where
they *mangia* "nice portions" of traditional eats, including "good plates
of pasta", while enjoying nightly piano music; too-"close tables" are
overlooked, as is the "old-fashioned" decor.

Vine 🅰 *American/Mediterranean*
25 | 23 | 24 | $57

Basking Ridge | 95 Morristown Rd. (bet. Finley & Maple Aves.) |
908-221-0017 | www.vinerestaurant.net

A "gracious" welcome precedes a "lovely meal" at this "classy"
Basking Ridge Med–New American "in the heart of horse country"; improved to "excellent in all areas", it also has a "lively" bar scene, but
regulars warn that "tabs are best suited to expense accounts."

Vivas Classic Latin Cuisine *Nuevo Latino*
26 | 21 | 22 | $44

Belmar | Belmar Plaza | 801 Belmar Plaza (bet. 8th & 10th Aves.) |
732-681-1213 | www.vivasrestaurant.com

Venezuelan-born chef Will Vivas (ex Bistro Olé) "has another hit" at
his Belmar BYO where he "works" Nuevo Latino "magic" on "inde-
scribably delicious" fare that's served, "unrushed", by a "willing and
helpful" staff; enjoy it both indoors in the "colorfully decorated"
"storefront" and (weather permitting) on the terrace – just "be prepared to wait" (no reservations).

Walpack Inn Ⓜ *American*
19 | 23 | 19 | $42

Walpack Center | Rte. 615 (Rte. 206) | 973-948-3890 |
www.walpackinn.com

"Where else can you dine with the deer?" than at this "large", "rustic" "country lodge" in Walpack with "a sweeping view of unspoiled
New Jersey"; many endure "long waits" to take in the "spectacular"
outside scenery (and the "taxidermied animals" within), along with
"solid but not spectacular" Traditional American fare that features
"amazing", "homemade" brown bread and a "very fresh" salad bar;
N.B. open Fridays–Sundays, but hours vary by season.

Wasabi Asian Plates *Japanese*
25 | 18 | 22 | $34

Somerville | 12 W. Main St. (Bridge St.) | 908-203-8881
Wasabi House *Japanese*
East Brunswick | Colchester Plaza | 77 Tices Ln. (Rte. 18) | 732-254-9988
A "mouthwatering array of sushi" and "sparkling sashimi" await at
these Japanese siblings, with East Brunswick a BYO and the roomier

Somerville branch also serving some other "amazing" Asian fare; with "kind and competent service" factored in, the "price-to-performance value is hard to beat."

🗹 Washington Inn *American* `27` `26` `26` `$62`

Cape May | 801 Washington St. (Jefferson St.) | 609-884-5697 | www.washingtoninn.com

Setting "the standard" for "fine dining" in Cape May and beyond is this "class act" voted "excellent in all respects", from the "top-tier" Traditional American fare and "wonderful", "deep" wine list to the "lovely" dining rooms set in a "beautiful" old plantation home; a "staff that goes the extra mile" helps make the predictably "high prices" easier to digest.

Waterfront Buffet *Eclectic* ▽ `19` `20` `18` `$36`
(fka Fantasea Reef Buffet)

Atlantic City | Harrah's | 777 Harrah's Blvd. (Brigantine Blvd.) | 609-441-5451 | www.harrahs.com

"Go when you're very hungry" to this casual, "cavernous" buffet in Harrah's, which some surveyors consider Atlantic City's "best" for its "dizzying selection" of "nicely prepared", "amply proportioned" Eclectic choices; service is basically limited to bringing drinks and clearing, yet still manages to be "spotty."

West Lake Seafood Restaurant *Chinese* `22` `10` `15` `$26`

Matawan | Pine Crest Plaza | 1016 Rte. 34 (Broad St.) | 732-290-2988 | www.westlakeseafood.com

There's more than just "run-of-the-mill" Chinese at this "authentic", "real-deal" Matawan BYO – simply "order from the Chinese menu" (it's translated) for food that conjures up "Chinatown", "Hong Kong" and/or "Canton" with its "bright flavors"; your fish is picked "fresh" from the room's tanks – if only the decor and service would "complement the unique food"; P.S. dim sum on weekends.

What's Your Beef? *Steak* `22` `15` `18` `$41`

Rumson | 21 W. River Rd. (Lafayette St.) | 732-842-6205 | www.whatsyourbeefrumson.com

"Walk in, pick your cut of beef" "from the display case", then help yourself to the "expansive" salad bar at this "informal" Rumson "institution"/steakhouse (which also features "quite delicious" fish); some say at 40-years-old it "needs a complete renovation" – but even so, "be prepared to wait" due to a no-reservations policy.

🗹 Whispers *American* `27` `24` `25` `$58`

Spring Lake | Hewitt Wellington Hotel | 200 Monmouth Ave. (2nd Ave.) | 732-974-9755 | www.whispersrestaurant.com

"Civility at the Shore" and "quiet elegance" can be found at this "intimate" Spring Lake BYO in a "lovely" Victorian inn; "always on top of its game", with "interesting" New American fare that "delivers big taste" and a "polished", "gracious" staff that "pays attention to the details", this "special-occasion mainstay" may be "a bit steep" but it's "worth it" for a "memorable" meal.

			FOOD	DECOR	SERVICE	COST

White House ⊅ *Sandwiches*   26 | 9 | 16 | $14

Atlantic City | 2301 Arctic Ave. (Mississippi Ave.) | 609-345-1564
It's "hoagie heaven" at this "legendary" 60-plus-years-old AC "landmark", a "sandwich" "icon" that may not "be good for your cholesterol – but is very satisfying"; credit the "lines-out-the-door" to the bread that's delivered multiple times daily from a nearby bakery to this "small", "worn" "time warp" where all overlook the decor ("there isn't any") and "pushy" but efficient staff.

Wild Ginger ⑤Ⓜ *Japanese*   22 | 16 | 20 | $42

Englewood | 6 E. Palisade Ave. (bet. Dean & Van Brunt Sts.) | 201-567-2660 | www.wild-ginger.biz
Fans of this "low-key, casual, funky" (and "cramped") Englewood Japanese BYO go wild for the "high-quality" "amazing sushi" in "interesting combinations"; "let the chef decide the menu and you can't go wrong", "but be prepared to drop some serious cash."

NEW William Douglas Steakhouse *Steak*   ∇ 22 | 24 | 22 | $61

Cherry Hill | Garden State Pk. | 941 Haddonfield Rd. (Rte. 70) | 856-665-6100 | www.williamdouglassteakhouse.com
This equestrian-themed "old-world-style" chophouse, which debuted at Cherry Hill's Garden State Park in 2008, is a project of McCormick & Schmick's (an outpost of which is just next door); early returns indicate it "competes well" with similar venues – including "high-priced" steakhouses – but stands out with "above-par" service and live piano Thursdays–Saturdays.

Windansea *Seafood*   17 | 20 | 18 | $36

Highlands | 56 Shrewsbury Ave. (Bay Ave.) | 732-872-2266 | www.windseanj.com
"Gorgeous" water views and "fresh" fare draw many to this Highlands seafooder; "families" applaud the scene for lunch or during early-dinner hours on Saturdays, all before "lively" crowds "invade the place" on the lookout for drinks and a "meat market."

WindMill, The *Hot Dogs*   19 | 8 | 14 | $12

Westfield | 256 E. Broad St. (Central Ave.) | 908-233-2001
Belmar | 1201 River Rd. (Rte. 71) | 732-681-9628 ◑
Brick | 856 Rte. 70 (Rte. 88) | 732-458-7774
Freehold | 3338 Hwy. 9 S. (Jackson Mills Rd.) | 732-303-9855
Long Branch | 200 Ocean Blvd. (Morris Ave.) | 732-870-6098
Long Branch | 586 Ocean Ave. (Brighton Ave.) | 732-229-9863 ◑
Ocean Grove | 18 S. Main St. (Lake Ave.) | 732-988-5277
Red Bank | 22 N. Bridge Ave. (Front St.) | 732-747-5958
www.windmillhotdogs.com
"Juicy" foot-long hot dogs that get a thumbs-up even from Martha Stewart and "freakin' incredible" cheese fries "keep people coming back" to these "quick-stop" "staples" at the Shore and now beyond (look for one to open in Hoboken); the original windmill-shaped location at 586 Ocean Avenue in Long Branch offers upstairs outdoor seating with a view.

| | FOOD | DECOR | SERVICE | COST |

Witherspoon Grill *Seafood/Steak* | 21 | 22 | 19 | $50 |

Princeton | 57 Witherspoon St. (bet. Hulfish & Wiggins Sts.) |
609-924-6011 | www.jmgroupprinceton.com
A "very active" bar scene and "casual"-yet-"cosmopolitan" digs (including an outdoor area facing Princeton's "lovely" library plaza)
make this steak-and-seafood grill "one happening place"; there are
complaints about "just-ok" eats at "NY prices" and a reservations
policy that excludes Fridays and Saturdays, but those "crowds"
keep coming nonetheless.

Wolfgang Puck American Grille *American* | 24 | 23 | 23 | $57 |

Atlantic City | Borgata Hotel, Casino & Spa | 1 Borgata Way (Huron Ave.) |
609-317-1000 | www.theborgata.com
"Master" restaurateur Wolfgang Puck's AC Borgata New American
is "a joy every time" for its "delicious" "typical Puck" fare, which
ranges from burgers and pizza in the "casual" tavern up front to
"high-end" "gourmet" offerings in the rear dining room of its "exciting", Tony Chi–designed space; "well-trained" service is one more
reason it's a "solid" bet.

Wondee's Thai Café *Thai* | 20 | 6 | 16 | $23 |

Hackensack | 296 Main St. (Camden St.) | 201-883-1700 |
www.wondeenj.com
"Traditional" soups and noodle dishes that are "cheap and tasty" attract patrons to this "unassuming", "authentic" Hackensack Thai
BYO; though the "atmosphere is rather stark", the "friendly and
helpful" staff delivers "fast" service, making it "good for lunch" if not
even "better for takeout."

Wonder Seafood *Chinese* | 23 | 10 | 17 | $25 |

Edison | 1984 Rte. 27 (Langstaff Ave.) | 732-287-6328
Carts bearing "yummy weekend lunchtime dim sum" attract those
craving "excellent Cantonese-style" fare to this Edison Chinese
BYO; though the "authentic" dishes "served family-style" are "wonderful", the "boring" digs and "not-so-great service, especially if you
don't know how to speak Chinese", make some opt for takeout.

Word of Mouth *American* | 25 | 24 | 23 | $41 |

Collingswood | 729 Haddon Ave. (bet. Collings & Washington Aves.) |
856-858-2228
Greg Fenski's "intimate", "upscale" New American BYO is a "favorite" of Collingswood locals on account of "excellent" and "inventive"
"fine-dining" fare that's "beautifully presented"; rounding out this
most "pleasant dining experience" is service that's "always on" in an
"elegant yet comfortable" space.

Yankee Doodle Tap Room *Pub Food* | 15 | 19 | 17 | $33 |

Princeton | Nassau Inn | 10 Palmer Sq. (Nassau St.) | 609-921-7500 |
www.nassauinn.com
"Reeking of Princeton tradition" is this "cozy" "Ivy League" taproom
inside the "very Princeton" Nassau Inn; it's "most memorable" for
the namesake Norman Rockwell mural above the bar, "dark-wood"

"booths bearing the carvings of past generations", and photos of famed graduates (Michelle Obama is a recent addition), but less memorable for its "dependable" bar food.

	FOOD	DECOR	SERVICE	COST

Ya Ya Noodles *Chinese* — 19 | 13 | 18 | $24
Skillman | Montgomery Shopping Ctr. | 1325 Rte. 206 N. (Rte. 518) | 609-921-8551 | www.yayanoodles.com
"Noodles and dumplings are especially well done" at this "casual" Skillman BYO serving "both American-Chinese and authentic Chinese" fare at a "reasonable price"; though there's "nothing special about the location" or service, the "huge menu" ensures "something for everyone."

Yellow Fin *American* — 26 | 18 | 20 | $52
Surf City | 104 24th St. (Beach Ave.) | 609-494-7001
"Crowded but fantastic", this Surf City New American BYO is spawning "spectacular", "artistically prepared" dishes (especially "first-rate" fish); for many, it's "Manhattan-meets-LBI", but that also extends to a "small", "tight" dining room, hard-to-get weekend reservations, a staff that some perceive as "snooty" – and "NYC prices" that are nonetheless "worth it."

Yumi *Pan-Asian* — 26 | 20 | 21 | $44
Sea Bright | 1120 Ocean Ave. (Church St.) | 732-212-0881 | www.yumirestaurant.com
"Yummy" is the word for the "wide and varied menu of raw and cooked dishes" with Pan-Asian "flair" at this "sublime" Sea Bright BYO – although "mouthwatering" and "jaw dropping" also apply; the "warm" and "attentive" owners and staff help deflect a "too dark" room and a tab that can get "a little pricey."

Zafra *Pan-Latin* — 24 | 16 | 19 | $31
Hoboken | 301 Willow Ave. (3rd St.) | 201-610-9801
"*Delicioso*" Pan-Latin fare and the "best fruit drinks imaginable" are served all day in a "festive", "homey" atmosphere at celeb chef and co-owner Maricel Presilla's "tiny" Hoboken BYO, "the low-key version" of sibling Cucharamama; *sí*, it's "cramped" and "fills up early", but the "curbside tables are a prime spot for people-watching."

NEW **Zen Den Bar & Grill** ◑Ⓜ *American* — - | - | - | M
(fka Bistro En)
Teaneck | 254 Degraw Ave. (Queen Anne Rd.) | 201-692-1002
Sushi is out – while mussels with white wine, burgers and rib-eye steaks are in at this former French-Japanese Teaneck storefront that has reinvented itself into an American bistro.

INDEXES

Cuisines

Includes restaurant names, locations and Food ratings.

AFGHAN

Pamir | **Morristown**	21

AMERICAN (NEW)

Acacia | **Lawrenceville**	23
☑ Amanda's | **Hoboken**	25
Amelia's Bistro | **Jersey City**	20
☑ André's | **Newton**	27
Anton's/Swan | **Lambertville**	22
Atlantic B&G | **S Seaside Pk**	25
NEW Avenue Bistro Pub | **Verona**	–
Barnsboro Inn | **Sewell**	22
☑ Bay Ave. | **Highlands**	27
Bazzini | **Ridgewood**	19
Belford Bistro | **Belford**	28
Bell's Mansion | **Stanhope**	17
☑ Bernards Inn | **Bernardsville**	26
Blackbird | **Collingswood**	26
Black Trumpet | **Spring Lake**	25
Blu | **Montclair**	24
Blue | **Surf City**	24
☑ Blue Bottle | **Hopewell**	27
NEW Blvd. Five 72 | **Kenilworth**	27
Brandl. | **Belmar**	24
Brass Rail | **Hoboken**	19
Brothers Moon | **Hopewell**	22
Cafe/Rosemont | **Rosemont**	20
Cafe Loren | **Avalon**	26
Cafe Madison | **Riverside**	20
☑ Chakra | **Paramus**	20
Church St. | **Montclair**	14
City Bistro | **Hoboken**	18
Clydz | **New Bruns.**	22
CoccoLa | **Hillsborough**	19
Continental | **A.C.**	23
Copeland | **Morristown**	25
Copper Fish | **Cape May**	20
Cork | **Westmont**	21
☑ CulinAriane | **Montclair**	27
daddy O | **Long Beach**	19
☑ Daryl | **New Bruns.**	24

David Burke | **Rumson**	25
☑ David Drake | **Rahway**	28
NEW Delicious Heights | **Berkeley Hts**	21
Dish | **Red Bank**	24
Doris/Ed's | **Highlands**	25
☑ Drew's | **Keyport**	26
☑ Ebbitt Rm. | **Cape May**	27
NEW elements | **Princeton**	–
Elements | **Haddon Hts**	24
Equus | **Bernardsville**	21
Esty St. | **Park Ridge**	24
NEW Farm 2 Bistro | **Nutley**	–
Ferry Hse. | **Princeton**	25
Fiddleheads | **Jamesburg**	22
55 Main | **Flemington**	20
NEW Fire/Oak | **Little Falls**	–
☑ Frog/Peach | **New Bruns.**	26
Gazelle | **Ridgewood**	24
GG's | **Mt Laurel**	24
Grenville | **Bay Hd.**	21
Grill 73 | **Bernardsville**	21
Harrison | **Asbury Pk**	22
Harvest Moon | **Ringoes**	23
☑ Highlawn | **W Orange**	25
High St. | **Mt Holly**	23
Huntley Taverne | **Summit**	22
Inlet | **Somers Point**	19
Isabella's | **Westfield**	18
Island Palm | **Spring Lake**	19
☑ Karen & Rei's | **Clermont**	26
Kitchen 233 | **Westmont**	20
Krave Café | **Newton**	23
Lahiere's | **Princeton**	22
Light Horse | **Jersey City**	23
Luke's | **Maplewood**	21
Madison B&G | **Hoboken**	20
Mahogany | **Manasquan**	23
Main St. Bistro | **Freehold**	21
Main St. Euro-Amer. | **Princeton**	19

Maize | **Newark**	18
Manna | **Margate**	24
Marco/Pepe ‡ **Jersey City**	22
Marie Nicole's | **Wildwood**	24
Martini Bistro | **Millburn**	18
Matisse | **Belmar**	21
Mattar's Bistro | **Allamuchy**	–
Matt's Rooster | **Flemington**	25
Metuchen Inn | **Metuchen**	21
Mill/Spring Lake | **Spring Lake Hts**	21
Mohawk Hse. | **Sparta**	19
Montville Inn | **Montville**	21
☑ Moonstruck | **Asbury Pk**	25
Napa Valley | **Paramus**	21
Nauvoo Grill | **Fair Haven**	16
☑ Nicholas | **Middletown**	28
NEW 9 North | **Wayne**	–
No. 9 | **Lambertville**	26
One 53 | **Rocky Hill**	23
Onieal's | **Hoboken**	18
NEW Orange Squirrel | **Bloomfield**	–
Orbis Bistro | **Upper Montclair**	20
Ox | **Jersey City**	23
Park Ave. | **Union City**	18
Pasta Fresca | **Shrewsbury**	19
☑ Peter Shields | **Cape May**	26
Pine Tavern | **Old Bridge**	18
Plan B | **Asbury Pk**	–
Plantation | **Harvey Cedars**	20
☑ Pluckemin Inn | **Bedminster**	26
NEW Prairie | **Monmouth Bch**	–
Raven/Peach | **Fair Haven**	25
Raymond's | **Montclair**	21
Red | **Red Bank**	20
Renault Winery | **Egg Harbor**	23
Rest. Latour | **Hamburg**	25
restaurant.mc | **Millburn**	23
Rosemary/Sage | **Riverdale**	26
☑ Saddle River Inn | **Saddle River**	28
Salt Water | **Asbury Pk**	18
Scarborough Fair | **Sea Girt**	21

Sergeantsville Inn | **Sergeantsville**	23
Shipwreck Grill | **Brielle**	25
Simply Radishing | **Lawrenceville**	19
Skylark | **Edison**	20
SoHo/George | **New Bruns.**	23
Sonsie | **A.C.**	21
Spargo's | **Manalapan**	24
Stage Hse. | **Scotch Plains**	22
Stage Left | **New Bruns.**	26
Steve/Cookie's | **Margate**	25
☑ Stonehouse | **Warren**	22
Sweet Basil's | **W Orange**	23
Table 8 | **Montclair**	23
Tabor Rd. | **Morris Plains**	21
Ted's/Main | **Medford**	25
Terrace | **Short Hills**	22
Tewksbury Inn | **Oldwick**	22
Theater Sq. | **Newark**	20
3 Forty | **Hoboken**	21
NEW Tim McLoone's | **Asbury Pk**	17
Tim Schafer's | **Morristown**	25
☑ Tisha's | **Cape May**	26
Trap Rock | **Berkeley Hts**	21
Trinity | **Keyport**	23
Union Park | **Cape May**	25
Verdigre | **New Bruns.**	21
Verve | **Somerville**	22
Village Green | **Ridgewood**	23
Vine | **Basking Ridge**	25
☑ Whispers | **Spring Lake**	27
Wolfgang Puck | **A.C.**	24
Word of Mouth | **Collingswood**	25
Yellow Fin | **Surf City**	26

AMERICAN (TRADITIONAL)

Alchemist/Barrister | **Princeton**	16
Allendale B&G | **Allendale**	17
A Toute Heure | **Cranford**	25
Avon Pavilion | **Avon-by-Sea**	19
NEW Backyards | **Hoboken**	–
Barnacle Bill's | **Rumson**	21
Basil T's | **Red Bank**	20
☑ Baumgart's | **multi.**	19

Bell's | **Lambertville**	21
Bell's Mansion | **Stanhope**	17
Bistro 44 | **Toms River**	24
Black Horse | **Mendham**	19
Blue Pig | **Cape May**	21
Braddock's | **Medford**	21
Brickwall | **Asbury Pk**	18
Buttonwood Manor | **Matawan**	14
Cabin | **Howell**	16
Charley's | **Long Branch**	18
☑ Cheesecake Factory | **multi.**	19
Chickie's/Pete's | **multi.**	16
Christopher's | **Colts Neck**	19
CJ Montana's | **Tinton Falls**	19
Clark's Landing | **Pt. Pleas.**	17
Country Pancake | **Ridgewood**	20
Cranbury Inn | **Cranbury**	15
Gaslight | **Hoboken**	19
Gladstone | **Gladstone**	21
Gotham City | **multi.**	18
Gusto Grill | **E Brunswick**	17
Hard Grove | **Jersey City**	15
Harry's | **Sea Bright**	21
Holsten's | **Bloomfield**	17
Inn/Millrace | **Hope**	21
Inn/Sugar Hill | **Mays Landing**	23
Inn/Hawke | **Lambertville**	18
Ivy Inn | **Hasbrouck Hts**	20
Java Moon | **Jackson**	18
Johnny Rockets | **multi.**	15
Lambertville Station | **Lambertville**	17
Liberty Hse. | **Jersey City**	20
Limestone Cafe | **Peapack**	21
Lucky Bones | **Cape May**	21
Mad Batter | **Cape May**	23
☑ Manor | **W Orange**	24
Mastoris | **Bordentown**	20
McLoone's | **multi.**	17
Meil's | **Stockton**	22
Merion Inn | **Cape May**	23
Molly Pitcher | **Red Bank**	23
Nag's Head | **Ocean City**	23
Next Door | **Montclair**	21

Nicky's | **Madison**	19
Old Man Rafferty's | **multi.**	18
Perryville Inn | **Union Twp**	23
Pheasants Landing | **Hillsborough**	19
P.J. Whelihan's | **multi.**	16
Pop Shop | **Collingswood**	20
☑ Ram's Head | **Galloway**	25
Redstone | **Marlton**	22
Redwood's | **Chester**	16
Robin's Nest | **Mt Holly**	22
Rod's Olde Irish | **Sea Girt**	18
Sallee Tee's | **Monmouth Bch**	19
Salt Creek | **multi.**	19
Smithville Inn | **Smithville**	21
South City | **multi.**	22
3 West | **Basking Ridge**	22
Toast | **Montclair**	20
Triumph Brew. | **Princeton**	16
Tuckers | **Beach Haven**	16
Tun Tavern | **A.C.**	17
Ugly Mug | **Cape May**	17
Walpack Inn | **Wallpack**	19
☑ Washington Inn | **Cape May**	27
Yankee Doodle | **Princeton**	15
NEW Zen Den | **Teaneck**	-

ASIAN

Coconut Bay | **Voorhees**	20
Metropolitan Cafe | **Freehold**	21
Taro | **Montclair**	20
Tina Louise | **Carlstadt**	24

ASIAN FUSION

Fusion | **Flemington**	22
Taro | **Montclair**	20

BAKERIES

Mastoris | **Bordentown**	20
Ponzio's | **Cherry Hill**	18

BARBECUE

Big Ed's BBQ | **Matawan**	19
Bourbon County | **Wyckoff**	19
Corky's | **A.C.**	18
Cubby's | **Hackensack**	18

D & L BBQ	**Asbury Pk**	22
GRUB Hut	**Manville**	21
Indigo Smoke	**Montclair**	21
Memphis Pig Out	**Atlantic Highlands**	21
Red Hot/Blue	**Cherry Hill**	19

BRAZILIAN

Brasilia Grill	**Newark**	21
Brasilia Rest.	**Newark**	21
Rio 22	**Union**	19

BRITISH

| Elephant/Castle | **Cherry Hill** | 13 |
| Ship Inn | **Milford** | 15 |

BURGERS

Barnacle Bill's	**Rumson**	21
NEW Bobby's	**Eatontown**	20
Five Guys	**multi.**	21
Hiram's	**Fort Lee**	20
JD's	**Fort Lee**	18
Johnny Rockets	**multi.**	15
Nifty Fifty's	**multi.**	18
Pop Shop	**Collingswood**	20
WindMill	**multi.**	19

CAJUN

Bayou Cafe	**Freehold**	21
Creole Café	**Sewell**	22
Oddfellows	**Hoboken**	18
Old Bay	**New Bruns.**	19

CALIFORNIAN

Napa Valley	**Paramus**	21
Surf Taco	**multi.**	20
Tomatoes	**Margate**	24

CARIBBEAN

| Bahama Breeze | **Cherry Hill** | 18 |
| Sister Sue's | **Asbury Pk** | 21 |

CHICKEN

NEW El Pollo Loco	**N Bergen**	-
NEW Pollo Campero	**W New York**	-
Pollo Tropical	**multi.**	-

CHINESE
(* dim sum specialist)

Cathay 22	**Springfield**	22
Chengdu 46	**Clifton**	24
Chez Elena Wu	**Voorhees**	23
Crown Palace*	**multi.**	20
Dim Sum Dynasty*	**Ridgewood**	20
Edo Sushi	**Pennington**	19
Far East Taste	**Eatontown**	23
Hunan Chinese	**Morris Plains**	22
Hunan Spring	**Springfield**	20
Hunan Taste	**Denville**	24
Joe's Peking*	**Marlton**	23
Lotus Cafe	**Hackensack**	24
Meemah	**Edison**	22
Mr. Chu	**E Hanover**	21
Z P.F. Chang's	**multi.**	20
Sakura Spring	**Cherry Hill**	22
Sally Ling	**Fort Lee**	18
Shanghai Jazz	**Madison**	21
Sunny Gdn.	**Princeton**	20
West Lake	**Matawan**	22
Wonder Seafood*	**Edison**	23
Ya Ya Noodles	**Skillman**	19

COFFEE SHOPS/DINERS

Fedora	**Lawrenceville**	18
Gotham City	**multi.**	18
Mastoris	**Bordentown**	20
Nifty Fifty's	**multi.**	18
Ponzio's	**Cherry Hill**	18
Skylark	**Edison**	20
Teplitzky's	**A.C.**	-
Tick Tock	**Clifton**	18
Tom Sawyer	**Paramus**	17

COLOMBIAN

| El Familiar | **multi.** | 19 |

CONTINENTAL

Black Forest Inn	**Stanhope**	22
Café Gallery	**Burlington**	23
Court St.	**Hoboken**	22
Farnsworth	**Bordentown**	23

CUISINES

Inn/Millrace	**Hope**	21
Lincroft Inn	**Lincroft**	18
Main St. Euro-Amer.	**Princeton**	19
Pheasants Landing	**Hillsborough**	19
Rest. L	**Allendale**	20
🔣 Stony Hill Inn	**Hackensack**	23

CREOLE

Bayou Cafe	**Freehold**	21
Clementine's	**Avon-by-Sea**	23
Creole Café	**Sewell**	22
410 Bank St.	**Cape May**	26
Mélange	**multi.**	25
Oddfellows	**Hoboken**	18
Old Bay	**New Bruns.**	19

CUBAN

Azúcar	**Jersey City**	21
Casona	**Collingswood**	22
Cuba Libre	**A.C.**	22
Cuban Pete's	**Montclair**	18
NEW Cubanu	**Rahway**	24
Hard Grove	**Jersey City**	15
Havana	**Highlands**	16
La Isla	**Hoboken**	26
Martino's	**Somerville**	22
Mi Bandera	**Union City**	23
Mundo	**N Bergen**	21
Rebecca's	**Edgewater**	25

DELIS/SANDWICH SHOPS

Eppes Essen	**Livingston**	19
Hobby's	**Newark**	23
Jack Cooper's	**Edison**	18
Jerry/Harvey's	**Marlboro**	18
Kibitz Rm.	**Cherry Hill**	22
Nana's Deli	**Livingston**	22
Richard's	**Long Branch**	21

DESSERT

🔣 Cheesecake Factory	**multi.**	19
Holsten's	**Bloomfield**	17
Old Man Rafferty's	**multi.**	18

EASTERN EUROPEAN

| Blue Danube | **Trenton** | 23 |
| Underground Café | **Princeton** | 19 |

ECLECTIC

Alstarz	**Bordentown**	16
Bistro/Red Bank	**Red Bank**	21
Black Duck	**W Cape May**	24
Blue	**Surf City**	24
Brix 67	**Summit**	18
🔣 Cafe Matisse	**Rutherford**	27
Cafe Metro	**Denville**	21
🔣 Cafe Panache	**Ramsey**	28
California Grill	**Flemington**	18
Eurasian	**Red Bank**	22
Fedora	**Lawrenceville**	18
Frenchtown Inn	**Frenchtown**	25
Full Moon	**Lambertville**	21
🔣 Gables	**Beach Haven**	25
Garlic Rose	**multi.**	20
Grand Colonial	**Union Twp**	23
Labrador	**Normandy Bch**	23
NEW Langosta	**Asbury Pk**	–
Lilly's/Canal	**Lambertville**	21
Little Café	**Voorhees**	25
Mkt. in the Middle	**Asbury Pk**	21
Market Roost	**Flemington**	21
Metropolitan Cafe	**Freehold**	21
Meyersville Inn	**Gillette**	17
🔣 Park/Orchard	**E Rutherford**	22
🔣 Red Square	**A.C.**	21
restaurant.mc	**Millburn**	23
Sallee Tee's	**Monmouth Bch**	19
Soho 33	**Madison**	19
Tomatoes	**Margate**	24
Triumph Brew.	**Princeton**	16
Village Gourmet	**Rutherford**	21
Waterfront Buffet	**A.C.**	19

ETHIOPIAN

| Makeda | **New Bruns.** | 25 |

FONDUE

| Magic Pot | **Edgewater** | 18 |
| Melting Pot | **multi.** | 18 |

FRENCH

Alexander's | **Cape May**	26
Andaman | **Morristown**	23
Aozora | **Montclair**	25
Chez Catherine | **Westfield**	26
Claude's | **N Wildwood**	25
Ferry Hse. | **Princeton**	25
Frenchtown Inn | **Frenchtown**	25
☑ Grand Cafe | **Morristown**	26
La Campagne | **Cherry Hill**	24
☑ Latour | **Ridgewood**	26
Le Jardin | **Edgewater**	18
Le Petit Chateau | **Bernardsville**	25
☑ Lorena's | **Maplewood**	28
Madeleine's | **Northvale**	25
Manon | **Lambertville**	25
☑ Origin | **multi.**	26
Passionne | **Montclair**	23
☑ Rat's | **Hamilton**	25
NEW Resto | **Madison**	21
☑ Saddle River Inn | **Saddle River**	28
☑ Serenade | **Chatham**	28
Silver Spring | **Flanders**	26
Siri's | **Cherry Hill**	24
Soufflé | **Summit**	22
Thai Chef | **multi.**	21
Verjus | **Maplewood**	25
Verve | **Somerville**	22

FRENCH (BISTRO)

Bienvenue | **Red Bank**	23
Bistro 44 | **Toms River**	24
☑ Chef's Table | **Franklin Lakes**	26
Circa | **High Bridge**	22
Elysian | **Hoboken**	20
Epernay | **Montclair**	20
Harvest Bistro | **Closter**	21
NEW JL Ivy | **Princeton**	19
Le Fandy | **Fair Haven**	25
Le Rendez-Vous | **Kenilworth**	26
Madame Claude | **Jersey City**	23
Sophie's | **Somerset**	22

FRENCH (BRASSERIE)

☑ Avenue | **Long Branch**	20

GERMAN

Black Forest Inn | **Stanhope**	22

GREEK

Athenian Gdn. | **Galloway Twp**	24
Axia | **Tenafly**	23
Greek Taverna | **multi.**	-
It's Greek To Me | **multi.**	17
Kuzina | **Cherry Hill**	20
NEW Limani | **Westfield**	22
My Little Greek | **Freehold**	18
NEW Nisi Estiatorio | **Englewood**	-
Pithari | **Highland Pk**	23
NEW Stamna | **Bloomfield**	23
Varka | **Ramsey**	26

GUATEMALAN

NEW Pollo Campero | **W New York**	-

HOT DOGS

Hiram's | **Fort Lee**	20
Rutt's Hut | **Clifton**	21
WindMill | **multi.**	19

ICE CREAM PARLORS

Holsten's | **Bloomfield**	17

INDIAN

Aamantran | **Toms River Twp**	21
Aangan | **Freehold Twp**	22
Akbar | **Edison**	19
Amiya | **Jersey City**	19
Bombay Curry | **Basking Ridge**	18
Bombay Gdns. | **E Brunswick**	23
Chand | **multi.**	23
Cinnamon | **Morris Plains**	23
Dabbawalla | **Summit**	18
India/Hudson | **Hoboken**	20
Karma Kafe | **Hoboken**	24
Mantra | **Paramus**	24
Mehndi | **Morristown**	24
Moghul | **Edison**	25

Moksha | **Edison**	22
Neelam | **multi.**	20
Passage/India | **Lawrenceville**	21
Raagini | **Mountainside**	22
Saffron | **E Hanover**	22

IRISH

Egan/Sons | **Montclair**	18
Irish Pub | **A.C.**	18
Quiet Man | **Dover**	20

ITALIAN

(N=Northern; S=Southern)

Acquaviva | N | **Westfield**	22
Alan@594 | **Upper Montclair**	21
Al Dente | N | **Piscataway**	23
Aldo/Gianni | **multi.**	21
Alessio 426 | N | **Metuchen**	19
A Mano | **Ridgewood**	21
Amarone | N | **Teaneck**	21
Amici Milano | N | **Trenton**	22
Angelo's | **A.C.**	21
Anjelica's | S | **Sea Bright**	24
Anna's | **Middletown**	25
Anthony David's | N | **Hoboken**	26
Anthony's | **Haddon Hts**	23
Antonia's | **N Bergen**	20
Aquila Cucina | **New Providence**	22
Armando's | **Fort Lee**	18
Arturo's | S | **Midland Pk**	23
A Tavola | **Old Bridge**	19
☑ Augustino's | S | **Hoboken**	26
Barone's/Villa Barone | **multi.**	20
Barrel's | **multi.**	17
Basilico | N | **Millburn**	24
Basil T's | **Red Bank**	20
☑ Bay Ave. | **Highlands**	27
Bazzarelli | **Moonachie**	21
Bazzini | **Ridgewood**	19
Bella Sogno | **Bradley Bch**	20
Bell's | **Lambertville**	21
Belmont Tavern | **Bloomfield**	23
Benito's | N | **Chester**	24
Berta's | N | **Wanaque**	21

Bistro di Marino | **Collingswood**	23
Brioso | **Marlboro**	22
Brio | **Cherry Hill**	19
Buca di Beppo | **Cherry Hill**	16
Cafe Arugula | **S Orange**	21
Café Azzurro | N | **Peapack**	24
Cafe Bello | **Bayonne**	24
Cafe Coloré | **Freehold Twp**	21
Cafe Cucina | **Branchburg**	21
Cafe Emilia | **Bridgewater**	21
Cafe Graziella | **Hillsborough**	20
Cafe Italiano | **Englewood Cliffs**	19
Caffe Aldo | **Cherry Hill**	24
Capriccio | **A.C.**	26
Carmine's | **A.C.**	21
Carmine's Asbury Pk. | S | **Asbury Pk**	20
Casa Dante | **Jersey City**	23
Casa Giuseppe | N | **Iselin**	24
Catelli | **Voorhees**	25
☑ Catherine Lombardi | **New Bruns.**	23
Cenzino | **Oakland**	24
☑ Chef Vola's | **A.C.**	27
Christie's | **Howell**	23
Ciao | **Basking Ridge**	21
Cinque Figlie | **Whippany**	21
CoccoLa | **Hillsborough**	19
Columbia Inn | **Montville**	21
Corso 98 | **Montclair**	23
Cucina Rosa | **Cape May**	21
da Filippo | **Somerville**	23
Dante's | **Mendham**	21
DeAnna's | **Lambertville**	22
Dimora | N | **Norwood**	23
Dinallo's | **River Edge**	22
NEW Dino's | **Harrington Pk**	–
DiPalma | **N Bergen**	22
NEW Due Mari | **New Bruns.**	26
Due Terre | **Bernardsville**	25
E & V | **Paterson**	23
Eccola | **Parsippany**	23
NEW Eno Terra | **Kingston**	–

Espo's | S | **Raritan**	21	Luchento's | **Millstone Twp**	–
Ⓩ Fascino | **Montclair**	26	ⓃⒺⓌ Luciano's | **Rahway**	–
Federici's | **Freehold**	22	Luigi's | **E Hanover**	23
Ferrari's | **Freehold Twp**	22	Luka's | **Ridgefield Pk**	22
Filomena Italiana | S | **Clementon**	23	Lu Nello | **Cedar Grove**	25
Filomena Lakeview | S | **Deptford**	24	Margherita's | **Hoboken**	21
Filomena Rustica | S | **W Berlin**	23	Marra's | **Ridgewood**	20
Fiorino | N | **Summit**	23	Mia | **A.C.**	25
Forno | **Maple Shade**	–	Michael's | **Manalapan**	19
Frankie Fed's | **Freehold Twp**	22	Mirabella | **Cherry Hill**	20
Frescos | **Cape May**	24	Nunzio | **Collingswood**	24
Gaetano's | **Red Bank**	20	Ⓩ Ombra | **A.C.**	26
Gaslight | **Hoboken**	19	Osteria Giotto | **Montclair**	25
Girasole | S | **A.C.**	25	Panico's | **New Bruns.**	23
Girasole | **Bound Brook**	26	Papa Razzi | **multi.**	17
Giumarello's | N | **Westmont**	24	Paula/Rigoletto | N | **Weehawken**	21
GoodFellas | N | **Garfield**	20	Pete/Elda's | **Neptune City**	22
Grissini | **Englewood Cliffs**	22	Ⓩ Piccola | **Ocean Twp**	27
Homestead Inn | **Trenton**	24	Piero's | **Union Beach**	21
I Cavallini | **Colts Neck**	23	Pietro's | **Marlton**	20
Ⓩ Il Capriccio | **Whippany**	26	Pino's | **Marlboro**	19
ⓃⒺⓌ Il Fiore | **Collingswood**	26	Pizzicato | **Marlton**	20
Il Michelangelo | **Boonton**	21	Portobello | N | **Oakland**	19
Ⓩ Il Mondo | N | **Madison**	25	Portofino | **Tinton Falls**	23
ⓏⓃⒺⓌ Il Mulino NY | **A.C.**	26	Porto Leggero | **Jersey City**	22
Il Villaggio | **Carlstadt**	23	Posillipo | **Asbury Pk**	22
In Napoli | **Fort Lee**	17	Primavera | **W Orange**	21
Jimmy's | S | **Asbury Pk**	23	Radicchio | N | **Ridgewood**	22
Joe Pesce | **Collingswood**	23	Raimondo's | **Ship Bottom**	24
Kinchley's | **Ramsey**	23	Reservoir | **Boonton**	22
La Campagna | N | **multi.**	22	Rest., The | **Hackensack**	19
Laceno | **Voorhees**	26	Richie Cecere's | **Montclair**	20
La Cipollina | **Freehold**	21	Rick's | **Lambertville**	20
La Focaccia | N | **Summit**	24	Risotto Hse. | **Rutherford**	23
La Pastaria | **multi.**	19	Rist. Benito | **Union**	24
ⓃⒺⓌ LaPrete's | **Belleville**	22	Roberto's | N | **Beach Haven**	22
La Scala | N | **Somerville**	22	Roberto's II | **Edgewater**	19
La Sorrentina | **N Bergen**	26	RoCCA | **Glen Rock**	23
La Spiaggia | **Ship Bottom**	24	Rosa Luca's | **Asbury**	24
La Strada | **Randolph**	22	Rosie's | **Randolph**	21
LouCás | **Edison**	23	San Remo | **Shrewsbury**	23
Luca's | **Somerset**	–	Sanzari's | **New Milford**	20
Luce | **Caldwell**	21	Sapori | **Collingswood**	24

Z Scalini Fedeli | N | **Chatham**	27	
Settebello | **Morristown**	21	
Sirena | **Long Branch**	22	
Sogno | **Red Bank**	22	
Solaia | **Englewood**	18	
Solari's | **Hackensack**	20	
Solo Bella | **Jackson**	21	
Squan Tavern | S | **Manasquan**	21	
NEW Stella Marina | **Asbury Pk**	–	
Z Stony Hill Inn | **Hackensack**	23	
Tattoni's | **Hamilton Twp**	21	
Teresa Caffe | **Princeton**	22	
Theresa's | **Westfield**	22	
NEW Torcello | **Red Bank**	–	
Z Tre Figlio | **Egg Harbor**	27	
Tre Piani | **Princeton**	22	
Trovato's | S | **multi.**	25	
Tutto a Modo Mio | **Ridgefield**	23	
Tuzzio's | **Long Branch**	20	
2Senza | **Red Bank**	21	
Undici | **Rumson**	21	
Ventura's | **Margate**	17	
Vespa's | **Edgewater**	17	
Vic's | **Bradley Bch**	20	
Villa Vittoria | **Brick**	22	

JAPANESE

(* sushi specialist)

Z Ajihei* | **Princeton**	28	
Akai* | **Englewood**	25	
Aligado* | **Hazlet**	24	
Aozora | **Montclair**	25	
Benihana | **multi.**	18	
Chez Elena Wu | **Voorhees**	23	
Dai-Kichi* | **Upper Montclair**	22	
East* | **Teaneck**	19	
Edo Sushi* | **Pennington**	19	
Elements Asia* | **Lawrenceville**	23	
Fuji | **Haddonfield**	24	
Ichiban* | **Princeton**	18	
Ikko* | **Brick**	25	
izakaya | **A.C.**	26	
NEW JL Ivy* | **Princeton**	19	
Kanji* | **Tinton Falls**	25	

Klein's* | **Belmar**	19	
K.O.B.E.* | **Holmdel**	22	
Komegashi* | **Jersey City**	23	
Konbu* | **Manalapan**	25	
Mahzu* | **multi.**	21	
Megu* | **Cherry Hill**	24	
Midori* | **Denville**	22	
Mikado* | **multi.**	23	
Minado* | **multi.**	19	
Monster Sushi* | **Summit**	20	
Nikko* | **Whippany**	24	
Nobi* | **Toms River Twp**	25	
Nori* | **multi.**	23	
Nouveau* | **Montclair**	24	
Ota-Ya* | **Lambertville**	22	
Oyako Tso's* | **Freehold**	23	
Rio 22* | **Union**	19	
Robongi | **Hoboken**	24	
Z Sagami* | **Collingswood**	27	
Sakura-Bana* | **Ridgewood**	25	
Sakura Spring | **Cherry Hill**	22	
SAWA Steak* | **multi.**	22	
Shogun* | **multi.**	22	
Shumi* | **Somerville**	25	
Sono Sushi* | **Middletown**	25	
Sumo* | **Wall**	25	
Sushi by Kazu* | **Howell**	26	
Sushi Lounge* | **multi.**	22	
Swanky Bubbles* | **Cherry Hill**	20	
Taka* | **Asbury Pk**	25	
Takara | **Oakhurst**	24	
Tokyo Bleu | **Cinnaminson**	22	
Tomo's | **Little Falls**	21	
Tsuki* | **Bernardsville**	22	
Wasabi* | **multi.**	25	
Wild Ginger* | **Englewood**	22	
Yumi* | **Sea Bright**	26	

JEWISH

Eppes Essen | **Livingston**	19	
Hobby's | **Newark**	23	
Kibitz Rm. | **Cherry Hill**	22	
Nana's Deli | **Livingston**	22	

Menus, photos, voting and more – free at ZAGAT.com

KOREAN

(* barbecue specialist)

So Moon Nan Jip* | **Palisades Pk** 25

KOSHER/ KOSHER-STYLE

Jerry/Harvey's | **Marlboro** 18

MALAYSIAN

Meemah | **Edison** 22

Penang | **multi.** 21

Taste of Asia | **Chatham** 21

MEDITERRANEAN

Europa Monroe | **Monroe Twp** 16

Frescos | **Cape May** 24

Hamilton's | **Lambertville** 25

Lodos | **New Milford** 23

Marmara | **Manalapan** 19

Mediterra | **Princeton** 21

Z Moonstruck | **Asbury Pk** 25

Sage | **Ventnor** 24

Seven Hills | **Highland Pk** 22

Terrace | **Short Hills** 22

Tre Piani | **Princeton** 22

2Senza | **Red Bank** 21

Verdigre | **New Bruns.** 21

Vine | **Basking Ridge** 25

MEXICAN

Aby's | **Matawan** 20

Baja | **multi.** 19

Baja Fresh | **multi.** 17

Casa Maya | **multi.** 21

Charrito's | **multi.** 22

Chilangos | **Highlands** 21

El Azteca | **Mt Laurel** 20

El Familiar | **multi.** 19

El Meson | **Freehold** 24

Jose's | **Spring Lake Hts** 24

Jose's Cantina | **multi.** 20

Juanito's | **multi.** 22

La Esperanza | **Lindenwold** 22

Los Amigos | **multi.** 22

Mexican Food | **Marlton** 20

Mexico Lindo | **Brick** 23

Pop's Garage | **multi.** 22

Senorita's | **Bloomfield** 20

Surf Taco | **multi.** 20

Taqueria | **Jersey City** 22

Tortilla Press | **Collingswood** 22

Tortuga's | **Princeton** 20

MIDDLE EASTERN

Ali Baba | **Hoboken** 20

Norma's | **Cherry Hill** 21

NOODLE SHOPS

Noodle Hse. | **N Brunswick** 18

NUEVO LATINO

Sabor | **multi.** 22

Vivas | **Belmar** 26

PAN-ASIAN

Bank 34 | **Somerville** 23

Z Baumgart's | **multi.** 19

Z Buddakan | **A.C.** 25

Elements Asia | **Lawrenceville** 23

Grand Shanghai | **Edison** 19

Z Hotoke | **New Bruns.** 21

Ming | **Edison** 21

Ming II | **Morristown** 24

Nori | **Caldwell** 23

Nouveau | **Montclair** 24

Ritz Seafood | **Voorhees** 24

Swanky Bubbles | **Cherry Hill** 20

Teak | **Red Bank** 20

Yumi | **Sea Bright** 26

PAN-LATIN

Casa Solar | **Belmar** 25

Lua | **Hoboken** 22

Park Ave. | **Union City** 18

Zafra | **Hoboken** 24

PIZZA

A Mano | **Ridgewood** 21

Benny Tudino's | **Hoboken** 20

Brooklyn's Pizza | **multi.** 23

Columbia Inn | **Montville** 21

Conte's | **Princeton** 24

🆉 DeLorenzo's Pies	multi.	27
DeLorenzo's Pizza	Trenton	–
Federici's	Freehold	22
Forno	Maple Shade	–
Frankie Fed's	Freehold Twp	22
Grimaldi's	Hoboken	24
Kinchley's	Ramsey	23
Luca's	Somerset	–
Margherita's	Hoboken	21
Nicky's	Madison	19
Pete/Elda's	Neptune City	22
Pietro's	Marlton	20
Pino's	Marlboro	19
Pizzicato	Marlton	20
Reservoir	Boonton	22
Tacconelli's	Maple Shade	22
Tony's	A.C.	18
Vic's	Bradley Bch	20

POLISH

Royal Warsaw	Elmwood Pk	23

PORTUGUESE

Adega	Newark	21
Bistro Olé	Asbury Pk	24
Don Pepe	multi.	21
Europa South	Pt. Pleas. Bch	19
Fernandes	Newark	23
Iberia	Newark	19
Maize	Newark	18
Pic-Nic	E Newark	24
Portuguese Manor	Perth Amboy	20
Segovia	Moonachie	22
Spain	Newark	22
Tony Da Caneca	Newark	23
Vila Nova	Newark	23

PUB FOOD

Alchemist/Barrister	Princeton	16
Allendale B&G	Allendale	17
Alstarz	Bordentown	16
Barnacle Bill's	Rumson	21
Black Horse	Mendham	19
Brickwall	Asbury Pk	18

Chickie's/Pete's	multi.	16
Elephant/Castle	Cherry Hill	13
Inn/Hawke	Lambertville	18
Irish Pub	A.C.	18
Light Horse	Jersey City	23
P.J. Whelihan's	multi.	16
Quiet Man	Dover	20
Rod's Olde Irish	Sea Girt	18
Ship Inn	Milford	15
Ugly Mug	Cape May	17
Yankee Doodle	Princeton	15

RUSSIAN

🆉 Red Square	A.C.	21

SANDWICHES

Hale/Hearty	Livingston	18
Little Food Café	multi.	25
Sallee Tee's	Monmouth Bch	19
Tony Luke's	A.C.	21
White Hse.	A.C.	26

SEAFOOD

Allen's	New Gretna	19
Athenian Gdn.	Galloway Twp	24
Atlantic B&G	S Seaside Pk	25
Axelsson's	Cape May	23
Bahrs Landing	Highlands	16
Bank 34	Somerville	23
Barnacle Ben's	Moorestown	20
Berkeley	S Seaside Pk	20
Blue Fish	Flemington	21
🆉 Blue Point	Princeton	25
Bobby Chez	multi.	24
Busch's	Sea Isle City	20
Capt'n Ed's	Pt. Pleas.	18
Chart Hse.	Weehawken	21
Chophouse	Gibbsboro	25
Clark's Landing	Pt. Pleas.	17
Copper Fish	Cape May	20
Crab House	Edgewater	16
Crab's Claw	Lavallette	18
Crab Trap	Somers Point	22
da Filippo	Somerville	23

Dock's | **A.C.**	26
Don Quijote | **Fairview**	17
Doris/Ed's | **Highlands**	25
NEW Due Mari | **New Bruns.**	26
Dune | **Margate**	25
Ferrari's | **Freehold Twp**	22
Fishery, The | **S Amboy**	–
Fresco | **Milltown**	25
Hamilton's | **Lambertville**	25
Harry's | **Sea Bright**	21
Harvey Cedars | **multi.**	22
Hunt Club | **Summit**	21
Inlet Café | **Highlands**	20
Joe Pesce | **Collingswood**	23
John Henry's | **Trenton**	24
Klein's | **Belmar**	19
Kunkel's | **Haddon Hts**	24
Laceno | **Voorhees**	26
Latitude 40N | **Pt. Pleas. Bch**	23
Z Legal Sea Foods | **multi.**	21
NEW Limani | **Westfield**	22
Little Tuna | **Haddonfield**	21
Lobster Hse. | **Cape May**	21
Z McCormick/Schmick | **multi.**	20
Milford Oyster Hse. | **Milford**	23
Mill/Spring Lake | **Spring Lake Hts**	21
Moonfish | **Cape May**	–
Mr. C's | **Allenhurst**	19
Mud City | **Manahawkin**	24
Navesink Fishery | **Navesink**	24
NEW Nisi Estiatorio | **Englewood**	–
Oceanos | **Fair Lawn**	23
Octopus's Gdn. | **Stafford**	23
Park Steak | **Park Ridge**	25
Phillips Seafood | **A.C.**	19
Ray's | **Little Silver**	22
Red's | **Pt. Pleas. Bch**	23
Ritz Seafood | **Voorhees**	24
Rod's Steak | **Morristown**	22
Rooney's | **Long Branch**	18
Z SeaBlue | **A.C.**	27
Sea Shack | **Hackensack**	21
Shipwreck Grill | **Brielle**	25

Smoke Chophse. | **Englewood**	23
Solaia | **Englewood**	18
South City | **multi.**	22
Spike's | **Pt. Pleas. Bch**	23
3 Forty | **Hoboken**	21
Vanthia's | **W Cape May**	21
Varka | **Ramsey**	26
West Lake | **Matawan**	22
Windansea | **Highlands**	17
Witherspoon | **Princeton**	21
Wonder Seafood | **Edison**	23

SMALL PLATES

(See also Spanish tapas specialist)

A Toute Heure | **Amer.** | **Cranford**	25
Z Daryl | **Amer.** | **New Bruns.**	24
Elements | **Amer.** | **Haddon Hts**	24
Grand Colonial | **Eclectic** | **Union Twp**	23
Lua | **Pan-Latin** | **Hoboken**	22
Marco/Pepe | **Amer.** | **Jersey City**	22

SOUL FOOD

Delta's | **New Bruns.**	23
Je's | **Newark**	24

SOUP

Hale/Hearty | **Livingston**	18

SOUTH AMERICAN

Cucharamama | **Hoboken**	25

SOUTHERN

Delta's | **New Bruns.**	23
Freshwater's | **Plainfield**	21
House of Blues | **A.C.**	16
Indigo Smoke | **Montclair**	21
Je's | **Newark**	24

SOUTHWESTERN

Copper Canyon | **Atlantic Highlands**	24
GRUB Hut | **Manville**	21
Los Amigos | **multi.**	22
Mojave | **Westfield**	23
Rattlesnake Rch. | **Denville**	15

SPANISH

(* tapas specialist)

Adega | **Newark**	21
Bistro Olé | **Asbury Pk**	24
Casa Vasca* | **Newark**	23
Don Pepe | **multi.**	21
Don Quijote | **Fairview**	17
El Cid | **Paramus**	21
Europa South | **Pt. Pleas. Bch**	19
Fernandes | **Newark**	23
Fornos/Spain | **Newark**	23
Havana* | **Highlands**	16
Iberia | **Newark**	19
Lola's* | **Hoboken**	21
Meson Madrid | **Palisades Pk**	18
Mompou* | **Newark**	21
Mundo | **N Bergen**	21
Pic-Nic | **E Newark**	24
Segovia | **Moonachie**	22
Spain | **Newark**	22
Spanish Tavern | **multi.**	22
Tapas de Espana* | **multi.**	21
Tony Da Caneca | **Newark**	23

STEAKHOUSES

Arthur's Steak | **N Brunswick**	19
Arthur's Tavern | **multi.**	18
Assembly | **Englewood Cliffs**	17
Blue Eyes | **Sewell**	20
☑ Bobby Flay | **A.C.**	25
Brennen's | **Neptune City**	23
Capt'n Ed's | **Pt. Pleas.**	18
NEW Char | **Raritan**	-
NEW Chelsea Prime | **A.C.**	-
Chophouse | **Gibbsboro**	25
Danny's | **Red Bank**	20
Don Pepe's Steak | **Pine Brook**	22
Fernandes | **Newark**	23
Fleming's | **multi.**	23
Fresco | **Milltown**	25
Gallagher's | **multi.**	22
Hunt Club | **Summit**	21
JD's | **Fort Lee**	18
Kanji | **Tinton Falls**	25

Kunkel's | **Haddon Hts**	24
Manhattan Steak | **Oakhurst**	19
Mignon Steak | **Rutherford**	22
Mill/Spring Lake | **Spring Lake Hts**	21
☑ Morton's | **Hackensack**	25
Nero's | **Livingston**	17
Old Homestead | **A.C.**	26
Palm | **A.C.**	25
Park Steak | **Park Ridge**	25
Pub | **Pennsauken**	19
Rare | **Little Falls**	20
Rio 22 | **Union**	19
☑ River Palm | **multi.**	24
Rod's Steak | **Morristown**	22
Roots | **Summit**	25
☑ Ruth's Chris | **multi.**	25
Sammy's | **Mendham**	21
Shogun | **multi.**	22
Smoke Chophse. | **Englewood**	23
NEW Steakhouse 85 | **New Bruns.**	-
Strip House | **Livingston**	23
What's Your Beef? | **Rumson**	22
NEW William Douglas | **Cherry Hill**	22
Witherspoon | **Princeton**	21

TAIWANESE

China Palace | **Middletown**	24

TEX-MEX

Texas Arizona | **Hoboken**	14

THAI

Aligado | **Hazlet**	24
Andaman | **Morristown**	23
Aroma | **Franklin Pk**	21
Bamboo Leaf | **multi.**	22
Bangkok Gdn. | **Hackensack**	22
Chao Phaya | **multi.**	24
Far East Taste | **Eatontown**	23
Ginger | **Freehold Twp**	16
Khun | **Short Hills**	23
Mie Thai | **multi.**	24
New Main Taste | **Chatham**	23
☑ Origin | **multi.**	26

Pad Thai | **Highland Pk**	21
Penang | **multi.**	21
Siam | **Lambertville**	20
Siam Gdn. | **Red Bank**	24
Sirin | **Morristown**	24
Siri's | **Cherry Hill**	24
Somsak | **Voorhees**	23
Sri Thai | **Hoboken**	23
Thai Chef | **multi.**	21
Thai Kitchen | **multi.**	24
Thai Thai | **Stirling**	23
Tuptim | **Montclair**	20
Wondee's | **Hackensack**	20

TURKISH

Beyti Kebab | **Union City**	23
Bosphorus | **Lake Hiawatha**	21

Lalezar | **Montclair**	18
Lodos | **New Milford**	23
Marmara | **Manalapan**	19
Samdan | **Cresskill**	23
Seven Hills | **Highland Pk**	22

VEGETARIAN
(* vegan)

Chand | **multi.**	23
Kaya's* | **Belmar**	20
Tuptim | **Montclair**	20

VIETNAMESE

Bamboo Leaf | **multi.**	22
Little Saigon | **A.C.**	25
Saigon R./Mo' Pho | **multi.**	24
Nha Trang Pl. | **Jersey City**	24

Locations

Includes restaurant names, cuisines and Food ratings.

Metro New York Area

ALLENDALE

Allendale B&G | *Pub* — 17
Rest. L | *Continental* — 20

BAYONNE

Cafe Bello | *Italian* — 24
Little Food Café | *Sandwiches* — 25

BELLEVILLE

NEW LaPrete's | *Italian* — 22

BERKELEY HEIGHTS

NEW Delicious Heights | *Amer.* — 21
Neelam | *Indian* — 20
Trap Rock | *Amer.* — 21

BLOOMFIELD

Belmont Tavern | *Italian* — 23
Holsten's | *Amer.* — 17
NEW Orange Squirrel | *Amer.* — –
Senorita's | *Mex.* — 20
NEW Stamna | *Greek* — 23

CALDWELL

Luce | *Italian* — 21
Nori | *Pan-Asian* — 23

CARLSTADT

Il Villaggio | *Italian* — 23
Tina Louise | *Asian* — 24

CEDAR GROVE

Lu Nello | *Italian* — 25

CLIFFSIDE PARK

It's Greek To Me | *Greek* — 17

CLIFTON

Chengdu 46 | *Chinese* — 24
Pollo Tropical | *Chicken* — –
Rutt's Hut | *Hot Dogs* — 21
Tick Tock | *Diner* — 18

CLOSTER

Harvest Bistro | *French* — 21

CRANFORD

A Toute Heure | *Amer.* — 25
Garlic Rose | *Eclectic* — 20

CRESSKILL

Samdan | *Turkish* — 23

EAST NEWARK

Pic-Nic | *Portug./Spanish* — 24

EAST RUTHERFORD

Baja Fresh | *Mex.* — 17
Z Park/Orchard | *Eclectic* — 22

EDGEWATER

Z Baumgart's | *Amer./Pan-Asian* — 19
Brooklyn's Pizza | *Pizza* — 23
Crab House | *Seafood* — 16
Fleming's | *Steak* — 23
Greek Taverna | *Greek* — –
Le Jardin | *French* — 18
Magic Pot | *Fondue* — 18
Rebecca's | *Cuban* — 25
Z River Palm | *Steak* — 24
Roberto's II | *Italian* — 19
Vespa's | *Italian* — 17

ELIZABETH

Johnny Rockets | *Burgers* — 15

ELMWOOD PARK

Royal Warsaw | *Polish* — 23
Trovato's | *Italian* — 25

ENGLEWOOD

Akai | *Japanese* — 25
Z Baumgart's | *Amer./Pan-Asian* — 19
It's Greek To Me | *Greek* — 17
NEW Nisi Estiatorio | *Greek* — –
Saigon R./Mo' Pho | *Viet.* — 24
Smoke Chophse. | *Seafood/Steak* — 23
Solaia | *Italian* — 18
Tapas de Espana | *Spanish* — 21
Wild Ginger | *Japanese* — 22

Menus, photos, voting and more – free at ZAGAT.com

ENGLEWOOD CLIFFS

Assembly | *Steak* — 17
Cafe Italiano | *Italian* — 19
Grissini | *Italian* — 22

FAIR LAWN

Gotham City | *Diner* — 18
Oceanos | *Seafood* — 23
Z River Palm | *Steak* — 24

FAIRVIEW

Don Quijote | *Spanish* — 17

FORT LEE

Armando's | *Italian* — 18
Hiram's | *Hot Dogs* — 20
In Napoli | *Italian* — 17
It's Greek To Me | *Greek* — 17
JD's | *Steak* — 18
Saigon R./Mo' Pho | *Viet.* — 24
Sally Ling | *Chinese* — 18

FRANKLIN LAKES

Z Chef's Table | *French* — 26

GARFIELD

GoodFellas | *Italian* — 20

GLEN ROCK

RoCCA | *Italian* — 23

HACKENSACK

Bangkok Gdn. | *Thai* — 22
Brooklyn's Pizza | *Pizza* — 23
Z Cheesecake Factory | *Amer.* — 19
Cubby's | *BBQ* — 18
Five Guys | *Burgers* — 21
Lotus Cafe | *Chinese* — 24
Z McCormick/Schmick | *Seafood* — 20
Z Morton's | *Steak* — 25
Z P.F. Chang's | *Chinese* — 20
Rest., The | *Italian* — 19
Sea Shack | *Seafood* — 21
Solari's | *Italian* — 20
Z Stony Hill Inn | — 23
    Continental/Italian

Thai Chef | *Thai* — 21
Wondee's | *Thai* — 20

HARRINGTON PARK

NEW Dino's | *Italian* — -

HASBROUCK HEIGHTS

Ivy Inn | *Amer.* — 20

HAWTHORNE

Sabor | *Nuevo Latino* — 22

HOBOKEN

Ali Baba | *Mideast.* — 20
Z Amanda's | *Amer.* — 25
Anthony David's | *Italian* — 26
Arthur's Tavern | *Steak* — 18
Z Augustino's | *Italian* — 26
NEW Backyards | *Amer.* — -
Baja | *Mex.* — 19
Benny Tudino's | *Pizza* — 20
Brass Rail | *Amer.* — 19
Charrito's | *Mex.* — 22
City Bistro | *Amer.* — 18
Court St. | *Continental* — 22
Cucharamama | *S Amer.* — 25
Elysian | *French* — 20
Gaslight | *Amer./Italian* — 19
Grimaldi's | *Pizza* — 24
India/Hudson | *Indian* — 20
It's Greek To Me | *Greek* — 17
Johnny Rockets | *Burgers* — 15
Karma Kafe | *Indian* — 24
La Isla | *Cuban* — 26
Lola's | *Spanish* — 21
Lua | *Pan-Latin* — 22
Madison B&G | *Amer.* — 20
Margherita's | *Italian* — 21
Melting Pot | *Fondue* — 18
Oddfellows | *Cajun/Creole* — 18
Onieal's | *Amer.* — 18
Robongi | *Japanese* — 24
Sri Thai | *Thai* — 23
Sushi Lounge | *Japanese* — 22
Texas Arizona | *Tex-Mex* — 14

3 Forty	*Amer.*	21
Zafra	*Pan-Latin*	24

JERSEY CITY

Amelia's Bistro	*Amer.*	20
Amiya	*Indian*	19
Azúcar	*Cuban*	21
Baja	*Mex.*	19
Casa Dante	*Italian*	23
Charrito's	*Mex.*	22
Hale & Hearty Soups	18
Hard Grove	*Amer./Cuban*	15
It's Greek To Me	*Greek*	17
Komegashi	*Japanese*	23
Liberty Hse.	*Amer.*	20
Light Horse	*Amer.*	23
Madame Claude	*French*	23
Marco/Pepe	*Amer.*	22
Nha Trang Pl.	*Viet.*	24
Ox	*Amer.*	23
Porto Leggero	*Italian*	22
South City	*Amer.*	22
Taqueria	*Mex.*	22

KENILWORTH

NEW Blvd. Five 72	*Amer.*	27
Le Rendez-Vous	*French*	26

LITTLE FALLS

NEW Fire/Oak	*Amer.*	-
Rare	*Steak*	20
Tomo's	*Japanese*	21

LITTLE FERRY

Minado	*Japanese*	19
Pollo Tropical	*Chicken*	-

LIVINGSTON

Z Baumgart's	*Amer./Pan-Asian*	19
Eppes Essen	*Deli*	19
Hale/Hearty	*Sandwiches/Soup*	18
It's Greek To Me	*Greek*	17
Nana's Deli	*Deli*	22
Nero's	*Steak*	17
Strip House	*Steak*	23

LODI

Penang	*Malaysian/Thai*	21

MAHWAH

Z River Palm	*Steak*	24

MAPLEWOOD

Z Lorena's	*French*	28
Luke's	*Amer.*	21
Verjus	*French*	25

MIDLAND PARK

Arturo's	*Italian*	23

MILLBURN

Basilico	*Italian*	24
Five Guys	*Burgers*	21
La Campagna	*Italian*	22
Martini Bistro	*Amer.*	18
restaurant.mc	*Amer./Eclectic*	23

MONTCLAIR

Aozora	*French/Japanese*	25
Blu	*Amer.*	24
Church St.	*Amer.*	14
Corso 98	*Italian*	23
Cuban Pete's	*Cuban*	18
Z CulinAriane	*Amer.*	27
Egan/Sons	*Irish*	18
Epernay	*French*	20
Z Fascino	*Italian*	26
Greek Taverna	*Greek*	-
Indigo Smoke	*BBQ/Southern*	21
Lalezar	*Turkish*	18
Next Door	*Amer.*	21
Nori	*Pan-Asian*	23
Nouveau	*Pan-Asian*	24
Osteria Giotto	*Italian*	25
Passionne	*French*	23
Raymond's	*Amer.*	21
Richie Cecere's	*Italian*	20
Table 8	*Amer.*	23
Taro	*Asian Fusion*	20
Thai Chef	*Thai*	21
Toast	*Amer.*	20
Tuptim	*Thai*	20

MONTVALE

Aldo/Gianni	*Italian*	21

MOONACHIE

Bazzarelli	*Italian*	21
Segovia	*Portug./Spanish*	22

MOUNTAINSIDE

Raagini	*Indian*	22
Spanish Tavern	*Spanish*	22

NEWARK

Adega	*Portug./Spanish*	21
Brasilia Grill	*Brazilian*	21
Brasilia Rest.	*Brazilian*	21
Casa Vasca	*Spanish*	23
Don Pepe	*Portug./Spanish*	21
Fernandes	*Portug./Spanish*	23
Fornos/Spain	*Spanish*	23
Gallagher's	*Steak*	22
Hobby's	*Deli*	23
Iberia	*Portug./Spanish*	19
Je's	*Soul Food*	24
Maize	*Amer.*	18
Mompou	*Spanish*	21
Spain	*Portug./Spanish*	22
Spanish Tavern	*Spanish*	22
Theater Sq.	*Amer.*	20
Tony Da Caneca	*Portug./Spanish*	23
Vila Nova	*Portug.*	23

NEW MILFORD

Lodos	*Med./Turkish*	23
Sanzari's	*Italian*	20

NEW PROVIDENCE

Aquila Cucina	*Italian*	22
Jose's Cantina	*Mex.*	20

NORTH BERGEN

Antonia's	*Italian*	20
DiPalma	*Italian*	22
NEW El Pollo Loco	*Chicken*	-
La Sorrentina	*Italian*	26
Mundo	*Cuban/Spanish*	21
Pollo Tropical	*Chicken*	-
Sabor	*Nuevo Latino*	22
Tapas de Espana	*Spanish*	21

NORTHVALE

Madeleine's	*Continental/French*	25

NORWOOD

Dimora	*Italian*	23

NUTLEY

NEW Farm 2 Bistro	*Amer.*	-

OAKLAND

Cenzino	*Italian*	24
Portobello	*Italian*	19
Trovato's	*Italian*	25

PALISADES PARK

Meson Madrid	*Spanish*	18
So Moon Nan Jip	*Korean*	25

PARAMUS

Z Chakra	*Amer.*	20
El Cid	*Spanish*	21
Johnny Rockets	*Burgers*	15
Z Legal Sea Foods	*Seafood*	21
Mantra	*Indian*	24
Napa Valley	*Amer.*	21
Papa Razzi	*Italian*	17
Tom Sawyer	*Diner*	17

PARK RIDGE

Esty St.	*Amer.*	24
Park Steak	*Seafood/Steak*	25

PATERSON

E & V	*Italian*	23

PLAINFIELD

Freshwater's	*Southern*	21

RAHWAY

NEW Cubanu	*Cuban*	24
Z David Drake	*Amer.*	28
NEW Luciano's	*Italian*	-

RAMSEY

Z Cafe Panache	*Eclectic*	28
Kinchley's	*Pizza*	23
Varka	*Greek/Seafood*	26

RIDGEFIELD

Gotham City | *Diner* — 18

Tutto a Modo Mio | *Italian* — 23

RIDGEFIELD PARK

Luka's | *Italian* — 22

RIDGEWOOD

A Mano | *Italian* — 21

Z Baumgart's | *Amer./Pan-Asian* — 19

Bazzini | *Amer./Italian* — 19

Brooklyn's Pizza | *Pizza* — 23

Country Pancake | *Amer.* — 20

Dim Sum Dynasty | *Chinese* — 20

Gazelle | *Amer.* — 24

It's Greek To Me | *Greek* — 17

Z Latour | *French* — 26

Marra's | *Italian* — 20

Radicchio | *Italian* — 22

Sakura-Bana | *Japanese* — 25

Village Green | *Amer.* — 23

RIVER EDGE

Dinallo's | *Italian* — 22

ROCHELLE PARK

South City | *Amer.* — 22

RUTHERFORD

Z Cafe Matisse | *Eclectic* — 27

Mignon Steak | *Steak* — 22

Risotto Hse. | *Italian* — 23

Village Gourmet | *Eclectic* — 21

SADDLE RIVER

Z Saddle River Inn | *Amer./French* — 28

SCOTCH PLAINS

Stage Hse. | *Amer.* — 22

SHORT HILLS

Benihana | *Japanese* — 18

Johnny Rockets | *Burgers* — 15

Khun | *Thai* — 23

Z Legal Sea Foods | *Seafood* — 21

Papa Razzi | *Italian* — 17

Terrace | *Med.* — 22

SOUTH HACKENSACK

Aldo/Gianni | *Italian* — 21

SOUTH ORANGE

Cafe Arugula | *Italian* — 21

Neelam | *Indian* — 20

SPRINGFIELD

Cathay 22 | *Chinese* — 22

Hunan Spring | *Chinese* — 20

SUMMIT

Brix 67 | *Eclectic* — 18

Dabbawalla | *Indian* — 18

Fiorino | *Italian* — 23

Hunt Club | *Seafood/Steak* — 21

Huntley Taverne | *Amer.* — 22

La Focaccia | *Italian* — 24

La Pastaria | *Italian* — 19

Monster Sushi | *Japanese* — 20

Roots | *Steak* — 25

Soufflé | *French* — 22

TEANECK

Amarone | *Italian* — 21

East | *Japanese* — 19

NEW Zen Den | *Amer.* — –

TENAFLY

Axia | *Greek* — 23

TOTOWA

Sushi Lounge | *Japanese* — 22

UNION

Rio 22 | *Brazilian* — 19

Rist. Benito | *Italian* — 24

UNION CITY

Beyti Kebab | *Turkish* — 23

Charrito's | *Mex.* — 22

Mi Bandera | *Cuban* — 23

Park Ave. | *Amer./Pan-Latin* — 18

UPPER MONTCLAIR

Alan@594 | *Italian* — 21

Dai-Kichi | *Japanese* — 22

Orbis Bistro | *Amer.* — 20

VERONA

NEW Avenue Bistro Pub | *Amer.* | - |

WANAQUE

Berta's | *Italian* | 21 |

WAYNE

Baja Fresh | *Mex.* | 17 |
Z Cheesecake Factory | *Amer.* | 19 |
NEW 9 North | *Amer.* | - |

WEEHAWKEN

Chart Hse. | *Amer.* | 21 |
Paula/Rigoletto | *Italian* | 21 |
Z Ruth's Chris | *Steak* | 25 |

WESTFIELD

Acquaviva | *Italian* | 22 |
Chez Catherine | *French* | 26 |
Isabella's | *Amer.* | 18 |
NEW Limani | *Greek* | 22 |
Mojave | *SW* | 23 |
Theresa's | *Italian* | 22 |
WindMill | *Hot Dogs* | 19 |

WEST NEW YORK

Z P.F. Chang's | *Chinese* | 20 |
NEW Pollo Campero | *Chicken* | - |

WEST ORANGE

Z Highlawn | *Amer.* | 25 |
Z Manor | *Amer.* | 24 |
Primavera | *Italian* | 21 |
Sweet Basil's | *Amer.* | 23 |

WESTWOOD

It's Greek To Me | *Greek* | 17 |
Melting Pot | *Fondue* | 18 |

WYCKOFF

Bourbon County | *BBQ* | 19 |

Central

BASKING RIDGE

Bombay Curry | *Indian* | 18 |
Ciao | *Italian* | 21 |

Z Origin | *French/Thai* | 26 |
3 West | *Amer.* | 22 |
Vine | *Amer./Med.* | 25 |

BEDMINSTER

Z Pluckemin Inn | *Amer.* | 26 |

BERNARDSVILLE

Z Bernards Inn | *Amer.* | 26 |
Due Terre | *Italian* | 25 |
Equus | *Amer.* | 21 |
Grill 73 | *Amer.* | 21 |
Le Petit Chateau | *French* | 25 |
Tsuki | *Japanese* | 22 |

BOONTON

Il Michelangelo | *Italian* | 21 |
Reservoir | *Italian* | 22 |

BOUND BROOK

Girasole | *Italian* | 26 |

BRANCHBURG

Cafe Cucina | *Italian* | 21 |

BRIDGEWATER

Cafe Emilia | *Italian* | 21 |
Z McCormick/Schmick | *Seafood* | 20 |
Thai Kitchen | *Thai* | 24 |

CHATHAM

New Main Taste | *Thai* | 23 |
Z Scalini Fedeli | *Italian* | 27 |
Z Serenade | *French* | 28 |
Taste of Asia | *Malaysian* | 21 |

CHESTER

Benito's | *Italian* | 24 |
Redwood's | *Amer.* | 16 |

CRANBURY

Cranbury Inn | *Amer.* | 15 |

DENVILLE

Cafe Metro | *Eclectic* | 21 |
Hunan Taste | *Chinese* | 24 |
Midori | *Japanese* | 22 |
Rattlesnake Rch. | *SW* | 15 |

LOCATIONS

CENTRAL NJ

DOVER

Quiet Man | *Pub* 20

EAST BRUNSWICK

Baja Fresh | *Mex.* 17
Bombay Gdns. | *Indian* 23
Gusto Grill | *Amer.* 17
Shogun | *Japanese/Steak* 22
Wasabi | *Japanese* 25

EAST HANOVER

Baja Fresh | *Mex.* 17
Luigi's | *Italian* 23
Mr. Chu | *Chinese* 21
Penang | *Malaysian/Thai* 21
Saffron | *Indian* 22

EAST WINDSOR

Mahzu | *Japanese* 21

EDISON

Akbar | *Indian* 19
Baja Fresh | *Mex.* 17
Benihana | *Japanese* 18
Z Cheesecake Factory | *Amer.* 19
Five Guys | *Burgers* 21
Grand Shanghai | *Pan-Asian* 19
Jack Cooper's | *Deli* 18
LouCás | *Italian* 23
Meemah | *Chinese/Malaysian* 22
Ming | *Pan-Asian* 21
Moghul | *Indian* 25
Moksha | *Indian* 22
Penang | *Malaysian/Thai* 21
Skylark | *Amer.* 20
Wonder Seafood | *Chinese* 23

FLANDERS

Silver Spring | *French* 26

FORDS

McLoone's | *Amer.* 17

FRANKLIN PARK

Aroma | *Thai* 21

GILLETTE

Meyersville Inn | *Eclectic* 17

GLADSTONE

Gladstone | *Amer.* 21

GREEN BROOK

Shogun | *Japanese/Steak* 22

HIGHLAND PARK

Pad Thai | *Thai* 21
Pithari | *Greek* 23
Seven Hills | *Turkish* 22

HILLSBOROUGH

Cafe Graziella | *Italian* 20
CoccoLa | *Amer./Italian* 19
Old Man Rafferty's | *Amer.* 18
Pheasants Landing | 19
   Amer./Continental
Thai Kitchen | *Thai* 24

ISELIN

Casa Giuseppe | *Italian* 24

JAMESBURG

Fiddleheads | *Amer.* 22

KENDALL PARK

Shogun | *Japanese/Steak* 22

KINGSTON

NEW Eno Terra | *Italian* -

LAKE HIAWATHA

Bosphorus | *Turkish* 21

MADISON

Garlic Rose | *Eclectic* 20
Z Il Mondo | *Italian* 25
Nicky's | *Amer.* 19
NEW Resto | *French* 21
Shanghai Jazz | *Chinese* 21
Soho 33 | *Eclectic* 19

MANVILLE

GRUB Hut | *BBQ* 21

MENDHAM

Black Horse | *Pub* 19
Dante's | *Italian* 21
Sammy's | *Steak* 21

METUCHEN

Alessio 426	*Italian*	19
Metuchen Inn	*Amer.*	21
Pollo Tropical	*Chicken*	–

MEYERSVILLE

Casa Maya	*Mex.*	21

MILLTOWN

Fresco	*Seafood/Steak*	25

MONROE TOWNSHIP

Europa Monroe	*Med.*	16

MONTVILLE

Columbia Inn	*Pizza*	21
Montville Inn	*Amer.*	21

MORRIS PLAINS

Arthur's Tavern	*Steak*	18
Cinnamon	*Indian*	23
Hunan Chinese	*Chinese*	22
Minado	*Japanese*	19
Tabor Rd.	*Amer.*	21

MORRISTOWN

Andaman	*French/Thai*	23
Copeland	*Amer.*	25
☒ Grand Cafe	*French*	26
La Campagna	*Italian*	22
Mehndi	*Indian*	24
Ming II	*Pan-Asian*	24
☒ Origin	*French/Thai*	26
Pamir	*Afghan*	21
Rod's Steak	*Seafood/Steak*	22
Settebello	*Italian*	21
Sirin	*Thai*	24
Sushi Lounge	*Japanese*	22
Tim Schafer's	*Amer.*	25

MOUNTAIN LAKES

South City	*Amer.*	22

NEW BRUNSWICK

☒ Catherine Lombardi	*Italian*	23
Clydz	*Amer.*	22
☒ Daryl	*Amer.*	24
Delta's	*Southern*	23
NEW Due Mari	*Italian*	26
☒ Frog/Peach	*Amer.*	26
☒ Hotoke	*Pan-Asian*	21
Makeda	*Ethiopian*	25
Old Bay	*Cajun/Creole*	19
Old Man Rafferty's	*Amer.*	18
Panico's	*Italian*	23
SoHo/George	*Amer.*	23
Stage Left	*Amer.*	26
NEW Steakhouse 85	*Steak*	–
Verdigre	*Amer.*	21

NORTH BRUNSWICK

Arthur's Steak	*Steak*	19
Mie Thai	*Thai*	24
Noodle Hse.	*Asian*	18

OLD BRIDGE

A Tavola	*Italian*	19
Pine Tavern	*Amer.*	18

PARSIPPANY

Chand	*Indian*	23
Eccola	*Italian*	23
Five Guys	*Burgers*	21
☒ Ruth's Chris	*Steak*	25

PEAPACK

Café Azzurro	*Italian*	24
Limestone Cafe	*Amer.*	21

PERTH AMBOY

Portuguese Manor	*Portug.*	20

PINE BROOK

Don Pepe	*Portug./Spanish*	21
Don Pepe's Steak	*Steak*	22

PISCATAWAY

Al Dente	*Italian*	23
Chand	*Indian*	23

POMPTON PLAINS

Little Food Café		25

RANDOLPH

La Strada	*Italian*	22
Rosie's	*Italian*	21

RARITAN

NEW Char | *Steak* | - |
Espo's | *Italian* | 21 |

RIVERDALE

Rosemary/Sage | *Amer.* | 26 |

ROCKY HILL

One 53 | *Amer.* | 23 |

SKILLMAN

Ya Ya Noodles | *Chinese* | 19 |

SOMERSET

Chao Phaya | *Thai* | 24 |
Luca's | *Italian* | - |
Sophie's | *French* | 22 |

SOMERVILLE

Bank 34 | *Pan-Asian/Seafood* | 23 |
Chao Phaya | *Thai* | 24 |
da Filippo | *Italian/Seafood* | 23 |
La Scala | *Italian* | 22 |
Martino's | *Cuban* | 22 |
Melting Pot | *Fondue* | 18 |
Z Origin | *French/Thai* | 26 |
Shumi | *Japanese* | 25 |
Verve | *Amer./French* | 22 |
Wasabi | *Japanese* | 25 |

SOUTH AMBOY

Fishery, The | *Seafood* | - |

SOUTH PLAINFIELD

Baja Fresh | *Mex.* | 17 |

STIRLING

Thai Thai | *Thai* | 23 |

WARREN

Jose's Cantina | *Mex.* | 20 |
Z Stonehouse | *Amer.* | 22 |
Thai Kitchen | *Thai* | 24 |

WATCHUNG

Baja Fresh | *Mex.* | 17 |
Five Guys | *Burgers* | 21 |

WHIPPANY

Cinque Figlie | *Italian* | 21 |
Z Il Capriccio | *Italian* | 26 |

Melting Pot | *Fondue* | 18 |
Nikko | *Japanese* | 24 |

WOODBRIDGE

Five Guys | *Burgers* | 21 |
Johnny Rockets | *Burgers* | 15 |
Mie Thai | *Thai* | 24 |

North Shore

ABERDEEN

Mahzu | *Japanese* | 21 |

ALLENHURST

Mr. C's | *Seafood* | 19 |

ASBURY

Rosa Luca's | *Italian* | 24 |

ASBURY PARK

Bistro Olé | *Portug./Spanish* | 24 |
Brickwall | *Pub* | 18 |
Carmine's Asbury Pk. | *Italian* | 20 |
D & L BBQ | *BBQ* | 22 |
Harrison | *Amer.* | 22 |
Jimmy's | *Italian* | 23 |
NEW Langosta | *Eclectic* | - |
Mkt. in the Middle | *Eclectic* | 21 |
Z Moonstruck | *Amer./Med.* | 25 |
Old Man Rafferty's | *Amer.* | 18 |
Plan B | *Amer.* | - |
Pop's Garage | *Mex.* | 22 |
Posillipo | *Italian* | 22 |
Salt Water | *Amer.* | 18 |
Sister Sue's | *Carib.* | 21 |
NEW Stella Marina | *Italian* | - |
Taka | *Japanese* | 25 |
NEW Tim McLoone's | *Amer.* | 17 |

ATLANTIC HIGHLANDS

Copper Canyon | *SW* | 24 |
Memphis Pig Out | *BBQ* | 21 |

AVON-BY-THE-SEA

Avon Pavilion | *Amer.* | 19 |
Clementine's | *Creole* | 23 |

BAY HEAD

Grenville | *Amer.* | 21

BEACH HAVEN

Z Gables | *Eclectic* | 25
Harvey Cedars | *Seafood* | 22
Roberto's | *Italian* | 22
Tuckers | *Amer.* | 16

BELFORD

Belford Bistro | *Amer.* | 28

BELMAR

Brandl. | *Amer.* | 24
Casa Solar | *Pan-Latin* | 25
Kaya's | *Veg.* | 20
Klein's | *Seafood* | 19
Matisse | *Amer.* | 21
Surf Taco | *Mex.* | 20
Vivas | *Nuevo Latino* | 26
WindMill | *Hot Dogs* | 19

BRADLEY BEACH

Bamboo Leaf | *Thai/Viet.* | 22
Bella Sogno | *Italian* | 20
Vic's | *Pizza* | 20

BRICK

Five Guys | *Burgers* | 21
Ikko | *Japanese* | 25
Mexico Lindo | *Mex.* | 23
Villa Vittoria | *Italian* | 22
WindMill | *Hot Dogs* | 19

BRIELLE

Shipwreck Grill | *Amer.* | 25

COLTS NECK

Christopher's | *Amer.* | 19
I Cavallini | *Italian* | 23

EATONTOWN

NEW Bobby's | *Burgers* | 20
Far East Taste | *Chinese/Thai* | 23
Johnny Rockets | *Burgers* | 15
SAWA Steak | *Japanese* | 22

FAIR HAVEN

Le Fandy | *French* | 25
Nauvoo Grill | *Amer.* | 16
Raven/Peach | *Amer.* | 25

FORKED RIVER

Surf Taco | *Mex.* | 20

FREEHOLD

Bayou Cafe | *Cajun/Creole* | 21
Z Cheesecake Factory | *Amer.* | 19
El Familiar | *Colombian/Mex.* | 19
El Meson | *Mex.* | 24
Federici's | *Pizza* | 22
Johnny Rockets | *Burgers* | 15
La Cipollina | *Italian* | 21
Mahzu | *Japanese* | 21
Main St. Bistro | *Amer.* | 21
Metropolitan Cafe | *Pac. Rim* | 21
My Little Greek | *Greek* | 18
Oyako Tso's | *Japanese* | 23
Z P.F. Chang's | *Chinese* | 20
WindMill | *Hot Dogs* | 19

FREEHOLD TOWNSHIP

Aangan | *Indian* | 22
Cafe Coloré | *Italian* | 21
Ferrari's | *Italian* | 22
Frankie Fed's | *Italian* | 22
Ginger | *Thai* | 16

HARVEY CEDARS

Harvey Cedars | *Seafood* | 22
Plantation | *Amer.* | 20

HAZLET

Aligado | *Japanese/Thai* | 24

HIGHLANDS

Bahrs Landing | *Seafood* | 16
Z Bay Ave. | *Amer./Italian* | 27
Chilangos | *Mex.* | 21
Doris/Ed's | *Amer./Seafood* | 25
Havana | *Cuban* | 16
Inlet Café | *Seafood* | 20
Windansea | *Seafood* | 17

HOLMDEL

It's Greek To Me | Greek | 17
K.O.B.E. | Japanese | 22

HOWELL

Bamboo Leaf | Thai/Viet. | 22
Cabin | Amer. | 16
Christie's | Italian | 23
Juanito's | Mex. | 22
Sushi by Kazu | Japanese | 26

JACKSON

Java Moon | Amer. | 18
Johnny Rockets | Burgers | 15
Solo Bella | Italian | 21
Surf Taco | Mex. | 20

KEYPORT

Z Drew's | Amer. | 26
Trinity | Amer. | 23

LAVALLETTE

Crab's Claw | Seafood | 18

LINCROFT

Lincroft Inn | Continental | 18

LITTLE SILVER

Ray's | Seafood | 22

LONG BEACH TOWNSHIP

daddy O | Amer. | 19

LONG BRANCH

Z Avenue | French | 20
Charley's | Amer. | 18
It's Greek To Me | Greek | 17
McLoone's | Amer. | 17
Richard's | Deli | 21
Rooney's | Seafood | 18
SAWA Steak | Japanese | 22
Sirena | Italian | 22
Surf Taco | Mex. | 20
Tuzzio's | Italian | 20
WindMill | Hot Dogs | 19

MANAHAWKIN

Mud City | Seafood | 24

MANALAPAN

Konbu | Japanese | 25
Marmara | Turkish | 19
Michael's | Italian | 19
Spargo's | Amer. | 24

MANASQUAN

Mahogany | Amer. | 23
Squan Tavern | Italian | 21
Surf Taco | Mex. | 20

MARLBORO

Brioso | Italian | 22
Crown Palace | Chinese | 20
Jerry/Harvey's | Deli | 18
Pino's | Italian | 19

MATAWAN

Aby's | Mex. | 20
Big Ed's BBQ | BBQ | 19
Buttonwood Manor | Amer. | 14
West Lake | Chinese | 22

MIDDLETOWN

Anna's | Italian | 25
Baja Fresh | Mex. | 17
China Palace | Taiwanese | 24
Crown Palace | Chinese | 20
Neelam | Indian | 20
Z Nicholas | Amer. | 28
Sono Sushi | Japanese | 25

MILLSTONE TOWNSHIP

Luchento's | Italian | -

MONMOUTH BEACH

NEW Prairie | Amer. | -
Sallee Tee's | Amer./Eclectic | 19

NAVESINK

Navesink Fishery | Seafood | 24

NEPTUNE CITY

Brennen's | Steak | 23
Pete/Elda's | Pizza | 22

Menus, photos, voting and more – free at ZAGAT.com

NORMANDY BEACH

Labrador | *Eclectic* — 23
Pop's Garage | *Mex.* — 22

OAKHURST/ OCEAN TOWNSHIP

Manhattan Steak | *Steak* — 19
Z Piccola | *Italian* — 27
Takara | *Japanese* — 24

OCEAN GROVE

WindMill | *Hot Dogs* — 19

POINT PLEASANT

Capt'n Ed's | *Seafood/Steak* — 18
Clark's Landing | *Amer./Seafood* — 17

POINT PLEASANT BEACH

Europa South | *Portug./Spanish* — 19
Latitude 40N | *Seafood* — 23
Red's | *Seafood* — 23
Spike's | *Seafood* — 23
Surf Taco | *Mex.* — 20

RED BANK

Basil T's | *Amer./Italian* — 20
Bienvenue | *French* — 23
Bistro/Red Bank | *Eclectic* — 21
Danny's | *Steak* — 20
Dish | *Amer.* — 24
Eurasian | *Eclectic* — 22
Gaetano's | *Italian* — 20
Juanito's | *Mex.* — 22
La Pastaria | *Italian* — 19
Melting Pot | *Fondue* — 18
Molly Pitcher | *Amer.* — 23
Red | *Amer.* — 20
Siam Gdn. | *Thai* — 24
Sogno | *Italian* — 22
Teak | *Pan-Asian* — 20
NEW Torcello | *Italian* — -
2Senza | *Italian/Med.* — 21
WindMill | *Hot Dogs* — 19

RUMSON

Barnacle Bill's | *Burgers* — 21
David Burke | *Amer.* — 25

Salt Creek | *Amer.* — 19
Undici | *Italian* — 21
What's Your Beef? | *Steak* — 22

SEA BRIGHT

Anjelica's | *Italian* — 24
Harry's | *Seafood* — 21
McLoone's | *Amer.* — 17
Yumi | *Pan-Asian* — 26

SEA GIRT

Rod's Olde Irish | *Pub* — 18
Scarborough Fair | *Amer.* — 21

SHIP BOTTOM

La Spiaggia | *Italian* — 24
Raimondo's | *Italian* — 24

SHREWSBURY

Pasta Fresca | *Amer.* — 19
San Remo | *Italian* — 23

SOUTH SEASIDE PARK

Atlantic B&G | *Amer./Seafood* — 25
Berkeley | *Seafood* — 20
Surf Taco | *Mex.* — 20

SPRING LAKE

Black Trumpet | *Amer.* — 25
Island Palm | *Amer.* — 19
Z Whispers | *Amer.* — 27

SPRING LAKE HEIGHTS

Jose's | *Mex.* — 24
Mill/Spring Lake | *Amer.* — 21

STAFFORD

Octopus's Gdn. | *Seafood* — 23

SURF CITY

Blue | *Amer./Eclectic* — 24
Yellow Fin | *Amer.* — 26

TINTON FALLS

CJ Montana's | *Pub* — 19
Kanji | *Japanese/Steak* — 25
Portofino | *Italian* — 23

TOMS RIVER

Benihana	*Japanese*	18
Bistro 44	*Amer./French*	24
Five Guys	*Burgers*	21
Queen Victoria	*Tea*	23
Surf Taco	*Mex.*	20

TOMS RIVER TOWNSHIP

Aamantran	*Indian*	21
El Familiar	*Colombian/Mex.*	19
Nobi	*Japanese*	25
Shogun	*Japanese/Steak*	22

UNION BEACH

Piero's	*Italian*	21

WALL

Shogun	*Japanese/Steak*	22
Sumo	*Japanese*	25

Delaware Valley

ALLAMUCHY

Mattar's Bistro	*Amer.*	-

FLEMINGTON

Blue Fish	*Seafood*	21
California Grill	*Eclectic*	18
55 Main	*Amer.*	20
Fusion	*Asian Fusion*	22
Market Roost	*Eclectic*	21
Matt's Rooster	*Amer.*	25

FRENCHTOWN

Frenchtown Inn	*Eclectic/French*	25

HAMBURG

Rest. Latour	*Amer.*	25

HAMILTON

☑ Rat's	*French*	25

HAMILTON TOWNSHIP

Tattoni's	*Italian*	21

HIGH BRIDGE

Casa Maya	*Mex.*	21
Circa	*French*	22

HOPE

Inn/Millrace	*Amer./Continental*	21

HOPEWELL

☑ Blue Bottle	*Amer.*	27
Brothers Moon	*Amer.*	22

LAMBERTVILLE

Anton's/Swan	*Amer.*	22
Bell's	*Amer./Italian*	21
DeAnna's	*Italian*	22
Full Moon	*Eclectic*	21
Hamilton's	*Med.*	25
Inn/Hawke	*Amer.*	18
Lambertville Station	*Amer.*	17
Lilly's/Canal	*Eclectic*	21
Manon	*French*	25
No. 9	*Amer.*	26
Ota-Ya	*Japanese*	22
Rick's	*Italian*	20
Siam	*Thai*	20

LAWRENCEVILLE

Acacia	*Amer.*	23
Elements Asia	*Pan-Asian*	23
Fedora	*Eclectic*	18
Passage/India	*Indian*	21
Simply Radishing	*Amer.*	19

MILFORD

Milford Oyster Hse.	*Seafood*	23
Ship Inn	*Pub*	15

NEWTON

☑ André's	*Amer.*	27
Krave Café	*Amer.*	23

OLDWICK

Tewksbury Inn	*Amer.*	22

PENNINGTON

Edo Sushi	*Chinese/Japanese*	19

PRINCETON

☑ Ajihei	*Japanese*	28
Alchemist/Barrister	*Amer.*	16
☑ Blue Point	*Seafood*	25

Menus, photos, voting and more – free at ZAGAT.com

Conte's | *Pizza*	24
NEW elements | *Amer.*	-
Ferry Hse. | *Amer./French*	25
Ichiban | *Japanese*	18
NEW JL Ivy | *French/Japanese*	19
Lahiere's | *Continental/French*	22
Main St. Euro-Amer. | *Amer./Continental*	19
Mediterra | *Med.*	21
Penang | *Malaysian/Thai*	21
☑ P.F. Chang's | *Chinese*	20
☑ Ruth's Chris | *Steak*	25
Salt Creek | *Amer.*	19
Sunny Gdn. | *Chinese*	20
Teresa Caffe | *Italian*	22
Tortuga's | *Mex.*	20
Tre Piani | *Italian/Med.*	22
Triumph Brew. | *Amer./Eclectic*	16
Underground Café | *E European*	19
Witherspoon | *Seafood/Steak*	21
Yankee Doodle | *Pub*	15

RINGOES

Harvest Moon | *Amer.*	23

ROBBINSVILLE

☑ DeLorenzo's Pies | *Pizza*	27

ROSEMONT

Cafe/Rosemont | *Amer.*	20

SERGEANTSVILLE

Sergeantsville Inn | *Amer.*	23

SPARTA

Mohawk Hse. | *Amer.*	19

STANHOPE

Bell's Mansion | *Amer.*	17
Black Forest Inn | *Continental/German*	22

STOCKTON

Meil's | *Amer.*	22

TRENTON

Amici Milano | *Italian*	22
Blue Danube | *E Euro.*	23
☑ DeLorenzo's Pies | *Pizza*	27
DeLorenzo's Pizza | *Pizza*	-
Homestead Inn | *Italian*	24
John Henry's | *Seafood*	24

UNION TOWNSHIP

Baja Fresh | *Mex.*	17
Grand Colonial | *Eclectic*	23
Perryville Inn | *Amer.*	23

WALLPACK CENTER

Walpack Inn | *Amer.*	19

South Shore

ATLANTIC CITY

Angelo's | *Italian*	21
☑ Bobby Flay | *Steak*	25
☑ Buddakan | *Pan-Asian*	25
Capriccio | *Italian*	26
Carmine's | *Italian*	21
☑ Chef Vola's | *Italian*	27
NEW Chelsea Prime | *Steak*	-
Continental | *Amer.*	23
Corky's | *BBQ*	18
Cuba Libre | *Cuban*	22
Dock's | *Seafood*	26
Gallagher's | *Steak*	22
Girasole | *Italian*	25
House of Blues | *Southern*	16
☑ **NEW** Il Mulino NY | *Italian*	26
Irish Pub | *Pub*	18
izakaya | *Japanese*	26
Johnny Rockets | *Burgers*	15
Little Saigon | *Viet.*	25
Los Amigos | *Mex./SW*	22
☑ McCormick/Schmick | *Seafood*	20
Melting Pot | *Fondue*	18
Mia | *Italian*	25
Old Homestead | *Steak*	26
☑ Ombra | *Italian*	26
Palm | *Steak*	25
☑ P.F. Chang's | *Chinese*	20
Phillips Seafood | *Seafood*	19
☑ Red Square | *Eclectic/Russian*	21

☑ Ruth's Chris | *Steak*	25
☑ SeaBlue | *Seafood*	27
Sonsie | *Amer.*	21
Teplitzky's | *Diner*	-
Tony Luke's | *Sandwiches*	21
Tony's | *Pizza*	18
Tun Tavern | *Amer.*	17
Waterfront Buffet | *Eclectic*	19
White Hse. | *Sandwiches*	26
Wolfgang Puck | *Amer.*	24

AVALON
Cafe Loren | *Amer.*	26

CAPE MAY
Alexander's | *French*	26
Axelsson's | *Seafood*	23
Blue Pig | *Amer.*	21
Copper Fish | *Amer./Seafood*	20
Cucina Rosa | *Italian*	21
☑ Ebbitt Rm. | *Amer.*	27
410 Bank St. | *Creole*	26
Frescos | *Italian/Med.*	24
Lobster Hse. | *Seafood*	21
Lucky Bones | *Amer.*	21
Mad Batter | *Amer.*	23
Merion Inn | *Amer.*	23
Moonfish | *Seafood*	-
☑ Peter Shields | *Amer.*	26
☑ Tisha's | *Amer.*	26
Ugly Mug | *Pub*	17
Union Park | *Amer.*	25
☑ Washington Inn | *Amer.*	27

CLERMONT
☑ Karen & Rei's | *Amer.*	26

EGG HARBOR
Chickie's/Pete's | *Pub*	16
Renault Winery | *Amer.*	23
☑ Tre Figlio | *Italian*	27

GALLOWAY
☑ Ram's Head | *Amer.*	25

GALLOWAY TOWNSHIP
Athenian Gdn. | *Greek*	24

LINWOOD
Barrel's | *Italian*	17

MARGATE
Barrel's | *Italian*	17
Bobby Chez | *Seafood*	24
Dune | *Seafood*	25
Manna | *Amer.*	24
Steve/Cookie's | *Amer.*	25
Tomatoes | *Calif./Eclectic*	24
Ventura's | *Italian*	17

MAYS LANDING
Bobby Chez | *Seafood*	24
Inn/Sugar Hill | *Amer.*	23
Johnny Rockets | *Burgers*	15

NORTH WILDWOOD
Claude's | *French*	25

OCEAN CITY
Nag's Head | *Amer.*	23

SEA ISLE CITY
Busch's | *Seafood*	20

SMITHVILLE
Smithville Inn | *Amer.*	21

SOMERS POINT
Crab Trap | *Seafood*	22
Inlet | *Amer.*	19

VENTNOR
Sage | *Med.*	24

WEST CAPE MAY
Black Duck | *Eclectic*	24
Vanthia's | *Seafood*	21

WILDWOOD
Marie Nicole's | *Amer.*	24

Suburban Philly Area

BORDENTOWN
Alstarz | *Eclectic*	16
Chickie's/Pete's | *Pub*	16
Farnsworth | *Continental*	23
Mastoris | *Diner*	20

Menus, photos, voting and more – free at ZAGAT.com

BURLINGTON

Café Gallery | *Continental* 23

CHERRY HILL

Bahama Breeze | *Carib.* 18
Bobby Chez | *Seafood* 24
Brio | *Italian* 19
Buca di Beppo | *Italian* 16
Caffe Aldo | *Italian* 24
Z Cheesecake Factory | *Amer.* 19
Elephant/Castle | *Pub* 13
Five Guys | *Burgers* 21
Kibitz Rm. | *Deli* 22
Kuzina | *Greek* 20
La Campagne | *French* 24
Z McCormick/Schmick | *Seafood* 20
Megu | *Japanese* 24
Mélange | *Creole/Southern* 25
Mikado | *Japanese* 23
Mirabella | *Italian* 20
Norma's | *Mideast.* 21
P.J. Whelihan's | *Pub* 16
Ponzio's | *Diner* 18
Red Hot/Blue | *BBQ* 19
Sakura Spring | *Chinese/Japanese* 22
Siri's | *French/Thai* 24
Swanky Bubbles | *Pan-Asian* 20
NEW William Douglas | *Steak* 22

CINNAMINSON

Tokyo Bleu | *Japanese* 22

CLEMENTON

Filomena Italiana | *Italian* 23
Nifty Fifty's | *Diner* 18

COLLINGSWOOD

Barone's/Villa Barone | *Italian* 20
Bistro di Marino | *Italian* 23
Blackbird | *Amer.* 26
Bobby Chez | *Seafood* 24
Casona | *Cuban* 22
NEW Il Fiore | *Italian* 26
Joe Pesce | *Italian/Seafood* 23
Nunzio | *Italian* 24

Pop Shop | *Amer.* 20
Z Sagami | *Japanese* 27
Sapori | *Italian* 24
Tortilla Press | *Mex.* 22
Word of Mouth | *Amer.* 25

DEPTFORD

Filomena Lakeview | *Italian* 24

GIBBSBORO

Chophouse | *Seafood/Steak* 25

HADDONFIELD

Fuji | *Japanese* 24
Little Tuna | *Seafood* 21
Mélange | *Creole/Southern* 25
P.J. Whelihan's | *Pub* 16

HADDON HEIGHTS

Anthony's | *Italian* 23
Elements | *Amer.* 24
Kunkel's | *Seafood/Steak* 24

LINDENWOLD

La Esperanza | *Mex.* 22

MAPLE SHADE

Forno | *Pizza* -
Mikado | *Japanese* 23
Penang | *Malaysian/Thai* 21
P.J. Whelihan's | *Pub* 16
Tacconelli's | *Pizza* 22

MARLTON

Fleming's | *Steak* 23
Joe's Peking | *Chinese* 23
Mexican Food | *Mex.* 20
Mikado | *Japanese* 23
Z P.F. Chang's | *Chinese* 20
Pietro's | *Pizza* 20
Pizzicato | *Italian* 20
Redstone | *Amer.* 22

MEDFORD

Braddock's | *Amer.* 21
Ted's/Main | *Amer.* 25

MEDFORD LAKES

P.J. Whelihan's | *Pub* 16

MOORESTOWN

Barnacle Ben's | *Seafood* 20

Barone's/Villa Barone | *Italian* 20

MOUNT EPHRAIM

Five Guys | *Burgers* 21

MOUNT HOLLY

High St. | *Amer.* 23

Robin's Nest | *Amer.* 22

MOUNT LAUREL

Baja Fresh | *Mex.* 17

Bobby Chez | *Seafood* 24

El Azteca | *Mex.* 20

GG's | *Amer.* 24

NEW GRETNA

Allen's | *Seafood* 19

PENNSAUKEN

Benihana | *Japanese* 18

Pub | *Steak* 19

RIVERSIDE

Cafe Madison | *Amer.* 20

SEWELL

Barnsboro Inn | *Amer.* 22

Blue Eyes | *Steak* 20

Bobby Chez | *Seafood* 24

Creole Café | *Cajun/Creole* 22

P.J. Whelihan's | *Pub* 16

TURNERSVILLE

Nifty Fifty's | *Diner* 18

VOORHEES

Catelli | *Italian* 25

Chez Elena Wu | 23
  Chinese/Japanese

Coconut Bay | *Asian* 20

Laceno | *Italian/Seafood* 26

Little Café | *Eclectic* 25

Ritz Seafood | *Pan-Asian/Seafood* 24

Somsak | *Thai* 23

WEST BERLIN

Filomena Rustica | *Italian* 23

Los Amigos | *Mex./SW* 22

WESTMONT

Cork | *Amer.* 21

Giumarello's | *Italian* 24

Kitchen 233 | *Amer.* 20

Special Features

Listings cover the best in each category and include names, locations and Food ratings. Multi-location restaurants' features may vary by branch.

BREAKFAST

(See also Hotel Dining)

Avon Pavilion | **Avon-by-Sea**	19
NEW Backyards | **Hoboken**	-
Christopher's | **Colts Neck**	19
Country Pancake | **Ridgewood**	20
Eppes Essen | **Livingston**	19
Full Moon | **Lambertville**	21
Hobby's | **Newark**	23
Java Moon | **Jackson**	18
Je's | **Newark**	24
Market Roost | **Flemington**	21
Mastoris | **Bordentown**	20
Meil's | **Stockton**	22
Nana's Deli | **Livingston**	22
Ponzio's | **Cherry Hill**	18
Toast | **Montclair**	20
Zafra | **Hoboken**	24

BRUNCH

Z Amanda's | **Hoboken**	25
Anthony David's | **Hoboken**	26
Brothers Moon | **Hopewell**	22
Cafe/Rosemont | **Rosemont**	20
Café Gallery | **Burlington**	23
Chart Hse. | **Weehawken**	21
Court St. | **Hoboken**	22
Crown Palace | **multi.**	20
NEW elements | **Princeton**	-
Fiddleheads | **Jamesburg**	22
Grenville | **Bay Hd.**	21
Grill 73 | **Bernardsville**	21
Harvest Bistro | **Closter**	21
La Campagne | **Cherry Hill**	24
Lambertville Station | **Lambertville**	17
Madame Claude | **Jersey City**	23
Marco/Pepe | **Jersey City**	22
Moghul | **Edison**	25
Molly Pitcher | **Red Bank**	23
Napa Valley | **Paramus**	21

NEW 9 North | **Wayne**	-
Z Rat's | **Hamilton**	25
Raymond's | **Montclair**	21
Rest., The | **Hackensack**	19
Taqueria | **Jersey City**	22
Terrace | **Short Hills**	22
Tortilla Press | **Collingswood**	22
Verjus | **Maplewood**	25
Zafra | **Hoboken**	24

BUFFET

(Check availability)

Aamantran | **Toms River Twp**	21
Aangan | **Freehold Twp**	22
Akbar | **Edison**	19
Alessio 426 | **Metuchen**	19
Allendale B&G | **Allendale**	17
Amiya | **Jersey City**	19
Assembly | **Englewood Cliffs**	17
Black Forest Inn | **Stanhope**	22
Bombay Curry | **Basking Ridge**	18
Bombay Gdns. | **E Brunswick**	23
Café Gallery | **Burlington**	23
Chand | **Parsippany**	23
Cinnamon | **Morris Plains**	23
Crab's Claw | **Lavallette**	18
Cranbury Inn | **Cranbury**	15
Europa Monroe | **Monroe Twp**	16
House of Blues | **A.C.**	16
Hunt Club | **Summit**	21
India/Hudson | **Hoboken**	20
Inlet | **Somers Point**	19
Karma Kafe | **Hoboken**	24
Kaya's | **Belmar**	20
Lambertville Station | **Lambertville**	17
Madison B&G | **Hoboken**	20
Z Manor | **W Orange**	24
Mantra | **Paramus**	24
McLoone's | **multi.**	17
Mehndi | **Morristown**	24

Meyersville Inn | **Gillette**	17
Mill/Spring Lake | **Spring Lake Hts**	21
Minado | **multi.**	19
Moghul | **Edison**	25
Moksha | **Edison**	22
Molly Pitcher | **Red Bank**	23
Neelam | **multi.**	20
New Main Taste | **Chatham**	23
Noodle Hse. | **N Brunswick**	18
Old Man Rafferty's | **multi.**	18
Passage/India | **Lawrenceville**	21
Rest., The | **Hackensack**	19
Rod's Steak | **Morristown**	22
Saffron | **E Hanover**	22
Salt Creek | **Rumson**	19
Shanghai Jazz | **Madison**	21
Smithville Inn | **Smithville**	21
Terrace | **Short Hills**	22
Waterfront Buffet | **A.C.**	19

BUSINESS DINING

Assembly | **Englewood Cliffs**	17
Benihana | **multi.**	18
Café Azzurro | **Peapack**	24
Chez Catherine | **Westfield**	26
Copeland | **Morristown**	25
☑ Daryl | **New Bruns.**	24
David Burke | **Rumson**	25
Due Terre | **Bernardsville**	25
NEW Eno Terra | **Kingston**	–
Equus | **Bernardsville**	21
☑ Fascino | **Montclair**	26
55 Main | **Flemington**	20
Fiorino | **Summit**	23
Fuji | **Haddonfield**	24
Gallagher's | **A.C.**	22
Gladstone | **Gladstone**	21
☑ Highlawn | **W Orange**	25
I Cavallini | **Colts Neck**	23
NEW Il Fiore | **Collingswood**	26
Kitchen 233 | **Westmont**	20
K.O.B.E. | **Holmdel**	22
NEW LaPrete's | **Belleville**	22

Lu Nello | **Cedar Grove**	25
Manhattan Steak | **Oakhurst**	19
Martini Bistro | **Millburn**	18
☑ McCormick/Schmick | **Cherry Hill**	20
Mill/Spring Lake | **Spring Lake Hts**	21
Moksha | **Edison**	22
☑ Morton's | **Hackensack**	25
NEW 9 North | **Wayne**	–
Old Homestead | **A.C.**	26
Panico's | **New Bruns.**	23
Papa Razzi | **Short Hills**	17
Passage/India | **Lawrenceville**	21
Phillips Seafood | **A.C.**	19
☑ Pluckemin Inn | **Bedminster**	26
Portofino | **Tinton Falls**	23
Raven/Peach | **Fair Haven**	25
☑ River Palm | **multi.**	24
Roots | **Summit**	25
☑ Ruth's Chris | **Princeton**	25
Sirena | **Long Branch**	22
Smoke Chophse. | **Englewood**	23
NEW Steakhouse 85 | **New Bruns.**	–
☑ Stonehouse | **Warren**	22
☑ Stony Hill Inn | **Hackensack**	23
Tabor Rd. | **Morris Plains**	21
Vine | **Basking Ridge**	25
Wasabi | **Somerville**	25
NEW William Douglas | **Cherry Hill**	22

BYO

Aamantran | **Toms River Twp**	21
Aangan | **Freehold Twp**	22
Aby's | **Matawan**	20
Acacia | **Lawrenceville**	23
☑ Ajihei | **Princeton**	28
Alan@594 | **Upper Montclair**	21
Aldo/Gianni | **S Hackensack**	21
Alessio 426 | **Metuchen**	19
Alexander's | **Cape May**	26
Ali Baba | **Hoboken**	20
Aligado | **Hazlet**	24
Allen's | **New Gretna**	19

Andaman | **Morristown**	23
Anjelica's | **Sea Bright**	24
Anna's | **Middletown**	25
Anthony David's | **Hoboken**	26
Anthony's | **Haddon Hts**	23
Aozora | **Montclair**	25
Aquila Cucina | **New Providence**	22
Aroma | **Franklin Pk**	21
A Tavola | **Old Bridge**	19
Athenian Gdn. | **Galloway Twp**	24
A Toute Heure | **Cranford**	25
Avon Pavilion | **Avon-by-Sea**	19
⍚ Backyards | **Hoboken**	–
Bamboo Leaf | **multi.**	22
Bank 34 | **Somerville**	23
Barnacle Ben's | **Moorestown**	20
Barone's/Villa Barone | **multi.**	20
Barrel's | **multi.**	17
Basilico | **Millburn**	24
⚡ Baumgart's | **multi.**	19
⚡ Bay Ave. | **Highlands**	27
Bayou Cafe | **Freehold**	21
Bazzini | **Ridgewood**	19
Belford Bistro | **Belford**	28
Bella Sogno | **Bradley Bch**	20
Benito's | **Chester**	24
Beyti Kebab | **Union City**	23
Bienvenue | **Red Bank**	23
Bistro/Red Bank | **Red Bank**	21
Bistro di Marino | **Collingswood**	23
Bistro 44 | **Toms River**	24
Bistro Olé | **Asbury Pk**	24
Blackbird | **Collingswood**	26
Black Duck | **W Cape May**	24
Black Trumpet | **Spring Lake**	25
Blu | **Montclair**	24
Blue | **Surf City**	24
⚡ Blue Bottle | **Hopewell**	27
Blue Fish | **Flemington**	21
⚡ Blue Point | **Princeton**	25
Bobby Chez | **multi.**	24
Bombay Curry | **Basking Ridge**	18
Bombay Gdns. | **E Brunswick**	23
Bosphorus | **Lake Hiawatha**	21
Brandl. | **Belmar**	24
Brasilia Rest. | **Newark**	21
Brioso | **Marlboro**	22
Brix 67 | **Summit**	18
Brooklyn's Pizza | **multi.**	23
Brothers Moon | **Hopewell**	22
Cafe Arugula | **S Orange**	21
Cafe/Rosemont | **Rosemont**	20
Café Azzurro | **Peapack**	24
Cafe Coloré | **Freehold Twp**	21
Cafe Graziella | **Hillsborough**	20
Cafe Loren | **Avalon**	26
⚡ Cafe Matisse | **Rutherford**	27
Cafe Metro | **Denville**	21
⚡ Cafe Panache | **Ramsey**	28
California Grill | **Flemington**	18
Capt'n Ed's | **Pt. Pleas.**	18
Casa Maya | **multi.**	21
Casa Solar | **Belmar**	25
Casona | **Collingswood**	22
Chand | **multi.**	23
Chao Phaya | **multi.**	24
Charrito's | **multi.**	22
⚡ Chef's Table | **Franklin Lakes**	26
⚡ Chef Vola's | **A.C.**	27
Chez Elena Wu | **Voorhees**	23
Christie's | **Howell**	23
Christopher's | **Colts Neck**	19
Church St. | **Montclair**	14
Cinnamon | **Morris Plains**	23
Clementine's | **Avon-by-Sea**	23
Coconut Bay | **Voorhees**	20
Copper Fish | **Cape May**	20
Corso 98 | **Montclair**	23
Country Pancake | **Ridgewood**	20
Creole Café | **Sewell**	22
Cuban Pete's | **Montclair**	18
Cucina Rosa | **Cape May**	21
⚡ CulinAriane | **Montclair**	27
Dabbawalla | **Summit**	18
da Filippo | **Somerville**	23
Dai-Kichi | **Upper Montclair**	22

D & L BBQ | **Asbury Pk**	22
Dante's | **Mendham**	21
Z DeLorenzo's Pies | **multi.**	27
DeLorenzo's Pizza | **Trenton**	–
Dim Sum Dynasty | **Ridgewood**	20
DiPalma | **N Bergen**	22
Dish | **Red Bank**	24
Z Drew's | **Keyport**	26
Dune | **Margate**	25
Edo Sushi | **Pennington**	19
El Azteca | **Mt Laurel**	20
Elements Asia | **Lawrenceville**	23
Elements | **Haddon Hts**	24
El Familiar | **multi.**	19
El Meson | **Freehold**	24
Epernay | **Montclair**	20
Eppes Essen | **Livingston**	19
Eurasian | **Red Bank**	22
Far East Taste | **Eatontown**	23
NEW Farm 2 Bistro | **Nutley**	–
Z Fascino | **Montclair**	26
Fedora | **Lawrenceville**	18
Ferrari's | **Freehold Twp**	22
Ferry Hse. | **Princeton**	25
Fiddleheads | **Jamesburg**	22
55 Main | **Flemington**	20
Fishery, The | **S Amboy**	–
Five Guys | **Watchung**	21
410 Bank St. | **Cape May**	26
Frankie Fed's | **Freehold Twp**	22
Fresco | **Milltown**	25
Freshwater's | **Plainfield**	21
Fuji | **Haddonfield**	24
Full Moon | **Lambertville**	21
Fusion | **Flemington**	22
Z Gables | **Beach Haven**	25
Gaetano's | **Red Bank**	20
Garlic Rose | **Madison**	20
Gazelle | **Ridgewood**	24
Ginger | **Freehold Twp**	16
Girasole | **Bound Brook**	26
Greek Taverna | **multi.**	–
Grill 73 | **Bernardsville**	21
GRUB Hut | **Manville**	21
Hamilton's | **Lambertville**	25
Harvey Cedars | **multi.**	22
Hunan Spring | **Springfield**	20
Ichiban | **Princeton**	18
Ikko | **Brick**	25
NEW Il Fiore | **Collingswood**	26
Z Il Mondo | **Madison**	25
Indigo Smoke | **Montclair**	21
Isabella's | **Westfield**	18
Island Palm | **Spring Lake**	19
It's Greek To Me | **multi.**	17
Jack Cooper's | **Edison**	18
Jerry/Harvey's | **Marlboro**	18
Joe Pesce | **Collingswood**	23
Joe's Peking | **Marlton**	23
Johnny Rockets | **A.C.**	15
Jose's | **Spring Lake Hts**	24
Jose's Cantina | **multi.**	20
Juanito's | **multi.**	22
Kanji | **Tinton Falls**	25
Z Karen & Rei's | **Clermont**	26
Kaya's | **Belmar**	20
Kibitz Rm. | **Cherry Hill**	22
K.O.B.E. | **Holmdel**	22
Konbu | **Manalapan**	25
Krave Café | **Newton**	23
Kunkel's | **Haddon Hts**	24
Kuzina | **Cherry Hill**	20
Labrador | **Normandy Bch**	23
La Campagna | **multi.**	22
La Campagne | **Cherry Hill**	24
Laceno | **Voorhees**	26
La Cipollina | **Freehold**	21
La Focaccia | **Summit**	24
La Isla | **Hoboken**	26
La Pastaria | **multi.**	19
La Scala | **Somerville**	22
La Spiaggia | **Ship Bottom**	24
Latitude 40N | **Pt. Pleas. Bch**	23
Z Latour | **Ridgewood**	26
Le Fandy | **Fair Haven**	25
Le Rendez-Vous | **Kenilworth**	26

Lilly's/Canal | **Lambertville**	21
🆕 Limani | **Westfield**	22
Limestone Cafe | **Peapack**	21
Little Café | **Voorhees**	25
Little Food Café | **Pompton Plains**	25
Little Saigon | **A.C.**	25
Little Tuna | **Haddonfield**	21
Lodos | **New Milford**	23
🇿 Lorena's | **Maplewood**	28
Lotus Cafe | **Hackensack**	24
LouCás | **Edison**	23
Luca's | **Somerset**	-
Luchento's | **Millstone Twp**	-
Luka's | **Ridgefield Pk**	22
Luke's | **Maplewood**	21
Madame Claude | **Jersey City**	23
Madeleine's | **Northvale**	25
Magic Pot | **Edgewater**	18
Mahzu | **multi.**	21
Main St. Bistro | **Freehold**	21
Manna | **Margate**	24
Manon | **Lambertville**	25
Margherita's | **Hoboken**	21
Market Roost | **Flemington**	21
Marmara | **Manalapan**	19
Marra's | **Ridgewood**	20
Martino's | **Somerville**	22
Matisse | **Belmar**	21
Matt's Rooster | **Flemington**	25
Meemah | **Edison**	22
Megu | **Cherry Hill**	24
Meil's | **Stockton**	22
Mélange | **multi.**	25
Mexico Lindo | **Brick**	23
Michael's | **Manalapan**	19
Midori | **Denville**	22
Mie Thai | **multi.**	24
Mignon Steak | **Rutherford**	22
Mikado | **multi.**	23
Ming | **Edison**	21
Mirabella | **Cherry Hill**	20
Moghul | **Edison**	25
Mojave | **Westfield**	23
Monster Sushi | **Summit**	20
Moonfish | **Cape May**	-
Saigon R./Mo' Pho | **multi.**	24
Mr. Chu | **E Hanover**	21
Mud City | **Manahawkin**	24
My Little Greek | **Freehold**	18
Navesink Fishery | **Navesink**	24
Neelam | **multi.**	20
New Main Taste | **Chatham**	23
Next Door | **Montclair**	21
Nha Trang Pl. | **Jersey City**	24
Nicky's | **Madison**	19
🆕 9 North | **Wayne**	-
Nobi | **Toms River Twp**	25
No. 9 | **Lambertville**	26
Noodle Hse. | **N Brunswick**	18
Nori | **multi.**	23
Norma's | **Cherry Hill**	21
Nouveau | **Montclair**	24
Nunzio | **Collingswood**	24
Octopus's Gdn. | **Stafford**	23
Orbis Bistro | **Upper Montclair**	20
🇿 Origin | **multi.**	26
Osteria Giotto | **Montclair**	25
Ota-Ya | **Lambertville**	22
Oyako Tso's | **Freehold**	23
Pamir | **Morristown**	21
Passionne | **Montclair**	23
Paula/Rigoletto | **Weehawken**	21
Penang | **multi.**	21
🇿 Peter Shields | **Cape May**	26
Pithari | **Highland Pk**	23
Pizzicato | **Marlton**	20
Plan B | **Asbury Pk**	-
Pop's Garage | **Normandy Bch**	22
Pop Shop | **Collingswood**	20
🆕 Prairie | **Monmouth Bch**	-
Radicchio | **Ridgewood**	22
Raimondo's | **Ship Bottom**	24
Raymond's | **Montclair**	21
Ray's | **Little Silver**	22
Rebecca's | **Edgewater**	25
Red | **Red Bank**	20

Red's | **Pt. Pleas. Bch**	23	Taka | **Asbury Pk**	25
NEW Resto | **Madison**	21	Taqueria | **Jersey City**	22
Richard's | **Long Branch**	21	Taro | **Montclair**	20
Rick's | **Lambertville**	20	Taste of Asia | **Chatham**	21
Risotto Hse. | **Rutherford**	23	Tattoni's | **Hamilton Twp**	21
Ritz Seafood | **Voorhees**	24	Ted's/Main | **Medford**	25
Roberto's | **Beach Haven**	22	Thai Chef | **Montclair**	21
Robongi | **Hoboken**	24	Thai Kitchen | **multi.**	24
RoCCA | **Glen Rock**	23	Thai Thai | **Stirling**	23
☑ Saddle River Inn | **Saddle River**	28	Theresa's | **Westfield**	22
Saffron | **E Hanover**	22	Tim Schafer's | **Morristown**	25
☑ Sagami | **Collingswood**	27	Tina Louise | **Carlstadt**	24
Sage | **Ventnor**	24	☑ Tisha's | **Cape May**	26
Sakura-Bana | **Ridgewood**	25	Toast | **Montclair**	20
Sakura Spring | **Cherry Hill**	22	Tokyo Bleu | **Cinnaminson**	22
San Remo | **Shrewsbury**	23	Tomo's | **Little Falls**	21
Sapori | **Collingswood**	24	**NEW** Torcello | **Red Bank**	-
Settebello | **Morristown**	21	Tortilla Press | **Collingswood**	22
Seven Hills | **Highland Pk**	22	Tortuga's | **Princeton**	20
Shumi | **Somerville**	25	Tsuki | **Bernardsville**	22
Siam | **Lambertville**	20	Tuptim | **Montclair**	20
Siam Gdn. | **Red Bank**	24	Tutto a Modo Mio | **Ridgefield**	23
Simply Radishing | **Lawrenceville**	19	Underground Café | **Princeton**	19
Sirin | **Morristown**	24	Union Park | **Cape May**	25
Siri's | **Cherry Hill**	24	Vanthia's | **W Cape May**	21
Sister Sue's | **Asbury Pk**	21	Village Gourmet | **Rutherford**	21
Sogno | **Red Bank**	22	Village Green | **Ridgewood**	23
Soho 33 | **Madison**	19	Vivas | **Belmar**	26
Solo Bella | **Jackson**	21	Wasabi | **E Brunswick**	25
Somsak | **Voorhees**	23	West Lake | **Matawan**	22
Sono Sushi | **Middletown**	25	☑ Whispers | **Spring Lake**	27
Soufflé | **Summit**	22	Wild Ginger | **Englewood**	22
Spargo's | **Manalapan**	24	Wondee's | **Hackensack**	20
Spike's | **Pt. Pleas. Bch**	23	Wonder Seafood | **Edison**	23
Sri Thai | **Hoboken**	23	Word of Mouth | **Collingswood**	25
NEW Stamna | **Bloomfield**	23	Ya Ya Noodles | **Skillman**	19
Sumo | **Wall**	25	Yellow Fin | **Surf City**	26
Sunny Gdn. | **Princeton**	20	Zafra | **Hoboken**	24
Surf Taco | **multi.**	20	**CATERING**	
Sushi by Kazu | **Howell**	26	Aamantran | **Toms River Twp**	21
Sweet Basil's | **W Orange**	23	Aangan | **Freehold Twp**	22
Table 8 | **Montclair**	23	☑ Amanda's | **Hoboken**	25
Tacconelli's | **Maple Shade**	22	Andaman | **Morristown**	23

Z André's	**Newton**	27
Anjelica's	**Sea Bright**	24
Anthony David's	**Hoboken**	26
Athenian Gdn.	**Galloway Twp**	24
Z Augustino's	**Hoboken**	26
Barone's/Villa Barone	**multi.**	20
Z Bernards Inn	**Bernardsville**	26
Bombay Gdns.	**E Brunswick**	23
Brioso	**Marlboro**	22
Brothers Moon	**Hopewell**	22
Cafe Loren	**Avalon**	26
Z Cafe Matisse	**Rutherford**	27
Z Cafe Panache	**Ramsey**	28
Caffe Aldo	**Cherry Hill**	24
Casa Dante	**Jersey City**	23
Catelli	**Voorhees**	25
Cucharamama	**Hoboken**	25
da Filippo	**Somerville**	23
Dock's	**A.C.**	26
Doris/Ed's	**Highlands**	25
Eppes Essen	**Livingston**	19
Far East Taste	**Eatontown**	23
Ferry Hse.	**Princeton**	25
Filomena Rustica	**W Berlin**	23
Z Gables	**Beach Haven**	25
Girasole	**Bound Brook**	26
Z Grand Cafe	**Morristown**	26
Harvest Moon	**Ringoes**	23
Hobby's	**Newark**	23
Joe's Peking	**Marlton**	23
Kibitz Rm.	**Cherry Hill**	22
La Campagne	**Cherry Hill**	24
Le Petit Chateau	**Bernardsville**	25
Limestone Cafe	**Peapack**	21
Little Café	**Voorhees**	25
Little Tuna	**Haddonfield**	21
Makeda	**New Bruns.**	25
Market Roost	**Flemington**	21
Mattar's Bistro	**Allamuchy**	–
Ming	**Edison**	21
Moghul	**Edison**	25
Mud City	**Manahawkin**	24
Z Nicholas	**Middletown**	28

No. 9	**Lambertville**	26
Norma's	**Cherry Hill**	21
Z Ombra	**A.C.**	26
Z Origin	**multi.**	26
Z Ram's Head	**Galloway**	25
Rebecca's	**Edgewater**	25
Red Hot/Blue	**Cherry Hill**	19
Robongi	**Hoboken**	24
Rosemary/Sage	**Riverdale**	26
Saigon R./Mo' Pho	**Englewood**	24
Siri's	**Cherry Hill**	24
Squan Tavern	**Manasquan**	21
Stage Hse.	**Scotch Plains**	22
Stage Left	**New Bruns.**	26
Tim Schafer's	**Morristown**	25
Tina Louise	**Carlstadt**	24
Z Washington Inn	**Cape May**	27
Z Whispers	**Spring Lake**	27
Zafra	**Hoboken**	24

CELEBRITY CHEFS

Z Avenue	*Antonio Mora*	**Long Branch**	20
Z Bay Ave.	*Joe Romanowski*	**Highlands**	27
Z Bernards Inn	*Corey Heyer*	**Bernardsville**	26
Blu	*Zod Arifai*	**Montclair**	24
Z Bobby Flay	*Bobby Flay*	**A.C.**	24
NEW Bobby's	*Bobby Flay*	**Eatontown**	20
Z Cafe Panache	*Kevin Kohler*	**Ramsey**	28
Z Chef's Table	*Claude Baills*	**Franklin Lakes**	26
Copeland	*Thomas Ciszak*	**Morristown**	25
Cucharamama	*Maricel Presilla*	**Hoboken**	25
Z Daryl	*David Drake*	**New Bruns.**	24
David Burke	*David Burke*	**Rumson**	25
Z David Drake	*David Drake*	**Rahway**	28

SPECIAL FEATURES

Ⓩ Fascino | *Ryan DePersio* | **Montclair** — 26

Fuji | *Matt Ito* | **Haddonfield** — 24

Ⓩ Karen & Rei's | *Karen Nelson* | **Clermont** — 26

Ⓩ Latour | *Michael Latour* | **Ridgewood** — 26

Le Petit Chateau | *Scott Cutaneo* | **Bernardsville** — 25

Ⓩ Lorena's | *Humberto Campos* | **Maplewood** — 28

Mélange | *Joe Brown* | **Cherry Hill** — 25

Mia | *G. Perrier, C. Scarduzio* | **A.C.** — 25

Ⓩ Nicholas | *Nicholas Harary* | **Middletown** — 28

Nunzio | *Nunzio Patruno* | **Collingswood** — 24

Ⓩ Ombra | *James Hennessey* | **A.C.** — 26

Orbis Bistro | *Nancy Caballes* | **Upper Montclair** — 20

Perryville Inn | *Paul Ingenito* | **Union Twp** — 23

Porto Leggero | *M. Cetrulo, A. Stella* | **Jersey City** — 22

Ⓩ Scalini Fedeli | *Michael Cetrulo* | **Chatham** — 27

Ⓩ SeaBlue | *Michael Mina* | **A.C.** — 27

Ⓩ Serenade | *James Laird* | **Chatham** — 28

NEW Stella Marina | *Michael Cetrulo* | **Asbury Pk** — -

Wolfgang Puck | *Wolfgang Puck* | **A.C.** — 24

Zafra | *Maricel Presilla* | **Hoboken** — 24

CHILD-FRIENDLY

(Alternatives to the usual fast-food places; * children's menu available)

Aby's* | **Matawan** — 20

Ⓩ Amanda's | **Hoboken** — 25

Ⓩ André's | **Newton** — 27

Anjelica's | **Sea Bright** — 24

Axelsson's* | **Cape May** — 23

Bahama Breeze* | **Cherry Hill** — 18

Bamboo Leaf | **Bradley Bch** — 22

Barone's/Villa Barone* | **multi.** — 20

Ⓩ Baumgart's* | **multi.** — 19

Bazzini* | **Ridgewood** — 19

Bell's | **Lambertville** — 21

Bell's Mansion* | **Stanhope** — 17

Beyti Kebab | **Union City** — 23

Big Ed's BBQ* | **Matawan** — 19

Black Duck | **W Cape May** — 24

Black Forest Inn | **Stanhope** — 22

Blue | **Surf City** — 24

Ⓩ Blue Point* | **Princeton** — 25

Bobby Chez | **multi.** — 24

Bombay Gdns. | **E Brunswick** — 23

Braddock's* | **Medford** — 21

Brioso | **Marlboro** — 22

Cabin* | **Howell** — 16

Cafe Loren | **Avalon** — 26

Capriccio | **A.C.** — 26

Casa Dante | **Jersey City** — 23

Casa Giuseppe | **Iselin** — 24

Casa Vasca | **Newark** — 23

Cenzino | **Oakland** — 24

Chao Phaya | **Somerville** — 24

Ⓩ Cheesecake Factory* | **multi.** — 19

Chengdu 46 | **Clifton** — 24

Christie's* | **Howell** — 23

Cucharamama | **Hoboken** — 25

da Filippo | **Somerville** — 23

Dock's* | **A.C.** — 26

E & V | **Paterson** — 23

El Azteca* | **Mt Laurel** — 20

Elephant/Castle* | **Cherry Hill** — 13

El Meson* | **Freehold** — 24

Espo's | **Raritan** — 21

Esty St. | **Park Ridge** — 24

Far East Taste | **Eatontown** — 23

Filomena Italiana* | **Clementon** — 23

Filomena Lakeview* | **Deptford** — 24

Filomena Rustica* | **W Berlin** — 23

Fornos/Spain | **Newark** — 23

410 Bank St. | **Cape May** — 26

Frankie Fed's* | **Freehold Twp** — 22

Frenchtown Inn | **Frenchtown** — 25

Ⓩ Grand Cafe | **Morristown** — 26

Harvest Moon* | **Ringoes**	23
Hobby's | **Newark**	23
Homestead Inn | **Trenton**	24
Ikko* | **Brick**	25
Inn/Hawke* | **Lambertville**	18
It's Greek To Me* | **multi.**	17
Java Moon* | **Jackson**	18
Kibitz Rm.* | **Cherry Hill**	22
La Campagne | **Cherry Hill**	24
La Esperanza* | **Lindenwold**	22
La Scala | **Somerville**	22
☑ Legal Sea Foods* | **multi.**	21
Little Tuna* | **Haddonfield**	21
Lu Nello | **Cedar Grove**	25
Margherita's | **Hoboken**	21
Meil's* | **Stockton**	22
Mexican Food* | **Marlton**	20
Mexico Lindo* | **Brick**	23
Midori | **Denville**	22
Mie Thai | **Woodbridge**	24
Mikado | **Cherry Hill**	23
Moghul | **Edison**	25
Mud City* | **Manahawkin**	24
Nag's Head* | **Ocean City**	23
Navesink Fishery | **Navesink**	24
New Main Taste | **Chatham**	23
Nifty Fifty's* | **multi.**	18
NEW 9 North* | **Wayne**	-
No. 9 | **Lambertville**	26
Norma's* | **Cherry Hill**	21
Ota-Ya | **Lambertville**	22
☑ Park/Orchard* | **E Rutherford**	22
Passage/India | **Lawrenceville**	21
☑ P.F. Chang's | **Marlton**	20
Pietro's* | **Marlton**	20
Pizzicato* | **Marlton**	20
Ponzio's* | **Cherry Hill**	18
Pop Shop* | **Collingswood**	20
Pub* | **Pennsauken**	19
Raimondo's* | **Ship Bottom**	24
☑ Ram's Head* | **Galloway**	25
☑ Rat's | **Hamilton**	25
Rebecca's | **Edgewater**	25

Red Hot/Blue* | **Cherry Hill**	19
Reservoir | **Boonton**	22
Robongi | **Hoboken**	24
Rosemary/Sage | **Riverdale**	26
Sabor | **N Bergen**	22
Saffron | **E Hanover**	22
☑ Sagami | **Collingswood**	27
Saigon R./Mo' Pho | **Englewood**	24
SAWA Steak* | **Eatontown**	22
Shipwreck Grill | **Brielle**	25
Siri's* | **Cherry Hill**	24
Sister Sue's | **Asbury Pk**	21
SoHo/George* | **New Bruns.**	23
Somsak | **Voorhees**	23
Sono Sushi* | **Middletown**	25
Steve/Cookie's* | **Margate**	25
Surf Taco* | **multi.**	20
Sushi by Kazu | **Howell**	26
Thai Kitchen | **multi.**	24
Thai Thai | **Stirling**	23
Theresa's* | **Westfield**	22
Tina Louise | **Carlstadt**	24
Tortilla Press* | **Collingswood**	22
☑ Tre Figlio* | **Egg Harbor**	27
Tuckers* | **Beach Haven**	16
Verjus | **Maplewood**	25
Wasabi | **multi.**	25
West Lake | **Matawan**	22
White Hse. | **A.C.**	26
Wild Ginger | **Englewood**	22
WindMill* | **multi.**	19
Word of Mouth | **Collingswood**	25
Zafra | **Hoboken**	24

DANCING

Alstarz | **Bordentown**	16
Azúcar | **Jersey City**	21
Busch's | **Sea Isle City**	20
Cabin | **Howell**	16
Casa Dante | **Jersey City**	23
Cuba Libre | **A.C.**	22
Delta's | **New Bruns.**	23
Filomena Rustica | **W Berlin**	23

SPECIAL FEATURES

Hunt Club	**Summit**	21
Z Manor	**W Orange**	24
Mohawk Hse.	**Sparta**	19
Portuguese Manor	**Perth Amboy**	20
Z Rat's	**Hamilton**	25
Rest., The	**Hackensack**	19
Sabor	**multi.**	22
Skylark	**Edison**	20
South City	**multi.**	22
Verdigre	**New Bruns.**	21
Windansea	**Highlands**	17

DELIVERY/TAKEOUT

(D=delivery, T=takeout)

Aamantran	D, T		21
Toms River Twp		
Aby's	D, T	**Matawan**	20
Athenian Gdn.	T	**Galloway Twp**	24
Bahama Breeze	T	**Cherry Hill**	18
Z Baumgart's	T	**multi.**	19
Bell's	T	**Lambertville**	21
Belmont Tavern	T	**Bloomfield**	23
Beyti Kebab	T	**Union City**	23
Big Ed's BBQ	T	**Matawan**	19
Blue Danube	T	**Trenton**	23
Bobby Chez	T	**multi.**	24
Brooklyn's Pizza	T	**multi.**	23
Cafe/Rosemont	T	**Rosemont**	20
California Grill	T	**Flemington**	18
Casa Maya	T	**Meyersville**	21
Chao Phaya	T	**Somerville**	24
Chilangos	T	**Highlands**	21
Crown Palace	T	**multi.**	20
Z DeLorenzo's Pies	T	**Trenton**	27
El Familiar	T	**Toms River Twp**	19
El Meson	T	**Freehold**	24
Eppes Essen	T	**Livingston**	19
Far East Taste	T	**Eatontown**	23
Federici's	T	**Freehold**	22
Filomena Italiana	T	**Clementon**	23
Filomena Lakeview	T	**Deptford**	24
Filomena Rustica	T	**W Berlin**	23
Frankie Fed's	T	**Freehold Twp**	22
Full Moon	T	**Lambertville**	21
Grimaldi's	D	**Hoboken**	24
Harvey Cedars	T	**Beach Haven**	22
Hobby's	D, T	**Newark**	23
Hunan Chinese	T	**Morris Plains**	22
India/Hudson	D	**Hoboken**	20
Indigo Smoke	T	**Montclair**	21
It's Greek To Me	T	**multi.**	17
Java Moon	T	**Jackson**	18
Je's	D, T	**Newark**	24
Joe's Peking	T	**Marlton**	23
Juanito's	T	**multi.**	22
Karma Kafe	D	**Hoboken**	24
Komegashi	D, T	**Jersey City**	23
Limestone Cafe	T	**Peapack**	21
Los Amigos	T	**multi.**	22
Lotus Cafe	D	**Hackensack**	24
Madison B&G	T	**Hoboken**	20
Mahzu	T	**Aberdeen**	21
Margherita's	D	**Hoboken**	21
Market Roost	T	**Flemington**	21
Mastoris	T	**Bordentown**	20
Meemah	T	**Edison**	22
Meil's	T	**Stockton**	22
Memphis Pig Out	T		21
Atlantic Highlands		
Mexico Lindo	T	**Brick**	23
Mie Thai	T	**Woodbridge**	24
Mikado	T	**Cherry Hill**	23
Moghul	T	**Edison**	25
New Main Taste	T	**Chatham**	23
Nobi	T	**Toms River Twp**	25
Noodle Hse.	T	**N Brunswick**	18
Norma's	T	**Cherry Hill**	21
Old Man Rafferty's	T	**multi.**	18
Ota-Ya	T	**Lambertville**	22
Pad Thai	T	**Highland Pk**	21
Passage/India	T	**Lawrenceville**	21
Penang	D, T	**multi.**	21
Z P.F. Chang's	T	**multi.**	20
Raagini	T	**Mountainside**	22
Reservoir	T	**Boonton**	22
Richard's	T	**Long Branch**	21
Robongi	D, T	**Hoboken**	24

Saffron | D | E Hanover	22
Saigon R./Mo' Pho | T | Englewood	24
Sakura-Bana | T | Ridgewood	25
Seven Hills | T | Highland Pk	22
Shogun | T | multi.	22
Shumi | T | Somerville	25
Siam | T | Lambertville	20
Sono Sushi | T | Middletown	25
Spike's | T | Pt. Pleas. Bch	23
Sri Thai | D | Hoboken	23
Sunny Gdn. | T | Princeton	20
Sushi Lounge | D, T | Hoboken	22
Taste of Asia | T | Chatham	21
Thai Chef | T | multi.	21
Thai Kitchen | T | multi.	24
Tina Louise | T | Carlstadt	24
Tortuga's | T | Princeton	20
Tuzzio's | T | Long Branch	20
Vic's | T | Bradley Bch	20
Wasabi | D, T | multi.	25
West Lake | T | Matawan	22
White Hse. | T | A.C.	26
Wonder Seafood | T | Edison	23

DESSERT SPECIALISTS

Aquila Cucina | New Providence	22
☑ Baumgart's | multi.	19
☑ Chakra | Paramus	20
☑ Cheesecake Factory | multi.	19
Copeland | Morristown	25
☑ Fascino | Montclair	26
Fedora | Lawrenceville	18
☑ Karen & Rei's | Clermont	26
Old Man Rafferty's | multi.	18
Raymond's | Montclair	21
Robin's Nest | Mt Holly	22

ENTERTAINMENT

(Call for days and times of performances)

Ali Baba | belly dancing | Hoboken	20
Atlantic B&G | varies | S Seaside Pk	25
Bahama Breeze | live music | Cherry Hill	18

☑ Bernards Inn | piano | Bernardsville	26
Blue Eyes | vocalist | Sewell	20
☑ Blue Point | jazz | Princeton	25
da Filippo | piano | Somerville	23
Dock's | piano | A.C.	26
☑ Ebbitt Rm. | jazz | Cape May	27
Filomena Italiana | live music | Clementon	23
Filomena Lakeview | varies | Deptford	24
Filomena Rustica | varies | W Berlin	23
☑ Grand Cafe | piano | Morristown	26
Harvest Moon | piano | Ringoes	23
☑ Il Capriccio | piano | Whippany	26
Lalezar | belly dancing | Montclair	18
Le Petit Chateau | jazz | Bernardsville	25
Makeda | African funk/jazz/reggae | New Bruns.	25
Marmara | belly dancing | Manalapan	19
Mattar's Bistro | varies | Allamuchy	-
McLoone's | jazz/rock | Sea Bright	17
Molly Pitcher | piano | Red Bank	23
Mompou | bossa nova/flamenco/jazz | Newark	21
☑ Moonstruck | jazz | Asbury Pk	25
Norma's | belly dancing | Cherry Hill	21
☑ Peter Shields | piano | Cape May	26
☑ Ram's Head | piano | Galloway	25
☑ Rat's | varies | Hamilton	25
Raven/Peach | guitar/piano | Fair Haven	25
Red Hot/Blue | blues | Cherry Hill	19
Sabor | DJ/flamenco | multi.	22
Shanghai Jazz | jazz | Madison	21

Shipwreck Grill | jazz | **Brielle**	25
Steve/Cookie's | jazz | **Margate**	25
NEW Tim McLoone's | live music | **Asbury Pk**	17
Tortilla Press | guitar | **Collingswood**	22
Z Tre Figlio | varies | **Egg Harbor**	27
Verve | varies | **Somerville**	22
Windansea | DJ/live music | **Highlands**	17

FAMILY-STYLE

Adega | **Newark**	21
Brio | **Cherry Hill**	19
Carmine's | **A.C.**	21
Z Chef Vola's | **A.C.**	27
Cinque Figlie | **Whippany**	21
Cuban Pete's | **Montclair**	18
Dinallo's | **River Edge**	22
Michael's | **Manalapan**	19
Pad Thai | **Highland Pk**	21
Papa Razzi | **multi.**	17
Z P.F. Chang's | **multi.**	20
Risotto Hse. | **Rutherford**	23
Spanish Tavern | **Mountainside**	22
Swanky Bubbles | **Cherry Hill**	20

FIREPLACES

Adega | **Newark**	21
Z Amanda's | **Hoboken**	25
Anna's | **Middletown**	25
Anton's/Swan | **Lambertville**	22
Arthur's Steak | **N Brunswick**	19
Z Avenue | **Long Branch**	20
Axia | **Tenafly**	23
Barrel's | **Linwood**	17
Z Bernards Inn | **Bernardsville**	26
Berta's | **Wanaque**	21
Black Forest Inn | **Stanhope**	22
Black Horse | **Mendham**	19
Black Trumpet | **Spring Lake**	25
Blue Pig | **Cape May**	21
NEW Blvd. Five 72 | **Kenilworth**	27
Braddock's | **Medford**	21
Cabin | **Howell**	16

Casona | **Collingswood**	22
Z Catherine Lombardi | **New Bruns.**	23
NEW Char | **Raritan**	-
Chickie's/Pete's | **Egg Harbor Twp**	16
Chophouse | **Gibbsboro**	25
Christopher's | **Colts Neck**	19
Ciao | **Basking Ridge**	21
Clydz | **New Bruns.**	22
Continental | **A.C.**	23
Cork | **Westmont**	21
Crab's Claw | **Lavallette**	18
Crab Trap | **Somers Point**	22
Cranbury Inn | **Cranbury**	15
da Filippo | **Somerville**	23
D & L BBQ | **Asbury Pk**	22
David Burke | **Rumson**	25
NEW Delicious Heights | **Berkeley Hts**	21
NEW Dino's | **Harrington Pk**	-
Z Ebbitt Rm. | **Cape May**	27
Elephant/Castle | **Cherry Hill**	13
NEW Eno Terra | **Kingston**	-
Europa Monroe | **Monroe Twp**	16
Filomena Italiana | **Clementon**	23
Filomena Lakeview | **Deptford**	24
Filomena Rustica | **W Berlin**	23
NEW Fire/Oak | **Little Falls**	-
Z Gables | **Beach Haven**	25
Giumarello's | **Westmont**	24
Gladstone | **Gladstone**	21
Z Grand Cafe | **Morristown**	26
Grenville | **Bay Hd.**	21
Harry's | **Sea Bright**	21
Harvest Bistro | **Closter**	21
Harvest Moon | **Ringoes**	23
High St. | **Mt Holly**	23
Huntley Taverne | **Summit**	22
Il Michelangelo | **Boonton**	21
Inn/Millrace | **Hope**	21
Inn/Sugar Hill | **Mays Landing**	23
Inn/Hawke | **Lambertville**	18
Ivy Inn | **Hasbrouck Hts**	20

Ẑ Karen & Rei's | **Clermont**	26
Kunkel's | **Haddon Hts**	24
La Campagne | **Cherry Hill**	24
Mad Batter | **Cape May**	23
Mahogany | **Manasquan**	23
Main St. Euro-Amer. | **Princeton**	19
Mastoris | **Bordentown**	20
McLoone's | **Sea Bright**	17
Metuchen Inn | **Metuchen**	21
Meyersville Inn | **Gillette**	17
Mohawk Hse. | **Sparta**	19
Molly Pitcher | **Red Bank**	23
Montville Inn | **Montville**	21
Nag's Head | **Ocean City**	23
Nauvoo Grill | **Fair Haven**	16
Nero's | **Livingston**	17
NEW Nisi Estiatorio | **Englewood**	-
Park Ave. | **Union City**	18
Perryville Inn | **Union Twp**	23
Ẑ Peter Shields | **Cape May**	26
Pheasants Landing | **Hillsborough**	19
P.J. Whelihan's | **Medford Lakes**	16
Plantation | **Harvey Cedars**	20
Ẑ Pluckemin Inn | **Bedminster**	26
Portobello | **Oakland**	19
Posillipo | **Asbury Pk**	22
Pub | **Pennsauken**	19
Ẑ Ram's Head | **Galloway**	25
Ẑ Rat's | **Hamilton**	25
Rest., The | **Hackensack**	19
Richie Cecere's | **Montclair**	20
Ẑ River Palm | **Mahwah**	24
Roberto's | **Beach Haven**	22
Salt Creek | **Princeton**	19
Samdan | **Cresskill**	23
Sanzari's | **New Milford**	20
Scarborough Fair | **Sea Girt**	21
Ẑ Serenade | **Chatham**	28
Sergeantsville Inn | **Sergeantsville**	23
Settebello | **Morristown**	21
Shanghai Jazz | **Madison**	21
Shogun | **Kendall Pk**	22

Sirena | **Long Branch**	22
Smithville Inn | **Smithville**	21
Solaia | **Englewood**	18
Stage Hse. | **Scotch Plains**	22
Stage Left | **New Bruns.**	26
Steve/Cookie's | **Margate**	25
Ẑ Stonehouse | **Warren**	22
Sushi Lounge | **Totowa**	22
Swanky Bubbles | **Cherry Hill**	20
Tabor Rd. | **Morris Plains**	21
3 West | **Basking Ridge**	22
Trap Rock | **Berkeley Hts**	21
Tuckers | **Beach Haven**	16
Undici | **Rumson**	21
Union Park | **Cape May**	25
Vila Nova | **Newark**	23
Walpack Inn | **Wallpack**	19
Ẑ Washington Inn | **Cape May**	27
Ẑ Whispers | **Spring Lake**	27
Windansea | **Highlands**	17
Wolfgang Puck | **A.C.**	24
Yankee Doodle | **Princeton**	15

HISTORIC PLACES

(Year opened; * building)

1682 | Farnsworth* | **Bordentown**	23
1685 | Grand Colonial* | **Union Twp**	23
1697 | Lincroft Inn* | **Lincroft**	18
1714 | Eno Terra* | **Kingston**	-
1734 | Sergeantsville Inn* | **Sergeantsville**	23
1737 | Stage Hse.* | **Scotch Plains**	22
1742 | Black Horse* | **Mendham**	19
1750 | Cranbury Inn* | **Cranbury**	15
1770 | Montville Inn* | **Montville**	21
1785 | Meyersville Inn* | **Gillette**	17
1787 | Smithville Inn* | **Smithville**	21
1800 | Bell's Mansion* | **Stanhope**	17
1800 | Cafe/Rosemont* | **Rosemont**	20
1800 | Robin's Nest* | **Mt Holly**	22
1800 | Tewksbury Inn* | **Oldwick**	22

1805	Frenchtown Inn*	Frenchtown	25
1818	Stony Hill Inn*	Hackensack	23
1823	Braddock's*	Medford	21
1840	David Drake*	Rahway	28
1840	Milford Oyster Hse.*	Milford	23
1840	Washington Inn*	Cape May	27
1841	La Campagne*	Cherry Hill	24
1843	Metuchen Inn*	Metuchen	21
1847	Gladstone*	Gladstone	21
1850	David Burke*	Rumson	25
1850	Delta's*	New Bruns.	23
1850	Light Horse*	Jersey City	23
1856	Equus*	Bernardsville	21
1856	High St.*	Mt Holly	23
1856	Il Michelangelo*	Boonton	21
1858	Trinity*	Keyport	23
1860	Inn/Hawke*	Lambertville	18
1863	Lambertville Station*	Lambertville	17
1864	Renault Winery*	Egg Harbor	23
1865	Park Ave.*	Union City	18
1868	Rick's*	Lambertville	20
1870	Silver Spring*	Flanders	26
1874	Saddle River Inn*	Saddle River	28
1879	Ebbitt Rm.*	Cape May	27
1880	Claude's*	N Wildwood	25
1880	410 Bank St.*	Cape May	26
1880	Moonstruck*	Asbury Pk	25
1882	Busch's	Sea Isle City	20
1882	Mad Batter*	Cape May	23
1883	Alexander's*	Cape May	26
1890	Gables*	Beach Haven	25
1890	Grenville*	Bay Hd.	21
1890	Matt's Rooster*	Flemington	25
1890	Red*	Red Bank	20
1890	Whispers*	Spring Lake	27
1892	Black Trumpet*	Spring Lake	25
1895	Amanda's*	Hoboken	25
1895	Elysian*	Hoboken	20
1895	Queen Victoria*	Toms River	23
1897	Dock's	A.C.	26
1897	Limestone Cafe*	Peapack	21
1900	Athenian Gdn.*	Galloway Twp	24
1900	Doris/Ed's*	Highlands	25
1900	Elements*	Haddon Hts	24
1900	Scarborough Fair*	Sea Girt	21
1903	Columbia Inn*	Montville	21
1905	Casona*	Collingswood	22
1906	Onieal's*	Hoboken	18
1909	Highlawn*	W Orange	25
1912	Grill 73*	Bernardsville	21
1912	Hobby's	Newark	23
1917	Bahrs Landing	Highlands	16
1919	Lahiere's	Princeton	22
1920	Ugly Mug*	Cape May	17
1921	Chef Vola's	A.C.	27
1921	Federici's	Freehold	22
1924	Stage Left*	New Bruns.	26
1926	Iberia	Newark	19
1926	Spike's	Pt. Pleas. Bch	23
1927	Berta's*	Wanaque	21
1928	Molly Pitcher*	Red Bank	23
1928	Rutt's Hut	Clifton	21
1929	Hunt Club	Summit	21
1929	Posillipo*	Asbury Pk	22
1930	Anthony's*	Haddon Hts	23
1930	Clementine's*	Avon-by-Sea	23
1930	Pheasants Landing*	Hillsborough	19
1930	Rosa Luca's*	Asbury	24
1932	Lobster Hse.	Cape May	21
1932	Spanish Tavern	Newark	22
1933	Buttonwood Manor	Matawan	14
1933	Harry's	Sea Bright	21
1933	Sammy's	Mendham	21
1935	Allendale B&G	Allendale	17

1935 | Angelo's | **A.C.** 21

1936 | Reservoir | **Boonton** 22

1936 | Steve/Cookie's* | **Margate** 25

1937 | Kinchley's | **Ramsey** 23

1937 | Yankee Doodle | **Princeton** 15

1938 | Mill/Spring Lake | **Spring Lake Hts** 21

1939 | Bell's | **Lambertville** 21

1939 | Holsten's | **Bloomfield** 17

1939 | Homestead Inn | **Trenton** 24

1939 | Solari's | **Hackensack** 20

1940 | La Spiaggia* | **Ship Bottom** 24

1941 | Conte's | **Princeton** 24

1941 | Walpack Inn* | **Wallpack** 19

1942 | Tuzzio's* | **Long Branch** 20

1945 | Berkeley | **S Seaside Pk** 20

1946 | White Hse.* | **A.C.** 26

1947 | DeLorenzo's Pies | **Trenton** 27

1947 | Vic's | **Bradley Bch** 20

1948 | Tick Tock* | **Clifton** 18

1950 | Main St. Euro-Amer.* | **Princeton** 19

1951 | Pub | **Pennsauken** 19

1951 | Rod's Steak | **Morristown** 22

1956 | Arthur's Tavern | **Morris Plains** 18

1956 | Manor | **W Orange** 24

1957 | Eppes Essen | **Livingston** 19

1957 | Pete/Elda's | **Neptune City** 22

HOTEL DINING

Alexander's Inn

Alexander's | **Cape May** 26

Best Western Robert Treat

Maize | **Newark** 18

Blue Bay Inn

Copper Canyon | **Atlantic Highlands** 24

Borgata Hotel, Casino & Spa

☒ Bobby Flay | **A.C.** 25

izakaya | **A.C.** 26

Old Homestead | **A.C.** 26

☒ Ombra | **A.C.** 26

☒ SeaBlue | **A.C.** 27

Tony Luke's | **A.C.** 21

Wolfgang Puck | **A.C.** 24

Caesars on the Boardwalk

Mia | **A.C.** 25

Carroll Villa Hotel

Mad Batter | **Cape May** 23

Chelsea Hotel

NEW Chelsea Prime | **A.C.** -

Teplitzky's | **A.C.** -

Clarion Hotel

Elephant/Castle | **Cherry Hill** 13

Congress Hall Hotel

Blue Pig | **Cape May** 21

Crystal Springs Resort

Rest. Latour | **Hamburg** 25

daddy O Hotel

daddy O | **Long Beach** 19

DoubleTree Mount Laurel

GG's | **Mt Laurel** 24

Gables Inn

☒ Gables | **Beach Haven** 25

Grand Summit Hotel

Hunt Club | **Summit** 21

Grenville Hotel

Grenville | **Bay Hd.** 21

Harrah's

☒ McCormick/Schmick | **A.C.** 20

Heldrich Hotel

☒ Daryl | **New Bruns.** 24

Hewitt Wellington Hotel

☒ Whispers | **Spring Lake** 27

Hilton at Short Hills

Terrace | **Short Hills** 22

Hilton Hotel

☒ Ruth's Chris | **Parsippany** 25

Holiday Inn

Red Hot/Blue | **Cherry Hill** 19

Madison Hotel

Rod's Steak | **Morristown** 22

Molly Pitcher Inn

Molly Pitcher | **Red Bank** 23

Nassau Inn		
Yankee Doodle	**Princeton**	15
Ocean Club Condos		
Girasole	**A.C.**	25
Quarter at the Tropicana		
Carmine's	**A.C.**	21
Cuba Libre	**A.C.**	22
Palm	**A.C.**	25
☑ P.F. Chang's	**A.C.**	20
☑ Red Square	**A.C.**	21
Resorts Casino & Hotel		
Capriccio	**A.C.**	26
Gallagher's	**A.C.**	22
Sandpiper Inn		
Black Trumpet	**Spring Lake**	25
Sheraton Hotel		
Tun Tavern	**A.C.**	17
Swan Hotel		
Anton's/Swan	**Lambertville**	22
Trump Taj Mahal		
☑ **NEW** Il Mulino NY	**A.C.**	26
Victoria on Main		
Queen Victoria	**Toms River**	23
Virginia Hotel		
☑ Ebbitt Rm.	**Cape May**	27
Westin Governor Morris		
Copeland	**Morristown**	25
Westminster Hotel		
Strip House	**Livingston**	23

JACKET REQUIRED

☑ Manor	**W Orange**	24
Molly Pitcher	**Red Bank**	23

LATE DINING

(Weekday closing hour)

Allendale B&G	1 AM	**Allendale**	17
Benny Tudino's	12:45 AM	**Hoboken**	20
Brickwall	1 AM	**Asbury Pk**	18
Carmine's	12 AM	**A.C.**	21
Chickie's/Pete's	varies	**multi.**	16
Clydz	1:30 AM	**New Bruns.**	22
Cuban Pete's	12 AM	**Montclair**	18

Danny's	1 AM	**Red Bank**	20
Elephant/Castle	varies	**Cherry Hill**	13
Gotham City	1:30 AM	**multi.**	18
Gusto Grill	2 AM	**E Brunswick**	17
House of Blues	12 AM	**A.C.**	16
Iberia	1:30 AM	**Newark**	19
Irish Pub	24 hrs.	**A.C.**	18
Johnny Rockets	12 AM	**multi.**	15
Kinchley's	12 AM	**Ramsey**	23
Lucky Bones	1 AM	**Cape May**	21
Mastoris	1 AM	**Bordentown**	20
Mattar's Bistro	12 AM	**Allamuchy**	-
Park Ave.	2 AM	**Union City**	18
Pete/Elda's	12 AM	**Neptune City**	22
☑ P.F. Chang's	varies	**A.C.**	20
P.J. Whelihan's	varies	**multi.**	16
Pollo Tropical	12 AM	**multi.**	-
Ponzio's	1 AM	**Cherry Hill**	18
Skylark	1 AM	**Edison**	20
So Moon Nan Jip	3 AM	**Palisades Pk**	25
Surf Taco	varies	**Jackson**	20
Tick Tock	24 hrs.	**Clifton**	18
Tom Sawyer	12 AM	**Paramus**	17
Tony's	3 AM	**A.C.**	18
Tun Tavern	varies	**A.C.**	17
Ugly Mug	2 AM	**Cape May**	17
WindMill	varies	**multi.**	19
NEW Zen Den	varies	**Teaneck**	-

MEET FOR A DRINK

Adega	**Newark**	21
Arturo's	**Midland Pk**	23
Atlantic B&G	**S Seaside Pk**	25
☑ Avenue	**Long Branch**	20
Barnacle Bill's	**Rumson**	21
Basil T's	**Red Bank**	20
Bell's	**Lambertville**	21
Black Horse	**Mendham**	19
Blue Pig	**Cape May**	21
Brickwall	**Asbury Pk**	18

Cenzino | **Oakland**	24	McLoone's | **Sea Bright**	17
Charley's | **Long Branch**	18	Mediterra | **Princeton**	21
NEW Char | **Raritan**	–	Metropolitan Cafe | **Freehold**	21
NEW Chelsea Prime | **A.C.**	–	Mia | **A.C.**	25
Chickie's/Pete's | **Bordentown**	16	Mompou | **Newark**	21
Chilangos | **Highlands**	21	Mr. C's | **Allenhurst**	19
Circa | **High Bridge**	22	Oddfellows | **Hoboken**	18
Clark's Landing | **Pt. Pleas.**	17	Old Bay | **New Bruns.**	19
Continental | **A.C.**	23	Old Man Rafferty's | **multi.**	18
Copper Canyon | **Atlantic Highlands**	24	Onieal's | **Hoboken**	18
		NEW Orange Squirrel | **Bloomfield**	–
Crab's Claw | **Lavallette**	18	Ox | **Jersey City**	23
Cuba Libre | **A.C.**	22	Park Ave. | **Union City**	18
Cucharamama | **Hoboken**	25	Pine Tavern | **Old Bridge**	18
daddy O | **Long Beach**	19	P.J. Whelihan's | **multi.**	16
Danny's | **Red Bank**	20	Plantation | **Harvey Cedars**	20
Z Daryl | **New Bruns.**	24	Quiet Man | **Dover**	20
David Burke | **Rumson**	25	Redstone | **Marlton**	22
Z David Drake | **Rahway**	28	Rest., The | **Hackensack**	19
Due Terre | **Bernardsville**	25	Rod's Olde Irish | **Sea Girt**	18
Equus | **Bernardsville**	21	Sallee Tee's | **Monmouth Bch**	19
Espo's | **Raritan**	21	Salt Creek | **Rumson**	19
Gaslight | **Hoboken**	19	Ship Inn | **Milford**	15
Gladstone | **Gladstone**	21	South City | **multi.**	22
Z Hotoke | **New Bruns.**	21	Stage Left | **New Bruns.**	26
House of Blues | **A.C.**	16	NEW Stella Marina | **Asbury Pk**	–
Hunt Club | **Summit**	21	**Z** Stonehouse | **Warren**	22
Huntley Taverne | **Summit**	22	Sushi Lounge | **Hoboken**	22
Inlet Café | **Highlands**	20	Swanky Bubbles | **Cherry Hill**	20
Inn/Hawke | **Lambertville**	18	Tabor Rd. | **Morris Plains**	21
Irish Pub | **A.C.**	18	Teak | **Red Bank**	20
izakaya | **A.C.**	26	Tewksbury Inn | **Oldwick**	22
Kitchen 233 | **Westmont**	20	Tokyo Bleu | **Cinnaminson**	22
NEW Langosta | **Asbury Pk**	–	Trap Rock | **Berkeley Hts**	21
Los Amigos | **multi.**	22	Trinity | **Keyport**	23
Lua | **Hoboken**	22	Triumph Brew. | **Princeton**	16
NEW Luciano's | **Rahway**	–	Tuckers | **Beach Haven**	16
Marco/Pepe | **Jersey City**	22	Tun Tavern | **A.C.**	17
Mkt. in the Middle | **Asbury Pk**	21	Ugly Mug | **Cape May**	17
Martini Bistro | **Millburn**	18	Undici | **Rumson**	21
Martino's | **Somerville**	22	Vine | **Basking Ridge**	25
Z McCormick/Schmick | **Cherry Hill**	20	Windansea | **Highlands**	17
		Witherspoon | **Princeton**	21

SPECIAL FEATURES

Wolfgang Puck | **A.C.**	24
Yankee Doodle | **Princeton**	15

MICROBREWERIES

Basil T's | **Red Bank**	20
Egan/Sons | **Montclair**	18
Ship Inn | **Milford**	15
Trap Rock | **Berkeley Hts**	21
Triumph Brew. | **Princeton**	16
Tun Tavern | **A.C.**	17

NOTEWORTHY NEWCOMERS

Avenue Bistro Pub | **Verona**	-
Backyards | **Hoboken**	-
Bobby's | **Eatontown**	20
Blvd. Five 72 | **Kenilworth**	27
Char | **Raritan**	-
Chelsea Prime | **A.C.**	-
Cubanu | **Rahway**	24
Delicious Heights | **Berkeley Hts**	21
Dino's | **Harrington Pk**	-
Due Mari | **New Bruns.**	26
elements | **Princeton**	-
El Pollo Loco | **N Bergen**	-
Eno Terra | **Kingston**	-
Farm 2 Bistro | **Nutley**	-
Fire/Oak | **Little Falls**	-
Il Fiore | **Collingswood**	26
☑ Il Mulino NY | **A.C.**	26
JL Ivy | **Princeton**	19
Langosta | **Asbury Pk**	-
LaPrete's | **Belleville**	22
Limani | **Westfield**	22
Luciano's | **Rahway**	-
9 North | **Wayne**	-
Nisi Estiatorio | **Englewood**	-
Orange Squirrel | **Bloomfield**	-
Pollo Campero | **W New York**	-
Prairie | **Monmouth Bch**	-
Resto | **Madison**	21
Stamna | **Bloomfield**	23
Steakhouse 85 | **New Bruns.**	-
Stella Marina | **Asbury Pk**	-

Tim McLoone's | **Asbury Pk**	17
Torcello | **Red Bank**	-
William Douglas | **Cherry Hill**	22
Zen Den | **Teaneck**	-

OFFBEAT

Aangan | **Freehold Twp**	22
Aby's | **Matawan**	20
Akai | **Englewood**	25
Ali Baba | **Hoboken**	20
Bangkok Gdn. | **Hackensack**	22
☑ Baumgart's | **multi.**	19
Bayou Cafe | **Freehold**	21
Beyti Kebab | **Union City**	23
Blue | **Surf City**	24
Blue Danube | **Trenton**	23
Bombay Curry | **Basking Ridge**	18
Buca di Beppo | **Cherry Hill**	16
Casa Solar | **Belmar**	25
Chand | **Parsippany**	23
Chao Phaya | **Somerville**	24
Charrito's | **Jersey City**	22
☑ Chef Vola's | **A.C.**	27
Chilangos | **Highlands**	21
China Palace | **Middletown**	24
Cucharamama | **Hoboken**	25
Dabbawalla | **Summit**	18
Elements Asia | **Lawrenceville**	23
El Meson | **Freehold**	24
Far East Taste | **Eatontown**	23
NEW Farm 2 Bistro | **Nutley**	-
Fedora | **Lawrenceville**	18
Garlic Rose | **multi.**	20
Grand Shanghai | **Edison**	19
Hard Grove | **Jersey City**	15
☑ Hotoke | **New Bruns.**	21
It's Greek To Me | **multi.**	17
Je's | **Newark**	24
Karma Kafe | **Hoboken**	24
K.O.B.E. | **Holmdel**	22
Labrador | **Normandy Bch**	23
La Esperanza | **Lindenwold**	22
La Isla | **Hoboken**	26
NEW Langosta | **Asbury Pk**	-

Little Café | **Voorhees**	25		Taro | **Montclair**	20
Madame Claude | **Jersey City**	23		Taste of Asia | **Chatham**	21
Mad Batter | **Cape May**	23		Teak | **Red Bank**	20
Makeda | **New Bruns.**	25		Tina Louise | **Carlstadt**	24
Manon | **Lambertville**	25		Trinity | **Keyport**	23
Marmara | **Manalapan**	19		West Lake | **Matawan**	22
Martino's | **Somerville**	22		Wild Ginger | **Englewood**	22
Meemah | **Edison**	22		Ya Ya Noodles | **Skillman**	19
Meil's | **Stockton**	22		Yumi | **Sea Bright**	26
Mexico Lindo | **Brick**	23			
Mie Thai | **Woodbridge**	24			

OUTDOOR DINING

(G=garden; P=patio; S=sidewalk; T=terrace)

Ming | **Edison**	21		Anthony David's | S | **Hoboken**	26
Moghul | **Edison**	25		Anton's/Swan | P | **Lambertville**	22
Moksha | **Edison**	22		Atlantic B&G | P | S **Seaside Pk**	25
Mompou | **Newark**	21		Avon Pavilion | T | **Avon-by-Sea**	19
Navesink Fishery | **Navesink**	24		Axelsson's | G | **Cape May**	23
New Main Taste | **Chatham**	23		Bamboo Leaf | S | **Bradley Bch**	22
Nha Trang Pl. | **Jersey City**	24		☑ Bernards Inn | T | **Bernardsville**	26
Nifty Fifty's | **Turnersville**	18		☑ Blue Point | P | **Princeton**	25
Norma's | **Cherry Hill**	21		Bobby Chez | P | **Margate**	24
Old Bay | **New Bruns.**	19		Brothers Moon | S | **Hopewell**	22
Ota-Ya | **Lambertville**	22		Café Gallery | T | **Burlington**	23
Pamir | **Morristown**	21		☑ Cafe Matisse | G | **Rutherford**	27
☑ Park/Orchard | **E Rutherford**	22		Caffe Aldo | P | **Cherry Hill**	24
Passage/India | **Lawrenceville**	21		Cucharamama | S | **Hoboken**	25
Penang | **Edison**	21		Danny's | S | **Red Bank**	20
Plan B | **Asbury Pk**	-		Elysian | P, S | **Hoboken**	20
Pop's Garage | **Asbury Pk**	22		Frenchtown Inn | P | **Frenchtown**	25
Pop Shop | **Collingswood**	20		☑ Frog/Peach | P | **New Bruns.**	26
Pub | **Pennsauken**	19		☑ Gables | P | **Beach Haven**	25
Raagini | **Mountainside**	22		Girasole | P | **A.C.**	25
☑ Rat's | **Hamilton**	25		Girasole | P | **Bound Brook**	26
Risotto Hse. | **Rutherford**	23		Giumarello's | P | **Westmont**	24
Saffron | **E Hanover**	22		☑ Grand Cafe | P | **Morristown**	26
Saigon R./Mo' Pho | **Englewood**	24		Hamilton's | P | **Lambertville**	25
Seven Hills | **Highland Pk**	22		India/Hudson | S | **Hoboken**	20
Siam | **Lambertville**	20		Inlet | T | **Somers Point**	19
Siam Gdn. | **Red Bank**	24		Inn/Hawke | P | **Lambertville**	18
Siri's | **Cherry Hill**	24		Klein's | P, T | **Belmar**	19
Sister Sue's | **Asbury Pk**	21		La Campagne | G, T | **Cherry Hill**	24
Somsak | **Voorhees**	23		☑ Latour | S | **Ridgewood**	26
Sunny Gdn. | **Princeton**	20		Le Rendez-Vous | S | **Kenilworth**	26
Taka | **Asbury Pk**	25			

Liberty Hse. | T | **Jersey City**	20
Lilly's/Canal | P | **Lambertville**	21
Matisse | T | **Belmar**	21
Mélange | S | **Cherry Hill**	25
Mexican Food | P | **Marlton**	20
Mill/Spring Lake | T | **Spring Lake Hts**	21
Z Moonstruck | T | **Asbury Pk**	25
Nag's Head | P | **Ocean City**	23
Perryville Inn | P | **Union Twp**	23
Z Peter Shields | T | **Cape May**	26
Z Rat's | T | **Hamilton**	25
Raven/Peach | P | **Fair Haven**	25
Rebecca's | P | **Edgewater**	25
Robin's Nest | T | **Mt Holly**	22
Robongi | S | **Hoboken**	24
Z Ruth's Chris | S | **Weehawken**	25
Shipwreck Grill | T | **Brielle**	25
Stage Hse. | G | **Scotch Plains**	22
Stage Left | P | **New Bruns.**	26
NEW Stella Marina | P | **Asbury Pk**	-
Z Tisha's | P | **Cape May**	26
Tuckers | T | **Beach Haven**	16
Village Green | S | **Ridgewood**	23
Windansea | T | **Highlands**	17
Zafra | P | **Hoboken**	24

PEOPLE-WATCHING

Z Bernards Inn | **Bernardsville**	26
Bistro di Marino | **Collingswood**	23
Z Bobby Flay | **A.C.**	25
Brio | **Cherry Hill**	19
Brix 67 | **Summit**	18
Z Buddakan | **A.C.**	25
Cafe Madison | **Riverside**	20
Caffe Aldo | **Cherry Hill**	24
Catelli | **Voorhees**	25
Chart Hse. | **Weehawken**	21
Chickie's/Pete's | **Bordentown**	16
Clark's Landing | **Pt. Pleas.**	17
Clydz | **New Bruns.**	22
Continental | **A.C.**	23
Copeland | **Morristown**	25
Cuba Libre | **A.C.**	22

Cucharamama | **Hoboken**	25
daddy O | **Long Beach**	19
Z Daryl | **New Bruns.**	24
Z David Drake | **Rahway**	28
Delta's | **New Bruns.**	23
Eccola | **Parsippany**	23
Equus | **Bernardsville**	21
Z Hotoke | **New Bruns.**	21
Huntley Taverne | **Summit**	22
Kitchen 233 | **Westmont**	20
NEW Langosta | **Asbury Pk**	-
Limestone Cafe | **Peapack**	21
Lua | **Hoboken**	22
Makeda | **New Bruns.**	25
Martini Bistro | **Millburn**	18
Z McCormick/Schmick | **Cherry Hill**	20
Mélange | **Haddonfield**	25
Mia | **A.C.**	25
Molly Pitcher | **Red Bank**	23
Mompou | **Newark**	21
Ox | **Jersey City**	23
Park Ave. | **Union City**	18
Plan B | **Asbury Pk**	-
Z Pluckemin Inn | **Bedminster**	26
Ponzio's | **Cherry Hill**	18
Pop Shop | **Collingswood**	20
Pub | **Pennsauken**	19
Salt Creek | **Rumson**	19
Sammy's | **Mendham**	21
South City | **Jersey City**	22
Swanky Bubbles | **Cherry Hill**	20
Tabor Rd. | **Morris Plains**	21
Tapas de Espana | **N Bergen**	21
Teak | **Red Bank**	20
3 West | **Basking Ridge**	22
Undici | **Rumson**	21
Witherspoon | **Princeton**	21
Wolfgang Puck | **A.C.**	24

POWER SCENES

Basilico | **Millburn**	24
Z Bernards Inn | **Bernardsville**	26
Z Bobby Flay | **A.C.**	25

🅉 Cafe Panache | **Ramsey**	28	
Caffe Aldo | **Cherry Hill**	24	
Casa Dante | **Jersey City**	23	
Catelli | **Voorhees**	25	
🅉 Catherine Lombardi | **New Bruns.**	23	
🅉 Chakra | **Paramus**	20	
Chez Catherine | **Westfield**	26	
Cuba Libre | **A.C.**	22	
🅉 Daryl | **New Bruns.**	24	
David Burke | **Rumson**	25	
🅉 Fascino | **Montclair**	26	
410 Bank St. | **Cape May**	26	
Gallagher's | **A.C.**	22	
Hunt Club | **Summit**	21	
🅉 Il Mondo | **Madison**	25	
🅉 McCormick/Schmick | **Cherry Hill**	20	
McLoone's | **Sea Bright**	17	
🅉 Morton's | **Hackensack**	25	
Old Homestead | **A.C.**	26	
Phillips Seafood | **A.C.**	19	
Ponzio's | **Cherry Hill**	18	
Redstone | **Marlton**	22	
🅉 Saddle River Inn | **Saddle River**	28	
🅉 SeaBlue | **A.C.**	27	
🅉 Serenade | **Chatham**	28	
Solari's | **Hackensack**	20	
Undici | **Rumson**	21	
🅉 Washington Inn | **Cape May**	27	
NEW William Douglas | **Cherry Hill**	22	
Wolfgang Puck | **A.C.**	24	

PRIVATE ROOMS

(Restaurants charge less at off times; call for capacity)

🅉 Amanda's | **Hoboken**	25	
🅉 André's | **Newton**	27	
Barone's/Villa Barone | **Moorestown**	20	
🅉 Bernards Inn | **Bernardsville**	26	
Bistro Olé | **Asbury Pk**	24	
Black Duck | **W Cape May**	24	
🅉 Cafe Matisse | **Rutherford**	27	

Caffe Aldo | **Cherry Hill**	24	
Catelli | **Voorhees**	25	
🅉 Chakra | **Paramus**	20	
Chez Catherine | **Westfield**	26	
Chez Elena Wu | **Voorhees**	23	
Chophouse | **Gibbsboro**	25	
🅉 Daryl | **New Bruns.**	24	
NEW elements | **Princeton**	-	
NEW Eno Terra | **Kingston**	-	
🅉 Fascino | **Montclair**	26	
Fiorino | **Summit**	23	
🅉 Gables | **Beach Haven**	25	
Giumarello's | **Westmont**	24	
Hamilton's | **Lambertville**	25	
Harvest Bistro | **Closter**	21	
🅉 Highlawn | **W Orange**	25	
🅉 Karen & Rei's | **Clermont**	26	
Le Jardin | **Edgewater**	18	
Le Petit Chateau | **Bernardsville**	25	
NEW Luciano's | **Rahway**	-	
Madeleine's | **Northvale**	25	
🅉 Manor | **W Orange**	24	
Mattar's Bistro | **Allamuchy**	-	
Nauvoo Grill | **Fair Haven**	16	
🅉 Nicholas | **Middletown**	28	
NEW Nisi Estiatorio | **Englewood**	-	
Perryville Inn | **Union Twp**	23	
Porto Leggero | **Jersey City**	22	
Pub | **Pennsauken**	19	
🅉 Serenade | **Chatham**	28	
Stage Hse. | **Scotch Plains**	22	
Stage Left | **New Bruns.**	26	
🅉 Stonehouse | **Warren**	22	
Tomatoes | **Margate**	24	
🅉 Washington Inn | **Cape May**	27	

PRIX FIXE MENUS

(Call for prices and times)

🅉 André's | **Newton**	27	
Anthony David's | **Hoboken**	26	
🅉 Bernards Inn | **Bernardsville**	26	
Cafe/Rosemont | **Rosemont**	20	
🅉 Cafe Matisse | **Rutherford**	27	
🅉 Cafe Panache | **Ramsey**	28	

SPECIAL FEATURES

Chez Catherine | **Westfield**	26
🆉 David Drake | **Rahway**	28
🆉 Ebbitt Rm. | **Cape May**	27
🆉 Fascino | **Montclair**	26
🆉 Frog/Peach | **New Bruns.**	26
🆉 Gables | **Beach Haven**	25
🆉 Latour | **Ridgewood**	26
Manon | **Lambertville**	25
🆉 Nicholas | **Middletown**	28
Norma's | **Cherry Hill**	21
Nunzio | **Collingswood**	24
Perryville Inn | **Union Twp**	23
🆉 Rat's | **Hamilton**	25
Rosemary/Sage | **Riverdale**	26
🆉 Scalini Fedeli | **Chatham**	27
🆉 Serenade | **Chatham**	28
Stage Hse. | **Scotch Plains**	22
Stage Left | **New Bruns.**	26
Verjus | **Maplewood**	25
Village Green | **Ridgewood**	23

QUICK BITES

Aby's | **Matawan**	20
Alchemist/Barrister | **Princeton**	16
Bobby Chez | **multi.**	24
🆕 Bobby's | **Eatontown**	20
Buttonwood Manor | **Matawan**	14
Chickie's/Pete's | **Bordentown**	16
CJ Montana's | **Tinton Falls**	19
Continental | **A.C.**	23
Cubby's | **Hackensack**	18
🆉 DeLorenzo's Pies | **multi.**	27
DeLorenzo's Pizza | **Trenton**	–
Fishery, The | **S Amboy**	–
Five Guys | **multi.**	21
Forno | **Maple Shade**	–
Full Moon | **Lambertville**	21
GRUB Hut | **Manville**	21
Hobby's | **Newark**	23
Irish Pub | **A.C.**	18
Jack Cooper's | **Edison**	18
Jerry/Harvey's | **Marlboro**	18
Johnny Rockets | **Eatontown**	15
Kibitz Rm. | **Cherry Hill**	22

Mastoris | **Bordentown**	20
Mexican Food | **Marlton**	20
Nana's Deli | **Livingston**	22
Nha Trang Pl. | **Jersey City**	24
Nifty Fifty's | **Turnersville**	18
Noodle Hse. | **N Brunswick**	18
Ox | **Jersey City**	23
Pic-Nic | **E Newark**	24
Ponzio's | **Cherry Hill**	18
Pop's Garage | **Asbury Pk**	22
Pop Shop | **Collingswood**	20
Rutt's Hut | **Clifton**	21
Simply Radishing | **Lawrenceville**	19
Takara | **Oakhurst**	24
Tick Tock | **Clifton**	18
Toast | **Montclair**	20
Tony Luke's | **A.C.**	21
Windansea | **Highlands**	17
WindMill | **multi.**	19
Witherspoon | **Princeton**	21

QUIET CONVERSATION

Black Trumpet | **Spring Lake**	25
Braddock's | **Medford**	21
Cafe Madison | **Riverside**	20
Chez Catherine | **Westfield**	26
Church St. | **Montclair**	14
🆉 David Drake | **Rahway**	28
🆕 elements | **Princeton**	–
Farnsworth | **Bordentown**	23
55 Main | **Flemington**	20
Fiorino | **Summit**	23
Frenchtown Inn | **Frenchtown**	25
🆕 Il Fiore | **Collingswood**	26
Krave Café | **Newton**	23
🆕 LaPrete's | **Belleville**	22
Luke's | **Maplewood**	21
Mahogany | **Manasquan**	23
Melting Pot | **Westwood**	18
Meyersville Inn | **Gillette**	17
Molly Pitcher | **Red Bank**	23
🆉 Pluckemin Inn | **Bedminster**	26
🆉 Rat's | **Hamilton**	25

Sergeantsville Inn | **Sergeantsville**	23
Soufflé | **Summit**	22
☑ Stonehouse | **Warren**	22
Ted's/Main | **Medford**	25
Village Green | **Ridgewood**	23
☑ Whispers | **Spring Lake**	27
NEW William Douglas | **Cherry Hill**	22

RAW BARS

☑ Avenue | **Long Branch**	20
Bahrs Landing | **Highlands**	16
Berkeley | **S Seaside Pk**	20
Blue Eyes | **Sewell**	20
☑ Blue Point | **Princeton**	25
Caffe Aldo | **Cherry Hill**	24
Carmine's Asbury Pk. | **Asbury Pk**	20
Catelli | **Voorhees**	25
CoccoLa | **Hillsborough**	19
Copeland | **Morristown**	25
Crab House | **Edgewater**	16
Dock's | **A.C.**	26
Don Quijote | **Fairview**	17
Fishery, The | **S Amboy**	–
Grill 73 | **Bernardsville**	21
Harvey Cedars | **Beach Haven**	22
Klein's | **Belmar**	19
Kunkel's | **Haddon Hts**	24
La Focaccia | **Summit**	24
☑ Legal Sea Foods | **multi.**	21
Liberty Hse. | **Jersey City**	20
NEW Limani | **Westfield**	22
Little Tuna | **Haddonfield**	21
Lobster Hse. | **Cape May**	21
☑ McCormick/Schmick | **Hackensack**	20
McLoone's | **multi.**	17
Nero's | **Livingston**	17
Old Homestead | **A.C.**	26
Pino's | **Marlboro**	19
Plantation | **Harvey Cedars**	20
Portobello | **Oakland**	19
Rare | **Little Falls**	20
Red's | **Pt. Pleas. Bch**	23
Rest. L | **Allendale**	20
Rooney's | **Long Branch**	18
Sallee Tee's | **Monmouth Bch**	19
Sea Shack | **Hackensack**	21
Shipwreck Grill | **Brielle**	25
Solaia | **Englewood**	18
South City | **multi.**	22
Spike's | **Pt. Pleas. Bch**	23
NEW Stella Marina | **Asbury Pk**	–
Steve/Cookie's | **Margate**	25
Varka | **Ramsey**	26

ROMANTIC PLACES

Acquaviva | **Westfield**	22
☑ Amanda's | **Hoboken**	25
Anton's/Swan | **Lambertville**	22
Atlantic B&G | **S Seaside Pk**	25
☑ Avenue | **Long Branch**	20
Blackbird | **Collingswood**	26
Black Trumpet | **Spring Lake**	25
Cafe Madison | **Riverside**	20
☑ Cafe Matisse | **Rutherford**	27
Catelli | **Voorhees**	25
☑ Catherine Lombardi | **New Bruns.**	23
Creole Café | **Sewell**	22
☑ CulinAriane | **Montclair**	27
David Burke | **Rumson**	25
☑ David Drake | **Rahway**	28
☑ Ebbitt Rm. | **Cape May**	27
NEW elements | **Princeton**	–
NEW Eno Terra | **Kingston**	–
Equus | **Bernardsville**	21
55 Main | **Flemington**	20
Frenchtown Inn | **Frenchtown**	25
Fuji | **Haddonfield**	24
☑ Gables | **Beach Haven**	25
Gaslight | **Hoboken**	19
Giumarello's | **Westmont**	24
☑ Grand Cafe | **Morristown**	26
Grenville | **Bay Hd.**	21
Harvest Moon | **Ringoes**	23
I Cavallini | **Colts Neck**	23

☑ Il Capriccio | **Whippany**	26
Inn/Millrace | **Hope**	21
Ivy Inn | **Hasbrouck Hts**	20
Jose's Cantina | **multi.**	20
K.O.B.E. | **Holmdel**	22
Krave Café | **Newton**	23
La Cipollina | **Freehold**	21
🆕 Langosta | **Asbury Pk**	–
Le Petit Chateau | **Bernardsville**	25
Le Rendez-Vous | **Kenilworth**	26
Lilly's/Canal | **Lambertville**	21
Melting Pot | **Westwood**	18
Metuchen Inn | **Metuchen**	21
Mia | **A.C.**	25
Molly Pitcher | **Red Bank**	23
Park Ave. | **Union City**	18
Perryville Inn | **Union Twp**	23
☑ Peter Shields | **Cape May**	26
Pino's | **Marlboro**	19
Plantation | **Harvey Cedars**	20
☑ Ram's Head | **Galloway**	25
☑ Rat's | **Hamilton**	25
Raven/Peach | **Fair Haven**	25
Rebecca's | **Edgewater**	25
Rod's Steak | **Morristown**	22
☑ Scalini Fedeli | **Chatham**	27
Scarborough Fair | **Sea Girt**	21
☑ SeaBlue | **A.C.**	27
Sergeantsville Inn | **Sergeantsville**	23
Sirena | **Long Branch**	22
☑ Stonehouse | **Warren**	22
☑ Stony Hill Inn | **Hackensack**	23
Taka | **Asbury Pk**	25
Ted's/Main | **Medford**	25
Tewksbury Inn | **Oldwick**	22
☑ Washington Inn | **Cape May**	27
☑ Whispers | **Spring Lake**	27

SENIOR APPEAL

Athenian Gdn. | **Galloway Twp**	24
Bahrs Landing | **Highlands**	16
Berkeley | **S Seaside Pk**	20
Bistro di Marino | **Collingswood**	23

Blackbird | **Collingswood**	26
Brio | **Cherry Hill**	19
Buca di Beppo | **Cherry Hill**	16
Buttonwood Manor | **Matawan**	14
Café Azzurro | **Peapack**	24
Cafe Madison | **Riverside**	20
California Grill | **Flemington**	18
Capt'n Ed's | **Pt. Pleas.**	18
Carmine's | **A.C.**	21
☑ Catherine Lombardi | **New Bruns.**	23
Chophouse | **Gibbsboro**	25
Christopher's | **Colts Neck**	19
Crab Trap | **Somers Point**	22
Don Pepe | **multi.**	21
Don Pepe's Steak | **Pine Brook**	22
E & V | **Paterson**	23
El Cid | **Paramus**	21
55 Main | **Flemington**	20
Fornos/Spain | **Newark**	23
Gallagher's | **A.C.**	22
Grenville | **Bay Hd.**	21
Iberia | **Newark**	19
🆕 Il Fiore | **Collingswood**	26
Jack Cooper's | **Edison**	18
Java Moon | **Jackson**	18
Joe Pesce | **Collingswood**	23
Kibitz Rm. | **Cherry Hill**	22
Kitchen 233 | **Westmont**	20
Klein's | **Belmar**	19
Krave Café | **Newton**	23
Kuzina | **Cherry Hill**	20
Lahiere's | **Princeton**	22
☑ Legal Sea Foods | **Short Hills**	21
Little Tuna | **Haddonfield**	21
Lobster Hse. | **Cape May**	21
LouCás | **Edison**	23
Luke's | **Maplewood**	21
☑ McCormick/Schmick | **multi.**	20
Meyersville Inn | **Gillette**	17
Mill/Spring Lake | **Spring Lake Hts**	21
Nifty Fifty's | **Turnersville**	18
Oceanos | **Fair Lawn**	23

Menus, photos, voting and more – free at ZAGAT.com

Octopus's Gdn. | **Stafford**	23
Pete/Elda's | **Neptune City**	22
Pop Shop | **Collingswood**	20
Portobello | **Oakland**	19
Portuguese Manor | **Perth Amboy**	20
Pub | **Pennsauken**	19
Rio 22 | **Union**	19
☑ SeaBlue | **A.C.**	27
Sea Shack | **Hackensack**	21
Smithville Inn | **Smithville**	21
☑ Stonehouse | **Warren**	22
Ted's/Main | **Medford**	25
Varka | **Ramsey**	26
Villa Vittoria | **Brick**	22
Waterfront Buffet | **A.C.**	19
NEW William Douglas | **Cherry Hill**	22
WindMill | **multi.**	19
Wolfgang Puck | **A.C.**	24

SINGLES SCENES

Atlantic B&G | **S Seaside Pk**	25
Blue Pig | **Cape May**	21
Brickwall | **Asbury Pk**	18
Brooklyn's Pizza | **Ridgewood**	23
☑ Buddakan | **A.C.**	25
Cenzino | **Oakland**	24
Chickie's/Pete's | **Bordentown**	16
Circa | **High Bridge**	22
City Bistro | **Hoboken**	18
Clark's Landing | **Pt. Pleas.**	17
Clydz | **New Bruns.**	22
Continental | **A.C.**	23
Copper Canyon | **Atlantic Highlands**	24
Corky's | **A.C.**	18
Cuba Libre | **A.C.**	22
Cucharamama | **Hoboken**	25
☑ Daryl | **New Bruns.**	24
Fleming's | **Edgewater**	23
Grissini | **Englewood Cliffs**	22
Gusto Grill | **E Brunswick**	17
House of Blues | **A.C.**	16
Inlet Café | **Highlands**	20

NEW Langosta | **Asbury Pk**	–
Lua | **Hoboken**	22
McLoone's | **Sea Bright**	17
Metropolitan Cafe | **Freehold**	21
Mia | **A.C.**	25
Mompou | **Newark**	21
Old Man Rafferty's | **multi.**	18
NEW Orange Squirrel | **Bloomfield**	–
Ox | **Jersey City**	23
Park Ave. | **Union City**	18
P.J. Whelihan's | **multi.**	16
Plantation | **Harvey Cedars**	20
Quiet Man | **Dover**	20
Red | **Red Bank**	20
Redstone | **Marlton**	22
Rest., The | **Hackensack**	19
Rooney's | **Long Branch**	18
Sage | **Ventnor**	24
Sallee Tee's | **Monmouth Bch**	19
Shipwreck Grill | **Brielle**	25
Sister Sue's | **Asbury Pk**	21
South City | **Jersey City**	22
Sushi Lounge | **multi.**	22
Swanky Bubbles | **Cherry Hill**	20
Teak | **Red Bank**	20
Texas Arizona | **Hoboken**	14
Tomatoes | **Margate**	24
Trap Rock | **Berkeley Hts**	21
Verve | **Somerville**	22
Windansea | **Highlands**	17
Witherspoon | **Princeton**	21

SLEEPERS

(Good food, but little known)

Alexander's | **Cape May**	26
Aligado | **Hazlet**	24
Andaman | **Morristown**	23
Athenian Gdn. | **Galloway Twp**	24
Belford Bistro | **Belford**	28
Benito's | **Chester**	24
Blue Danube | **Trenton**	23
Bombay Gdns. | **E Brunswick**	23
Cafe Bello | **Bayonne**	24

Cafe Loren | **Avalon**	26
China Palace | **Middletown**	24
Claude's | **N Wildwood**	25
Clementine's | **Avon-by-Sea**	23
Elements | **Haddon Hts**	24
Filomena Italiana | **Clementon**	23
Filomena Lakeview | **Deptford**	24
Filomena Rustica | **W Berlin**	23
GG's | **Mt Laurel**	24
Grand Colonial | **Union Twp**	23
High St. | **Mt Holly**	23
Ikko | **Brick**	25
Inn/Sugar Hill | **Mays Landing**	23
izakaya | **A.C.**	26
Je's | **Newark**	24
John Henry's | **Trenton**	24
Jose's | **Spring Lake Hts**	24
Konbu | **Manalapan**	25
Krave Café | **Newton**	23
Kunkel's | **Haddon Hts**	24
La Sorrentina | **N Bergen**	26
Little Food Café | **multi.**	25
Manna | **Margate**	24
Marie Nicole's | **Wildwood**	24
Megu | **Cherry Hill**	24
Mexico Lindo | **Brick**	23
Milford Oyster Hse. | **Milford**	23
Ming II | **Morristown**	24
Nag's Head | **Ocean City**	23
Nobi | **Toms River Twp**	25
Oyako Tso's | **Freehold**	23
Pic-Nic | **E Newark**	24
Queen Victoria | **Toms River**	23
Rosa Luca's | **Asbury**	24
Sapori | **Collingswood**	24
Silver Spring | **Flanders**	26
Sirin | **Morristown**	24
So Moon Nan Jip | **Palisades Pk**	25
Somsak | **Voorhees**	23
Sumo | **Wall**	25
Sushi by Kazu | **Howell**	26
Takara | **Oakhurst**	24
Ted's/Main | **Medford**	25

Trovato's | **multi.**	25
Tutto a Modo Mio | **Ridgefield**	23
Vila Nova | **Newark**	23

SPECIAL OCCASIONS

🛛 Blue Bottle | **Hopewell**	27
🛛 Bobby Flay | **A.C.**	25
🛛 Cafe Matisse | **Rutherford**	27
🛛 Cafe Panache | **Ramsey**	28
Catelli | **Voorhees**	25
🛛 Chakra | **Paramus**	20
Chart Hse. | **Weehawken**	21
🛛 Chef's Table | **Franklin Lakes**	26
Chengdu 46 | **Clifton**	24
Chez Catherine | **Westfield**	26
Cucharamama | **Hoboken**	25
🛛 CulinAriane | **Montclair**	27
🛛 Daryl | **New Bruns.**	24
🛛 David Drake | **Rahway**	28
Doris/Ed's | **Highlands**	25
Due Terre | **Bernardsville**	25
Equus | **Bernardsville**	21
Ferry Hse. | **Princeton**	25
55 Main | **Flemington**	20
Frenchtown Inn | **Frenchtown**	25
🛛 Frog/Peach | **New Bruns.**	26
Gallagher's | **A.C.**	22
Giumarello's | **Westmont**	24
🛛 Grand Cafe | **Morristown**	26
Harvest Moon | **Ringoes**	23
🛛 Highlawn | **W Orange**	25
🛛 Hotoke | **New Bruns.**	21
I Cavallini | **Colts Neck**	23
🛛 Il Capriccio | **Whippany**	26
Ivy Inn | **Hasbrouck Hts**	20
🛛 Karen & Rei's | **Clermont**	26
K.O.B.E. | **Holmdel**	22
🛛 Latour | **Ridgewood**	26
Madeleine's | **Northvale**	25
Maize | **Newark**	18
🛛 Manor | **W Orange**	24
Mattar's Bistro | **Allamuchy**	-
Napa Valley | **Paramus**	21

☑ Nicholas	**Middletown**	28
No. 9	**Lambertville**	26
Nunzio	**Collingswood**	24
☑ Peter Shields	**Cape May**	26
Posillipo	**Asbury Pk**	22
☑ Ram's Head	**Galloway**	25
☑ Rat's	**Hamilton**	25
Raven/Peach	**Fair Haven**	25
Rebecca's	**Edgewater**	25
NEW Resto	**Madison**	21
Robin's Nest	**Mt Holly**	22
Rod's Steak	**Morristown**	22
Rosa Luca's	**Asbury**	24
☑ Saddle River Inn	**Saddle River**	28
☑ SeaBlue	**A.C.**	27
☑ Serenade	**Chatham**	28
Shanghai Jazz	**Madison**	21
Stage Hse.	**Scotch Plains**	22
Stage Left	**New Bruns.**	26
☑ Stonehouse	**Warren**	22
☑ Stony Hill Inn	**Hackensack**	23
Taro	**Montclair**	20
3 West	**Basking Ridge**	22
Trinity	**Keyport**	23
☑ Washington Inn	**Cape May**	27
Wild Ginger	**Englewood**	22
NEW William Douglas	**Cherry Hill**	22
Witherspoon	**Princeton**	21
Wolfgang Puck	**A.C.**	24

TASTING MENUS

Anthony David's	**Hoboken**	26
☑ Bernards Inn	**Bernardsville**	26
Bienvenue	**Red Bank**	23
Black Trumpet	**Spring Lake**	25
Cafe Madison	**Riverside**	20
☑ Cafe Panache	**Ramsey**	28
Chez Catherine	**Westfield**	26
Copeland	**Morristown**	25
da Filippo	**Somerville**	23
☑ David Drake	**Rahway**	28
NEW Due Mari	**New Bruns.**	26

Due Terre	**Bernardsville**	25
☑ Ebbitt Rm.	**Cape May**	27
NEW elements	**Princeton**	-
NEW Eno Terra	**Kingston**	-
☑ Fascino	**Montclair**	26
Fuji	**Haddonfield**	24
La Campagne	**Cherry Hill**	24
La Cipollina	**Freehold**	21
☑ Latour	**Ridgewood**	26
Le Petit Chateau	**Bernardsville**	25
Le Rendez-Vous	**Kenilworth**	26
Mediterra	**Princeton**	21
Mélange	**Cherry Hill**	25
☑ Nicholas	**Middletown**	28
Norma's	**Cherry Hill**	21
Nouveau	**Montclair**	24
Nunzio	**Collingswood**	24
Old Homestead	**A.C.**	26
☑ Ombra	**A.C.**	26
Passionne	**Montclair**	23
Perryville Inn	**Union Twp**	23
☑ Piccola	**Ocean Twp**	27
☑ Pluckemin Inn	**Bedminster**	26
☑ Rat's	**Hamilton**	25
☑ Red Square	**A.C.**	21
Rest. Latour	**Hamburg**	25
RoCCA	**Glen Rock**	23
Rosemary/Sage	**Riverdale**	26
☑ Serenade	**Chatham**	28
Spargo's	**Manalapan**	24
Stage Hse.	**Scotch Plains**	22
Stage Left	**New Bruns.**	26
Village Green	**Ridgewood**	23
Vine	**Basking Ridge**	25

TRENDY

Anna's	**Middletown**	25
Aozora	**Montclair**	25
Atlantic B&G	**S Seaside Pk**	25
A Toute Heure	**Cranford**	25
Axelsson's	**Cape May**	23
Bank 34	**Somerville**	23
Blu	**Montclair**	24

Blue | **Surf City**	24
🅩 Blue Bottle | **Hopewell**	27
🅩 Bobby Flay | **A.C.**	25
NEW Bobby's | **Eatontown**	20
🅩 Buddakan | **A.C.**	25
🅩 Cafe Matisse | **Rutherford**	27
🅩 Chakra | **Paramus**	20
NEW Char | **Raritan**	–
🅩 Chef Vola's | **A.C.**	27
Conte's | **Princeton**	24
Continental | **A.C.**	23
Cuba Libre | **A.C.**	22
Cucharamama | **Hoboken**	25
daddy O | **Long Beach**	19
🅩 Daryl | **New Bruns.**	24
David Burke | **Rumson**	25
🅩 DeLorenzo's Pies | **Trenton**	27
Delta's | **New Bruns.**	23
Dock's | **A.C.**	26
🅩 Drew's | **Keyport**	26
Dune | **Margate**	25
Equus | **Bernardsville**	21
NEW Farm 2 Bistro | **Nutley**	–
🅩 Fascino | **Montclair**	26
Frescos | **Cape May**	24
Fusion | **Flemington**	22
Girasole | **Bound Brook**	26
Harvest Moon | **Ringoes**	23
Homestead Inn | **Trenton**	24
🅩 Hotoke | **New Bruns.**	21
🅩 Il Mondo | **Madison**	25
K.O.B.E. | **Holmdel**	22
Labrador | **Normandy Bch**	23
La Campagna | **Morristown**	22
NEW Langosta | **Asbury Pk**	–
🅩 Latour | **Ridgewood**	26
Lobster Hse. | **Cape May**	21
🅩 Lorena's | **Maplewood**	28
Lua | **Hoboken**	22
Mad Batter | **Cape May**	23
Mahzu | **Aberdeen**	21
Makeda | **New Bruns.**	25
Marco/Pepe | **Jersey City**	22
Martino's | **Somerville**	22
Matt's Rooster | **Flemington**	25
Mélange | **multi.**	25
Mia | **A.C.**	25
Minado | **multi.**	19
Mojave | **Westfield**	23
Mud City | **Manahawkin**	24
Nikko | **Whippany**	24
NEW 9 North | **Wayne**	–
Nunzio | **Collingswood**	24
Old Homestead | **A.C.**	26
NEW Orange Squirrel | **Bloomfield**	–
🅩 Origin | **Somerville**	26
Ox | **Jersey City**	23
Park Ave. | **Union City**	18
Pete/Elda's | **Neptune City**	22
Plan B | **Asbury Pk**	–
Plantation | **Harvey Cedars**	20
🅩 Pluckemin Inn | **Bedminster**	26
Pop's Garage | **Asbury Pk**	22
NEW Prairie | **Monmouth Bch**	–
🅩 Rat's | **Hamilton**	25
Rebecca's | **Edgewater**	25
Reservoir | **Boonton**	22
NEW Resto | **Madison**	21
🅩 River Palm | **multi.**	24
Rosemary/Sage | **Riverdale**	26
Sage | **Ventnor**	24
Saigon R./Mo' Pho | **Englewood**	24
🅩 SeaBlue | **A.C.**	27
Shanghai Jazz | **Madison**	21
Sister Sue's | **Asbury Pk**	21
NEW Steakhouse 85 | **New Bruns.**	–
NEW Stella Marina | **Asbury Pk**	–
Steve/Cookie's | **Margate**	25
Swanky Bubbles | **Cherry Hill**	20
Tabor Rd. | **Morris Plains**	21
Taste of Asia | **Chatham**	21
Theresa's | **Westfield**	22
3 West | **Basking Ridge**	22
Tim Schafer's | **Morristown**	25

Toast | **Montclair**	20
Tokyo Bleu | **Cinnaminson**	22
Tony Luke's | **A.C.**	21
Trap Rock | **Berkeley Hts**	21
Undici | **Rumson**	21
Verve | **Somerville**	22
White Hse. | **A.C.**	26
Witherspoon | **Princeton**	21
Wolfgang Puck | **A.C.**	24
Yellow Fin | **Surf City**	26
Zafra | **Hoboken**	24

VIEWS

Atlantic B&G | **S Seaside Pk**	25
Z Avenue | **Long Branch**	20
Avon Pavilion | **Avon-by-Sea**	19
Bahrs Landing | **Highlands**	16
Barnacle Bill's | **Rumson**	21
Z Baumgart's | **Edgewater**	19
Berkeley | **S Seaside Pk**	20
Z Buddakan | **A.C.**	25
Buttonwood Manor | **Matawan**	14
Café Gallery | **Burlington**	23
Z Cafe Matisse | **Rutherford**	27
Capriccio | **A.C.**	26
Chart Hse. | **Weehawken**	21
NEW Chelsea Prime | **A.C.**	-
Chophouse | **Gibbsboro**	25
City Bistro | **Hoboken**	18
Continental | **A.C.**	23
Crab Trap | **Somers Point**	22
Doris/Ed's | **Highlands**	25
Frenchtown Inn | **Frenchtown**	25
Hamilton's | **Lambertville**	25
Z Highlawn | **W Orange**	25
House of Blues | **A.C.**	16
Inlet | **Somers Point**	19
Inlet Café | **Highlands**	20
Komegashi | **Jersey City**	23
Lambertville Station | **Lambertville**	17
Liberty Hse. | **Jersey City**	20
Lilly's/Canal | **Lambertville**	21
Lua | **Hoboken**	22

Matisse | **Belmar**	21
McLoone's | **multi.**	17
Meson Madrid | **Palisades Pk**	18
Milford Oyster Hse. | **Milford**	23
Mill/Spring Lake | **Spring Lake Hts**	21
Molly Pitcher | **Red Bank**	23
Z Moonstruck | **Asbury Pk**	25
Mr. C's | **Allenhurst**	19
Phillips Seafood | **A.C.**	19
P.J. Whelihan's | **Medford Lakes**	16
Plantation | **Harvey Cedars**	20
Porto Leggero | **Jersey City**	22
Z Rat's | **Hamilton**	25
Rebecca's | **Edgewater**	25
Rest. Latour | **Hamburg**	25
Robin's Nest | **Mt Holly**	22
Rooney's | **Long Branch**	18
Z Ruth's Chris | **Weehawken**	25
Z Saddle River Inn | **Saddle River**	28
Sallee Tee's | **Monmouth Bch**	19
Salt Creek | **Rumson**	19
SAWA Steak | **Long Branch**	22
Ship Inn | **Milford**	15
Sirena | **Long Branch**	22
Smithville Inn | **Smithville**	21
Sonsie | **A.C.**	21
NEW Stella Marina | **Asbury Pk**	-
3 Forty | **Hoboken**	21
NEW Tim McLoone's | **Asbury Pk**	17
Z Tisha's | **Cape May**	26
Tuckers | **Beach Haven**	16
Union Park | **Cape May**	25
Ventura's | **Margate**	17
Walpack Inn | **Wallpack**	19
Windansea | **Highlands**	17

VISITORS ON EXPENSE ACCOUNT

Z Avenue | **Long Branch**	20
Bienvenue | **Red Bank**	23
Z Bobby Flay | **A.C.**	25
Brennen's | **Neptune City**	23
Z Buddakan | **A.C.**	25

SPECIAL FEATURES

Cafe Madison | **Riverside**	20
Capriccio | **A.C.**	26
Z Catherine Lombardi | **New Bruns.**	23
NEW Chelsea Prime | **A.C.**	-
Chez Catherine | **Westfield**	26
Z CulinAriane | **Montclair**	27
Z Daryl | **New Bruns.**	24
David Burke | **Rumson**	25
Esty St. | **Park Ridge**	24
Z Fascino | **Montclair**	26
Z Gables | **Beach Haven**	25
Gallagher's | **A.C.**	22
Girasole | **A.C.**	25
Z Grand Cafe | **Morristown**	26
Harry's | **Sea Bright**	21
I Cavallini | **Colts Neck**	23
Z NEW Il Mulino NY | **A.C.**	26
Il Villaggio | **Carlstadt**	23
Lahiere's | **Princeton**	22
NEW LaPrete's | **Belleville**	22
Le Petit Chateau | **Bernardsville**	25
Lu Nello | **Cedar Grove**	25
Mahogany | **Manasquan**	23
Manhattan Steak | **Oakhurst**	19
Mantra | **Paramus**	24
Z McCormick/Schmick | **Cherry Hill**	20
Mia | **A.C.**	25
Z Morton's | **Hackensack**	25
Z Nicholas | **Middletown**	28
Old Homestead | **A.C.**	26
Panico's | **New Bruns.**	23
Park Ave. | **Union City**	18
Z Pluckemin Inn | **Bedminster**	26
Portofino | **Tinton Falls**	23
Z Ram's Head | **Galloway**	25
Rist. Benito | **Union**	24
Z Ruth's Chris | **Princeton**	25
Z Scalini Fedeli | **Chatham**	27
Z SeaBlue | **A.C.**	27
Sirena | **Long Branch**	22
Smoke Chophse. | **Englewood**	23

Stage Left | **New Bruns.**	26
Z Stonehouse | **Warren**	22
3 West | **Basking Ridge**	22
Undici | **Rumson**	21
Witherspoon | **Princeton**	21
Wolfgang Puck | **A.C.**	24

WARM WELCOME

Z Amanda's | **Hoboken**	25
Angelo's | **A.C.**	21
Benito's | **Chester**	24
Berta's | **Wanaque**	21
Z Blue Point | **Princeton**	25
Casa Giuseppe | **Iselin**	24
Chez Catherine | **Westfield**	26
Church St. | **Montclair**	14
Cinnamon | **Morris Plains**	23
Cucharamama | **Hoboken**	25
da Filippo | **Somerville**	23
Z DeLorenzo's Pies | **multi.**	27
Doris/Ed's | **Highlands**	25
Far East Taste | **Eatontown**	23
NEW Farm 2 Bistro | **Nutley**	-
Labrador | **Normandy Bch**	23
NEW Langosta | **Asbury Pk**	-
NEW LaPrete's | **Belleville**	22
Le Rendez-Vous | **Kenilworth**	26
Madeleine's | **Northvale**	25
Nana's Deli | **Livingston**	22
NEW 9 North | **Wayne**	-
Nunzio | **Collingswood**	24
Plan B | **Asbury Pk**	-
Plantation | **Harvey Cedars**	20
Pop's Garage | **Asbury Pk**	22
Quiet Man | **Dover**	20
Risotto Hse. | **Rutherford**	23
Rist. Benito | **Union**	24
Rod's Olde Irish | **Sea Girt**	18
Rosa Luca's | **Asbury**	24
Sage | **Ventnor**	24
Sister Sue's | **Asbury Pk**	21
Taqueria | **Jersey City**	22
NEW Torcello | **Red Bank**	-

WATERSIDE

Atlantic B&G | **S Seaside Pk**   25
Z Avenue | **Long Branch**   20
Avon Pavilion | **Avon-by-Sea**   19
Axelsson's | **Cape May**   23
Bahrs Landing | **Highlands**   16
Barnacle Bill's | **Rumson**   21
Z Baumgart's | **Edgewater**   19
Café Gallery | **Burlington**   23
Capriccio | **A.C.**   26
Chart Hse. | **Weehawken**   21
Chophouse | **Gibbsboro**   25
Crab House | **Edgewater**   16
Crab Trap | **Somers Point**   22
Hamilton's | **Lambertville**   25
Inlet | **Somers Point**   19
Inlet Café | **Highlands**   20
Inn/Sugar Hill | **Mays Landing**   23
It's Greek To Me | **Long Branch**   17
Klein's | **Belmar**   19
Komegashi | **Jersey City**   23
Lambertville Station | **Lambertville**   17
NEW Langosta | **Asbury Pk**   –
Liberty Hse. | **Jersey City**   20
Lilly's/Canal | **Lambertville**   21
Lua | **Hoboken**   22
Matisse | **Belmar**   21
McLoone's | **multi.**   17
Mill/Spring Lake | **Spring Lake Hts**   21
Molly Pitcher | **Red Bank**   23
Mr. C's | **Allenhurst**   19
Z Peter Shields | **Cape May**   26
Pop's Garage | **Asbury Pk**   22
Red's | **Pt. Pleas. Bch**   23
Robin's Nest | **Mt Holly**   22
Rooney's | **Long Branch**   18
Sallee Tee's | **Monmouth Bch**   19
Salt Water | **Asbury Pk**   18
Sirena | **Long Branch**   22
NEW Stella Marina | **Asbury Pk**   –
Teplitzky's | **A.C.**   –

3 Forty | **Hoboken**   21
NEW Tim McLoone's | **Asbury Pk**   17
Z Tisha's | **Cape May**   26
Tuckers | **Beach Haven**   16
Union Park | **Cape May**   25
Ventura's | **Margate**   17
Windansea | **Highlands**   17

WINNING WINE LISTS

Z Bernards Inn | **Bernardsville**   26
Berta's | **Wanaque**   21
Black Forest Inn | **Stanhope**   22
Bobby Chez | **Sewell**   24
Z Bobby Flay | **A.C.**   25
Brass Rail | **Hoboken**   19
Cafe Madison | **Riverside**   20
Z Catherine Lombardi | **New Bruns.**   23
Z Chakra | **Paramus**   20
Chengdu 46 | **Clifton**   24
Court St. | **Hoboken**   22
Crab's Claw | **Lavallette**   18
Cucharamama | **Hoboken**   25
Z Daryl | **New Bruns.**   24
David Burke | **Rumson**   25
Z David Drake | **Rahway**   28
Doris/Ed's | **Highlands**   25
Due Terre | **Bernardsville**   25
Equus | **Bernardsville**   21
Esty St. | **Park Ridge**   24
Z Frog/Peach | **New Bruns.**   26
Gladstone | **Gladstone**   21
Harvest Moon | **Ringoes**   23
Kitchen 233 | **Westmont**   20
Le Petit Chateau | **Bernardsville**   25
Z Manor | **W Orange**   24
Mediterra | **Princeton**   21
Mia | **A.C.**   25
Napa Valley | **Paramus**   21
Z Nicholas | **Middletown**   28
Z Ombra | **A.C.**   26
Ox | **Jersey City**   23
Z Park/Orchard | **E Rutherford**   22

WORTH A TRIP

SPECIAL FEATURES

Wine Vintage Chart

This chart, based on our 0 to 30 scale, is designed to help you select wine. The ratings (by **Howard Stravitz,** a law professor at the University of South Carolina) reflect the vintage quality and the wine's readiness to drink. We exclude the 1991–1993 vintages because they are not that good. A dash indicates the wine is either past its peak or too young to rate. Loire ratings are for dry white wines.

Whites	89	90	94	95	96	97	98	99	00	01	02	03	04	05	06	07
French:																
Alsace	24	25	24	23	23	22	25	23	25	26	22	21	24	25	24	-
Burgundy	23	22	-	27	26	23	21	25	25	24	27	23	26	27	25	23
Loire Valley	-	-	-	-	-	-	-	-	24	25	26	22	23	27	24	-
Champagne	26	29	-	26	27	24	23	24	24	22	26	21	-	-	-	-
Sauternes	25	28	-	21	23	25	23	24	24	29	25	24	21	26	23	27
California:																
Chardonnay	-	-	-	-	-	-	-	24	23	26	26	25	26	29	25	-
Sauvignon Blanc	-	-	-	-	-	-	-	-	-	-	-	26	27	26	27	26
Austrian:																
Grüner Velt./Riesling	-	-	-	25	21	26	26	25	22	23	25	26	26	25	24	-
German:	26	27	24	23	26	25	26	23	21	29	27	24	26	28	24	-

Reds	89	90	94	95	96	97	98	99	00	01	02	03	04	05	06	07
French:																
Bordeaux	25	29	21	26	25	23	25	24	29	26	24	26	24	28	25	23
Burgundy	24	26	-	26	27	25	22	27	22	24	27	25	24	27	25	-
Rhône	28	28	23	26	22	24	27	26	27	26	-	26	24	27	25	-
Beaujolais	-	-	-	-	-	-	-	-	-	-	22	24	21	27	25	23
California:																
Cab./Merlot	-	28	29	27	25	28	23	26	-	27	26	25	24	26	23	-
Pinot Noir	-	-	-	-	-	-	-	24	23	25	28	26	27	25	24	-
Zinfandel	-	-	-	-	-	-	-	-	-	25	23	27	22	23	23	-
Oregon:																
Pinot Noir	-	-	-	-	-	-	-	-	-	-	27	25	26	27	26	-
Italian:																
Tuscany	-	25	23	24	20	29	24	27	24	27	-	25	27	25	24	-
Piedmont	27	27	-	-	26	27	26	25	28	27	-	24	23	26	25	24
Spanish:																
Rioja	-	-	26	26	24	25	-	25	24	27	-	24	25	26	24	-
Ribera del Duero/Priorat	-	-	26	26	27	25	24	25	24	27	20	24	27	26	24	-
Australian:																
Shiraz/Cab.	-	-	24	26	23	26	28	24	24	27	27	25	26	26	24	-
Chilean:	-	-	-	-	-	24	-	25	23	26	24	25	24	26	25	24